THE CATHOLIC UNIVERSITY OF AMERICA
CANON LAW STUDIES
No. 243

Marriage Legislation for the Catholics of the Oriental Rites in the United States and Canada

BY THE
REV. JOSEPH FRANCIS MARBACH, A.B., J.C.L.
Priest of the Archdiocese of New York

A DISSERTATION

Submitted to the Faculty of the School of Canon Law of the Catholic University of America in Partial Fulfillment of the Requirements for the Degree of Doctor of Canon Law

THE CATHOLIC UNIVERSITY OF AMERICA PRESS
WASHINGTON, D. C.
1946

Nihil Obstat:
CLEMENS V. BASTNAGEL, S.T.L., J.U.D.,
Censor Deputatus.

Washingtonii, D. C., die 6 maii, 1946.

Imprimatur:
✠ FRANCISCUS CARDINAL SPELLMAN,
Archiepiscopus Neo-Eboracensis.

Neo-Eboraci, die 6 maii, 1946.

Printed by
THE PAULIST PRESS
401 WEST 59TH STREET
NEW YORK 19, N. Y.

51

DEDICATED

TO

MY PARENTS

TABLE OF CONTENTS

CHAPTER II

FOREWORD

An Oriental rite is a distinct world of its own, with a distinct legal sphere existing apart from that of all other rites, and with a distinct social ethos derived from a solidarity of historical and cultural traditions amid the other social groups that existed by its side in the East long before the Latin world developed its present unity of basic law.

The Church, conscious of the fact that each Oriental rite is a distinct entity in itself with its own history and laws, has not interfered with the legitimate laws, liturgies, and customs of the divers Oriental Churches. For example, the most well-known fact in the East that is alien to our Latin customs is that a married man may become a priest and retain his wife. The words of Pope Pius XI concerning this differing feature reflect the Latin attitude towards the extant differences: "We do not wish that what we said in commendation of clerical celibacy should be interpreted as though it were in Our mind in any way to blame, or, as it were, disapprove the different discipline legitimately prevailing in the Oriental Church." [1]

Since the geographical and national factors of each Oriental rite as well as its legal traditions current through the centuries occasioned the rise of a legal independence, this dissertation will attempt to present a separate analysis of each Oriental group which has some organization in the United States or Canada. The historical part is given in summary form, and the reader is urged to consult the books mentioned, for they furnish further details, and furthermore carry references to more extensive bibliographies.

The first chapter intends to give a survey of the early marriage legislation in the East. The interplay of canon law and civil law is presented briefly. The sources here used are limited to those of the first eight centuries, with the incidental exceptions which em-

[1] Litt. encycl., *"Ad catholici sacerdotii,"—Acta Apostolicae Sedis*, XXVIII (1936), 28.

brace a few canons of Patriarch Nicephorus of Constantinople (806-815), a few references to the celebrated reply of Pope St. Nicholas I in 866 to the questions proposed by the Bulgarians, and a few later civil law decrees concerning the form of marriage. Throughout the following centuries, and even at the present time, the early Eastern councils of the Church exercise in the East a major degree of influence which they did not have in the West, where in later centuries there were held innumerable synods and many ecumenical councils whose decrees did not extend to the East.

As the scope of this dissertation is limited to the Oriental Catholics who have some organization in the United States and Canada, it is exclusively the rites of these Catholics that are treated in the subsequent chapters, although it is to be admitted that the decrees treated in the first chapter of this study were such as to wield an influence upon every Oriental rite in some degree. The second chapter attempts to give a synopsis of the history, of the general legal traditions, and of the particular marriage laws of these rites from the beginning of the Church to the Council of Florence. The third chapter considers the period between the Council of Florence and the year 1800. The fourth summarizes the historical and legal events in the nineteenth century. However, it is to be noted that, though the second chapter considers the history, the laws, and the marriage rules of these rites in their status of schism, of heresy, or of union with Rome, the following two chapters limit their consideration in the main to the history and the laws of the Catholics, which fact explains why so little space is given to some of the rites at those periods.

As the extensive immigration of the Oriental Catholics to the United States and Canada began towards the end of the nineteenth century, this dissertation in its fifth chapter foregoes the study of their European and Near Eastern twentieth century history in order to limit its survey to the situation in the United States. The sixth chapter presents a brief survey of these rites in Canada. The seventh chapter discusses some problems common to all the Oriental rites, in their relations with one another or with Latin Catholics and Latin Ordinaries.

To canonists who are now accustomed to the succinct canons

of the Latin Code the contrast between the varying legislation for the Oriental Rites and the uniform code for the Latin Church will show the great need for the Code for the Oriental Churches, which is now being prepared by the Holy See. The laws of one Oriental Rite cannot be applied to the people of another Oriental Rite, which fact makes difficult a uniform presentation of the Oriental marriage discipline. This dissertation strives to present the extant legislation for the Oriental Catholics who have an organization in the United States and Canada, as far as the sources at hand will allow. It is to be noted here that a consideration of the marriage legislation which stems from the divine law, such as legislation concerning impotence, force and fear, evil intentions *contra bona matrimonii,* substantial error in the marriage contract, the impossibility of divorce after a ratified, consummated marriage, and the impediment of an existing valid marriage bond, has been omitted, with a few exceptions, since these questions need little explanation concerning their force in the Eastern Churches.

In Appendix I are found some documents concerning some marriage questions of the Eastern Catholics in the United States and Canada. For permission to quote these documents the writer is indebted to the Most Reverend Joseph T. McGucken, D.D., S.T.D., Auxiliary Bishop of Los Angeles, the Most Reverend Raymond J. Kearney, D.D., J.C.D., Auxiliary Bishop of Brooklyn, the Most Reverend Constantine Bohachevsky, D.D., Ordinary for the Ukrainians from Galicia in the United States, the Most Reverend Basil Takach, D.D., Ordinary for the Ruthenians from Podcarpathia, Hungary, Slovakia, and Jugoslavia in the United States, and the Right Reverend George J. Casey, J.C.D., Vicar-General of the Archdiocese of Chicago. In Appendix II there is presented a list of the Oriental pastors and churches in the United States and Canada, to assist those priests who in relation to an Eastern Catholic seek information from the proper Oriental Rite pastor of the party.

A special mention of gratitude should be made for the kindness of the Patriarch of the Armenians, His Eminence, Gregory Peter XV Cardinal Agagianian, and of the Reverend Mesrob Terzian of the Pontifical Armenian College at Rome, in sending valuable information about the marriage laws of the Armenians.

A special mention of gratitude should likewise be made for the kindness of His Beatitude, the Maronite Patriarch of Antioch and of all the Orient, Anthony Peter Arida, in sending valuable information concerning the marriage legislation of the Maronites.

Gratitude is also due to the Reverend Louis E. Bélanger, J.C.D., of the Archdiocese of Ottawa, to the Right Reverend James H. Griffiths, S.T.D., Chancellor of the Military Ordinariate for the United States, to the Very Reverend Joseph M. McShea, D.D., Ph.D., Secretary of the Apostolic Delegation to the United States, to the Reverend Stephen C. Gulovich, S.T.D., Chancellor of the Pittsburgh Ordinariate of the Byzantine-Slavonic Rite, and to the Reverend Anthony Simbalist, secretary to His Excellency Bishop Ladyka of Winnipeg, Canada, for repeated acts of kindness; to the Reverend William F. King, S.E.O.D., Professor of Church History at St. Joseph's Seminary, Yonkers, N. Y., to several other priests from the Archdiocese of New York, and to many other priests, both secular and regular, both Latin and Oriental, who have assisted the writer; and to the Faculty of the School of Canon Law of the Catholic University of America for their aid and encouragement. Most of all, the writer wishes to express his gratitude to His Eminence, Francis Cardinal Spellman, Archbishop of New York, for the opportunity to pursue graduate study in Canon Law.

CHAPTER I

MARRIAGE LEGISLATION IN THE EAST IN THE FIRST EIGHT CENTURIES

ARTICLE I. THE DIGNITY OF MARRIAGE

ST. PAUL in his letter to the Christians of Ephesus revealed the great dignity of the sacrament of marriage, by proclaiming the matrimonial union as a symbol of the union between Christ and His Church.[1] This union of Christ with His Church, being essentially supernatural, is a source of grace for us. In an analogous manner, the union of husband and wife should be supernatural and a source of grace for both.

The early Christian writers were conscious of this dignity of Christian marriage. St. Ignatius of Antioch (d. 107), in his letter to St. Polycarp (d. ca. 156), quoted the words of St. Paul to the Ephesians, in requesting St. Polycarp to "exhort my brothers in the name of Jesus Christ that 'they should love their wives as Christ loved His Church.' "[2] Tertullian (160-222) wrote to his wife: "How shall we be able to describe the happiness of that marriage which the Church ratifies, the Mass strengthens, the blessing seals, the angels announce and of which the Father approves?"[3] Origen (185-254), in his commentaries on the Gospel of St. Matthew, wrote: "Indeed it is God Who has united the two into one, so that they are no longer two after the marriage. Since God has joined them, therefore grace is in them who were so joined by God; St. Paul knew this

[1] Chapter V, verses 25-32.

[2] 5, 1: «Ὁμοίως καὶ τοῖς ἀδελφοῖς μου παράγγελλε ἐν ὀνόματι Ἰησοῦ Χριστοῦ, 'ἀγαπᾶν τὰς συμβίους ὡς ὁ Κύριος τὴν ἐκκλησίαν.'»— Funk-Bihlmeyer, *Die Apostolischen Väter* (Tübingen, 1924), p. 112.

[3] *Ad Uxorem,* II, 9: "Unde sufficiamus ad enarrandam felicitatem eius matrimonii, quod ecclesia conciliat et confirmat oblatio, et obsignat benedictio, angeli renuntiant, Pater rato habet?"—Migne, *Patrologiae Cursus Completus, Series Latina* (221 vols., Parisiis, 1844-1864), I, 1302 (hereafter cited as *MPL*).

well, when he declared that marriage according to the will of Christ is a grace, just as a pure unmarried life is a grace." [4]

The sanctification of marriage at the wedding feast at Cana is mentioned among the Eastern writers. Thus St. Cyril of Alexandria (d. 444), commenting on the second chapter of St. John's Gospel, declared that Our Lord came to Cana not to feast, but to work a miracle, and so to sanctify the source of human procreation.[5]

From the first centuries the Christians realized the sanctity and dignity of marriage, and regarded it as a sacred institution of God for the welfare of the human race. Unfortunately, some false teachings about Christian marriage appeared in various heretical sects, such as that of the Encratites, begun by Tatian (120-?), that of the Manichaeans, followers of Manichaeus of Persia (215-276), and that of the Hieracians, disciples of Hieracas of Egypt (270?-360?), all of whom condemned marriage as an evil thing. In the early part of the fourth century, Eustathius of Sebaste (300-380?) taught an exaggerated asceticism, out of admiration of the monastic life. He condemned all marriages in general, and declared that no one who lived in the married state could have any hope of eternal happiness. At this teaching many husbands left their wives and likewise many wives left their husbands; many refused to attend the public ceremonies of the Church on the pretext that they could not communicate with the priests who were married.[6]

[4] Tom. 14, n. 16: «Καὶ ὁ Θεός ἐστιν ὁ συζεύξας τὰ δύο εἰς ἕν, ἵνα μηκέτι ὦσι δύο παρ' οὗ ἁρμόζεται ἀνδρὶ γυνή. Καὶ ἐπεὶ ὁ Θεὸς συνέζευξε διὰ τοῦτο χάρισμά ἐστιν ἐν τοῖς ὑπὸ Θεοῦ συνεζευγμένοις, ὅπερ ὁ Παῦλος ἐπιστάμενος, ἐπίσης τῷ εἶναι τὴν ἁγνὴν ἀγαμίαν χάρισμά φησι καὶ τὸν κατὰ Λόγον Θεοῦ γάμον εἶναι χάρισμα.»—Migne, *Patrologiae Cursus Completus, Series Graeca* (161 vols., Parisiis, 1856-1866), XIII, 1229 (hereafter cited as *MPG*).

[5] Lib. 2, cap. 1: « . . . Θαυματουργήσων μᾶλλον ἤπερ συνεστιασόμενος, ἔτι τε πρὸς τούτῳ καὶ αὐτὴν ἁγιάσων τῆς ἀνθρώπου γενέσεως τὴν ἀρχήν . . . »—*MPG*, LXXIII, 224.

[6] Bingham, *The Antiquities of the Christian Church* (2 vols., London, 1845), bk. XXII, chapter i, sections 5-8 (hereafter cited as Bingham); De Smet, *De Sponsalibus et Matrimonio* (4. ed., Brugis: Beyaert, 1927), pp. 69-70 (hereafter cited as De Smet); Cayré, *Manual of Patrology* (trans. by Howitt, 2 vols., Paris: Desclée, 1936-1940), I, 318; Bobak, *De caelibatu ecclesiastico deque impedimento Ordinis Sacri apud Orientales et praesertim*

The Council of Gangra (in Paphlagonia, 340-341) first deposed Eustathius, and then issued many canons against his teaching. The first canon anathematized anyone who upbraided the married state, or put any blame on a pious woman who cohabited with her husband, as if to say that she could not enter heaven because of such cohabitation.[7]

The fourth canon anathematized anyone who stood aloof from a married priest on the pretext that it was not lawful to partake of the Mass of such a priest.[8] The ninth anathematized anyone who retired from the world out of an abomination of marriage, rather than from a worthy motive.[9] The fourteenth anathematized a wife who left her husband for a similar reason, i. e., out of abhorrence of marriage itself.[10]

The *Canons of the Apostles* in the fifty-first canon inveighed

apud Ruthenos (Romae: Officium Libri Catholici, 1941), pp. 39-40, 64-65 (hereafter cited as Bobak, *De caelibatu*).

[7] «Εἴ τις τὸν γάμον μέμφοιτο καὶ τὴν καθεύδουσαν μετὰ τοῦ ἀνδρὸς αὐτῆς, οὖσαν πιστὴν καὶ εὐλαβῆ, βδελύσσοιτο ἢ μέμφοιτο ὡς ἂν μὴ δυναμένην εἰς βασιλείαν εἰσελθεῖν, ἀνάθεμα ἔστω.» The four quoted canons of this council can be found in: Lauchert, *Die Kanones der wichtigsten altkirchlichen Concilien nebst den apostolischen Kanones* (Leipzig, 1896), pp. 80-82 (hereafter cited as Lauchert); Bruns, *Canones Apostolorum et Conciliorum Saeculorum IV, V, VI, VII* (2 vols., Berolini, 1839), I, 107-108 (hereafter cited as Bruns); Pitra, *Iuris Ecclesiastici Graecorum Historia et Monumenta* (2 vols., Romae, 1864-1868), I, 489-491 (hereafter cited as Pitra). For a detailed commentary on these canons from the Council of Gangra, cf. *Synodus Gangrensis evangelicae promulgationis anno circiter trecentesimo congregata* (Parisiis, 1560).

[8] «Εἴ τις διακρίνοιτο παρὰ πρεσβυτέρου γεγαμηκότος, ὡς μὴ χρῆναι λειτουργήσαντος αὐτοῦ προσφορᾶς μεταλαμβάνειν, ἀνάθεμα ἔστω.» Cf. Esmein, *Le Mariage en Droit canonique* (2. éd. par R. Génestal et J. Dauvillier, 2 vols., Paris: Sirey, 1929, 1935), I, 315. Hereafter this work will be cited as Esmein.

[9] «Εἴ τις παρθενεύοι ἢ ἐγκρατεύοιτο, ὡς ἂν βδελύττων τῶν γάμων ἀναχωρήσας καὶ μὴ δι' αὐτὸ τὸ καλὸν καὶ ἅγιον τῆς παρθενίας, ἀνάθεμα ἔστω.»

[10] «Εἴ τις γυνὴ καταλιμπάνοι τὸν ἄνδρα καὶ ἀναχωρεῖν ἐθέλοι βδελυττομένη τὸν γάμον, ἀνάθεμα ἔστω.» This canon (in Latin) is also found in the *Codificazione Canonica Orientale, Fonti* (Parte I, 16 vols., Città del Vaticano: Tipografia Poliglotta Vaticana, 1930-1937; Parte II, 3 Serii, Roma, 1937-), IX, n. 575. Hereafter this collection will be cited as *Fonti*, and the citations will be from Part One, unless otherwise noted.

against bishops, priests, deacons, or any other "of the sacred list," and laymen also who abstained from marriage, or meat, or wine, not for the exercise of the ascetic life, but out of abhorrence, thereby "blaspheming and calumniating the workmanship of God." [11]

Article II. Impediments to Marriage

1. *Espousals*

Under Roman Law, a marriage with a person in violation of an espousal with another resulted in pretorian infamy for the parties.[12] Betrothal also gave rise to a kind of affinity which made illegal the marriage of one party to the betrothal with the parent or child of the other; according to Ulpian (d. 228), a father could not marry his son's fiancée, nor a son his father's.[13]

The Byzantine Church added a religious ceremony to the civil elements connected with betrothal, and thus added a special sanction to the force of a betrothal and marriage as but two elements of the one marriage contract. Thus the juridical effects of betrothal and marriage became almost the same. It was in view of this rising feeling in the East that the Council in Trullo (692) [14] decreed that if a

[11] «Eἴ τις ἐπίσκοπος ἢ πρεσβύτερος ἢ διάκονος ἢ δλως τοῦ καταλόγου τοῦ ἱερατικοῦ γάμου καὶ κρεῶν καὶ οἴνου οὐ δι' ἄσκησιν ἀλλὰ διὰ βδελυρίαν ἀπέχεται . . . βλασφημῶν διαβάλλει τὴν δημιουργίαν . . . τῆς ἐκκλησίας ἀποβαλλέσθω· ὡσαύτως καὶ λαϊκός.»—Funk, *Didascalia et Constitutiones Apostolorum* (2 vols. in 1, Paderbornae, 1905), I, 580 (hereafter cited as Funk; the numbering of the *Canons of the Apostles* as found in this work will be followed); Bruns, I, 8; Pitra, I, 26; Lauchert, p. 8.

[12] *Corpus Iuris Civilis,* Vol. I (*Institutiones* recognovit Paulus Kreuger, *Digesta* recognovit Theodorus Mommsen, retractavit Paulus Kreuger, 15. ed., Berolini: Apud Weidmannos, 1928), *Digesta* (3.2) 1; (3.2) (13.1-4). Hereafter the *Institutiones* will be cited as Inst., and the *Digesta* as D.

[13] D. (23.2) (12.1-2). Cf. Corbett, *The Roman Law of Marriage* (Oxford: The Clarendon Press, 1930), p. 16. Hereafter cited as Corbett.

[14] There were no disciplinary canons issued by the Fifth and Sixth Ecumenical Councils held at Constantinople in 553 and 680; Justinian II (685-695) wanted to fill this lack, and in 692 summoned a council to supplement these ecumenical councils. This council met in the domed hall (Τροῦλλος) of the palace at Constantinople, as had the Sixth Ecumenical Council in 680, and received its name from the place of meeting, the "troullos" at the palace. Strictly

man married a woman who was espoused to a living fiancé, such a man was to be punished as an adulterer.[15]

The *Ecloga* of Emperor Leo III (717-741) and his son Constantine (741-775) gave the force of the civil law to this penalty as enacted by the Council in Trullo, by decreeing the facial mutilation of a man who seduced a betrothed woman.[16]

The early Council of Ancyra (314) had declared that if anyone stole a woman who was espoused to another, she should be taken from that abductor, although he might have done violence to her, and restored to the one who espoused her, indicating that at an early period in the Church espousals impeded a marriage with a third person.[17]

taken, the council of 692 should be called the Second Council in Trullo, but it alone is usually called "the Trullan Synod," "the Trullanum," "the Council in Trullo," and as it was meant to complete the Fifth and Sixth Ecumenical Councils, it is also called "the Quini-sextum," "the Fifth-Sixth" (Σύνοδος πενθέκτη). It drew up 102 disciplinary canons (canons 3, 6, 10, 12, 26, 53, 54, 87, 92, 93, and 98 concern marriage), but issued no dogmatic definitions; most of the canons merely repeat older canons; some of the new ones show hostility to Rome. Pope Sergius I (687-701) refused to sign the canons, and Pope John VII (705-707) sent back the copy they wanted him to sign (this has been considered as an implied act of approbation); eventually some canons were approved and were assigned to the Sixth Ecumenical Council. The Council in Trullo has been a main source of law for the churches allied to Constantinople, and it can be said that the peculiarly Byzantine legislation had its beginning in this Council. Cf. Coussa, *Epitome Praelectionum de Iure Ecclesiastico Orientali* (Vol. I, Romae, 1940; Vol. II, Venetiis, 1941), I, 10. In the following pages, this Council will be called "the Council in Trullo," as Dauvillier and De Clercq do in their scholarly work, *Le Mariage en Droit canonique oriental* (Paris: Recueil Sirey, 1936). This work will be cited as Dauvillier and De Clercq. Cf. also White, *De Forma Celebrationis Matrimonii seu de Clandestinatate apud Byzantinos Catholicos* (Romae: Pontificium Institutum Utriusque Juris, 1935), pp. 14-15. Hereafter cited as White, *De forma celebrationis matrimonii.*

[15] Canon 98: «Ὁ ἑτέρῳ μνηστευθεῖσαν γυναῖκα, ἔτι τοῦ μνηστευσαμένου ζῶντος, πρὸς γάμου κοινωνίαν ἀγόμενος τῷ τῆς μοιχείας ὑποκείσθω ἐγκλήματι.»—Lauchert, p. 137; Bruns, I, 63; *Fonti,* IX, n. 505; Pitra, II, 69; Pargoire, *L'Eglise Byzantine de 527 à 847* (Paris, 1905), p. 227 (hereafter cited as Pargoire); Esmein, I, 149.

[16] XVII, 32. References to the *Ecloga* will be taken from *A Manual of Roman Law, The Ecloga,* trans. by Edwin Freshfield, Cambridge: The University Press, 1926.

[17] Canon 11: «Τὰς μνηστευθείσας κόρας καὶ μετὰ ταῦτα ὑπὸ ἄλλων

2. *Vows*

The Council of Ancyra declared that those who vowed virginity and disregarded the vow were to be considered as bigamists, and thus were irregular concerning ordination.[18] The Council of Chalcedon (451) decreed that marriage was not allowed for a virgin or a monk, since they had dedicated themselves to God, and that they were to be excommunicated if they attempted marriage.[19] The same canon added, however, that the bishop of the place had the power to temper the severity of this punishment.[20] The Council in Trullo (692) declared that a monk who married was to be subjected to the canonical penalties exacted against fornication.[21] The Patriarch Nicephorus of Constantinople (806-815) in his *Constitutiones* decreed that

ἁρπαγείσας ἔδοξεν ἀποδίδοσθαι τοῖς προμνηστευσαμένοις, εἰ καὶ βίαν ὑπ' αὐτῶν πάθοιεν.»—Lauchert, p. 32; Bruns, I, 68; *Fonti,* IX, n. 504; Pitra, I, 445. Cf. Bingham, bk. XXII, chapt. iii, sect. 9.

[18] Canon 19: «Ὅσοι παρθενίαν ἐπαγγελλόμενοι ἀθετοῦσι τὴν ἐπαγγελίαν, τὸν τῶν διγάμων ὅρον ἐκπληρούτωσαν.»—Lauchert, p. 34; Bruns, I, 69; *Fonti,* IX, n. 515 (listed as from the Council of Neocaesarea); Pitra, I, 447. Cf. Bingham, bk. VII, chapt. iv, sect. 3; *Fonti,* Serie II, Fasc. V, p. 114.

[19] Canon 16: «Παρθένον ἑαυτὴν ἀναθεῖσαν τῷ δεσπότῃ Θεῷ, ὡσαύτως δὲ καὶ μονάζοντα μὴ ἐξεῖναι γάμῳ προσομιλεῖν· εἰ δέ γε εὑρεθεῖεν τοῦτο ποιοῦντες, ἔστωσαν ἀκοινώνητοι.»—Lauchert, p. 93; Bruns, I, 29; *Fonti,* IX, n. 469; Pitra, I, 528; c. 22, C. XXVII, q. 1.

[20] « . . . ὡρίσαμεν δὲ ἔχειν τὴν αὐθεντίαν τῆς ἐπ' αὐτοῖς φιλανθρωπίας τὸν κατὰ τόπον ἐπίσκοπον.» Cf. *Fonti,* IX, n. 470; Bingham, bk. VII, chapt. iii, sect. 24.

[21] Canon 44: «Μοναχὸς . . . πρὸς γάμου κοινωνίαν καὶ συμβίωσιν γυναῖκα ἀγαγόμενος τοῖς τῶν πορνευόντων ἐπιτιμίοις κατὰ τοὺς κανόνας ὑποβληθήσεται.»—Lauchert, p. 121; Bruns, I, 51; *Fonti,* IX, n. 471; Pitra, II, 48. Papp-Szilagyi (*Enchiridion Iuris Ecclesiae Orientalis Catholicae* [2. ed., Magno-Varadini, 1880], p. 256) stated that this points to the invalidity of such a marriage. (Hereafter this work will be cited at Papp-Szilagyi.) Today the main Oriental monastic Orders with solemn vows are the following: the Order of St. Basil the Great among the Ruthenians, the Order of St. Basil the Great among the Melkites, the Order of St. Hormisdas among the Chaldeans, the Order of St. Basil among the Italo-Greeks, the Baladitae, the monks of Aleppo and the monks of St. Anthony among the Maronites, the Order of St. Basil the Great among the Rumanians.

a monk who did not repent of his marriage was to be excommunicated.[22]

3. Previous Marriage

A. If the First Spouse Was Still Alive

The *Canons of the Apostles* declared excommunicated any lay person who married another after dismissing his own wife, or who married a woman dismissed from her husband.[23] The Council in Trullo emphasized the indissolubility of marriage in decreeing long public penances for a man who had left his wife and then married another.[24]

In his *Constitutiones* Nicephorus, the Patriarch of Constantinople, pointed to five years as the duration of penance for a man who had left his wife and married another,[25] while the duration of penance for a woman who had given up her husband and attempted marriage with another was set for seven years. The priest who knowingly blessed such an attempted second marriage was to be deposed.[26]

B. If the Death of a Spouse Was Not Certainly Known

The Council in Trullo declared that the wife of a man who had left and did not return committed adultery if she cohabited with another spouse before ascertaining the death of her first spouse. The

[22] Canon 91: «'Εὰν μοναχὸς . . . γυναῖκα λάβῃ δεῖ μὴ ἐπιστρέφοντα τοῦτον ἀναθέματι καθυποβληθῆναι . . . »—Pitra, II, 336; *Fonti*, IX, n. 474.

[23] Canon 48: «Εἴ τις λαϊκὸς τὴν ἑαυτοῦ γυναῖκα ἐκβαλὼν ἑτέραν λάβοι ἢ παρὰ ἄλλου ἀπολελυμένην, ἀφοριζέσθω.»—Funk, I, 578; Bruns, I, 8; Lauchert, p. 7; *Fonti*, IX, n. 574; Pitra, I, 24. Cf. Bingham, bk. XVI, chapt. xi, sect. 6.

[24] Canon 87: «Κεκανόνισται γὰρ παρὰ τῶν πατέρων ἡμῶν, τοὺς τοιούτους ἐνιαυτὸν προσκλαίεν, διετίαν ἐπακροάσθαι, τριετίαν ὑποπίπτειν καὶ τῷ ἑβδόμῳ συνίστασθαι τοῖς πιστοῖς καὶ οὕτω τῆς προσφορᾶς καταξιοῦσθαι.»—Lauchert, p. 134; Bruns, I, 60; *Fonti*, IX, nos. 577-578; Pitra, II, 64. Cf. Pargoire, p. 227.

[25] Canon 139: «Εἴ τις ἀνὴρ ἀφήσῃ τὴν γυναῖκα αὐτοῦ καὶ ἐπάρῃ ἄλλην, ἔχει ἐπιτίμιον ἔτη ε'.»—Pitra, II, 340; *Fonti*, IX, n. 482.

[26] Canon 140: «Εἴ τις γυνὴ ἀφήσῃ τὸν ἄνδρα αὐτῆς καὶ ἐπάρῃ ἄλλον, ἔχει ἐπιτίμιον ἔτη ζ'. εἰ δὲ καὶ εὐλογηθῇ γινώσκων ὁ ἱερεὺς τὸ σφάλμα, καθαιρείσθω.»—Pitra, II, 340; *Fonti*, IX, n. 482-a.

charge of adultery also attached in a case of similar cohabitation on the part of the wives of soldiers who did not return, but whose death was not certainly known; if the soldier returned after some time, he could take back his wife, for he was free to condone in her and her consort what they had done through ignorance of the fact that he was alive.[27]

C. If the First Spouse Had Died

At the time of the Roman Republic a widower could remarry at once, but the widow was penalized if she remarried within the first ten months after the death of her husband. The penalty consisted in the offering of sacrifices, and thus at first implied a religious sanction, but the praetor later added infamy in the eyes of the law as a penalty. To show imperial disfavor to subsequent marriages, the Emperors Gratian (d. 383), Valentinian II (d. 392) and Theodosius I (d. 395) in 381 extended the time interval to twelve months, and added certain pecuniary penalties, such as the loss of the widow's inheritance due from her first husband.[28] The Christian Emperors legislated against second marriages; even a first marriage was no longer insisted upon after Constantine the Great (306-337) had abolished the penalties for celibacy.[29] When there were children from a first marriage, then a remarriage of the widow brought with it monetary losses in the property inherited,[30] but an abstention from remarriage brought monetary gains.[31] In 439 Theodosius II (d. 450) and Valentinian (d. 455) extended the same rules to the remarriage

[27] Canon 93: «Ἡ ἀναχωρήσαντος τοῦ ἀνδρὸς καὶ ἀφανοῦς ὄντος πρὸ τοῦ πεισθῆναι περὶ τοῦ θανάτου αὐτοῦ, ἑτέρῳ συνοικοῦσα μοιχᾶται· ὡσαύτως καὶ αἱ στρατιώτιδες . . . ὥσπερ καὶ αἱ διὰ τὴν ἀποδημίαν τοῦ ἀνδρὸς . . πλὴν ἔχει τινὰ συγγνώμην τὸ πρᾶγμα . . . εἰ δὲ γε ὁ στρατιώτης ἐπανέλθοι . . . οὗτος εἰ προαιρεῖται τὴν οἰκείαν αὖθις ἀναλαμβανέτω γυναῖκα, συγγνώμης . . . ἐπὶ τῇ ἀγνοίᾳ δεδομένης . . .»—Lauchert, p. 135; Bruns, I, 62; *Fonti,* IX, n. 481; Pitra, II, 66-67. Cf. Bingham, bk. XXII, chapt. ii, sect. 9; Pargoire, p. 227.

[28] *Corpus Iuris Civilis,* Vol. II, *Codex Iustinianus* (10. ed., recognovit et retractavit Paulus Kreuger, Berolini: Apud Weidmannos, 1929), (5.9) 1 and 2 (hereafter cited as C.). Cf. Dauvillier and De Clercq, p. 196.

[29] C. (8.57) 1.

[30] C. (5.9) 3.

[31] *Corpus Iuris Civilis,* Vol. III, *Novellae* (5. ed., recognovit Rudolfus

of widowers who had children. In 535 Justinian I (527-565) published a comprehensive statute, wherein remarriage was viewed as a dishonor to the children of the first marriage, and wherein the main points of the preceding legislation were maintained. The presence of children from a preceding union was an important factor, for the same penalties were not incurred if there were no children. The woman had to wait a year before remarriage, but the man could remarry at once.[32]

Among the clerics lectors were allowed to marry, but Justinian also decreed that a lector who married a second time could never attain a higher rank in the clergy.[33]

The early councils tried to discourage second marriages, though they did not condemn them as violently as the Montanists and the Novatians. The Council of Neocaesarea (314-325) decreed that a definite term of penance was established for those who entered second marriages.[34] It also forbade a priest from being a guest at the marriage feasts of those who married a second time, inasmuch as his presence would be taken for approval.[35] The I Council of Nicaea (325) imposed on the Novatian clergy who returned to the Church the duty of certifying in writing that they would associate with those who had entered second marriages.[36]

The *Canons of the Apostles* declared that one who had married a

Schoell, absolvit Gulielmus Kroll, Berolini: Apud Weidmannos, 1928), (127.3). Hereafter these *Novellae* of Justinian will be cited as Nov.

[32] Nov. (22.23 and 27). Cf. Corbett, pp. 249-251, for these rules of the Roman Law up to and including the time of Justinian; cf. Dauvillier, *Le Mariage dans le Droit classique de L'Eglise* (Paris: Recueil Sirey, 1933), p. 448, for the legislation of the later Eastern Emperors concerning third and fourth marriages. Hereafter this work will be cited as Dauvillier.

[33] Nov. (6.5).

[34] Canon 3: «Περὶ τῶν πλείστοις γάμοις περιπιπτόντων ὁ μὲν χρόνος σαφὴς ὁ ὡρισμένος, ἡ δὲ ἀναστροφὴ καὶ ἡ πίστις αὐτῶν συντέμνει τὸν χρόνον.»—Lauchert, p. 35; Bruns, I, 71; *Fonti*, IX, n. 688; Pitra, I, 451. Cf. Bingham, bk. XVI, chapt. xi, sect. 7.

[35] Canon 7: «Πρεσβύτερον εἰς γάμους διγαμούντων μὴ ἑστιᾶσθαι ἐπεὶ μετάνοιαν αἰτοῦντος τοῦ διγάμου, τίς ἔσται ὁ πρεσβύτερος, ὁ διὰ τῆς ἑστιάσεως συγκατατιθέμενος τοῖς γάμοις.»—Lauchert, *loc. cit.*; Bruns, *loc. cit.*; Pitra, I, 452. Cf. Pargoire, p. 338; Bingham, bk. XXII, chapt. iv, sect. 2.

[36] Canon 8: «πρὸ πάντων . . . ὁμολογῆσαι . . . ἐγγράφως . . . διγάμοις κοινωνεῖν.»—Lauchert, p. 39; Bruns, I, 16.

widow could not be a bishop or priest or deacon or cleric of any rank; [37] anyone who married twice after baptism was similarly irregular for ordination.[38] The Council in Trullo renewed this strong expression of Eastern feeling against second marriages.[39]

The Council of Laodicea (343-381) in its first canon declared that those who entered second marriages freely and legitimately could be received back into the communion of the Church after a period of penance.[40] The Patriarch Nicephorus in his *Typicum* ordered that one who had married twice was not to receive the crowning, and was to do penance for two years.[41] In his *Constitutiones* he also ordered that a widower who married a widow was not to receive the nuptial prayers, and both were to undergo the penances established for second marriages.[42]

According to Bingham (1668-1723) the ceremony of crowning in the contracting of marriage served as a symbol that the two parties had conquered all temptations to impurity, and thus the crowns were regarded as marks of victory. So, in a secondary sense, because of this symbolism, this ceremony was seldom used in second or third

[37] Canon 18: «ὁ χήραν λαβὼν . . . οὐ δύναται εἶναι ἐπίσκοπος ἢ πρεσβύτερος ἢ διάκονος ἢ ὅλως τοῦ καταλόγου τοῦ ἱερατικοῦ.»—Funk, I, 568; Bruns, I, 3; Lauchert, p. 3; *Fonti,* IX, n. 512; Pitra, I, 17.

[38] Canon 17: «ὁ δυσὶ γάμοις συμπλακεὶς μετὰ τὸ βάπτισμα . . . οὐ δύναται εἶναι ἐπίσκοπος ἢ πρεσβύτερος ἢ ὅλως τοῦ καταλόγου τοῦ ἱερατικοῦ.»—Funk, *loc. cit.*; Bruns, *loc. cit.*; Lauchert, *loc. cit.*; *Fonti,* IX, n. 511; Pitra, I, 16.

[39] Canon 3: « . . . ὁρίζοντες ἀπὸ τοῦ παρόντος καὶ ἀνανεούμενοι τὸν κανόνα τὸν διαγορεύοντα, τὸν δυσὶ γάμοις συμπλακέντα μετὰ τὸ βάπτισμα . . . μὴ δύνασθαι εἶναι ἐπίσκοπον ἢ πρεσβύτερον ἢ διάκονον ἢ ὅλως τοῦ καταλόγου τοῦ ἱερατικοῦ . . . »—Lauchert, p. 103; Bruns, I, 38; *Fonti,* IX, n. 72; Pitra, II, 25-26. Cf. Dauvillier, p. 457.

[40] «Περὶ τοῦ δεῖν κατὰ τὸν ἐκκλησιαστικὸν κανόνα τοὺς ἐλευθέρως καὶ νομίμως συναφθέντας δευτέροις γάμοις . . . ὀλίγου χρόνου παρελθόντος καὶ σχολασάντων ταῖς προσευχαῖς καὶ νηστείαις, κατὰ συγγνώμην ἀποδίδοσθαι αὐτοῖς τὴν κοινωνίαν ὡρίσαμεν.»—Lauchert, p. 72; Bruns, I, 73; *Fonti,* IX, n. 684; Pitra, I, 495.

[41] Canon 8: «ὁ δίγαμος οὐ στεφανοῦται ἀλλ' ἕξει ἐπιτίμιον ἔτη δύο.»—Pitra, II, 328; *Fonti,* IX, n. 687.

[42] Canon 149: «Ἐάν τις ἀπὸ χηρείας ὢν καὶ θέλῃ λαμβάνειν γυναῖκα ἀπὸ χηρείας . . . καὶ ἀκολουθίαν οὐκ ἔχει· τὰ δὲ ἐπιτίμια τῆς διγαμίας δουλεύσουσι.»—Pitra, II, 341; *Fonti,* IX, n. 687-a. Cf. Pargoire, p. 338.

marriages since, even though such unions were not condemned as entirely unlawful, they were not considered as honorable as the first marriage.[43]

Pargoire, in describing the marriage rites among the Byzantines in this early period, writes that it was the custom to have the crowning of the two parties followed with the reception of Holy Communion by both, and then all would proceed, the priest included, to the marriage feast. However, he remarks, "All that, note well, is reserved for a first wedding; for the others, nothing of the crowning, the Communion, the presence of the priest at the marriage feast." [44] This lack of the usual rites of marriage did not mean that the second marriages were invalid; rather it indicated the displeasure of the Church at second marriages.[45]

St. Theodore the Studite (759-826) wrote to Naucrates, "You have asked me if those who marry a second time ought to be crowned as those who marry for the first time. . . . How can you judge worthy of crowning those who are not victorious but conquered? Which priest would crown them when the priest is forbidden by the Fathers to assist at their wedding feast? . . . But then, you may ask, what will be the formalities?—formalities purely human as are used in marriages of those who enter third marriages or even further unions." [46] He admitted, however, that the contrary custom, to crown second marriages, had already been introduced.[47]

[43] *The Antiquities of the Christian Church,* bk. XXII, chapt. iv, sect. 6.

[44] "Mais tout cela, notez-le-bien, est réservé aux premières noces; pour les autres, point de couronnes, point de Communion, point de prêtre au festin."—*L'Eglise Byzantine de 527 à 847,* p. 338.

[45] Cf. Deslandes, "Le mariage clandestin des Orientaux est-il valide?"—*Echos d'Orient,* XXVIII (1929), 9; Spácil, "Commentarium de theologia dogmatica,"—*Orientalia Christiana,* XVIII (1930), 178.

[46] «Ἡ ἐρώτησίς σου περὶ τῶν διγάμων· ὅτι ἀμφισβητούμενόν ἐστι περὶ τῆς συναφείας αὐτῶν, ἆρα στεφανοῦσθαι αὐτοὺς, ὡς ἐπὶ τῶν μονογάμων, ἢ μή; . . . Πῶς γὰρ ἂν καὶ στεφανώσεως ἄξιος, ἡττηθεὶς, ἀλλ' οὐ νικήσας; τίς δὲ καὶ ὁ στεφανώσων τοῦτον πρεσβύτερος, ὃς καὶ τοῦ ἁπλῶς ἑστιαθῆναι ἐν τῷ κατ' αὐτὸν ἀρίστῳ Πατρικῶς κεκώλυται; . . . Φαίης δ' ἄν· Καὶ πῶς ἔλθωσιν ἐπὶ τὴν συνάφειαν; Τοῖς ἀνθρωπίνοις καθήκουσιν ὥσπερ καὶ οἱ τρίγαμοι καὶ πολύγαμοι.»—*MPG,* XCIX, 1092-1093; White, *De forma celebrationis matrimonii,* pp. 53-55.

[47] *MPG,* XCIX, 973.

4. Affinity

The legislation of the Church regarding affinity was influenced by both the Mosaic Law and the Roman Law. The Book of Leviticus had forbidden a man to marry his affines in the first and second degrees of the direct line, and in the first and second degrees of the collateral line.[48] The laws of the levirate removed the ban against marrying the widow of a deceased brother, if there were no children born to that couple.[49]

Roman Law in the fourth century prohibited marriages between persons related in the first degree of the collateral line of affinity.[50] In the law of Justinian, marriage was also forbidden between a man and the fiancée of his son or father in view of the fiction of affinity which existed between them; similarly, marriage was forbidden between a man and the stepmother of his deceased wife; the children of a husband and a wife begotten by them in prior marriages could intermarry.[51]

In the *Ecloga,* marriage was forbidden among "those who are recognized as relations by marriage, stepfather and stepdaughter, father-in-law and daughter-in-law, son-in-law and mother-in-law, brother and bride, that is to say, a brother's wife, likewise father and son of one family and mother and daughter of another family, two brothers of one family with two sisters of another family." [52]

The Church applied to women as well as to men the rule concerning affinity in the first degree of the collateral line, to cover the case wherein a woman might marry her deceased husband's brother. The Council of Neocaesarea (314-325) declared that if a woman successively married two brothers, she was to remain excommunicated to the day of her death, and only in danger of death could she be reconciled after she had promised that she would dissolve the marriage if she recovered; the Council concluded this canon solemnly by stating

[48] Ch. XVIII, vv. 14-18; XX, vv. 11, 12, 14, 20, 21.

[49] Deut. XXV, 5.

[50] C. (5.5) 5.

[51] Inst. (1.10) 8; D. (23.2) 14; D. (38.10) 4; C. (5.4) 17. Cf. Corbett, p. 50; Dauvillier and De Clercq, p. 137.

[52] II, 2.

that if the woman or the man died in such a marriage, repentance would be difficult in eternity.[53]

The *Canons of the Apostles* decreed that a man who successively married two sisters could not be a cleric.[54] The Council in Trullo decreed that a father and his son who attempt marriage with persons who are mother and daughter, or who are sisters, and also two brothers who attempt similar marriages, were deserving of a long penance and were to be separated publicly from their consorts.[55] This canon shows how the degrees of affinity as impediments to marriage had become multiplied by this time in the East.

5. *Consanguinity*

Roman Law, following the natural law, forbade all marriages between blood relatives in the direct line; in the collateral line the marriages of brothers and sisters were not allowed. The Emperor Claudius (41-54) for his own benefit, it is said, legalized marriage between a man and his brother's daughter, but Diocletian (284-305) and then also Constantine the Great (306-337) restored the ancient law which forbade such a marriage.[56] The Emperor Theodosius I in 384 forbade marriages between cousins,[57] but this rule was abrogated

[53] Canon 2: «Γυνὴ ἐὰν γήμηται δύο ἀδελφοῖς, ἐξωθείσθω μέχρι θανάτου, πλὴν ἐν θανάτῳ διὰ τὴν φιλανθρωπίαν, εἰποῦσα ὡς ὑγιάνασα λύσει τὸν γάμον, ἕξει τὴν μετάνοιαν. ἐὰν δὲ τελευτήσῃ ἡ γυνὴ ἐν τοιούτῳ γάμῳ οὖσα ἤτοι ὁ ἀνὴρ δυσχερὴς τῷ μείναντι ἡ μετάνοια.»—Lauchert, p. 35; Bruns, I, 71; *Fonti*, IX, n. 463; Pitra, I, 451.

[54] Canon 19: «ὁ δύο ἀδελφὰς ἀγαγόμενος . . . οὐ δύναται εἶναι κληρικός.»—Funk, I, 568; Bruns, I, 3; Lauchert, p. 3; *Fonti*, IX, n. 513; Pitra, I, 17. Cf. Bingham, bk. XVI, chapt. xi, sect. 3.

[55] Canon 54: « . . . ὁρίζοντες ἀπὸ τοῦ νῦν . . . πρὸς γάμου κοινωνίαν συναπτόμενον . . . πατέρα καὶ υἱὸν μητρὶ καὶ θυγατρί, ἢ δυσὶ κόραις ἀδελφαῖς πατέρα καὶ υἱόν, ἢ ἀδελφοῖς δυσὶ μητέρα καὶ θυγατέρα, ἢ ἀδελφοὺς δυὸ δυσὶν ἀδελφαῖς ὑπὸ τὸν τῆς ἑπταετίας πίπτειν κανόνα, ἀφισταμένων αὐτῶν προδήλως τοῦ παρανόμου συνοικεσίου.»—Lauchert, p. 124; Bruns, I, 53; *Fonti*, IX, n. 478; Pitra, II, 52. Cf. Pargoire, p. 226.

[56] Cf. Moyle, *Imperatoris Justiniani Institutiones* (Oxford: Clarendon Press, 1923), in his footnote to Inst. (1.10) 3. Cf. also Corbett, *The Roman Law of Marriage*, pp. 47-51.

[57] *Codex Theodosianus* (ed. Paulus Kreuger, Berolini: Apud Weidmannos, 1928), (3.10) 1. Hereafter this will be cited as C.Th.

for the eastern part of the Empire by Arcadius about twenty years later.[58] The law of Justinian revealed the traditional civil limitation on this impediment, for his rule extended the impediment to all the degrees of the direct line, but in the collateral line only to the case in which at least one of the parties was but one degree removed from the common ancestor; this excluded a marriage not only between an uncle and a niece, or an aunt and a nephew, but also between a great-uncle and a grand-niece, i. e., neither party could be related to the common ancestor in the first degree if they were to be free from this impediment.[59]

The *Ecloga* extended the impediment to the children of first cousins, i. e., to the sixth degree of the collateral line, according to the Roman and Eastern computation.[60]

The *Canons of the Apostles* viewed a marriage with a niece as constituting an irregularity against entering the clerical state.[61] The Christians for a long time simply obeyed the civil law concerning this impediment, and the Church in the East did not legislate beyond the civil degrees of this impediment. The Council in Trullo however returned to the prohibition against marriages between cousins, in decreeing that one who married his cousin was to be subjected to a long penance and separated publicly from such a union.[62]

[58] C. (5.4) 19. Cf. Esmein, I, 374; Bingham, bk. XVI, chapt. xi, sect. 4; Dauvillier and De Clercq, p. 124; Petrovits, *The New Church Law on Matrimony* (2. ed., Philadelphia: John Joseph McVey, 1926), n. 323.

[59] Inst. (1.10) 3.

[60] II, 2. This method of counting degrees, which was adopted in many civil codes, and which was used in the Eastern Church, consisted simply in counting all the persons on both sides of the collateral line, with the common ancestor omitted from the count. For the first six centuries this method of computation was used also in the Latin Church. Finally Peter Damian and "Jurisperitus de Ravenna" debated the point for the benefit of Pope Alexander II (1061-1073), who in a council at Rome prescribed that the Germanic method of computation, which was being followed in the West, be made the official method of computation. Cf. Papp-Szilagyi, p. 263. The Germanic method of computation has influenced the computation employed in canon 96 of the Latin Code.

[61] Canon 19: «ὁ . . . ἀγαγομένος . . . ἀδελφιδὴν οὐ δύναται εἶναι κληρικός» Cf. footnote n. 54.

[62] Canon 54: «ὁρίζοντες ἀπὸ τοῦ νῦν τὸν τῇ οἰκείᾳ ἐξαδέλφῃ πρὸς

6. *Sacred Orders*

The first canon of the Council of Neocaesarea (314-325) prohibited a priest from marrying, and imposed the penal sanction of deposition if he attempted marriage.[63] Though a married man could become a priest,[64] the *Canons of the Apostles* declared that among the unmarried clerics only those who were lectors or singers could marry.[65] These same *Canons* forbade a bishop, a priest or a deacon to send away his wife on the pretext of religion; if he nevertheless did so, he was to be excommunicated, and if he refused to amend, he was to be deposed.[66]

The Council of Ancyra (314) allowed a deacon to marry upon his ordination if in the ceremony of ordination he had told the bishop that he wanted to contract marriage in the future, but if he had said nothing about this during the ordination, but later on contracted marriage, he was to cease from the exercise of his office.[67]

γάμου κοινωνίαν συναπτόμενον . . . ὑπὸ τὸν τῆς ἑπταετίας πίπτειν κανόνα, ἀφιστομένων αὐτῶν προδήλως τοῦ παρανόμου συνοικεσίου.»—Lauchert, p. 124; Bruns, I, 53; *Fonti,* IX, n. 468; Pitra, II, 52. Cf. Dauvillier, p. 452; Assemani, *Bibliotheca Iuris Orientalis (Clementino-Vaticana)* (3 vols. in 4, Romae, 1719-1728), Vol. II, Pars Secunda, p. 325; Fleury, *Recherches historiques sur les Empêchements de Parenté dans le Mariage canonique* (Paris: R. Sirey, 1933), pp. 81-84; Janin, *Les Églises orientales et les Rites orientaux* (3. éd., Paris: La Bonne Press, 1926), p. 74. Hereafter this work will be cited as Janin, *Les Églises orientales.*

63 «Πρεσβύτερος ἐὰν γήμῃ, τῆς τάξεως αὐτὸν μετατίθεσθαι.» — Lauchert, p. 35; Bruns, I, 71; *Fonti,* IX, n. 489; Pitra, I, 451; c. 9, D. XXVIII. Cf. Gilbert, *Le Mariage des Prêtres* (Paris, 1904), p. 5; Papp-Szilagyi, p. 256; Dauvillier, p. 460; Esmein, I, 315.

64 Cf., e. g., canon 4 of the Council of Gangra, quoted *supra* in the discussion of the dignity of marriage; cf. Pitzipios, *L'Église orientale* (Rome: Propaganda, 1855), Part I, p. 102.

65 Canon 26: «Τῶν εἰς κλῆρον παρελθόντων ἀγάμων κελεύομεν βουλομένους γαμεῖν ἀναγνώστας καὶ ψάλτας μόνους.»—Funk, I, 570; Bruns, I, 4; Lauchert, p. 4; *Fonti,* IX, n. 237; Pitra, I, 18. Cf. *Fonti,* Serie II, Fasc. V, pp. 54, 155.

66 Canon 5: «Ἐπίσκοπος ἢ πρεσβύτερος ἢ διάκονος τὴν ἑαυτοῦ γυναῖκα μὴ ἐκβαλλέτω προφάσει εὐλαβείας· ἐὰν δὲ ἐκβάλῃ, ἀφοριζέσθω, ἐπιμένων δὲ καθαιρείσθω.»—Funk, I, 564; Bruns, I, 2; Lauchert, p. 2; *Fonti,* IX, n. 236; Pitra, I, 14. Cf. Bobak, *De caelibatu,* p. 64.

67 Canon 10: «Διάκονοι ὅσοι καθίστανται, παρ' αὐτὴν τὴν κατάστα-

Justinian (527-565) wrote to one of his praetorian prefects that he considered deposition from the priesthood not a sufficient sanction to prevent the marriages of those who were in sacred priestly orders; he accordingly decreed that the civil law would not recognize the children of such marriages, not even with the technical recognition given by the law to illegitimate children. In this prohibitive enactment he included subdeacons and deacons as well as priests.[68]

The Council in Trullo (692) declared that a subdeacon, a deacon or a priest who attempted to marry was to be deposed.[69] The Council in effect nullified the earlier exception, in favor of deacons who had signified their intention to marry, as made by the Council of Ancyra (314) in its tenth canon.[70] In another canon the Council in Trullo decreed that if the priest married through ignorance of the law, the

σιν εἰ ἐμαρτύραντο καὶ ἔφασαν χρῆναι γαμῆσαι, μὴ δυνάμενοι οὕτως μένειν, οὗτοι μετὰ ταῦτα γαμήσαντες ἔστωσαν ἐν τῇ ὑπηρεσίᾳ διὰ τὸ ἐπιτραπῆναι αὐτοὺς ὑπὸ ἐπισκόπου· τοῦτο δὲ εἴ τινες σιωπήσαντες καὶ καταδεξάμενοι ἐν τῇ χειροτονίᾳ μένειν οὕτως μετὰ ταῦτα ἦλθον ἐπὶ γάμον, πεπαῦσθαι αὐτοὺς τῆς διακονίας.»—Lauchert, p. 32; Bruns, I, 68; *Fonti*, IX, n. 174; Pitra, I, 445. Cf. Bingham, bk. IV, chapt. v, sect. 8; Dauvillier, p. 459; Bobak, *De caelibatu*, pp. 59-60.

[68] C. (1.3) 44; Nov. (6.5) ordered the one who attempted such a marriage to be expelled from his order and to become a layman. Cf. Esmein, I, 318. Bobak (*De caelibatu*, p. 147) contends that these two decrees of Justinian do not expressly declare that such marriages were invalid.

[69] Canon 6: «. . . ὁρίζομεν, ἀπὸ τοῦ νῦν μηδαμῶς ὑποδιάκονον ἢ διάκονον ἢ πρεσβύτερον μετὰ τὴν . . . χειροτονίαν ἔχειν ἄδειαν, γαμικὸν ἑαυτῷ συνιστᾶν συνοικέσιον. εἰ δέ τις τοῦτο τολμήσει ποιῆσαι, καθαιρείσθω.» —Lauchert, p. 104; Bruns, I, 39; *Fonti*, IX, n. 178; Pitra, II, 26; Galante, *Fontes Iuris Canonici Selecti* (Oeniponte, 1906), p. 381; c. 7, D. XXXII. Dauvillier and De Clercq (p. 172) lean to the view that this canon indicates a diriment impediment, though they admit the earlier councils did not declare such marriages invalid. Esmein (*loc. cit.*) declares the East considered it as rather referring to an impedient impediment. Bobak (*De caelibatu*, pp. 144-150) asserts that the council issued, in grave words, threats of deposition if a priest attempted marriage, but that the council did not expressly declare such attempted marriages to be invalid. He also notes (p. 162) that at that time (692) the priesthood was not a diriment impediment in the Latin Church.

[70] Cf. Souarn, "Impedimentum Ordinis in Ecclesia Graeca,"—*Jus Pontificium*, XIII (1933), 47, and "L'ordre, empêchement canonique du mariage chez les Grecs,"—*Echos d'Orient*, IV (1900-1901), 67.

union was to be dissolved. While he could have a place at the cathedral, yet he was restrained from all his priestly functions, since he was thought to have lost the holiness which he was to transmit to others.[71]

If a married priest, deacon or subdeacon attempted a second marriage after the dissolution of his first, the Council prescribed that he should be deposed in the case of unrepentance; if he was repentant, he could keep his place of honor at the cathedral, but could never be advanced to another order, and the marital union itself was to be dissolved.[72] The Council also forbade priests or deacons to dismiss their wives; it claimed to follow "the ancient canon of apostolic perfection" in decreeing that the marriages of those who had become priests were to be given continued recognition, and that at ordination the candidates were not to be required to leave their wives.[73]

[71] Canon 26: «Πρεσβύτερον τὸν κατὰ ἄγνοιαν ἀθέσμῳ γάμῳ περιπαρέντα καθέδρας μὲν μετέχειν . . . τῶν δὲ λοιπῶν ἐνεργειῶν ἀπέχεσθαι.» —Lauchert, p. 112; Bruns, I, 45; *Fonti,* IX, n. 493; Pitra, II, 37.

[72] Canon 3: «συνορῶμεν, ὥστε τοὺς δυσὶ γάμοις περιπαρέντας . . . ἐνάτου δουλωθέντας τῇ ἁμαρτίᾳ καὶ μὴ ἐκνῆψαι ταύτης προελομένους καθαιρέσει κανονικῇ ὑποβαλεῖν . . . τοὺς μετὰ τὴν χειροτονίαν γάμῳ ἑνὶ παρανόμῳ προσομιλήσαντας, τουτέστι πρεσβυτέρους καὶ διακόνους καὶ ὑποδιακόνους . . . ἐπιτιμηθέντας . . . ἀποκαταστῆναι . . . προδήλως διαλυθέντος αὐτοῖς τοῦ ἀθέσμου συνοικεσίου.»—Lauchert, p. 103; Bruns, I, 38; *Fonti,* IX, nos. 490-491; Pitra, II, 24-25; Pope Benedict XIV in paragraph 38 of his Instruction to the missionaries of Egypt "*Eo quamvis semper,*" May 4, 1745 (*Codicis Iuris Canonici Fontes cura Emi Petri Gasparri editi* [9 vols., Romae (postea Civitate Vaticana): Typis Polyglottis Vaticanis, 1923-1939 (Vols. VII, VIII, et IX ed. *cura et studio Emi Iustiniani Card. Serédi*)], n. 357; hereafter cited as *Fontes*) referred to these words to show the main argument of those who maintained that such marriages of priests in the East were not only illicit but also invalid, without taking a definite position on the question himself. The Pope decreed that each case should be sent to Rome, which refers however only to returning schismatic clerics. Cf. *Fonti,* I, 267-269. Cf. Mansella, *De Impedimentis Matrimonium dirimentibus ac de Processu Iudiciali in causis Matrimonialibus* (Romae, 1881), pp. 92-93 (hereafter cited as *De Impedimentis*). Papp-Szilagyi (pp. 253-256) asserts vigorously that this canon of the Council in Trullo indicated that such marriages of subdeacons, deacons, and priests were invalid, and not only gravely illicit.

[73] Canon 13: «ἡμεῖς τῷ ἀρχαίῳ ἐξακολουθοῦντες κανόνι τῆς ἀποστολικῆς ἀκριβείας καὶ ταξέως, τὰ τῶν ἱερῶν ἀνδρῶν κατὰ νόμους συνοικέσια

7. Spiritual Relationship

The Council in Trullo not only canonized the decree of Justinian which forbade a man to marry a woman for whom he had been the sponsor at baptism in view of the spiritual tie between them,[74] but also expanded this enactment by declaring that the sponsor could not marry the infant's mother, and consequently ordered that those who in violation of this law had attempted such marriages were to be separated, and were to atone for this misdeed by performing the penance which the law imposed for the guilt of fornication.[75]

The *Ecloga* declared that "the man who has baptized a woman cannot marry her, or her mother or her daughter, nor can his son do so, for the marital relations cannot be combined with the spiritually paternal." [76]

καὶ ἀπὸ τοῦ νῦν ἐῤῥῶσθαι βουλόμεθα . . . μήτε μὴν ἐν τῷ τῆς χειροτονίας καιρῷ ἀπαιτείσθω ὁμολογεῖν, ὡς ἀποστήσεται τῆς νομίμου πρὸς τὴν οἰκείαν γαμετὴν ὁμιλίας.»—Lauchert, p. 107; Bruns, I, 42; *Fonti*, IX, n. 239; Pitra, II, 31. Cf. Bingham, bk. IV, chapt. v, sect. 8; Jugie, "Joseph de Maistre et le Schisme Gréco-Russe,"—*Echos d'Orient*, XXI (1922), 131; Dauvillier, p. 463; Esmein, I, 317; Bobak, *De caelibatu*, pp. 75-76.

[74] C. (5.4) 26.

[75] Canon 53: «. . . ἔγνωμεν δὲ ἔν τισι τόποις τινὰς ἐκ τοῦ ἁγίου καὶ σωτηριώδους βαπτίσματος παῖδας ἀναδεχομένους καὶ μετὰ τοῦτο ταῖς ἐκείνων μητράσι χηρευούσαις γαμικὸν συναλλάττοντας συνοικέσιον . . . εἰ δέ τινες μετὰ τὸν παρόντα κανόνα φωραθεῖεν τοῦτο ποιοῦντες, πρωτοτύπως μὲν οἱ τοιοῦτοι ἀφιστάσθωσαν τοῦ παρανόμου τούτου συνοικεσίου ἔπειτα δε καὶ τοῖς τῶν πορνευόντων ἐπιτιμίοις ὑποβληθήτωσαν.»—Lauchert, p. 123; *Fonti*, IX, n. 475; Pitra, II, 51. Cf. De Angelis, *Praelectiones Iuris Canonici* (5 vols. in 9 [Vols. 4, 5 prosequi curavit Nazarenus Gentilini, 1881-1891], Romae, 1877-1891), Tom. III, Pars I, p. 204; cf. c. 1, C. XXX, q. 3, which repeated the words of Pope St. Nicholas I (858-867) in his reply to the Bulgarians: "Est inter fratres et filios spirituales gratuita et sancta communio quae dicenda non est consanguinitas, sed habenda spiritualis proximitas."—*Monumenta Germaniae Historica, Epistolae, Tom. VI, pars 2, fasc. 1: Epistolae Karolini Aevi* (ed., E. Perels, Berolini, 1912), p. 569 (hereafter this volume will be cited *MGH, Epistolae*); Jaffé, *Regesta Pontificum Romanorum ab condita Ecclesia ad annum post Christum natum MCXCVIII* (2. ed., correctam et auctam auspiciis Gulielmi Wattenbach curaverunt S. Loewenfeld, F. Kaltenbrunner, P. Ewald, 2 tomes in 1 vol., Lipsiae, 1885-1888), n. 2812 (hereafter cited as Jaffé). Cf. Papp-Szilagyi, p. 266; Janin, *Les Églises orientales*, p. 74; *Fonti*, Serie II, Fasc. XXVII, p. 103.

[76] II, 3.

The *Constitutiones* of Nicephorus, Patriarch of Constantinople (806-815), forbade a man to marry the sister of the man who had baptized his son, and imposed a penalty of five years' penance on the one who entered such a marriage.[77]

The impediment of spiritual relationship did not comprise a distinct relationship arising from the ministration of the sacrament of confirmation, inasmuch as this sacrament was usually administered in the East immediately after baptism.

8. *Abduction*

The *Canons of the Apostles* decreed that if anyone by force kept in his power a virgin who was not betrothed, he was to be excommunicated. He was not to be allowed to marry anyone other than the one whom he thus had seized, even though she was a person of no material means.[78] If she was betrothed, she had to be returned to her intended husband, declared the Council of Ancyra (314).[79]

The Council of Chalcedon (451) enacted the penalty of deposition for this crime if the man was a cleric, and excommunication if he was a lay person. These penalties applied also to all who coöperated in the crime.[80] The Council in Trullo (692) used similar words in repeating this prohibition against abduction.[81]

[77] Canon 124—Pitra, II, 339; *Fonti,* IX, n. 476.

[78] Canon 67: «Εἴ τις παρθένον ἀμνήστευτον βιασάμενος ἔχῃ, ἀφοριζέσθω· μὴ ἐξεῖναι δὲ αὐτῷ ἑτέραν λαμβάνειν, ἀλλ' ἐκείνην κατέχειν, ἣν καὶ ἠρετίσατο, κἂν πενιχρὰ τυγχάνῃ.»—Funk, I, 584; Bruns, I, 10; Lauchert, p. 10; *Fonti,* IX, n. 498; Pitra, I, 29.

[79] Canon 11: «Τὰς μνηστευθείσας κόρας καὶ μετὰ ταῦτα ὑπὸ ἄλλων ἁρπαγείσας ἔδοξεν ἀποδίδοσθαι τοῖς προμνηστευσαμένοις.» — Lauchert, p. 32; Bruns, I, 68; *Fonti,* IX, n. 504; Pitra, I, 445.

[80] Canon 27: «Τοὺς ἁρπαζόντας γυναῖκας καὶ ἐπ' ὀνόματι συνοικεσίου, ἢ συμπράττοντας ἢ συναινοῦντας τοῖς ἁρπάζουσιν, ὥρισεν ἡ ἁγία σύνοδος, εἰ μὲν κληρικοὶ εἶεν, ἐκπίπτειν τοῦ οἰκείου βαθμοῦ· εἰ δὲ λαϊκοί, ἀναθεματίζεσθαι αὐτούς»—Lauchert, p. 96; Bruns, I, 32; *Fonti,* IX, n. 499; Pitra, I, 532; c. 1, C. XXXVI, q. 2. Schroeder, in his *Disciplinary Decrees of the General Councils* (St. Louis: Herder, 1937), p. 124, in commenting on this canon, gives a synopsis of the evil of abduction in the early centuries. Hereafter this work will be cited as Schroeder.

[81] Canon 92—Lauchert, p. 135; Bruns, I, 62; *Fonti,* IX, n. 500; Pitra, II, 66; Pargoire, p. 227.

The contraction of the marriage was gravely illicit, but nevertheless valid. In this point the Church was less severe than the Roman civil law. Constantine the Great had prohibited marriage between any abductor and the victimized young woman regardless of the presence or absence of her consent.[82] He did this to counteract the leniency of the ancient Roman Law in this matter which had led to many abuses. The Emperor Justinian I likewise forbade such marriages, and barred the abductor from marrying the girl, even though her parents had fully consented.[83]

9. *Difference of Religion*

The punishment for intermarriage with heretics and pagans was not everywhere the same in the early Church, though the councils prohibited and discouraged such a union as dangerous and sinful. Some canons merely forbade the marriage, without attaching any penalty as a sanction to this prohibition. Thus, in the Council of Laodicea (343-381) it was decreed that Catholics were not indifferently to give their children to heretics in marriage.[84] Another canon of the same council enacted that Catholics were not to marry any and every kind of heretics, nor were they to give their sons and daughters in marriage to heretics unless the latter promised to be converted.[85]

The Council of Chalcedon (451) in its fourteenth canon noted that in some provinces the lectors and cantors were allowed to enter marriage, but the Council forbade any of them to marry a heterodox

[82] C. Th. (9.24) 1.

[83] Nov. 143.

[84] Canon 10: « . . . μὴ δεῖν τοὺς τῆς ἐκκλησίας ἀδιαφόρως πρὸς γάμου κοινωνίαν συνάπτειν τὰ ἑαυτῶν παιδία αἱρετικοῖς.»—Lauchert, p. 73; *Fonti*, IX, n. 486; Pitra, I, 496. Hefele and Le Clercq (*Histoire des Conciles* [10 vols. in 19, Paris: Letouzey and Ané, 1907-1938], Vol. I, Pars II, p. 1002) refer to the opinion of Fuchs, that the word "indifferently" (ἀδιαφόρως) does not mean that mixed marriages were to be approved if a good and careful selection was made among the heretics, but that all mixed marriages were prohibited.

[85] Canon 31: «῞Οτι οὐ δεῖ πρὸς πάντας αἱρετικοὺς ἐπιγαμίας ποιεῖν ἢ διδόναι υἱοὺς ἢ θυγατέρας, ἀλλὰ μᾶλλον λαμβάνειν, εἴγε ἐπαγγέλλοιντο Χριστιανοὶ γίνεσθαι.»—Lauchert, p. 75; *Fonti*, IX, n. 487; Pitra, I, 499. Cf. Bingham, bk. XXII, chapt. ii, sect. 1; Papp-Szilagyi, p. 257.

woman.[86] The canon then added the requirement of a kind of *cautiones* in decreeing that, if the lectors and cantors had already married women of the heterodox faith and had already permitted that their children be baptized as heretics, they should bring them into the communion of the Catholic Church, but that any unbaptized children should not be baptized among the heretics.[87] The children were not to be given in marriage to a heretic, Jew or pagan unless such a one promised to be converted.[88]

The Council in Trullo (692) decreed that it was not allowed for a Catholic man to marry a heretical woman, nor could a Catholic woman marry a heretical man. If such a marriage was nevertheless contracted, the marriage was to be thought null and the unlawful union was to be ended.[89]

[86] «'Επειδὴ ἔν τισιν ἐπαρχίαις συγκεχώρηται τοῖς ἀναγνώσταις καὶ ψάλταις γαμεῖν, ὥρισεν ἡ ἁγία σύνοδος, μὴ ἐξεῖναι τινα αὐτῶν ἑτερόδοξον γυναῖκα λαμβάνειν.»—Lauchert, p. 92; Bruns, I, 29; *Fonti*, IX, nn. 483-485; Pitra, I, 527-528; c. 16, D. XXXII. Cf. Dauvillier, p. 380; Schroeder (pp. 105-107), in his comments on this canon, gives a synopsis of the position and duties of the lectors and cantors (on p. 521 he presents the Greek text of this canon). Papp-Szilagyi (p. 259) speaks of this canon as referring only to clerics, and it would appear that he is correct and that this canon should not be extended as implying a prohibition of all marriages with non-Catholics.

[87] «Τοὺς δὲ ἤδη ἐκ τοιούτων γάμων παιδοποιήσαντες, εἰ μὲν ἔφθασαν βαπτίσαι τὰ ἐξ αὐτῶν τεχθέντα παρὰ τοῖς αἱρετικοῖς, προσάγειν αὐτὰ τῇ κοινωνίᾳ τῆς καθολικῆς ἐκκλησίας, μὴ βαπτισθέντα δέ, μὴ δύνασθαι ἔτι βαπτίζειν αὐτὰ παρὰ τοῖς αἱρετικοῖς.»

[88] «μήτε μὴν συνάπτειν πρὸς γάμον αἱρετικῷ ἢ 'Ιουδαίῳ ἢ "Ελληνι, εἰ μὴ ἄρα ἐπαγγέλλοιτο μετατίθεσθαι εἰς τὴν ὀρθόδοξον πίστιν τὸ συναπτόμενον πρόσωπον τῷ ὀρθοδόξῳ.» The *Fonti* (IX, 484) adopt the Latin rendition of this part of the canon from Pitra (I, 528): "Sed neque copulari debet nuptura haeretico, iudaeo, vel pagano, nisi forte promittat ad orthodoxam fidem se personam orthodoxe copulandam transferre." But the word "*nuptura*" in its equivalent does not appear in the Greek text, which seems only to be forbidding such marriages to the children of clerics, and does not seem to be making such a general statement, as the Latin text would indicate, about all mixed marriages.

[89] Canon 72: «Μὴ ἐξέστω ὀρθόδοξον ἄνδρα αἱρετικῇ συνάπτεσθαι γυναικί, μήτε μὴν αἱρετικῷ ἀνδρὶ γυναῖκα ὀρθόδοξον ζευγνύσθαι· ἀλλ' εἰ καὶ φανῇ τι τοιοῦτον ὑπό τινος τῶν ἁπάντων γινόμενον, ἄκυρον ἡγεῖσθαι τὸν

The civil law also legislated on this prohibition against marrying outside the Church. Valentinian II, Theodosius I and Arcadius in 388 attached the penalties of adultery to a marriage between a Christian and a Jew; Justinian incorporated this law in his Code.[90]

Article III. The Pauline Privilege

The Council in Trullo, in its 72nd canon, after enacting its prohibition against mixed marriages, implied the usual conditions for the use of the Pauline Privilege. It determined that if two infidels contracted a legitimate marriage, and one of them "ran to the light of the truth," the privilege could be used, unless, of course, the infidel

γάμον καὶ τὸ ἄθεσμον διαλύεσθαι συνοικέσιον.»—Lauchert, p. 129; Bruns, I, 60; *Fonti,* IX, n. 488; Pitra, II, 59. Cf. Pargoire, p. 226; Dauvillier, p. 380. Authors dispute the origin of the universal impediment of disparity of cult. Wernz (*Ius Decretalium* [2. ed., 6 vols., Romae et Prati, 1906-1913], IV, n. 504, nota 19) points to this 72nd canon of the Council in Trullo as the possible origin. It does not seem that canon 14 of the Council of Chalcedon is the source of the impediment. Wernz (*op. cit.*, IV, n. 505) wrote: ". . . iure vero ecclesiastico, non scriptis legibus, sed generali ecclesiae occidentalis et orientalis consuetudine constituto matrimonia propter disparitatem cultus . . . absolute hominibus baptizatis interdicuntur. . . . " Cf. Schenk, *The Matrimonial Impediments of Mixed Religion and Disparity of Cult,* The Catholic University of America Canon Law Studies, n. 51 (Washington, D. C.: The Catholic University of America, 1929), p. 27; De Becker, *De Matrimonio Praelectiones Canonicae* (ed. nova, Lovanii, 1931), p. 89; De Smet, pp. 512-513; Esmein, II, 300; Mansella, *De Impedimentis,* p. 77; Papp-Szilagyi, pp. 257-259. Petrovits declared: "The practically unanimous opinion of canonists holds that the diriment impediment of disparity of worship was introduced by virtue of an accepted custom prevailing in the Eastern and Western Church in the period intervening between the ninth and the twelfth century."—*The New Church Law on Matrimony,* n. 219. Pope Benedict XIV (1740-1758) declared: ". . . qua quidem in re omnes sentiunt, ob cultus disparitatem irrita matrimonia esse, non quidem iure sacrorum canonum, sed generali ecclesiae more, qui pluribus abhinc saeculis viget, ac vim legis obtinet."—epist. *"Singulari,"* 9 febr. 1749, n. 10—*Fontes,* n. 394.

[90] C. (1.9) 6; cf. *Nomocanon in XIV Titles,* XII, 2—Pitra, II, 600. Cf. Herman, "Ius Justinianeum qua ratione conservatum sit in iure ecclesiastico orientali,"—*Acta Congressus Iuridici Internationalis* (5 vols., Romae, 1935-1937), II, 153. After mentioning this law Herman declared: "Impedimentum vero ut hodie viget, ortum posteriorem habet et potius consuetudini debetur."

party was willing to live peacefully with the new convert, for in such a case the converted spouse would sanctify the other party.[91]

ARTICLE IV. THE "FORBIDDEN TIME"

The first prohibition that appears concerning the time for the celebration of marriage is that of the Council of Laodicea (343-381), which forbade all celebration of marriages and birthday feasts in Lent.[92] Pope St. Nicholas I (858-867), in 866, writing in answer to

[91] «. . . εἱ δέ τινες ἔτι ἐν τῇ ἀπιστίᾳ τυγχάνοντες καὶ οὔπω τῇ τῶν ὀρθοδόξων ἐγκαταλεγέντες ποίμνῃ ἀλλήλοις γάμῳ νομίμῳ ἡρμόσθησαν· εἶτα ὁ μὲν τὸ καλὸν ἐκλεξάμενος τῷ φωτὶ τῆς ἀληθείας προσέδραμεν, ὁ δὲ ὑπὸ τοῦ τῆς πλάνης κατεσχέθη δεσμοῦ μὴ πρὸςτὰς θείας ἀτενίσαι ἀκτῖνας ἑλόμενος· εὐδοκεῖ δὲ τῷ πιστῷ ἡ ἄπιστος συνοικεῖν ἢ τὸ ἔμπαλιν ὁ ἄπιστος τῇ πιστῇ, μὴ χωριζέσθωσαν κατὰ τὸν θεῖον ἀπόστολον· Ἡγίασται γὰρ ὁ ἄπιστος ἀνὴρ ἐν τῇ γυναικί, καὶ ἡγίασται ἡ ἄπιστος γυνὴ ἐν τῷ ἀνδρί.» —Lauchert, *loc. cit.;* Bruns, *loc. cit.; Fonti,* IX, n. 793; Pitra, II, 59. Cf. Pargoire, p. 226; cf. *Fonti,* Serie II, Fasc. V, p. 101, for the comment of Balsamon on this canon, and pp. 224-225, for the comment of Blastares; cf. also Wernz-Vidal, *Ius Canonicum* (7 vols. in 8, Romae: Universitas Gregoriana, 1923-1938), V, n. 631, nota 57. Dauvillier and De Clercq (p. 165, n. 3) feel that this part of the canon, which refers to the words of St. Paul (I Cor. VII, 12-15), should not have been made to refer to the words of St. Paul, since they feel that this latter part of the canon is concerned with the marriage of two heretics, and not of two infidels. However, while the first three sentences of this canon do refer to the marriage of a Catholic with a heretical woman («αἱρετικῇ») or with a heretical man («αἱρετικῷ»), the fourth sentence begins, "If however certain ones who still are in unbelief. . . . " («εἱ δὲ τινες ἔτι ἐν τῇ ἀπιστίᾳ τυγχάνοντες . . .»). If heretics were meant, it seems that the word for "heresy" (αἶρεσις) would have been used, rather than "unbelief" or "infidelity" (ἀπιστία). Gregory (*The Pauline Privilege,* The Catholic University of America Canon Law Studies, n. 68 [Washington, D. C.: The Catholic University of America, 1931], p. 20, note 40) quotes only the first three sentences of the canon in his footnote to the words: "To whatever kind of marriages canon 72 of this council referred. . . ." In a previous sentence within the same paragraph he had stated: " . . . another Council, this time in the East, apparently mentioned the Privilege, the pseudo—Council in Trullo." Cf. *supra,* footnote n. 89, for the previous part of this canon 72.

[92] Canon 52: «Ὅτι οὐ δεῖ ἐν τεσσαρακοστῇ γάμους ἢ γενέθλια ἐπιτελεῖν.»—Lauchert, p. 77; Bruns, I, 78; *Fonti,* IX, n. 690; Pitra, I, 502; c. 8, C. XXXIII, q. 4. Cf. Bingham, bk. XXII, chapt. ii, sect. 14.

the questions proposed by the Bulgarians, noted the prohibition against marriage in Lent.[93]

Article V. The Form of Marriage

1. *The Civil Law*

At the time of the classical jurists, there could be a marriage with *manus,* which implied that the woman passed over from her family to the family of her husband, and there could be a marriage without *manus,* which acknowledged that the woman remained in her original family. *Manus* was acquired in three ways, by *confarreatio,* by *coemptio* or by *usus.*[94] As the word *confarreatio* indicates, this ceremony consisted in the offering to the Roman deities of a piece of corn bread together with the pronouncing of solemn words before ten witnesses. This was a religious ceremony reserved to the aristocrats and the priests.[95] Besides this religious ceremony there was the civil marriage of plebeians by *coemptio,* which consisted in a fictitious sale (*per mancipationem, id est per quandam imaginariam venditionem*) before five witnesses. If either of these ceremonies was omitted, but the parties lived as husband and wife continuously for a year, the title of *usus* arose. The marriage without *manus* was formed by a simple exchange of true consent without any determined form, but was accompanied usually with the act of the husband bringing the wife to his house.

When the state became Christian, it modified certain parts of the

[93] Cap. XLVIII: "Unde nec uxorem ducere nec convivia facere in quadragesimali tempore convenire posse ullatenus arbitramur. Verum quid hinc sacri canones dicant episcopo vestro docente scietis."—*MGH, Epistolae,* Vol. VI, Pars altera, p. 586. This thought of the Pope is incorporated into the work of Gratian—c. 11, C. XXXIII, q. 4.

[94] Gaius, *Institutiones* (ed. Joannes Baviera in *Fontes Iuris Romani Antejustiniani,* Florentiae, 1909), I, 109-115. Cf. Leage, *Roman Private Law* (2. ed. by C. Ziegler, London: Macmillan, 1942), pp. 99-104.

[95] Cf. Deslandes, "Le mariage clandestin des Orientaux est-il valide?"—*Echos d'Orient,* XXVIII (1929), 6; cf. also Cappello, *Tractatus Canonico-Moralis de Sacramentis* (3 vols. in 6, Romae: Marietti, 1932-1939), Vol. III, Partes I et II, *De Matrimonio* (4. ed., 1939), II, n. 658. Hereafter this work *De Matrimonio* will be cited as Cappello.

marriage legislation. Theodosius I and Valentinian II demanded the presence of witnesses among persons of the same rank, if certain due solemnities were missing.[96] Certain abuses in this matter crept in, and Justinian in 537 ordered that persons of high rank manifest their consent before the Church, as a *proof* of their marriage, if they wanted to omit the ante-nuptial contracts required by the civil law.[97] The persons of lower rank enjoyed as before the faculty of contracting marriage without any formality. Later, the Emperor Leo the Philosopher (886-912) imposed the obligation of religious ceremonies as the condition of a valid civil marriage for all free persons.[98] As a civil law, however, this could not affect the validity of Christian marriage.[99]

[96] C. Th., (3.7) 3. Cf. White, *De forma celebrationis matrimonii*, p. 19.

[97] *Novella* LXXIV, *Caput* IV. Pargoire (*L'Église Byzantine*, p. 97), in discussing the period from 527 to 628, writes: "In marriage, as is proved by the word 'crowning' given to it by Byzantine authors when they mention the union of Heraclius and Eudoxia, the most remarkable ceremony is that of the crowns placed on the heads of the couple. But the law would still recognize the legitimacy of conjugal union without the intervention of the church." This is reconcilable with this *Novella* of Justinian, because in it he required that the couple go before the church so that their marriage would be recorded on the marriage books of the church; they did not have to do this if they were willing to go through the ceremonies required by the civil law for people of their rank.

[98] *Novella* LXXXIX: «... οὕτω δὴ καὶ τὰ συνοικέσια τῇ μαρτυρίᾳ τῆς ἱερᾶς εὐλογίας ἐῤῥῶσθαι κελεύομεν, ὡς ἔνθα γε μὴ ὁρῷτο τοῖς συνοικεῖν βουλομένοις, τοιαύτη διαιτῶσα ἁρμογή, οὐδὲ τὴν ἀρχὴν ῥηθήσεται συνοικέσιον, οὐδ' ἐπιτεύξεται τῶν τοιούτου δικαίων ἡ τοιαύτη συμβίωσις.» —*MPG*, CVII, 601. The text is also found in *Ius Graecoromanum*, Vol. I, *Novellae et Aureae Bullae Imperatorum post Justinianum* (ed. Zacharias von Lingenthal, Athenis, 1930), p. 156. Cf. Scott, *The Civil Law* (17 vols. in 7, Cincinnati: The Central Trust Co., 1932), XV, 277. Cf. also Dauvillier and De Clercq, pp. 41-42; Esmein, I, 149; White, *De forma celebrationis matrimonii*, p. 20.

[99] Cf. Papp-Szilagyi, p. 273. Cf. also Pope Benedict XIV, epist. *"Singulari"* 9 febr. 1749, n. 7—*Fontes*, n. 394; cf. the Instruction of the Sacred Congregation for the Propagation of the Faith in 1858 to the Greek-Rumanian bishops—*Collectanea Sacrae Congregationis de Propaganda Fide* (2 vols., Romae: Typographia Polyglotta S.C. de Propaganda Fide, 1907), n. 1154 (hereafter referred to as *Collectanea*).

2. The Church Law

Though the faithful early followed the advice expressed by St. Ignatius (d. 107) in his letter to St. Polycarp (d. ca. 156), that their intended marriages should be made known to the bishop,[100] there is no canon of the early councils which required a religious ceremony for the validity of the marriage.[101] The legislation and the express sentiment of the Church against those who married after their spouses had died [102] support the view that, though the Church ceremonies were neglected by those who were marrying for the first time, or if such ceremonies were disapproved for those who were marrying a second time, the marriage still was viewed as a valid union if true marriage consent was present and no impediment existed.

The Patriarch of Constantinople, Nicephorus, in his *Constitutiones,* which were written in the early ninth century, answered the following question: "Is it lawful to allow at Mass and Communion servants who were joined in marriage by their masters without the blessing of the priest?" with these words: "A union without the blessing of the priest is fornication whether the person be a free man or a servant, and so the ones who have contracted such a union should not at all be received into the house of God." [103] However, in another canon of the same work, he ordered that if a widower wished to marry a widow, he should prepare a banquet and invite ten men of the family to it and say to them privately, "See, masters and brothers, that I take this woman as my wife," but that he should not have the nuptial prayers, and both were to undergo the penance assigned for those who entered a second marriage.[104] In yet another canon he for-

[100] 5, 1—Funk-Bihlmeyer, *Die Apostolischen Väter,* p. 112.

[101] Cf. Duchesne, *Christian Worship* (3. ed., trans. by M. McClure, London, 1903), p. 428; cf. also Jugie, "Mariage dans l'Église gréco-russe,"—*Dictionnaire de théologie catholique* (Paris, 1903—), IX (Part 2), Coll. 2318-2319 (hereafter cited as *DTC*).

[102] Cf. *supra,* pp. 8-11.

[103] Canon 199: «'Επίμιξις ἄνευ ἱερολογίας πορνεία ἐστὶν κἄν τε δοῦλος κἄν τε ἐλεύθερος· ὡς οὔτε γὰρ εἰς δωροθορίαν, οὕτως οὐκ εἰς οἴκους Θεοῦ εἰσδέχονται οἱ πορνεύοντες.»—Pitra, II, 346; *Fonti,* IX, n. 573.

[104] Canon 149—Pitra, II, 341. Cf. *supra,* p. 10.

bade a priest to bless those who are marrying for the third time.[105] Thus he seems to be demanding the intervention of the priest at a first marriage, while denying the giving of the blessing to those who married a second or a third time. It does seem then that, in his canon 199 about the marriage of servants, he meant that their marriage without the blessing of the priest was illicit, and therefore their marital life would be illicit.[106]

In the present discussion it is to be remembered that in the East the "blessing of the priest" was not the equivalent of the interrogations of the priest and the presence of witnesses, but in the strict sense a priest's blessing unaccompanied with any exchange of consent either asked or received by the priest. In the early marriage ceremonies of all those churches which were linked with the Church of Constantinople, the marriage consent was not expressed vocally, for among the Byzantines the blessing along with the crowning ceremony gave external manifestation of the consent of the parties.[107]

Pope St. Nicholas I (858-867), in answer to a query sent him by the Bulgarians, who said that Byzantine priests at Constantinople demanded a set form for validity, reviewed the customary usages connected with the making of espousals and the contraction of marriage in the Roman Church, but declared that not all these ceremonies were necessary for the validity of the marriage, for the marriage consent itself was the essential element.[108]

105 Canon 153—Pitra, *loc. cit.*

106 Cf. Cappello, n. 926. Gulovich ("Matrimonial laws of the Catholic Eastern Churches,"—*The Jurist,* IV [1944], 225) and White (*De forma celebrationis matrimonii,* pp. 37, 52-53) seem to put too great stress on this canon 199.

107 Dauvillier, "La formation du mariage dans les Eglises Orientales,"—*Revue des Sciences Religieuses,* XV (1935), 387. As the Byzantines for many centuries had no external vocal expressions of consent, the blessing was more than a liturgical blessing and approached being canonically necessary. The language of canonists often becomes difficult to follow when they are treating the history of the form among the Byzantines, since the Latin notions of today are alien to those of the early Byzantines. Further, the early writers did not distinguish between valid and licit marriages.

108 *MGH, Epistolae,* Vol. VI, Pars Altera, p. 570; *MPL,* CXIX, 980. His words here are found in Gratian in c. 3, C. XXX, q. 5; c. 2, C. XXVII, q. 2; c. un., C. XXX, q. 2, to be read in that order. Duchesne (*op. cit.*, p. 429) gives an outline of this response; cf. also Joyce, *Christian Marriage* (New

Cappello asserts that some canonists speak "at least less accurately" when they imply that the Church "adopted" her teaching on consent as the efficient cause of marriage from Roman Law; the Church has always taught this doctrine as part of the Divine Law itself, for the reason that God, as the author of marriage, has also established its essence, its nature, its purpose and its properties.[109]

It is not certain whether it was a common practice among the early Christians of the East (or of the West) to have their marriages blessed by a priest. It was to be expected that many took the advice of such leaders as St. John Chrysostom (d. 407), who pleaded that they should "call for the priest and by prayer and benediction tie the knot of unity in marriage, that the husband's love might increase and the wife's chastity might be strengthened."[110] Pope Hormisdas (514-523) decreed that no one should enter a clandestine marriage; but by receiving the benediction of the priest should marry publicly in the Lord.[111]

After the benediction of the priest, there was the rite of the crowning of the two parties with garlands, symbols of victory, which usage became very important in the marriage ceremonies of the East. It was first considered as a pagan symbol (although innocent in its own nature),[112] but during the latter part of the third century it became a general custom among the Christians.[113]

York: Sheed and Ward, 1933), pp. 44 and 52; White, *De forma celebrationis matrimonii,* pp. 17-18; Donovan, *The Pastor's Obligation in Pre-Nuptial Investigation,* The Catholic University of America Canon Law Studies, n. 115 (Washington. D. C.: The Catholic University of America, 1938), p. 21.

[109] *De Matrimonio,* n. 573, nota 5.

[110] Hom. 48 in Gen.: « . . . καὶ ἱερέας καλεῖν καὶ δι' εὐχῶν καὶ εὐλογιῶν τὴν ὁμόνοιαν τοῦ συνοικεσίου συσφίγγειν, ἵνα καὶ ὁ πόθος τοῦ νυμφίου αὔξηται, καὶ τῆς κόρης ἡ σωφροσύνη ἐπιτείνηται.»—*MPG,* LIV, 443.

[111] "Nullus fidelis, cuiuscumque conditionis sit, occulte nuptias faciat, sed benedictione accepta a sacerdote publice nubat in Domino."—*Bullarum Diplomatum et Privilegiorum Sanctorum Pontificum Taurinensis editio* (24 vols. in 25, Augustae Taurinorum, 1857-1872), App. I, p. 458 (hereafter cited as *Bull. Rom.*); c. 2, C. XXX, q. 5; Jaffé, n. 867; *MPL,* LXIII, 525.

[112] Tertullian, *De Corona,* cap. 13: ". . . Est omnis publicae laetitiae luxuria captatrix . . . coronant et nuptiae sponsos, ideo non nubamus ethnicis, ne nos ad idololatriam usque deducant, a qua apud illos nuptiae incipiunt. . . . Coronat libertas saecularis."—*MPL,* II, 96.

[113] Schrijnen ("La couronne nuptiale dans l'antiquité chrétienne,"—*Mé-*

St. John Chrysostom mentioned the ceremony and said about it: "Crowns are therefore put upon their heads as symbols of victory, because being invincible they entered the bridal chamber without ever having been subdued by any unlawful pleasure." [114]

In summary, it may be repeated that for many centuries in the early Church there was no certain formula in either the East or the West, inasmuch as the Christians most probably merely followed the usual marriage ceremonies of the places where they lived, though they omitted everything in the marriage ceremonies that was contrary to Christian faith or morals. The use of the priestly blessing appeared in the fourth century as a custom which warranted the licit contracting of marriage, in that it served to remove the evils consequent on any lack of outward signs as proof for the contraction of marriage. The use of this priestly blessing was quickly fostered by the piety of the people. It gradually became part of the civil law, and finally was demanded by the civil law in the ninth century as binding upon all. In its nature of a civil law it could not bind the Christians to follow it under pain of nullity for their marriages, but the Christians usually adopted the civil prescriptions as their own whenever they found it possible to do so.[115]

langes d'archéologie et d'histoire, XXI [1911], 309-319) gives quotations from Tertullian, Clement of Alexandria, Justin, Minucius Felix, St. John Chrysostom to show its evolution from a pagan symbol to a Christian one. Cf. *Fonti,* Serie II, Fasc. XXVII, pp. 120-121.

[114] Hom. 9 in 1 Tim.: «Διὰ τοῦτο στέφανοι ταῖς κεφαλαῖς ἐπιτίθενται, σύμβολον τῆς νίκης, ὅτι ἀήττηται γενόμενοι, οὕτω προσέρχονται τῇ εὐνῇ, ὅτι μὴ κατηγωνίσθησαν ὑπὸ τῆς ἡδονῆς.» — *MPG,* LXII, 546. Cf. White, *De forma celebrationis matrimonii,* p. 68.

[115] For a scholarly summary of the early Eastern sources concerning the form of marriage, cf. Herman, "De benedictione nuptiali quid statuerit ius byzantinum sive ecclesiasticum sive civile,"—*Orientalia Christiana Periodica,* IV (1938), 189-234.

CHAPTER II

A SUMMARY OF THE MARRIAGE LEGISLATION BEFORE THE COUNCIL OF FLORENCE OF THOSE ORIENTAL RITES WHICH ARE REPRESENTED IN THE UNITED STATES AND CANADA

ARTICLE I. THE ARMENIANS

1. A synopsis of their history before the Council of Florence [1]

Armenia, north of Kurdistan between the Caspian Sea and the Black Sea, was made a Roman province by Trajan (98-117), but about a hundred years later it passed over to the power of Persia. In 261 King Tiridates drove out the Persians and again made the country dependent on Rome. St. Gregory the Illuminator baptized Tiridates (after being persecuted by him), and so Armenia justly claims to be the first nation to accept the faith officially and as a single body. During this time Armenia perfected an organization for its Church, dependent on Caesarea in Cappadocia in the Patriarchate of Antioch.[2]

[1] Fortescue, *The Lesser Eastern Churches* (London, 1913), pp. 383-423; Attwater, *The Catholic Eastern Churches* (Milwaukee: Bruce, 1937), pp. 203-205; Janin, *The Separated Eastern Churches* (trans. by Boylan, St. Louis: B. Herder, 1933), pp. 173-178; *Sacra Congregazione Orientale, Statistica con cenni storici della Gerarchia e dei Fedeli di Rito Orientale* (Roma: Typografia Poliglotta Vaticana, 1932), pp. 77-80 (hereafter cited as *Statistica*); Ledit, *Praelectiones de Theologia Orientali* (Quebec: Universitas Lavallensis, 1942), pp. 34-39; Dauvillier and De Clercq, pp. 24-27.

[2] Near the end of the third century, St. Gregory the Illuminator had the title of *Katholikos*, i. e., universal delegate, as he was the delegate of the Exarch of Caesarea in Cappadocia. Cf. Cicognani, *Commentarium ad Librum Primum Codicis Iuris Canonici*, recognitum et auctum a Dino Staffa (2 vols., Romae, 1939, 1942), I, 11. Hereafter this work will be cited as Cicognani-Staffa, *Commentarium*.

After Jovian (363-364) Armenia was again handed over to Persia. Later, Theodosius I (379-395) made the mistake of dividing Armenia between Rome and Persia, with Persia getting four-fifths of it. Thus Christian Armenia, sympathetic at first to the empire at Constantinople, was put under pagan Persian kings. In the seventh century the Arabs pillaged the country; there was, however, from 856-1071 a line of semi-independent kings of Armenia of the Bagratid dynasty. In 1071 came the Turks who devastated the land of the Armenians, turned their cathedral into a mosque, and forever broke the political unity of Armenia. Because of the Turkish oppression then and that of the Mongols of the thirteenth century, great numbers of Armenians wandered about Asia and Europe seeking refuge and founding colonies in many countries. The colony in Cilicia became friendly to the Holy See in view of the assistance received from the Crusaders, and in 1198 became united to Rome. This Kingdom of Little Armenia in Cilicia, with Sis as its capital, lasted until 1393. Armenia sent four representatives to the Council of Florence (1438-1445), which published a reunion decree for the Armenians, but no real union was effected.

In 374 the Armenian Church rejected its canonical dependence on the Church at Caesarea, and formed a new body under its own *Katholikos*. In the first part of the fifth century, the Patriarch Isaac (Sahak) the Great (390-439) introduced the national language into the liturgy. The Armenian Church had no share in Monophysitism until forty years after the Council of Chalcedon, when a synod at Valarshapat (491) repudiated that Council (at which ten Armenian bishops had been present and had signed the acts); it cut itself off from the Catholic Church in approving Zeno's *Henotikon* in this synod, and widened the breach at the synod of Tovin (554) under the *Katholikos* Nerses II (548-557). Constantinople made many attempts in vain to unite the Armenian Church with itself. Especially was its effort in vain after the Council in Trullo condemned some of the Armenian religious practices in canons 32, 33 and 56. The attempts of Photius (d. 891), and later those of the Emperor Comnenus (1057-1059) in the eleventh century, were also in vain as the Armenian Church continued to develop along strictly national lines.

2. *Their laws* [3]

After the fifth century, when the Armenian Church followed its own course, it developed its own set of laws, but it retained also the early elements that came to it from the Greek Church at Caesarea in Cappadocia. The Church of Armenia accepted the authority of the three ecumenical councils of I Nicaea (325), of I Constantinople (381) and of Ephesus (431). According to Hatzuni they probably also accepted that of Chalcedon (451).[4] The particular councils of the fourth century, which were a chief source of the canon law of Byzantium, found their way into the Armenian collections, though in them there are variant readings and numberings of the conciliar canons. As for their own early councils which issued disciplinary decrees, there were those at Ashtishat (364 under Nerses I), Sahapivan (447), Duin (645 under Nerses III), another probably at Duin (719) and at Partav (771).[5]

After the Kingdom of Little Armenia was established, councils were held at Sis in the years 1204, 1246, 1307 and 1342. Canons on various matters were issued in these councils with the exception of the last one mentioned, which was occupied solely with a formulation of the answers to the 117 "accusations" which had been sent to Rome concerning them. In these answers are found many points of their canon law.[6] Canons are also attributed to the leading figures in the

[3] Cf. the Preface of the VIIth volume of the *Fonti,* which gives the Armenian law from the fourth to the seventeenth century; cf. also, *Fonti,* VIII, pp. 141-168; Doens, "Armenian Canon Law,"—*The Eastern Churches Quarterly,* III (1938-1939), 419-429, 460-473; Dauvillier and De Clercq, pp. 25-27.

[4] *Fonti,* VIII, 150.

[5] The text of the canons of these councils, with the exception of those of the Council of Ashtishat, can be found in Mai, *Scriptorum Veterum Nova Collectio,* X (e vaticanis codicibus edita, Romae, 1838), 290-310. Hereafter this tenth volume of his collection will be referred to as Mai. The *Canones selecti ecclesiae Armeniorum* are found on pages 269-316 of the second half of this book.

[6] The acts of the last two councils held at Sis, in 1307 and 1342, can be found in Mansi, *Sacrorum Conciliorum Nova et Amplissima Collectio* (53 vols. in 60, Parisiis, Arnhem, Lipsiae, 1901-1927), XXV, 134-140, 1185-1270. Hereafter this collection will be cited as Mansi. It appears that these "accusations"

Armenian church. Thirty canons are attributed to St. Gregory the Illuminator (d. ca. 332), fifty-five to Isaac the Great (d. 439) and thirty-nine to Nerses II (d. 557). Worthy of note also is the encyclical of Nerses IV (d. 1173) in 1166, which treats many points of Armenian canon law. In 1184 Mekhitar Gosh from Greater Armenia published a code of Armenian law, which Sempad used in 1264 to compile a body of laws as existing at that date. This code was officially introduced by King Leo IV of Lesser Armenia in 1331.[7]

3. A survey of their marriage legislation

In considering in a general way the marriage legislation of the Armenians before the Council of Florence (1438-1445), one notices many similarities with the points enumerated in the first chapter.

1. *The dignity of marriage.* A man could not send away his wife on the pretext of religion.[8]

2. *Vow.* One who vowed virginity to God should not dare to marry; if marriage was attempted, he was to be excommunicated, expelled and even deposed. The penalty for the violation of a vow of chastity was to be a penance of seven years.[9]

3. *Previous Marriage.* Second and third marriages were forbidden. This strictness was relaxed after the union with Rome in 1198. But dissidents in Greater Armenia in the fourteenth century regarded a third or fourth marriage as invalid.[10] A second marriage could be

arose after some uneducated faithful groups had been asked some theological questions of a technical nature. The two principal authors of the accusations were Bishop Nerses of Ourmiah and Bishop Simeon of Garin; the former sent them to the Holy See. An Armenian Franciscan, Fr. Daniel, answered these charges with a long *apologia* directed to the pope. The synod held in 1342 developed these responses of Fr. Daniel. Cf. Tournebize, "Les cent dix-sept accusations présentées à Benoît XII contre les Arméniens,"—*Revue de l'Orient Chrétien,* XI (1906), 163-181, 274-301, 352-370.

[7] *Fonti,* VIII, 163-164.

[8] Canon 24 of St. Gregory—Mai, p. 270; *Fonti,* VII, n. 442.

[9] Canons 13 and 30 of St. Gregory—Mai, pp. 269-270; *Fonti,* VII, nn. 121 and 122 (n. 120 repeats the thought of the 19th canon of the Council of Ancyra (314), namely, that one who married after a vow was to be considered a bigamist).

[10] Cf. Dauvillier and De Clercq, pp. 203-204.

permitted if one of the partners had not returned from captivity after seven years, according to an early Armenian council.[11] One of the charges made about the Armenians of Little Armenia to Rome was that they considered second marriages unlawful. The answer to this charge as given in the Council of Sis (1342) was in the same tenor as most of their answers, "That may be true of Greater Armenia, but it is not true of us here." [12]

4. *Affinity.* There were various penances for the forbidden marriage with a brother's widow or with the widow of any blood relative or affine.[13] In the fourteenth century, the impediment of affinity went to the third degree of the collateral line.[14]

5. *Consanguinity.* This impediment extended to all the degrees in the direct line, and, at first, up to and including the second degree of the collateral line in the now current mode of computation (fourth degree according to the Roman and Armenian way).[15] Nerses IV (1166-1173) prescribed the fourth (the Armenian eighth) degree because "the fourth generation has only the fourth part of the blood of the original parent, and this is the term of the propinquity of blood." [16] The Council of Sis in 1342 prescribed the Armenian fifth degree, "though according to the ancient custom we kept the impediment of the seventh degree." [17]

6. *Sacred Orders.* A priest could not marry after his wife died.[18]

[11] Council of Duin (645)—Mai, p. 311; *Fonti,* VII, n. 436. The Mekhitar Gosh allowed real divorce and remarriage if a spouse committed adultery. (Cf. *Fonti,* VII, nn. 440-441).

[12] Mansi, XXV, 1231; *Fonti,* VII, n. 529.

[13] Canon 12 of Sahapivan (447)—Mai, p. 294; *Fonti,* VII, n. 401; Dauvillier and De Clercq, p. 144.

[14] Council of Sis (1342)—Mansi, XXV, 1264; *Fonti,* VII, n. 408.

[15] Canon 13 of Sahapivan (447)—Mai, p. 294; *Fonti,* VII, n. 403. Cf. Canon 16 of Partav (771)—Mai, p. 308; *Fonti,* VII, n. 404.

[16] *Fonti,* VII, n. 405.

[17] Mansi, XXV, 1264; *Fonti,* VII, n. 408. Dauvillier and De Clercq (*op. cit.,* pp. 134-135) feel that their use of "fifth" and "seventh" degrees in this council was in the Latin method of computing degrees, and not in the Eastern way; also, "fifth" and "seventh" here do not point to the last prohibited degree, but rather to the first degree that lies outside of the enacted prohibitions.

[18] Canon 2 of Sahapivan (447)—Mai, p. 292; *Fonti,* VII, n. 524. (Nor

The Synod of Sis (1342) answered the charge that the Armenians allowed a deacon to marry by saying that if a deacon married, he could not be promoted to the priesthood.[19] However, those in Greater Armenia, not united with Rome, kept the old law among them which restricted the priest, but not the deacon. This restriction was not in the nature of a diriment impediment, but the priest who remarried was to be deposed.[20]

7. *Spiritual Relationship.* There was no conciliar legislation on this impediment.

8. *Abduction.* If anyone married a woman whom he had taken by force, the marriage was null, and the woman was free to marry whomever she willed.[21] The Council of Sahapivan (447), after decreeing that the woman was to be given back to her parents, set the monetary fines the man was made to pay.[22]

9. *Difference of religion.* A marriage with an infidel was regarded as no marriage at all, but as an evil and sacrilegious union.[23]

10. *The forbidden time.* The enactment of the Council of Laodicea (343-381), that marriages should not be celebrated in Lent, is restated in the Council of Duin (719).[24]

11. *Age.* Nerses IV (1166-1173) had required an age of fifteen for the man and of twelve for the woman,[25] but the Council of Sis in 1246 declared an age of fourteen sufficient for the man.[26]

12. *The form of marriage.* A charge against the Armenian Catholic clergy in Cilicia was that they did not prescribe for the con-

could the widow of a priest remarry). The Armenian Council at Rome in 1911 recalled this early decree. Cf. *Acta et Decreta Concilii Nationalis Armenorum Romae habiti ad Sancti Nicolai Tolentinatis anno MDCCCCXI* (Romae: Typis Polyglottis Vaticanis, 1913), p. 278.

19 Mansi, XXV, 1261; *Acta et Decreta, loc. cit.*

20 Dauvillier and De Clercq, p. 179.

21 Canon 9 of St. Gregory. According to *Fonti,* VII, n. 418, the word *"raptam"* is used; according to Mai, p. 269, the word *"concubinam."* But in the context the meaning of this canon of St. Gregory is no doubt the same.

22 Canon 7. *Fonti,* VII, n. 421, shows with relation to Mai, p. 293, the same discrepancy that was noted in the previous reference.

23 Canon 11 of the Council of Partav (771)—Mai, p. 308; *Fonti,* VII, n. 410.

24 Canon 5—*Fonti,* VII, n. 521.

25 *Fonti,* VII, n. 383.

26 *Ibid.,* n. 407.

tracting of marriage any determined form which would reveal the express consent of the spouses and that this consent was not required for the marriage. The Council of Sis in 1342 replied: "Among the Armenians there is a form of words which express the matrimonial consent between the man and his wife. First, through the intervention of the parents, the parties speak to one another and, if they consent, they become espoused mutually through the handing over of a ring. When they come to the door of the church, then they promise their faith to each other in this manner. The priest asks the man, 'If this woman would become blind, lame, leprous, sick, do you wish to take her?' Then the man replies, 'I consent to take her.' The bride is asked and replies in similar fashion. (An account of such things you will find in the book we sent to you.) They go into the church, receive the blessing of the priest, and then return to the house. This is the general custom of all the Armenians." [27]

St. Gregory had declared that if anyone contracted a clandestine marriage, the one who crowned him was to be deposed.[28] Nerses IV in his encyclical (1166) forbade priests to crown a couple secretly, without witnesses, and ordered that the crowning should be done publicly, for otherwise it would be "unstable and illicit." This requirement of witnesses and of a public crowning existed for those grooms who had no parents, or who had left them. If the groom's parents were alive and he wanted to live with them, then their previous consent and will had to be obtained, and thus it seems that they could also be the witnesses.[29]

[27] Mansi, XXV, 1264; *Fonti,* VII, n. 318; cf. Raes, "Le consentement matrimonial dans les rites orientaux,"—*Ephemerides Liturgicae,* XLVII (1933), 442-443.

[28] Canon 8—*Fonti,* VII, n. 386. Mai (p. 269) gives the following reading for this canon: "If anyone shall have contracted a clandestine marriage, let that be null."

[29] *Fonti,* VII, n. 388. Dauvillier (pp. 428-429) says that this insistence on the consent of the parents applied only to the man living with his parents because of the constitution of the Armenian family; as the son would bring the wife to the parents' home, his parents' consent was required; if the son wanted to leave his family, he had merely to leave the family house. The constant use of the word "crowning" (cf. e.g., *Fonti,* VII, nn. 380, 382, 387, 391, among others) shows the Greek origin of part of the marriage ceremonies.

It may be concluded, then, that for a valid marriage there was required the presence of a priest and witnesses, and if the couple were to live with the groom's parents, then also the previous consent of the latter was needed for licitness. Similarly it may be concluded that a marriage was branded as clandestine when no witnesses were present to constitute it as a public ceremony, even though a priest had assisted at the marriage.[80]

Article II. The Chaldeans

1. *A synopsis of their history before the Council of Florence* [81]

Beyond the eastern boundary line of the *Oriens* Praefecture of the Roman Empire there existed another empire, that of Persia. Catholicism penetrated into Persia through Edessa, which in the first century was the capital of an autonomous state. From Edessa the faith spread along the Tigris River into Chaldea and other parts of the Persian Empire. War broke out between the Persians and the Romans in 340. The Christians were persecuted by the Persians, since Christianity was regarded then as the official state religion of the Roman Empire. At that time the Church had several dioceses in Persia, and the bishop of Seleucia-Ctesiphon began to claim a certain rule over the other sees. The position of this bishop was confirmed in the synod of the Persian Church at Seleucia in 410,

[80] Cf. Dauvillier and De Clercq, pp. 72-76, for additional legislation and the liturgy concerning the form of marriage among the Armenians. It is important to emphasize the fact that among the Orientals in past centuries the term "clandestine" was referred to a marriage which was contracted in the presence of a priest, but not as a public ceremony, i. e., apart from the presence of witnesses, or of the parents of the couple. This term was not understood in the later Tridentine sense, as pointing to a marriage in which there was no intervention of either priest or witnesses. Cf. White, *De forma celebrationis matrimonii,* p. 80; Papp-Szilagyi, p. 274; Benedetti, *Votum, Acta Sanctae Sedis,* XLI (1908), 260.

[81] Fortescue, *The Lesser Eastern Churches,* pp. 88-100; Janin, *The Separated Eastern Churches,* pp. 199-202; Dvornik, "National Churches and the Church Universal"—*The Eastern Churches Quarterly,* V (1942-1944), 173-180; *Statistica,* pp. 229-235; Dauvillier and De Clercq, pp. 10-11; Attwater, *The Catholic Eastern Churches,* pp. 227-228.

when the Primate of Persia assumed the title of *Katholikos*. This synod accepted the decisions of the I Council of Nicaea (325) and of the I Council of Constantinople (381). In 424 a synod at Seleucia-Ctesiphon decreed that thereafter no appeal from their *Katholikos* to the Patriarch of Antioch or to the Metropolitan of Edessa was to be granted. The exact reason for this decree is disputed, but a likely cause was the wish to show the pagan Persian kings that their Christian subjects were not allied politically with the Christians of the Roman Empire.

The great promise of the Persian Church as an instrument for the spreading of the faith in Asia was impaired by that Church's refusal to accept the condemnation of Nestorius in the Council of Ephesus in 431. Accordingly the Catholic Persian Church became the schismatic Nestorian Church. It retained at first the rite of Antioch, but in the course of time it adopted so many changes that it gradually developed a distinct rite. This Nestorian church flourished from within, and even under the Caliphate in Bagdad it had sees in China, Cyprus, Turkestan and Southern India. The invasion of Tamerlane (1336-1405), the rebel Mongol chieftain whose wild hordes in the latter part of the fourteenth century swept like a hurricane over Asia, crushing the Turks and the Mongols and devastating Syria, Persia, India and China, subjected the country, and brought about the gradual decline of the people and their Church. At the Council of Florence, Archbishop Timothy of Tarsus, Metropolitan of Cyprus, became united with Rome, along with all the Nestorians under his jurisdiction.[32] But after his death and after the occupation of Cyprus by the Turks, the Chaldeans of this island gradually adopted the Latin rite.

2. *Their laws* [33]

Marûthâ, Bishop of Maiferat, a city between the River Tigris and Lake Van, went to Persia as the ambassador of Theodosius II to

[32] Cf. *Fonti*, Serie III, Fasc. VI, p. 190; Giamil, *Genuinae Relationes inter Sedem Apostolicam et Assyriorum Orientalium seu Chaldaeorum Ecclesiam* (Romae, 1902), pp. 9-12.

[33] *Fonti*, IV, 1, 3-6; VIII, 649-693; Dauvillier and De Clercq, pp. 11-14.

represent the "Western Fathers" in the synod at Seleucia in 410. He tried to have the Persian Church accept all the early church legislation, but only that of the two ecumenical councils held up to that time, I Nicaea (325) and I Constantinople (381), was accepted. The decrees of the Council of Chalcedon (451), in which the Persians had not taken any part, found their way into the Nestorian canon law through Mar Aba I (d. 552), who brought them back from Constantinople, where he had stayed a year between 525-533. The Council's condemnation of Eutyches (378—d. after 451) proved acceptable to the Nestorians.

Many synods were held (15 between 410 and 905) and many attempts to codify the canons were made. The outstanding collection among the Nestorians is that of Abdisho of Nisibis, also known as Ebedjesus (d. 1318). He codified the various Nestorian decrees in his *Epitome of the synodal canons,* designated under the name of the *Nomocanon of Ebedjesus.* This compilation comprised two books, one of civil law and the other of church law.[34] The *Nomocanon* even today has the force of law among the Nestorians. The collection of Ebedjesus incorporated the acts of the early eastern councils and also the *Canons of the Apostles.* (A collection of the synods of the Patriarchs of Seleucia was drawn up at the end of the eighth century under the title of "*Eastern Synods.*") Ebedjesus made another collection, called *Rules for Church Courts.*[35] His collections were declared authentic in a synod of 1318, held by the *Katholikos* Timothy II (1318-1328?).

3. *A survey of their marriage legislation*

1. *The dignity of marriage.* A cleric could not dismiss his wife on the pretext of seeking chastity.[36]

[34] Assemani presented a detailed analysis of this Nomocanon in his *Bibliotheca Iuris Orientalis,* Vol. III, Pars I, pp. 332 sqq. and Cardinal Mai edited this with the translation of Aloysius Assemani in the first part of the tenth volume of his *Scriptorum Veterum Nova Collectio* (all of the 27 chapters of the second part of the *Nomocanon* concern marriage).

[35] This has been edited and put into Latin by Vosté in the *Fonti,* Serie II, Fasc. XV, Romae, 1940.

[36] Canon 5—Ebedjesus, *Epitome Canonum Apostolorum (qui dati fuerunt*

2. *Vow.* The early Nestorian Church did not know monastic vows; however, Ebedjesus required that the Nestorian religious who contemplated marriage first obtain the permission of the bishop, and also that the ceremony of their marriage be of a private nature.[37]

3. *Previous marriage.* Successive polygamy was not reproved in the canons codified by Ebedjesus.[38] He allowed a spouse to marry again, if the other party to the marriage had been held in captivity for three years.[39] If husband and wife both agreed to enter the religious life, it was licit for them to do so.[40]

4. *Affinity.* The synod of Mar Aba I (544) repeated the second canon of the Council of Neocaesarea (314-325) by decreeing that a woman who successively married men who were brothers was to remain excommunicated to the day of her death; the same synod also in effect repeated the prohibition of such marriages as were prohibited in the Book of Leviticus (XVIII, 6-18; XX, 10-12).[41] In the collection of Ebedjesus affinity received a very wide interpretation. The blood relatives of the man were considered as related by affinity to the blood relatives of the woman.[42]

5. *Consanguinity.* The synod of Mar Aba I (544) forbade marriages between blood relatives in the entire direct line, but in the collateral line only between brother and sister, between uncle and niece, and between nephew and aunt. Under later Byzantine influence the prohibition was extended to include the intermarriage of first cousins. But this greater restrictiveness in the law was later

per sanctum Clementem discipulum Apostolorum) as found in Mai, p. 9; *Fonti,* IV, 45.

[37] *Nomocanon,* II, 11—Mai, p. 47.

[38] Cf. Dauvillier, p. 449.

[39] *Nomocanon,* II, 21—Mai, pp. 50-51. However, the *Ordo Iudiciorum Ecclesiasticorum* (L. II, tr. 3, cap. 13) declared that a man should wait 10 years —*Fonti,* Serie II, Fasc. XV, p. 188. Hereafter this will be cited as *Ordo.*

[40] *Ordo,* L. II, tr. 3, cap. 20—*Fonti,* Serie II, Fasc. XV, pp. 198-199.

[41] Canon 16—Chabot, *Syndicon Orientale* (Paris, 1902), pp. 557-558 (hereafter cited as Chabot); *Fonti,* IV, 15.

[42] Cf. the long, detailed list of prohibited marriages as presented in the *Nomocanon,* II, 1—Mai, p. 41; *Ordo,* L. I, tr. 3, cap. 3; Assemani, *op. cit.,* III, 2, 319, sqq.; cf. Dauvillier and De Clercq, p. 142; *Fonti,* Serie II, Fasc. XV, p. 177.

withdrawn by the return of the Nestorians to the limited prohibitions as set in the synod of 544. This relaxation is still followed as the law among the Nestorians of the present day.[43]

6. *Sacred Orders.* The synod of Mar Akak (486) abolished this impediment for deacons. It also allowed an unmarried priest to marry after his ordination, and a married priest to remarry after the death of his wife.[44]

7. *Spiritual relationship.* Marriage with one's spiritual children through baptism was prohibited inasmuch as they were likened to physical children, and because of this analogy the minister of baptism could not marry the party whom he baptized, or a person who was a sponsor at the baptism.[45]

8. *Difference of religion.* The synod of Mar Aba I (544) prohibited the intermarriage of a Christian and a non-Christian.[46] The synod of George I (676) forbade the marriages of Christians with non-Christians because of the danger of perversion, especially for the Christian woman.[47] Ebedjesus repeated this prohibition in the 65th case in the list of marriages forbidden to a woman.[48] He mentioned as the special reason for this prohibition the fact that it was the custom after marriage for a woman to go over to the religion of the man, just as she goes over to his tribe and family; hence a Christian woman naturally could not marry an infidel, but a man could marry a pagan woman in the hope of aiding her conversion.[49]

9. *Age.* Ebedjesus placed the ages at sixteen for the man and at twelve for the woman.[50]

10. *Abduction.* If the girl was not an engaged woman (mekhirtà),

[43] Dauvillier and De Clercq, pp. 127-128.

[44] Canon 3—Chabot, p. 305; *Fonti,* IV, 47.

[45] *Ordo,* L, II, tr. 3, cap. 3—*Fonti,* IV, 175. Cf. also *Fonti,* Serie II, Fasc. XV, p. 175.

[46] Chabot, p. 336; *Fonti,* IV, 175.

[47] Canon 14—Chabot, p. 488; *Fonti,* IV, 185.

[48] *Nomocanon* II, 1—Mai, p. 43; *Fonti,* IV, 173.

[49] *Nomocanon,* II, 14 and 15—Mai, p. 48; *Fonti,* IV, 183.

[50] *Ordo,* L. II, tr. 3, cap. 9—*Fonti,* IV, 15; *Fonti,* Serie II, Fasc. XV, p. 185.

the abductor could marry her if she and her family consented to the marriage.[51]

11. *The form of marriage.* The betrothals were important ceremonies among the Nestorians, for in these ceremonies were decided the free consent of the parties and the details of the dowry to be exchanged by the parties. Ebedjesus listed the details of the ceremony which took place in the presence of the priest and of the faithful; the blessing of the priest, the use of the crucifix and the holy water, the symbolism of the acceptance of the ring by the woman, the drinking from the chalice by both, the writing on two tablets of the consent of the couple, the man signifying his betrothal of this particular woman and his settlement on her of a definite dowry, and the woman doing likewise, signifying her voluntary betrothal and the receiving of a certain dowry from the goods of her father. The priests and guests then witnessed these documents, and the parties thereupon received their tablets. Any betrothal done outside of this prescribed form was held invalid.[52]

Ebedjesus in the succeeding paragraph described the ceremony for betrothal if there was no priest in the region available for the man who desired to be betrothed. The man was to call together four or five of the faithful who could be the witnesses, take the crucifix, the ring and the holy water, and then recite the *Our Father* and the *"Trisagion."* Thus the betrothal was complete until such time that a priest could come and bless it. If a priest was not available at the time which was set for the marriage itself, then the marriage ceremony

[51] *Nomocanon,* II, 12—Mai, p. 47.

[52] *Nomocanon,* II, 2: . . . "Ubi autem mutuum sibi invicem consensum dederint adolescens et adolenscentula, scribatur consensus amborum in duabus tabulis; una quidem tabula in testimonium sit sponso, seu ore ac voce ipsius ita: voluntate mea desponsavi *talem* filiam *talis;* et dotem *sic* et *sic* constitui ei. In alia vero nomine sponsae sic scribatur: voluntate mea desponsavi me ipsam *tali* filio *talis per* sponsores meos *talem* et *talem;* zebda (dos) data est mihi e domo patris mei *sic* et *sic.* Et ambae tabulae confirmentur testimonio sacerdotum et invitatorum, et unicuique ex eis detur scriptura sua. Quaevis desponsatio quae extra praescriptum modum ineatur, nulla reputatur a nobis. . . ."—Mai, p. 44 (cf. *Fonti,* IV, 181, which summarizes this quotation down to the words, "Et ambae tabulae" with these words: "Iamvero requirebatur ut consensus sponsi et sponsae scripto consignentur, in duabus tabulis una nomine sponsi danda sponsae et altera nomine sponsae danda sponso.")

was to be conducted in a manner similar to that of the betrothal.[53] Ebedjesus also listed the details of the betrothal for a woman who had no relatives, and for the one who came from another city. The priest acted as her father in the ceremony; the priest also asked the man about his qualities, his religion and his free status.[54]

All these various ceremonies appear to refer rather to a betrothal than to an actual marriage rite itself. Thus it may be said that Ebedjesus did not indicate the actual juridical form for the contraction of marriage as in use among the Nestorians.[55]

In any analysis of the ceremonies current among the Nestorians for the engagement contract and the contract of actual marriage, it must be remembered that the Nestorians were imbued with the concept that the betrothal and its sealing in marriage proper were but

[53] *Nomocanon,* II, 3: "Ille, qui existat in regione in qua sacerdotes non reperiantur, ex fidelibus convocet quatuor aut quinque, qui testimonium perhibeant, et accipient crucem, et annulum, ac hananam, et alta voce recitent orationem: pater noster qui es in coelis: et sanctus Deus: et hoc pacto perficiatur desponsatio, donec ad sacerdotes accedant (*veniant*) aut sacerdos ad eos veniat et suppleat id quod defuit desponsationi quam inierunt. At si non pervenerit ad eos sacerdos ante tempus thalami (*nuptiarum*) simili modo perficiant thalamum (*nuptias per verba de praesenti, uti vulgo dicitur, contrahant*)." —Mai, p. 44.

[54] *Nomocanon,* II, 6—Mai, p. 45; *Fonti,* IV, 179.

[55] Gulovich ("The Matrimonial Laws of the Catholic Eastern Churches"—*The Jurist,* IV [1944], 224) claims that Ebedjesus did indicate the form of marriage by showing the ceremonies of betrothal and then saying that the marriage takes place "in a like manner." But these words of Ebedjesus were used in his instructions regarding the ceremonies which were to be employed in the *absence* of the priest, and hence this set of circumstances ought not to be associated with the ordinary case when a priest was available. The marriage ceremonies proper are not listed by Ebedjesus. So, while it can be denied that the betrothal ceremony was said by him also to constitute the marriage ceremony, no positive description of the usual marriage ceremony among the Nestorians can apparently be given. Also, the word that Ebedjesus used for the ceremony he described is *Mekhuryá,* which means "betrothal." However, it must not be overlooked that the Nestorians placed more emphasis on betrothals (in which a consent *de praesenti* was given) than is found in the Western Church, and also, that it was Peter Lombard who distinguished between *desponsatio per verba de praesenti* and *desponsatio per verba de futuro.* Cf. Raes, "Le consentement matrimonial dans les rites orientaux,"—*Ephemerides Liturgicae,* XLVII (1933), 135; XLVIII (1934), 316.

two successive stages or elements in one and the same marriage contract. This concept is somewhat similar to, but not derived from, the Roman Law concept of betrothal and marriage. The concept was derived rather from the Jewish law as it was binding at the time of Our Lord, for the Jews attached the terms "husband" and "wife" to those who in strict parlance were only engaged, and accordingly regarded the cohabitation of "husband" and "wife" as the factor which initiated the existence of their "marriage."[56] The first witnesses regarding the practices of the Persian Church show in the fourth century how the Christians were carefully trying to reconcile the Jewish observances with the Christian traditions and the recognized sacramental dignity of marriage. The amount and the importance of the purchase (*mekhar*) of the woman was gradually lessened. In the eighth century the pact of engagement (*mekhirutha*) consisted in the symbolic act of the exchange of the ring, and the engagement was blessed by the priests and other clerics before some of the faithful as witnesses. Betrothals without the intervention of the priests or without Christian witnesses were null.

For the "second moment" of the marriage (the *sautaputha*), no definite form seems to have been prescribed under pain of nullity. The priest usually appeared at the wedding banquet, and blessed the

[56] The Syriac version of the Scriptures, the *Peshito,* has the term *"mekhira"* (engagement) to describe the relation between the Blessed Virgin and St. Joseph, and later in the texts they are called "husband" and wife," though in their relationship "the second moment of marriage" as understood in the Jewish sense never became an actuality. Cf. Dauvillier and De Clercq, p. 50, note 2. Dauvillier ("La formation du mariage dans les Eglises orientales,"—*Revue des Sciences Religieuses,* XV [1935], 389-390) stated that the Eastern canonists of the middle ages did not view marriage as a *res simplicissima* which cannot be divided, since marriage in their eyes was formed in several moments. What they call the first moment of marriage (which is not however *per se* the mere espousal) has therefore some of the properties of marriage itself. De Clercq, in speaking of this Eastern concept of "two moments" of marriage, declared: "C'est alors que se donne le consentement au nom des parties et celui-ci ne doit dès lors, plus être renouvelé; le mariage n'est qu'une solennelle exécution, une prise de possession de ce qui a été accordé."—*Ordre, Mariage, Extrême-Onction* (Paris: Bloud et Gay, 1939), p. 81.

couple. It was understood that thus the couple acquired the right of marital cohabitation.[57]

Article III. The Antiochene Rite

1. *The Syrians*

A. A synopsis of their history before the Council of Florence [58]

The antipathy of the Syrians for the Greeks who were centered around Constantinople in the first centuries became very definite at the time of the Monophysite struggle. Urged on also by those in Egypt, who viewed the stand taken at the Council of Chalcedon (451) as implying a betrayal of their St. Cyril of Alexandria (d. 444), they refused to accept the decrees of the Council of Chalcedon, and tried to capture the existing sees for their sect. They succeeded at first, even at Jerusalem and at Antioch, but the Emperors at Constantinople, especially the Emperor Justin (518-527) and his nephew Justinian (527-565) soon drove them out. Justinian imposed the decrees of the Council of Chalcedon on the Empire, and tried to suppress the Syrian heretics.

The Monophysites were about to become extinct when the Empress Theodora (d. 548), Justinian's royal consort, intervened. Under her protection, James Baradai (d. 578) was consecrated Bishop of Edessa in 543 by Theodosius, Monophysite Patriarch of Alexandria (535-567), who was in prison at Constantinople. For nearly forty years, this James labored unceasingly in Syria, Egypt, Thrace and the islands of the Archipelago, and everywhere he renewed the people's interest in Monophysitism and organized new churches. He consecrated a bishop for Antioch, and from this line comes the

[57] For a detailed study of the evolution of the Nestorian form of betrothal and marriage, cf. Dauvillier and De Clercq, pp. 48-61. Cf. also Denzinger, *Ritus Orientalium, Coptorum, Syrorum et Armenorum in Administrandis Sacramentis* (2 vols., Wirceburgi, 1863), II, 419-450.

[58] Fortescue, *The Lesser Eastern Churches,* pp. 323-336; Janin, *The Separated Eastern Churches,* pp. 191-194; *Fonti,* VIII, 117-125; *Statistica,* pp. 64-65; Ledit, *Praelectiones de Theologia Orientali,* pp. 27-29; Attwater, *The Dissident Eastern Churches* (Milwaukee: Bruce, 1937), pp. 269-271.

Jacobite Patriarch of Antioch existing side by side with the Melkite Patriarch.

For the next thirteen centuries the Jacobites (the Syrians who took their name from James Baradai) had a rather uneventful history. They were more numerous than the Melkites who remained faithful to the teachings of the Council of Chalcedon. Under the Moslem Arabs they became a *millet* (nation) of Christians. Their dealings with the Crusaders were for the most part friendly. In the time of the Crusades they were in a flourishing condition, as the Patriarch then had about 118 bishops subject to him in Syria, Asia Minor, Cyprus and Persia. From 1292 to 1495 they had schisms among themselves which weakened them, especially the continuous rivalry between the Patriarch and the *Mafrian,* his legate in Persia, and the repeated setting up of rival Patriarchs.

Latin missionaries in the thirteenth century brought some of the Jacobites back to union with Rome, but as a whole the body of Monophysites was unaffected. At the time of the Council of Florence (1438-1445) a temporary union was effected when the Jacobites of Egypt, Ethiopia and Libya sent envoys to the Pope at Florence to bring about a union. On February 4, 1442, the decree of their union, *"Cantate Domino,"* was promulgated by the Council. In the fall of 1443, Pope Eugene IV (1431-1447) transferred the Council from Florence to Rome, and continued to receive the Orientals into the Church. Abdallah, the Syrian Patriarch for the Jacobites between the Tigris and the Euphrates, submitted to the Holy See on September 30, 1444.[59] These unions however gradually disappeared.

B. Their laws [60]

The Syrians used a collection of their councils at the beginning of the sixth century, but a practical guide for a survey of their laws is the codification of the Jacobite laws as made by Gregory Abdul-

[59] Cf. *Bulla unionis Syrorum—Fonti,* Serie III, Fasc. VI, pp. 188-190.

[60] *Fonti,* VIII, 128-138; Duval, *Anciennes Littérature Chrétiennes,* II, *La Littérature Syriaque* (Paris, 1907), pp. 167-168; Dauvillier and De Clercq, pp. 16-18; Chabot, *Littérature Syriaque,* Bibliothèque Catholique des Sciences Religieuses, n. 66 (Paris: Bloud et Gay, 1934), *passim.*

Faraj (1226-1286) (as he was of Jewish descent he was called BarHebraeus) in the late thirteenth century. He gathered in his collection, entitled *"The Book of Directions,"* the juridical texts of the Western Syrians, embracing both the church canons and the civil laws. The work is divided into forty chapters, covering an extensive field of law. Because of its combination of canon and civil law, it is known as the *Nomocanon* of BarHebraeus.[61] In the early part of the present century Nau translated into French the canonical writings of some of the bishops and patriarchs, covering the period from 412-896. All of these prelates were Jacobites, except Bishop Rabboula, who governed the see of Edessa from 412 to 435.[62]

C. A survey of their marriage legislation [63]

The *Nomocanon* of BarHebraeus contained the following prescriptions concerning marriage:

1. *The dignity of marriage.* A cleric could not dismiss his wife on the pretext of seeking chastity.[64]

2. *Previous marriage.* A second marriage was considered a venial offense, a third was branded as a transgression of the law, and a fourth was stigmatized as a type of depravity.[65] A second marriage was not to be contracted until ten months after the death of the

[61] Cardinal Mai, in the second part of the tenth volume of his *Scriptorum Veterum Nova Collectio,* has a Latin translation of it as made by Aloysius Assemani. The great amount of legal details that it contains can be judged from the fact that it comprises 265 pages in the work of Mai. The influence of the early general legislation in the East, particularly that of the fourth century, is seen in the very frequent quotations by BarHebraeus from the early councils, not only with reference to marriage, but also regarding various other sections of the law.

[62] Nau, *Les Canons et les Resolutions Canoniques de Rabboula, Jean de Tella, Cyriaque d'Amid, Jacques d'Edesse, Georges des Arabes, Cyriaque d'Antioche, Jean III, Theodose d'Antioche et des Perses* (Paris, 1906).

[63] For an analysis of the early Syrian marriage legislation, divided according to the chapters as they are found in the Latin Code, cf. *Fonti,* Serie II, Fasc. XXVII, pp. 237-279.

[64] VII, 5—Mai, p. 47; *Fonti,* III, 33.

[65] VIII, 2—Mai, p. 64.

husband.[66] In a second marriage there was to be no blessing of the rings or of the crowns, but a prayer could be said over the contracting parties. No provision was made for any ritual ceremony at a third betrothal, but in necessity prayers could be said over the parties after previous fasting and almsgiving.[67]

3. *Affinity.* This impediment extended to all the degrees of the direct line and was extended by BarHebraeus to the seventh (in their reckoning) in the collateral.[68] The easiest way to calculate affinity and the reason for its existence as an impediment were indicated by BarHebraeus thus: since the two parties are as one flesh, the husband of the deceased woman (and vice versa) is to be put in the place of the woman (or man) in the schema of her (his) blood relatives, and the calculation is to be made as in the case of consanguinity.[69]

4. *Consanguinity.* This impediment extended to all the degrees of the direct line and to the seventh (in their reckoning) in the collateral line.[70]

5. *Sacred Orders.* BarHebraeus repeated the first canon of the Council of Neocaesarea (314-325), which declared that a priest or a deacon who married was to be deposed from his office.[71]

6. *Vow.* BarHebraeus quoted the decree of the early Council of Ancyra (314), which had declared that those who vowed virginity

[66] VIII, 6—Mai, p. 79; *Fonti,* III, 123. No strict rule is set for a man, but in the same section it was declared fitting that he wait five months.

[67] VIII, 2—Mai, p. 64; *Fonti, loc. cit.*

[68] Hindo (*Fonti,* Serie II, Fasc. XXVII, *Introduction,* pp. 102-103) quotes David as saying that BarHebraeus, in extending this impediment to the seventh degree of the collateral line, represented the Greek discipline rather than that of his own Church.

[69] VIII, 3: "Et illa prima affinitas sponsae quae obiit (aut derelicta fuit verbo legali) ad typum affinitatis genericae commensuratur, eo quod vir et mulier una sunt caro, ut dixit Deus. Itaque filia mulieris, filia est mariti eius quamvis ex alio marito sit; et mater eius (*mulieris*) mater eius (*mariti*); et soror eius, soror eius; et cetera talia, quae inquiruntur in generationem generationum; aut usque ad complementum septem facierum"—Mai, pp. 67-68; cf. *Fonti,* III, 89; Dauvillier and De Clercq, p. 142.

[70] VIII, 3—Mai, p. 66; cf. *Fonti,* III, 85. Hindo (*ibid.,* pp. 100-101) asserts that BarHebraeus was the first of the Syrians to extend this impediment to the seventh degree, but that his rule was not followed.

[71] VII, 4—Mai, p. 46; *Fonti,* III, 33.

but later married were to have the penances of bigamists imposed upon them.[72]

7. *Spiritual relationship.* The godfather was accounted with the real father, and the godmother with the real mother, and so the one baptized was considered as a real child. The relationship created by the spiritual bond accordingly occasioned a matrimonial impediment between the recipient of baptism and the members of the godparents' families unto the seventh degree (in their reckoning) of the collateral line.[73]

8. *Difference of religion.* Six general types of "infidelity" were listed: pagans, *magi* (probably refers to the Persians), Jews, Saracens, Christians doubting in their faith regarding the divinity of Christ, namely, the Arians, and Christians dividing the natural and personal unity of Christ. (In this last type the Monophysite BarHebraeus referred to Nestorians and Catholics). After the women of the first five types had through their reception into the Church been baptized and instructed, it was allowed to marry them. If women of the sixth type were received, they had no need of baptism, but only of "sound instruction." The same rule applied to "infidel" men.[74]

9. *Forbidden time.* Marriages were not to be celebrated in Lent, "according to the canons of the Council of Laodicaea," nor at the time of Pentecost.[75]

10. *Age.* The woman was required to be at least twelve years of age;[76] the man at least fourteen.[77]

[72] VII, 10—Mai, p. 56. The Syrian Church did not know monastic vows in the present understanding of the terms. Cf. Dauvillier and De Clercq, p. 181.

[73] VIII, 3—Mai, p. 67; *Fonti,* III, 87.

[74] VIII, 3: "Infidelitatis autem sex novimus diversitates genericas: ethnicos, magos, iudaeos, saracenos, christianos de deitatis fide dubios, qui sunt Ariani, ac socii eorum christianos dividentes unitatem naturalem et personalem. . . . Et mulieres quae sunt ex quinque generibus primis, cum baptizantur, suscipimus ad nuptias: at mulieres quae ex genere sexto, non baptizamus, sed solum cum recte instituuntur, recipimus: similiter et viris infidelibus. . . ."—Mai, p. 69; cf. *Fonti,* III, 93; cf. Dauvillier and De Clercq, pp. 169-170; Hindo, *ibid.,* p. 95.

[75] VIII, 1—Mai, p. 63; *Fonti,* III, 119.

[76] VIII, 1—Mai, p. 63; *Fonti,* III, 93.

[77] XIV, 3—Mai, p. 131; *Fonti,* III, 95.

11. *The form of marriage.* Among the Jacobites there was an evolution in the concept of betrothal and marriage as constituting but two moments or stages of the same contract, similarly as it existed in the Nestorian Church. At the time of BarHebraeus the form of betrothal was very solemn. Another ceremony, usually a nuptial banquet and a blessing of the crowns that were to be worn by the spouses, initiated the common life of the contracting parties.[78] At the time of BarHebraeus, the time-interval between the betrothal and the blessing of the crowns sometimes lasted as much as seven years. After his death, the two rituals became blended into one.[79]

2. *The Maronites*

A. A synopsis of their history before the Council of Florence [80]

Lebanon, the home of the Maronites, on the Mediterranean Coast above Palestine, is approximately the same territory as ancient Phoenicia. The Maronites take their name from the saintly Maron (350-433), model of the cenobitic life in Northern Syria and founder of a religious community at Apamea, which was a center of Catholic literature and faith (some 350 of these monks were martyred for the faith about 517). The Maronites claim that they never fell into schism, but that they withdrew into the hills of Lebanon to preserve their faith in 680 when the Mohammedans were overrunning Syria.[81]

[78] Cf. *Nomocanon,* VIII, 2—Mai, p. 63; *Fonti,* III, 121. Cf. Dauvillier and De Clercq, pp. 61-64. Cf. also *Nomocanon,* VIII, 5—Mai, p. 74; *Fonti,* III, 155.

[79] Cf. *Fonti,* Serie II, Fasc. XXVII, pp. 111-112.

[80] Eid, *A l'Ombre des Cèdres ou L'Épopée de Liban* (Fall River, Mass., 1940), pp. 39-60; Abraham, *The Maronites of Lebanon* (Wheeling, W. Va., 1931), pp. 1-79. These two authors give many references to source books and works of reference. Cf. *Statistica,* pp. 54-55. Janin, *Les Églises orientales,* pp. 551-554; Dib, "Les Maronites et leur liturgie,"—*Le Canoniste Contemporain,* XL (1917), 302-314, 401-418.

[81] It appears however that at the Council of Florence a group of Maronites from Cyprus "returned" to union with Rome. Cf. Anaissi, *Bullarium Maronitarum* (Romae, 1911), pp. 14-16. Cf. *Fonti,* Serie III, Fasc. VI, p. 191: ". . . Deinde similem per omnia professionem dilectus in Christo filius Ysach nuntius venerabilis fratris Nostri Eliae episcopi Maronitarum ipsius vice et nomine reprobando Macharii de unica voluntate in Christo haeresim, cum

The few thousand who thus went to the hills formed the nucleus of the Maronite nation. Their great leader was a monk from the convent of St. Maron, John Maron, the first Patriarch of the Maronites after their separation from the other Catholic groups in Syria.

When the Crusaders came, the Maronites helped them, but they suffered greatly for this proffered assistance after the Crusaders had left. The Maronite Patriarch Joseph George went to Rome with Godfrey de Bouillon's messenger, who was to announce to Pope Urban II (1088-1099) that the Crusaders had captured Jerusalem. The Maronites again fought on the side of the Crusaders with St. Louis, King of France (1226-1270).

Patriarch Jeremias attended the IV General Council of the Lateran (1215), and Pope Innocent III (1198-1216) accorded to him the use of the pallium. In the same century, Pope Alexander IV (1254-1261) gave to Patriarch Simeon II the right to the use of the title: "Patriarch of Antioch."

B. Their laws [82]

In 1058 the superior of the Maronite monks asked the Maronite Bishop David to make an Arabic translation of the canons. Bishop David however compiled a Syriac treatise, entitled, *"Perfection,"* which explained dogma and elucidated the law, both civil and canon. The Maronite monks of the eleventh century did not understand Syriac, and so about the year 1105 a translation was made by Bishop Thomas of Kephartab, who furnished a personal interpretation for what he judged to be obscure passages. The first part of this translation consisted of a treatise in 19 chapters on the sacraments (the 17th concerns marriage) and on the principal duties of Christians; the second part is a general discourse on the various

multa veneratione emisit." The Maronites of the present day are all Catholics and they alone of the Eastern rites have no "Orthodox" counterpart. As to the debate whether the Maronites ever lapsed into heresy, Ledit (*Praelectiones de Theologia Orientali,* p. 32) advises: "Res tamen forte mitius erga hunc fidelissimum populum dijudicari potest." Cf. Attwater, *The Catholic Eastern Churches,* pp. 181-182.

[82] *Fonti,* VIII, 92-100 and XII, v-viii; Duval, *La Littérature Syriaque,* p. 168; Dauvillier and De Clercq, pp. 19 and 20.

duties of Christians, and embraces the commands of the Apostles and of the Fathers of the Church; the third part reproduces the canons of the early Church councils, and also the text of the *Syro-Roman Book,* which contains the decrees of the Emperors Constantine (306-337), Theodosius II (408-450), and Leo the Philosopher (886-912). This translated *Nomocanon* remained as the canon law of the Maronite Church from the twelfth century to the Plenary Council of the Lebanon in 1736, with the exception of the minor synodal law enacted in the year 1596 by two Synods held by the Patriarchs Sergius and Joseph. Another legal collection used by the Maronites was the *Book of the Law,* the compilation of Ibn-al-Assal, a Coptic writer of the thirteenth century. The Maronites adopted this compilation to supply the omissions in their own law.

C. A survey of their marriage legislation [83]

1. *Vows.* The Maronites did not know the impediment of vows.[84]

2. *Previous marriage.* It seems that the Maronites did not allow the crowning ceremony in a second marriage.[85]

3. *Affinity.* This impediment affected all in the direct line. In the collateral line a man could not marry the wife of his deceased brother, nephew or uncle. At a later time the wider prohibitions of the Council in Trullo were introduced, but the law of a council held in 1580 returned to the earlier and more limited prohibitions.[86]

4. *Consanguinity.* A man could not marry his sister, his aunt, his niece, his grandniece, or anyone in the direct line of relationship.[87]

5. *Sacred Orders.* A priest could not marry after his wife died.[88]

6. *Spiritual relationship.* This impediment was more extensive

[83] The translation of the Maronite *Nomocanon* exists in an unedited manuscript. However, Dauvillier and De Clercq in their work on the marriage laws of the Orientals (*Le Mariage en Droit canonique oriental*) had access to the manuscript, and their summaries of the early Maronite marriage laws are used here.

[84] Dauvillier and De Clercq, p. 182.

[85] *Ibid.*, p. 202.

[86] *Ibid.*, p. 143.

[87] *Ibid.*, p. 130.

[88] *Ibid.*, p. 176.

among the Maronites than among the Latins, inasmuch as it was made to derive not only from baptism (abstracting from any distinct relationship through confirmation, which at this period was conferred together with baptism), but also from marriage. The godfather could not marry the girl at whose baptism he had acted as sponsor, her mother, grandmother, sister, aunt, daughter or even her parents' godmothers. Similarly, a person could not upon the death of his consort marry the one who had acted as a witness at his marriage, nor could he marry the daughter of this witness.[89]

7. *Abduction.* This impediment was not known.[90]

8. *Difference of religion.* The faithful could not give their daughters in marriage to infidels, heretics or schismatics, unless these had first been converted to the Church. An attempted marriage with such a non-Catholic was regarded as null, even though this person had been baptized previously, and accordingly the parties of such a union were to be separated.[91]

9. *The form of marriage.* The presence of some priest was required for validity. After the Crusades, the influence of the Latins induced the Maronites to reduce their "first moment of marriage" to a simple espousal, and to introduce a certain Latinized solemnity for the form of marriage proper.[92]

Article IV. The Byzantine Rite

1. *The position of Constantinople*

Of the greatest influence among the Eastern Churches was the position of the Patriarch of Constantinople, who became the leading Church figure in the East through the support of the Eastern Emperors. Byzantium was the rather insignificant suffragan see of Heraclea before Constantine brought the seat of his government there. The bishop of Byzantium (Constantinople), relying on the accepted custom in the East that the rank of a bishop is to be proportionate to the rank of the civil ruler of the city, sought to

[89] *Ibid.*, p. 150.
[90] *Ibid.*, p. 189.
[91] *Ibid.*, p. 170.
[92] *Ibid.*, pp. 65-66.

have his see recognized as the leading see in the East. Later in the fourth century his hopes were realized when the I Council of Constantinople in 381 declared, "The bishop of Constantinople shall have the primacy of honor after the bishop of Rome, because the same is the new Rome." [93]

This conciliar recognition was later expanded by the Council of Chalcedon (451) in its 28th canon into an acknowledgment of explicit jurisdiction in the dioceses of Pontus, Asia and Thrace, because "the city which is honored with the sovereignty and the senate, and enjoys equal privileges with old imperial Rome, should in ecclesiastical matters also be magnified as she is and rank next after her." The Pope, however, did not recognize this canon. The accepted notion in the East of linking the church in a city with the civil rulers reveals the seed of the later schisms, not only the schism from Rome because of the growing power of the Eastern Emperor at Constantinople, but also the schisms within the Church of the Eastern Empire itself, for the various oriental nationalities became opposed to the rule at Constantinople and its power over their own groups. In the East nationality became identified with religion. The two concepts were so linked that, while in the West the fall of the Empire did not imply the fall of the Church, in the East the desire to break away from the Byzantine rulers at Constantinople implied a breaking away from the Church at Constantinople, which was considered the State-Church and the instrument of the imperial ecclesiastical policy.

Soon after 395 (the year of the death of Theodosius I, after whose reign Constantinople became the definitive capital of the Eastern Roman Empire) the Bishop of Constantinople ruled over six provinces in Thrace and twenty-two in Asia-Minor. Seventy-five years later he exercised jurisdiction over more than 400 dioceses,

[93] Canon 3: «Τὸν μέντοι Κωνσταντινουπόλεως ἐπίσκοπον ἔχειν τὰ πρεσβεῖα τῆς τιμῆς μετὰ τὸν τῆς Ῥώμης ἐπίσκοπον, διὰ τὸ εἶναι αὐτὴν νέαν Ῥώμην.» —Pitra, I, 509; *Fonti*, IX, n. 756. Cf. Schroeder, *Disciplinary Decrees of the General Councils*, pp. 65-67; Bingham, bk. II, chapt. xvii, sect. 21; Dawson, *The Making of Europe* (New York: Sheed & Ward, 1945), pp. 111-113, 179-180; Raab, *The Twenty Ecumenical Councils of the Catholic Church* (New York: Longmans, Green, 1937), p. 13; Dauvillier and De Clercq, p. 1; De Clercq, *Les Églises unies d'Orient*, Bibliothèque catholique des Sciences Religieuses, n. 65 (Paris: Bloud et Gay, 1934), p. 44.

and at the beginning of the tenth century he ruled over 624.[94] Thus it was only natural that such a vast organization could spread into the Ukraine, into Russia and into the Balkans, and thenceforth maintain its hold on these churches for centuries, in addition to the extensive influence it wielded in Asia Minor.

2. *A survey of the Byzantine law sources*[95]

The best known early systematic collection of the Byzantine Canon Law is that of John the Scholastic, who was a lawyer at Antioch. He went from Antioch to Constantinople as a deputy to Emperor Justinian; he became Patriarch in 564, and ruled until 578. About the year 550 he collected the existing church laws under fifty titles.[96] After the death of the Emperor he collected the civil laws into a work called *The Collection of the 87 Chapters.* Later these Church laws and civil laws were put together in a collection called *The Nomocanon of 50 Titles;* this was translated into the early Slavic language of Moravia and later the disciples of St. Methodius (d. 885) probably brought it to the Bulgarians; from Bulgaria it passed into Russia.[97]

The marriage legislation which the early *Collection of 50 Titles* contained was a repetition of the early decrees already considered in the first chapter of this dissertation. For example, cantors and lectors alone among the clerics could marry, but not with heretics;[98] a priest could not send away his wife on the pretext of piety;[99] no

[94] Janin, *The Separated Eastern Churches,* p. 44.

[95] Cf. Van Hove, *Commentarium Lovaniense in Codicem Iuris Canonici,* Vol. I, Tom. I, *Prolegomena* (ed. altera, Mechliniae-Romae: Dessain, 1945), pp. 163-169.

[96] Cf. Benesevic, *Iohannis Scholastici Synagoga L titulorum,* in *Abhandungen der bayerischen Akademie der Wissenschaften,* N. F., Heft 14, München, 1937. Cf. also Cimetier, *Les Sources du Droit ecclésiastique* (Paris: Bloud et Gay, 1930), p. 16.

[97] Cf. Herman in the *Fonti,* Serie II, Fasc. VI, p. 7.

[98] Title XXVI—Pitra, II, 381. The early *Collection of 50 Titles* is contained in pages 375-385 of this second volume of Cardinal Pitra's collection; the *Nomocanon of 50 Titles* is found in summary form on pages 416-420.

[99] Title XXVII—*ibid.,* p. 382.

one could rightfully abhor marriage; [100] repeated marriages were not approved.[101]

The *Nomocanon of 50 Titles* did not combine the canon and civil laws (it merely placed them side by side), but such a legal interweaving of these laws was undertaken in the *Nomocanon of XIV Titles,* first drawn up in the seventh century by an anonymous writer who is called Enantiophanes, then revised, and ultimately issued in 883 under Photius as the second part of a collection of laws, the first part containing the early canons accepted in the East, most of the canons of the Council in Trullo, 22 canons from the II Council of Nicaea (787) and the twenty canons of two councils (861 and 879) held under Photius. This collection is substantially the same as the previous *Nomocanon,* but presents a more finished work.[102] Each title is divided into many chapters. Each chapter in turn first lists the canons of the councils or the canons of the *Canons of the Apostles* that pertain to its subject, and then the civil law as found mainly in the *Code* and the *Novellae* of Justinian. Repeated references to the early canons on marriage are given.[103]

While Photius lived, this collection, translated into Syriac and Arabic, was brought to many places in the East. After his death in 891 no further collections of Byzantine canon law were made. The Byzantine canonists from then on devoted themselves to commentaries on the collection issued under Photius, which was adopted as the official Byzantine canonical collection at a council held at Con-

[100] Title XXIX—*loc. cit.*

[101] Title XLIII—*ibid.,* p. 384.

[102] It can also be found in the work of Pitra, II, 433-636.

[103] Legislation both canon and civil on the following marriage questions can be found in this *Nomocanon:*

I. Dignity of marriage. A. Title 9, chapter 28—Pitra, II, 563. B. Title 13, chapter II—*ibid.,* p. 621.

II. Vows. Title 9, chapter 29—*ibid.,* p. 563.

III. Previous marriage. A. In same reference as for Vows. B. Title 13, chapter 2—*ibid.,* p. 610. C. Title 14, chapter 3—*ibid.,* p. 612.

IV. Sacred Orders. A. Title 1, chapter 33—*ibid.,* p. 479. B. Title 9, chapter 29—*ibid.,* p. 563.

V. Abduction. A. Title 9, chapter 30—*ibid.,* pp. 566-567. B. Title 13, chapter 8—*ibid.,* p. 619.

VI. Difference of religion. Title 12, chapter 13—*ibid.,* p. 608.

stantinople in 920; a third recension was made in 1080 by Theodore Bestes (at this time Constantinople was definitively separated from Rome). The better known commentators in the twelfth century were John Zonaras, Alexius Aristenus and Theodore Balsamon, of whom the last was the most outstanding.[104] Among those who developed a canon law science in Byzantine law the best known writer was Matthew Blastares in the fourteenth century. He made an abstract of the *Nomocanon of 14 Titles,* and disposed the material in alphabetical order by headings.[105]

It can be said then that the Byzantine laws for the Church at Constantinople down to almost modern times can be found in the collection of Photius along with the commentaries of Zonaras, Aristenus and Balsamon, with the abstract of Blastares, besides other minor commentators and abbreviators. In modern times even the churches which have broken away from the Patriarchate of Constantinople have retained this Byzantine law as handed down since the fourteenth century. This law is especially known through the *Pidalion,* a collection made by two monks of Mt. Athos, printed for the first time in Leipzig in 1802, and reprinted in a new edition in 1841. The *Pidalion* was translated into Russian in 1839, and into Rumanian in 1842. Several times reprinted and translated into various languages, it forms the basis of law for the modern branches of the Byzantine Church.

3. Some Byzantine rules concerning marriage

A legal concept that went through centuries of evolution was the concept of clandestinity in relation to marriage. In the first chapter of the present study mention was made of the *Novella* of Leo the

104 The collection of Migne (*PG.,* Vol. 137) contains the logically combined commentaries of Zonaras, Aristenus and Balsamon on the six early particular councils, the Council in Trullo and the early seven eastern ecumenical councils. Vol. 138 continues this combined commentary for the Council of Carthage which was held in 419, and for the canonical letters of the Fathers (col. 953 sqq. is devoted to Balsamon alone).

105 This dictionary of Byzantine law can be found in Migne, *PG.,* Vol. 144, coll. 959-1400, and Vol. 145, coll. 9-210. The section dealing with marriage can be found in Vol. 144, coll. 1147-1214. Cf. *Fonti,* Serie II, Fasc. VI, pp. 33-35.

Philosopher in 895, which required the benediction of the priest for the validity of any marriage between free persons, and of the almost inconsistent decisions of the Patriarch Nicephorus, who ruled the See of Constantinople from 806 to 815. The Emperor Alexius I Comnenus (1081-1118) demanded the benediction of the priest for all marriages, even those of serfs, yet the crowning was still forbidden for second or third marriages. The Patriarch Lucas Chrysoberges (1156-1169) likewise demanded the blessing of the priest for both free persons and slaves. A few years later a synodal decree of Michael Anchialos in 1177 declared that it was not the will of the contracting parties, but the fulfilling of the rite, which made the marriage; Balsamon said the same. In effect, the crowning rite did not carry with it an exchange of consent. A synod of 1306, approved by Andronicus II Paleologus (1283-1328), declared that for the future a marriage was not to be contracted without the knowledge and permission of the proper parish priest.[106]

[106] Dauvillier, p. 381; Dauvillier and De Clercq (pp. 41-45), after presenting these various decrees of the Byzantine Emperors, declared that the Holy See "has put in doubt the juridical value of the practice which demands the presence of a priest for validity, since that practice rests, in the last analysis, on some edicts of the Emperors or on some ecclesiastical decisions taken after the rupture with Rome. It seems that custom would be able precisely to justify this practice, but the Holy See has not judged it sufficiently established. On the other hand, the Holy See is opposed to that which, on their own initiative without the approval of the Holy See, some Catholic groups would introduce as a juridic form of marriage similar to that of the Latin Church." In a recent article Gulovich suggests the same thought when he writes: "As for the Byzantine legislation requiring sacerdotal blessing for all marriages there can be no doubt as to the existence of the law, but at present we have no proof that this law received the approval of the supreme authority in the Church. Hence, since this supreme approval—not the existence of the law itself—is doubtful, the obligatory force of the law cannot be invoked. Therefore, until such time as it can be proved that the 199th canon of St. Nicephorus of Constantinople was approved either by an ecumenical council or by a decree of the Supreme Pontiff, marriages contracted without the sacerdotal blessing cannot be condemned as concubinages."—"The Principle Underlying the Validity of Oriental Marriage Law,"—*The Jurist,* VI (1946), 45. As noted *supra* (p. 27), it would seem that Gulovich puts too much stress on the 199th canon. Cf. Staffa, "De transitu ad alium Ritum,"—*Apollinaris,* XIII (1940), 185.

Another Byzantine legal controversy concerned the number of successive marriages a man could enter. The attitude of the early councils towards repeated marriages has been previously outlined in the first chapter. The *Prochiron* (870-879) of Basil the Macedonian (867-886) declared a third union to be subject to canonical penalties, and a fourth marriage to be null. This legislation was renewed by Leo the Philosopher (886-912). However, this Emperor himself later decided to marry a fourth time. The clergy of Constantinople upheld the ancient customs and laws against such a marriage. The Patriarch Nicholas the Mystic asserted that a fourth marriage was forbidden by the Divine Law itself. Accordingly, he excommunicated the Emperor, but he himself was then deposed in 907 by the Emperor, and the new Patriarch, Euthymius (d. 917) removed the censure from the Emperor. The Emperor then decided to convoke a council, and he invited representatives also from the three other Eastern Patriarchs; legates were likewise sent in 907 by Pope Sergius III (904-911). Since the Latin Church knew of no restrictions on the number of successive marriages, the papal legates rendered a decision favorable to the Emperor; but by so doing they aroused much bitter feeling, so that many considered their decision to be a violation of Christian morality. After the death of Emperor Leo a council in 920 declared a third marriage to be null and at the same time severely punishable; this decree made no mention of the marriages of the deceased Emperor. This feeling in the East against successive marriages continued for centuries, as can be deduced from the fact that the profession of faith demanded of the Emperor Michael VIII Paleologus (1261-1282) by the II General Council of Lyons (1274) contained an admission of the licitness of second and third marriages.[107]

In the eleventh century there was a development in the early Byzantine Church tendency to consider the betrothal and the actual marriage crowning as but two elements of the same marriage contract.[108] A synodal decision of Patriarch Xiphilinos in 1066,

[107] Dauvillier, pp. 448-451; Duchesne, *The Churches Separated from Rome* (trans. by Mathew, New York: Benziger Bros., 1907), pp. 148-149; Schroeder, p. 35, note 78; Dauvillier and De Clercq, p. 199.

[108] Cf. *supra*, p. 4. Cf. *Fonti*, Serie II, Fasc. III, n. 31.

which was confirmed by the Emperor Nicephorus in 1080, declared that the impediment of affinity between brother-in-law and sister-in-law thenceforth derived from a betrothal as well as from a marriage. The Emperor Alexius Comnenus in 1084 decreed solemn betrothals to be completely assimilated to marriage, so that from that time onward betrothal and marriage pointed simply to two separate stages in the same contract. Some natural consequences of this juridical view were: (1) betrothal as a diriment impediment of *ligamen* stood in the way of all marriages other than that between the betrothed; (2) the same impediments arose from betrothal as from marriage; (3) betrothals could be dissolved only for the same reasons for which divorce was justified in Byzantine law; (4) if one of the parties died between the betrothal and the crowning ceremony, the surviving partner's marriage was viewed as successive bigamy. Also, a logical liturgical development of this juridic view appeared in the later middle ages when the rites both of the betrothal and of the crowning were held on the same day.[109]

The impediment of consanguinity in the collateral line was extended in the early middle ages to the seventh degree, but the Patriarchs did not expressly declare marriages within the seventh degree to be null, e.g., in 1038 Patriarch Alexius forbade such marriages under the penalty of spiritual punishments, but made no specific mention of the penalty of nullity. The Patriarch Michael Caerularius (1043-1058) in 1057 declared that such marriages were

[109] Dauvillier and De Clercq, pp. 34-35. The Byzantine Church received at first the notion of espousals, *sponsalia,* the simple promise of marriage, from the Roman Law. But in the course of the centuries the promise to marry took on a solemn aspect, and in the ceremony the parties actually signified their marital consent, and could be called husband and wife, but they could not live as husband and wife until the crowning ceremony. Thus, as seen above in the discussion of the Chaldean and Syrian Churches, the English terms "espousal," "betrothal" or "engagement" do not fully connote the later Byzantine concept that true matrimonial consent was given, and not a mere promise to marry in the future. What seems foreign to our thought of today, they did not think that the matrimonial contract was made in its entire essence at one moment, but they considered that there could be two time-elements in one and the same matrimonial contract. Cf. Dauvillier "La formation du mariage dans les Églises orientales,"—*Revue des Sciences Religieuses,* XV (1935), 386-395.

null, but this decree was not generally observed. In 1166 a synod at Constantinople, held by the Patriarch Lucas Chrysoberges, ordered that all marriages in the future contracted within the seventh degree were to be declared null.[110] This impediment in its extension to the seventh degree has continued as the law of the Church of Constantinople up to the present time.

4. The Melkites

A. A synopsis of their history before the Council of Florence.[111]

After the decrees of the Council of Chalcedon were announced (451), many of the people in Syria, Palestine and Egypt became Monophysites, because they regarded these decrees as constituting a betrayal of St. Cyril of Alexandria (d. 444), the outstanding figure of Egypt. When the Emperor Marcian (450-457) in 452 approved the decrees of the Council of Chalcedon as the law of the Empire and fortified their observance with severe sanctions, adherence to these conciliar decrees became identified with loyalty to the Emperor in the minds of the people. Followers of the Council of Chalcedon were therefore called "imperialists" or "king's men," i.e., "Melkites" (Syriac root plus a Greek ending).[112]

Under the Moslems the Monophysites disintegrated into local sects, while the Melkite minority stubbornly clung to the Empire and the Church at Constantinople. After the death of the Patriarch Stephen of Antioch in 744, Theophylact Bar Kanbara, jeweler of Merwan the Caliph, became the Patriarch for the next six years.

[110] Mansi, XXII, 13. Cf. Dauvillier and De Clercq, pp. 124-125; Janin, *Les Églises orientales*, p. 74; *Fonti*, Serie II, Fasc. V, p. 223.

[111] *Fonti*, VIII, 376-383; Fortescue, *The Uniate Eastern Churches* (ed. G. Smith, London: Burns, Oates, 1923), pp. 185-195; Janin, *The Separated Eastern Churches*, pp. 65-68; Abraham, *The Maronites of Lebanon*, pp. 20, 43-44; *Statistica*, pp. 134-139.

[112] Cf. Ayrout, "The Melkites and the Mohammedans,"—*The Eastern Churches Quarterly*, IV (1940-1941), 64-67; Janin, *The Separated Eastern Churches*, p. 66; Assemani, *Bibliotheca Iuris Orientales*, I, 507. Ricciotti, writing about the Syrians in the *Fonti*, claims (VIII, 119) that the name means "realists," inasmuch as the term is derivable from the Syriac word *malka*, which stands for the Latin word *res*.

It was during his rule that the separation of the Melkites and the Maronites became complete, since the Maronites maintained their status of independence in the Lebanon hills, while the Melkites, true to their name, remained loyal to Constantinople. Michael Caerularius in 1054 was opposed by the Melkite Patriarch Peter III, who was evidently a staunch Catholic, but the latter's successor, Theodosius III Chrysoberges, who became Patriarch in 1057, was the ally of Caerularius. It was under this Patriarch that the Melkites obediently removed the Pope's name from the Diptychs, thereby withdrawing from Rome. At first they kept their own liturgy, but at the end of the twelfth century Theodore Balsamon, the Greek Patriarch of Antioch residing at Constantinople, prevailed on the weakened Patriarchate to change its liturgy of St. James to that of Constantinople.

It appears that the actions of the Crusaders, especially the establishment of a Latin Patriarch at Antioch (1098-1268), increased the hostility of the Melkites against Rome. The Melkite Bishop Theodosius Villehardouin however signed the reunion decree at the II General Council of Lyons in 1274, and resigned his see when the Emperor Andronicus II (1282-1328) rejected the union. Probably others in the fourteenth and fifteenth centuries united with Rome. The Patriarch of Antioch, Dorotheos I, accepted the decree of union formulated at the Council of Florence, but the capture of Constantinople by the Turks in 1453 hindered the work of a successful union in the East. However, several Melkite Patriarchs remained in union with Rome. In Egypt, at the beginning of the thirteenth century, the Melkite Patriarch of Alexandria, Nicholas I, showed himself favorable to Rome, but his successors were hostile to the Holy See.

B. Their laws [118]

A manuscript collection, dating from 1378, and giving the Melkite canonical sources, was found at Mt. Lebanon in the library of the Aleppan Basilian priests. Besides the usual *Canons of the Apostles*, the canons of the ecumenical and early particular councils, and the

[118] *Fonti*, VIII, 310-349, 383-403; Cheiko, "Catalogue Raisonné des Manuscrits de la Bibliothèque Orientale,"—*Mélanges de l'Université Saint Joseph de Beyrouth*, XI (1926), 216-225.

decrees of the Emperors Theodosius II, Leo the Philosopher, and others, this collection contains precepts of St. Peter, St. Matthew and St. Paul. Abela, in his analytical classification of the various parts of the Melkite law,[114] refers frequently to the canons of the Council in Trullo, while the next source is dated after their definitive union with Rome in 1724. Thus it may be said that up to the eighteenth century the Melkites followed the canon law of Constantinople. However, Charon (Korolevskij) claimed that, if it be contended that the canon law of the Melkites was "the same as that of Constantinople," one must understand by this the truly early law of Constantinople, since the commentaries of Zonaras, Aristenus, Balsamon, and Blasteres were not known among the Melkites, who also were not influenced by any Melkite *Pidalion* as mirroring for them the canon law of Constantinople in the early middle ages.[115]

C. A survey of their marriage legislation

In view of their adherence to Constantinople in the early centuries, and in view of the reasoned position of Charon, namely, that they were not in contact with the laws of Constantinople in the early middle ages, it can be said that the marriage laws of the Melkites before their reunion with Rome in the eighteenth century remained the same as the laws outlined above in the first chapter.[116]

5. The Ruthenians [117]

[114] *Fonti,* VIII, 310-349.

[115] *Histoire des Patriarcats Melkites* (Vol. II, Fasc. 1, and Vol. III, Rome, 1910, 1911), III, 362-365.

[116] Cf. the introduction to Volume XV of the *Fonti*; also, Darblade, "La collection canonique Melkite d'après les manuscrits arabes des XIIIe-XVIIe siècles,"—*Orientalia Christiana Periodica,* IV (1938), 85-119.

[117] The term "Ruthenians" is used in the documents of the Holy See in reference to those of the Byzantine-Slavonic rite who inhabit the northern and southern slopes of the Carpathian Mountains; the northern part constitutes Galicia, and the southern comprises the eastern part of Czecho-Slovakia and also part of Hungary. This terminology ("Ruthenians" or "Greek-Ruthenians") connotes a legal custom at the present time rather than a popular custom, as the people of Galicia prefer to be called Ukrainians, ever since their nationalist revival in the nineteenth century. (After World War I, Galicia became the southeastern part of Poland.) The word *Rutheni* is first found in the writings of the

A. A synopsis of their history before the Council of Florence.[118]

Without discussing the controversy whether the Rusins living around Kiev became Christianized through the influence of the West or of the East,[119] it can be said that the Kievian Rusins date their organized Christianity from the baptism of Vladimir (d. 1015), Prince of Kiev, in 988, near Kiev by a Bishop Paul, and from the mass baptism of his people in 990 in the Byzantine rite. For almost fifty

Polish annalist Martinus Gallus of the twelfth century; before that these people usually called themselves *Rusini,* derived from *Rus,* the abstract word for the vast territory that became the home of the Slavic people and the Russian fatherland. This land was first limited to that portion of Europe which we call the Ukraine. Therefore, when speaking of the first inhabitants around Kiev in the early Middle Ages, one finds it difficult to use a term which would not give a modern connotation; those people could be called "Rus-Ukrainians." The Ruthenians of the present day claim that they were these original Rusins, and that the present Russia and Russians owe their name and territory to the conquest of the former "Rus-Ukrainians." Cf. *A Memorial of Andrew J. Shipman* (edited by Condé B. Pallen, New York: Encyclopedia Press, 1916), pp. 188-189; *Statistica,* p. 169. Cf. also Holoweckyj in his summary of the Ruthenian Church sources (*Fonti,* VIII, 593): " . . . the Ruthenian Church cannot be viewed as Russian in the modern sense, in the manner of the Church of Peter the Great, for, while the Russian Church took its origin from the Ruthenian, it now has a very different form and spirit." At first the area around Kiev was alone called Rus, but the same name was kept as other groups merged with the Rusins and as the country developed into the present Russia. The word "Ruthenian" is derived from the late Latin word *Ruthenia,* which designates the territory that gradually became the modern Russia.

[118] *Fonti,* IX, iii-viii; *Statistica,* pp. 169-177, 198-199; Koncevicius, *Russia's Attitude Towards Union with Rome (9th-16th Centuries),* Washington, D. C.: The Catholic University, 1927, *passim* (hereafter cited as Koncevicius); Fedotov, "Le baptême de Saint Vladimir et la conversion de la Russie,"—*Irenikon,* XV (1938), 417-436; De Baumgarten, "Aux origines de la Russie,"—*Orientalia Christiana Analecta,* no. 119 (1939); Danzas, *The Russian Church* (trans. by Bennigsen, London: Sheed & Ward, 1936), pp. 1-20; Hrushevsky, *A History of Ukraine* (ed. by O. Frederiksen, New Haven: Yale University Press, 1941), pp. 20-138 (hereafter cited as Hrushevsky).

[119] Cf. Vernadsky, "The Status of the Russian Church during the first half-century following Vladimir's conversion,"—*The Slavonic and East European Review,* XX (1941), 294-314, and "Byzantium and Southern Russia,"—*Byzantion: International Journal of Byzantine Studies,* XV (1940-1941), 67-86; cf. Hrushevsky, p. 65; Dauvillier and De Clercq, p. 9.

years the Rusins tried to develop a church organization which would be independent of the Patriarch of Constantinople, lest their Church would exist merely as one of the metropolitan provinces of the Byzantine Patriarchate. However, in 1036 the nation was weakened by internal war, and so it accepted as Metropolitan the Greek Theopemptum, named by the Byzantine Emperor and consecrated by the Byzantine Patriarch.

After this time the Metropolitans at Kiev were practically appointees from Constantinople with two notable exceptions, the Metropolitan Hilarion, elected in 1051, and the Metropolitan Clement Smolatyn, elected in 1147 at the synod of Kiev.[120] Constantinople did not recognize either of these. At the schism of 1054 the Rusins did not at once break away from Rome, but internal disorder and political upheavals eventually caused a break with Rome, which cannot be accurately dated. For the four subsequent centuries until the union of Brest in 1595, the history of the Rusins is one of alternate periods of union and separation. Isidor, the Metropolitan of Kiev (1437-1463), at the time of the Council of Florence attempted to create a permanent union.

Kiev was captured by the Tatars on December 2, 1240, and this date is given as the end of the history of the kingdom of Kiev, which had been gradually weakened by civil wars and by conflicts with the nomads from the East; the Tatars ruled the Ukrainian provinces for fifty years. The following century also saw an end of the independence of the Ukrainian groups, for Poland took Galicia, while the Dukes of Lithuania controlled Volhynia and also the provinces around Kiev and Chernigov.

Galicia was the first to separate from the political unity at Kiev, and became the strongest of the early Ukrainian regions. Coloman (1208-1241) the son of King Andrew II of Hungary (1205-1235), who sought to annex Galicia, married Salome, a daughter of the Polish King Lieszko V (1194-1227), and received at Halicz the rule of Galicia, while the Polish king took for himself the provinces of Przemysl and Brest. Pope Innocent III (1198-1216) negotiated with Coloman for reunion, but revolts broke out at this attempt. The Hungarians and the Poles a little later waged war against one

[120] Cf. *Fonti,* Serie II, Fasc. VI, p. 12.

another, and the Hungarians were driven from Galicia; however, a century later they renewed their alliance, and Poland appropriated Galicia which she kept until 1772.

In 1246 Pope Innocent IV (1243-1254) negotiated with Prince Daniel of Galicia who wanted to be crowned by the Pope, and who therefore promised that he would strive for reunion and fight with the Christian powers of Europe against the Tatars.[121] In the following year the Pope wrote to Daniel that the people in Galicia could retain their rites as long as they did not conflict with faith.[122] In 1253 the Pope sent a legate to crown the prince as King of Galicia, but only a few years later, in 1257, Pope Alexander IV (1254-1261) had to reprove the king for not fulfilling his promises. In 1299 Rome established Galicia as a separate province, but this arrangement was ended in 1345; it was renewed for a brief period after 1371, but in 1389 it was united with the province of Kiev.[123]

The Rusins also spread throughout the southern slopes of the Carpathian Mountains in the regions of eastern Czechoslovakia, northeastern Hungary, and also to Transylvania, Bucovina and Croatia. After the attempts of King Louis I of Hungary (1342-1382) in the latter part of the fourteenth century to annex Galicia had failed, there was fixed a boundary line in the Carpathian Mountains, and this line has remained down to modern times as the boundary between Hungary and Galicia.

At the time of the Council of Florence (1438-1445), reunion of the Rusins with Rome was linked with the name of the Metropolitan of Kiev, Isidor (1437-1463). He attended the Council of Florence, signed the Acts, and in 1439 was created a Cardinal and Papal Legate to Lithuania, Rus, Livonia and Poland. In the Lithuania of that time he was well received; in the larger cities of the

[121] Baronius, *Annales Ecclesiastici* (37 vols., ed. Theiner, Vols. I-XXVIII, Barri-Ducis, 1864-1875; Vols. XXIX-XXXVII, Parisiis, 1876-1883), XXI, 326-327. Hereafter this work will be cited as Baronius.

[122] " . . . Eapropter, carissime in Christo fili, tuis supplicationibus inclinati, episcopis et aliis presbyteris de Russia ut liceat eis more suo ex fermentato conficere et alios eorum ritus, qui fidei Catholicae quam Ecclesia Romana tenet non obviant, observare auctoritate praesentium indulgemus."—Baronius, XXI, 346.

[123] Koncevicius, pp. 152-153.

Rusins, such as at Kiev and Smolensk, in his double capacity as Papal Legate and Metropolitan, he promulgated the reunion decrees. His rejection at Moscow can be regarded as marking the definite break from Rome on the part of the rising state of modern Russia.

B. Their laws [124]

Vladimir I (d. 1015) issued a Church Statute or Constitution (996-1011), the fourth section of which declared that the *Nomocanon* of the Greek Church, i.e., the one issued under Photius, was to be the common law of the land. This was natural, as the Rusins were baptized in the rite of Constantinople, and even though they tried to establish an independent church organization, they felt that they would accept the Christian laws which Constantinople followed. In the succeeding centuries, as practically all their Metropolitans were Greek bishops from Constantinople, their canon law was almost the same as that of their mother church. The Greek *Nomocanones* (that of John the Scholastic and that issued under Photius) existed among the Rusins in the old Slavonic language in the eleventh century. The edition of that of Photius as commented on by Zonaras appeared in 1120, and was translated into the Bulgarian language by Prince Sviatoslav of that country in 1262. It was shown to the Metropolitan of Kiev, Cyril II, and adopted by the synod of Vladimir-Kiev (1274) as obligatory on all. This collection became known as the *Kormca Knyha* or *Pilot Book*. It contains synopses of the canons of the ecumenical and particular councils of the first nine centuries in the East, canons of the Eastern Fathers, seventeen canons of St. Paul, seventeen of St. Peter and St. Paul, and two canons of "all" the apostles. Other sources of Ruthenian law before the Union of Brest were the provincial synods of Kiev in 1147, of Vladimir-Kiev in 1274, of Novgorod (in Lithuania) in 1415 and of Vilna in 1509.

C. A survey of their marriage legislation

Among the Rusins, even at the end of the eleventh century, the religious ceremonies connected with marriage, such as the blessing of the priest, were in use only for the princes and the boyars. Docu-

[124] *Fonti,* VIII, pp. 590-594; Dauvillier and De Clercq, p. 9.

ments reveal that for centuries, until the seventeenth century, marriages among the people were contracted without a religious blessing.[125] The people still preserved the old pre-Christian forms which consisted in the "stealing" and the "buying" of the bride, and for a long time these forms were viewed as the essential ceremonies of marriage. After the price was fixed, the bride was solemnly conducted to the house of the bridegroom, where she received the name of a legitimate wife (*vodimaja*, the Latin *deducta*), and on the following morning the amount of the previously arranged price was brought to the parents of the bride.[126] There did not, at first, exist among the Greek Byzantines any verbal expression of consent; it was introduced as a liturgical innovation among the Ruthenians only under Peter Moghlia, the dissident Metropolitan of Kiev, in his ritual of 1646.[127]

In the eleventh and twelfth centuries there were many intermarriages between the ruling families of the Kievian dynasty and those of Western Catholic Europe. The accounts of these marriages reveal that there was no thought that any impediment of mixed religion existed, and so perhaps they were considered as members of the same faith.[128]

[125] Dauvillier and De Clercq, pp. 37, 43; Dauvillier, p. 425.

[126] For these ancient customs of marriage among the Rusins, cf. Hrushevsky, pp. 32-33.

[127] Dauvillier, "La formation du mariage dans les Églises orientales,"—*Revue des Sciences Religieuses*, XV (1935), 386-395.

[128] Koncevicius, p. 52. Dauvillier and De Clercq (pp. 165-166), after saying that the Council in Trullo (which became part of the *Nomocanon of 14 Titles* and thus found its way among the Kievian Rusins) forbade marriages with heretics, declared that "the notion of heresy had not been defined by the Council in Trullo, and it was interpreted soon at Constantinople in the restricted sense of a sect condemned by an ecumenical council. Under this meaning fall the dissident Nestorian and Monophysite Churches, but not at all the Latin Church. However, Balsamon, while admitting the validity of marriages with Latins, wanted them first to reject their errors. But his opinion was not generally followed in the thirteenth century or in the first half of the fourteenth." Dauvillier and De Clercq in this discussion refer to an article by Petrides (name used by Father Sophrone Rabois-Bousquet, A.A.), "Chrysobulle de l'impératrice Theodora (1283),"—*Echos d'Orient*, XIV (1911), 25-29, concerning the profession of faith exacted from the Empress Theodora by the synod of 1283 under Andronicus II. As the widow of Michael VIII Paleologus who had sought union with Rome at the II General Council of Lyons (1274), the Em-

At the end of the eleventh century the Metropolitan John II, who was of Greek origin, imposed on the Rusins the Byzantine prescriptions against marriage with second cousins, but the Ruthenians did not follow this rule.[129] It was this same Metropolitan who rebuked the Rusin princes for allowing their daughters to marry "heterodox" princes, and made the bishops promise before their consecration that they would not allow in their territories marriages of the faithful with heretics, under which term were included Armenians and Latins.[130]

In the thirteenth century there were many "accusations" in Rus against the Latins. Among these was the charge that the Latins forbade marriage to deacons, and that permission was granted for a marriage with the sister of a deceased wife. This charge reveals the contrary current discipline on these marriage questions among the Rusins of that time.[131]

In the thirteenth century the schismatic Rusins who married Latin women had them rebaptized according to the rite of the Rusins, and forced them to adhere to their schismatic faith. For this reason Pope Gregory IX (1227-1241) issued an edict forbidding Latins to marry schismatic Rusins.[132]

press was required to make a profession of faith and to repudiate the union which her husband had made. In her statement the Empress declared that all who had helped the reunion were "enemies of the church of God" (« . . . πολεμίους . . . τῆς τοῦ Θεοῦ ἐκκλησίας»), "plotters against their own salvation" («ἐπιβούλους δε τῆς ἑαυτῶν σωτηρίας»), "helpers of the loss of souls" («προξένους ἀπωλείας ψυχῶν . . . »).

129 Dauvillier and De Clercq, p. 126.

130 *Ibid.*, p. 166.

131 Koncevicius, p. 70.

132 *"Quaeque nobis erronea,"* 24 febr. 1233—Potthast, *Regesta Pontificum Romanorum* (2 vols., Berolini, 1874-1875), n. 9105 (hereafter cited as Potthast). Dauvillier (*Le Mariage dans le Droit Classique de l'Église*, p. 373) asserts that this is the only Papal decretal forbidding a "mixed" marriage between Latins and Schismatics, and even in this case the local, not universal, prohibition can be explained in the demand for rebaptism and the adherence to the "orthodox" errors. He refers also to a council at Presburg, in Hungary, in 1309, which forbade Catholics to allow their daughters, nieces or cousins to marry a Rusin or Bulgarian or Lithuanian, because they also drew their Catholic spouses to their beliefs and because they also repeated baptism and scorned the Latin Sacraments. This decree is found in Mansi, XXV, 222 . . . "schismatico vel alteri fidei Christianae contrario maxime Ruthenis, Bulgaris, Rasciis, Lituanis

6. The Rumanians [133]

The Rumanians, or Wallachians, find their origin in the early Roman colonists who settled in the Roman province of Dacia and the neighboring provinces early in the Christian era, after the conquests of Trajan (105). They intermarried with the groups they found there—Dacians, Slavs, Bulgars, etc., but kept their original language, though it assimilated many words of the language groups around them. They settled in the various parts of the Roman Praefecture of Illyricum, [134] and so in 860 Pope St. Nicholas I defended his right over this praefecture against the Byzantine Emperor Michael III (842-867).[135]

in errore manentibus . . . filiam, neptem, consanguineam suam connubio tradere. . . ." Thus the prohibition affected the women only, and only in the territory affected by this Council. Dauvillier then proceeds to give a few examples of cases wherein the Pope approved certain marriages between Latins and the Byzantines, which approval was motivated by a hope that intermarriage would hasten reunion. Disapproval of a mixed marriage which was intended to create a union of the East with a Latin power against the Holy See was voiced in the I General Council of Lyons in 1245, which listed, among the reasons for the excommunication of Frederick II (1212-1250), his arrangement of the marriage in 1244 between his daughter Constance and John Vatatzes (1222-1254). " . . . Batatio Dei et ecclesiae inimico a communione fidelium per excommunicationis sententiam cum adiutoribus, consiliatoribus et fautoribus suis, solemniter separato, filiam suam tradidit in uxorem."—Mansi, XXIII, 618.

[133] *Fonti,* VIII, 472-478; *Statistica,* pp. 152-156; Janin, *The Separated Eastern Churches,* pp. 147-148.

[134] The Roman Empire was divided by Diocletian (284-305) into four great Praefectures; (1) Gaul (i. e., Spain, Gaul and Britain), placed under Constantius Chlorus; (2) Italy (Italy and Africa) under Maximian; (3) Illyricum (Dacia, Macedonia, Greece, Crete, thus nearly all the Balkan lands) under Galerius; (4) the East (Thrace, Asia Minor, Syria and Egypt) under Diocletian himself. The East (*Oriens*) alone constituted the Eastern Patriarchate and contained the following civil dioceses: (I) *Thrace* in Europe (chief town Constantinople); (II) *Asia* (Mysia, Lydia, Pisidia and part of Phrygia [chief town Ephesus]); (III) *Pontus* (Galatia, Paphlagonia, Pontus and Cappadocia [chief town Caesarea]); (IV) *Diocese of the East* (Syria, Palestine and eastward to the Persian border [chief town Antioch]); (V) *Egypt* (chief town Alexandria). Cf. Fortescue, *The Orthodox Eastern Church,* pp. 21-22.

[135] Epist. *"Principatum itaque,"* 25 sept. 860—*MGH, Epistolae,* VI, Pars Altera, p. 438. Cf. Ledit, *Praelectiones de Theologia Orientali,* p. 47.

It is not known with certainty when Christianity was first preached to them after they arrived in Dacia, though most probably some of the first colonists were Catholics. Their conversion seems due to missionaries from the West, as in the fourth and fifth centuries the Latin language and the Latin Liturgy were in use. St. Nicetas (335-414), the reputed author of the *Te Deum,* is said to have effected a widespread conversion. The invasions of the eastern barbarians along with the Bulgarian conquest in 634 extinguished Rumanian Catholicism; in 870 the enlarged kingdom of Bulgaria passed to the jurisdiction of Photius, because King Boris had become an enemy of the Latins, forcing the Latin priests to become Byzantines or to leave the country. Thus the Rumanian people of that period lost their Latin rite, and for many centuries their history was the same as that of the Bulgars in both politics and religion. However, in 1290 a separate principality was established in Wallachia, and another in Moldavia in 1363. Transylvania was subject to Hungary from 896 to 1526, when it became subject to the Turks.

At the end of the twelfth century the rule of this land of Bulgarians and Rumanians was in the hands of a Rumanian family, the Assani, who tried to effect a union with Rome. Many obstacles arose, but Pope Innocent III sent a legate to crown their king, and also wrote a letter urging them under their new king to return to the Catholic practices of their ancestors.[186] However, in 1256 the Assani lost the control of the throne. For a long time any communication with Rome was impossible. At the Council of Florence the Metropolitan Damian of Moldavia signed the reunion decree, but the period of reunion was very brief.[187]

Up to the year 870 the Rumanians followed the discipline of Rome. The Bishop of Thessalonica was the vicar of the Pope, and the other bishops of Illyricum referred to him their more serious cases. Moreover, the Pope sent many letters to them, but they

[186] *"Apostolicae Sedes,"* 27 nov. 1202—Baronius, Vol. XX, p. 124, n. 34. The Pope also recalled to them that at the time of Pope St. Nicholas I their king had been baptized, but that the Bulgarians became "corrupted" by the gifts and promises of the Greeks ("Bulgari corrupti donis Graecorum et promissionibus circumventi, Romanis ejectis, Graecos presbyteros receperunt"). This letter is found summarized in Potthast, n. 1775.

[187] Mansi, XXXI^{a}, 1035.

claimed that the celebrated replies of Pope St. Nicholas I in 866 to the questions of the Bulgarians did not apply to them. After the action of Boris in 870 of bringing all the country under the rule of Constantinople, the Rumanians followed the imposed law of the Byzantine Church; they used the law of the Latin Church if a norm was lacking in the laws from the East. In the thirteenth century there again were addressed to them Papal letters from Pope Innocent III (1198-1216) and from Pope Gregory IX (1227-1241), especially during the temporary reunion with the West under the Assani; these were principally concerned with administrative affairs. After the fall of the Assani the union with Rome was disrupted, and only in rare cases could the Pope send them letters.[138]

7. *The Italo-Greeks* [139]

For centuries before the birth of Christ, Greek colonists settled in Sicily and lower Italy. During this time Greek was their language and Rome was almost a foreign country in the north. The Athenians, Spartans and later the Byzantines were considered their fellow countrymen, so that when the capital of the Empire was moved to Constantinople no change was effected among these Greeks who remained zealously loyal to the government at Constantinople. The Code of Justinian became their law, though the Lombard customs introduced modifications; they dated their acts by the ruling reign at Constantinople. Sicily, Calabria, Apulia and Terra d'Otranto were parts of the Empire of Justinian. Yet, the Greek cities in Italy were in truth only loosely united with the city of the Emperor; occasional tribute was paid and the views of the Eastern capital were generally followed.

As to the origin of the Churches, it was St. Peter and St. Paul who first came to lower Italy. St. Paul is said to have created a

[138] Cf. *Fonti,* VIII, 483-489.

[139] Fortescue, *The Uniate Eastern Churches,* pp. 47-124. The brief summary given here will concern more the relation of these people to Constantinople than the historical events in their territory itself, such as the conquests of the Lombards and the Normans, and the various political factions which occupied the land. Cf. also *Statistica,* pp. 96-97, 116-119; *A Memorial of Andrew J. Shipman,* pp. 106-113.

certain Stephen as Bishop of Rhegium, and the Sicilians begin the line of their bishops with him. Indeed, even in Rome Greek was the liturgical language for the first two or three centuries. Greece, and later Constantinople, sent bishops to Sicily, Calabria and Apulia. Until the Moslems came, it can be said that Catholicism in Southern Italy and Sicily was mainly Greek.

The most definite and formal imposition of the Byzantine rite came from the Eastern Emperors in the eighth century when they ordered a new legal organization of the Church. This was a new thing, for the Pope had been considered their Metropolitan, even though by language and custom they had been linked to Constantinople. Now the Byzantine Emperors made Sicily a province under the Archbishop of Syracuse, and created other Metropolitan Sees in lower Italy. Gradually these Greeks then became strictly subject to the Patriarch of Constantinople. Rome would probably have tolerated this system of jurisdiction for the Greeks living in her patriarchate, inasmuch as usurpation did not necessarily mean schism, and no essential point of faith or morals was involved. But in the height of the discussion came the two schisms, that of Photius (Gregory Asbestas of Syracuse had ordained him) in 867, and then that of Caerularius in 1054.

The Normans, Latins of the Roman Rite, after their conquests in lower Italy in the early part of the eleventh century, did not persecute the Greeks nor the pagan Moslems in the country. However, they did not allow traffic with Constantinople, and so they prevented the schism of 1054 from reaching Sicily and Lower Italy. They restored the Roman Rite to those churches which had been made Byzantine by the eastern Emperors. Many of the sees received Latin bishops, while there remained Byzantine churches, monasteries, priests and institutions of various kinds for centuries. These Byzantine elements began to disappear, first of all because for nearly five centuries after 1054 almost all the Eastern Christians were schismatics and bitter opponents of the Pope with the consequence that suspicion fell also on the Greek Catholics in Italy, then also because these Catholics were subject to Latin Ordinaries, and, finally, because it was simpler to conform to the usages of the country.

In the fifteenth century, however, when the Byzantine rite in

Italy was almost extinct, it received new life through the colonies from the East which were seeking refuge from the ravages of the Turks. Most of those who came to Sicily and Southern Italy were from Albania, beginning about 1448. The use of the Greek Rite became restricted to monasteries, religious houses and country towns, and was saved from extinction only by these colonists from Albania. Albania, the ancient Epirus of the Greeks, early became Christianized and followed the Oriental rite; its people had their own language, but used Greek in the Mass much as the Roman Rite uses Latin, i.e., as a dead language. They maintained their independence against the Bulgarian Slavs, the Eastern Greeks, and for a long time also against the Turks. Their freedom from dependence on Constantinople helped them remain loyal to Rome in the days of the schism.

Early in the fifteenth century the Turks and the Saracens invaded Albania, subjecting it to themselves. They took as a hostage the son of the hereditary prince, the boy George Castriota (1403?-1468), and brought him up at the Ottoman Court as an officer in the Turkish Army. He received the name of Alexander Bey (named by the Albanians Scanderbeg). In 1443, at the death of his father, he became the prince of Albania. After the defeat of the Turkish Army in 1456 by Jánas Hunyadi (1387-1456) he proclaimed himself to be a Christian prince, and for the next decade fought with his countrymen a fierce but unsuccessful campaign for the liberty of his country. As he was repeatedly defeated, large emigrations of Albanians settled in Sicily. After the death of Scanderbeg in 1468 and the increasing victories of the Turks even larger numbers of Albanians came to Sicily. Mixing with the Italian Greek Catholics and using the same liturgical language and rite, they revived the Byzantine Rite in lower Italy and Sicily.

8. *The Russians* [140]

It is difficult to find any historical date indicating a division between the Russians and the Ruthenians. In the twelfth century "Russia" had started to withdraw to the northeast of Kiev, and formed a new center of national life at Suzdal, and later at Moscow.

[140] Cf. Koncevicius, *Russia's Attitude Towards Union with Rome (9th-16th Centuries)*, *passim*.

The sack of Kiev in 1240 by the Tatars diminished the centralizing force of that city. In 1242 the Russian Kniazs (Dukes) submitted themselves to the Tatar leader, Batu Khan (d. 1255), and asked him to confirm them as provincial rulers under him. All of Russia thus had come under the dominion of the Tatars except what was held by Lithuania in the southwest and by the independent states of Livonia and Novgorod in the northwest. For over two hundred years the Tatar influence ruled Russia, and consequently Russian life underwent many changes in politics, social life and religion. The political centers of the country gradually moved to the central and northern sections. Because of the union of Church and State, the religious centers shifted likewise. The Metropolitan See was first transferred, in 1299, from Kiev to Vladimir-on-the-Kliazma, and in 1325 (while keeping the title of Kiev) to Moscow itself, which received initial mention in Russian history as late as the year 1147, but soon thereafter achieved political importance. As a rule the Tatars allowed the Russians to govern their own religious affairs, and some of them also became converted, especially in the fourteenth century.

Cardinal Isidor (d. 1463), Metropolitan of "Kiev and all Russia," brought the reunion decrees of the Council of Florence to Moscow on March 19, 1441. He gave the Kniaz Vasilii III (1425-1462) two letters, one from the Pope and one from the Greek Emperor, urging the Kniaz to foster the reunion of the churches. However, on considering the matter the Kniaz on the fourth day ordered Isidor to be taken to prison, where he stayed until September 15, 1441. Vasilii thus created a final break between the Church of Moscow and the Roman Church. In 1448, without the approval of Constantinople, he appointed Jonas as Metropolitan of Russia. The beginnings of modern Russia can then be seen in the rise of Moscow and its surrounding Muscovites, and after the rejection of Cardinal Isidor the policy of Russia in regard to the Holy See and to the question of reunion became increasingly inimical.

CHAPTER III

THE PERIOD FROM THE COUNCIL OF FLORENCE TO THE YEAR 1800

Article I. The Armenians [1]

For centuries the Armenians remained a scattered nation throughout Asia Minor, especially in the north between the Black and the Caspian Seas, and also in the Balkan States and in Poland. In matters of religion they remained estranged from both Rome and Constantinople. The movement toward reunion at the Council of Florence did not have lasting effect, especially after the death of the *Katholikos* Constantine V who had sent legates to the Council. In the succeeding centuries the history of Armenia reveals a sad list of wars and massacres of contending Turkish and Persian armies, so that the Armenians lived as outlaws in their own original land. There were not many Catholics during these difficult times.

In 1680 the *Katholikos* in Greater Armenia, Stephen V, united with Rome as did many of his successors. At that time the work of the Jesuit missionaries was outstanding. However, grave harm was done to the Church by the action of Count Ferriol, Minister of Louis XIV at Constantinople (1689-1709), who sent to the Inquisition at Paris the dissident patriarch, Avedik of Tohat; this caused severe persecutions which lasted until 1830. Despite these persecutions, the number of Catholic Armenians increased, and in 1742 Pope Benedict XIV (1740-1758) established a patriarchal see at Kraim in the Lebanon. It is from this date that the Armenians mark their modern, official "reunion."

The Mechitarists owe their origin to Mechitar, born at Sebaste in Asia Minor in 1676. After becoming a Catholic he founded in 1701 an order of Armenian monks under a modified Benedictine

[1] Fortescue, *The Lesser Eastern Churches*, pp. 416-419; Attwater, *The Catholic Eastern Churches*, pp. 205-210; Adeney, *The Greek and Eastern Churches* (New York, 1908), pp. 547-549.

rule. Pope Clement XI (1700-1721) gave his approval, and made Mechitar the head of the order with the title of abbot. The monks of this order resided at Modon in the Morea Peninsula, then under Venetian rule, but the conquest of this peninsula by the Turks caused the monks to flee to Venice in 1715, where the Senate granted them the Island of San Lazzaro. They became a valuable group through missionary and educational work, and contributed remarkably to the printing and diffusion of books. A branch of this congregation settled in Trieste in 1773, and later in Vienna. On May 30, 1775, Maria Theresa (1740-1780) granted them many privileges.

Between 1630 and 1681 most of the Armenians who were in Galicia (southern Poland) submitted to Rome, many of them joining the Latin rite. As early as 1635 Pope Urban VIII (1623-1644) placed an archbishop at Lemberg as the head of the Catholic Armenians there.

On October 1, 1785, the Sacred Congregation for the Propagation of the Faith sent an Instruction to the Vicar Apostolic of Constantinople concerning the marriages of Catholic Armenians before a Turkish civil magistrate, which marriages were held as valid because "their error that they are not able to contract marriage validly before a Turkish judge does not thereby make that marriage null." [2] The Instruction also declared that those who say the Armenians always claimed that a priest was necessary for a valid marriage do not realize that the Armenians had lost sight of the distinction between a valid and a licit marriage.

Article II. The Chaldeans [3]

In 1450 the Nestorian *Katholikos* Simon IV decreed that the office of *katholikos* was to pass from uncle to nephew. In 1551, after

[2] "Il loro errore di non potersi contrarre validamente il matrimonio avanti il guidice turco, non può renderlo nullo."—*Collectanea,* n. 580; cf. White, *De forma celebrationis matrimonii,* p. 61; Deslandes, "Le mariage clandestin des orientaux est-il valide?"—*Echos d'Orient,* XXVIII (1929), 14-15.

[3] Tisserant, "Nestorienne (l'Église), union à Rome,"—*DTC,* XI, 228-244; *Fonti,* VIII, 696-698; Badger, *The Nestorians and their Rituals* (2 vols., London, 1852), I, 145-148, 176-181; Attwater, *The Catholic Eastern Churches,* pp. 228-230; Adeney, *The Greek and Eastern Churches,* pp. 497-500; Giamil,

the succession in this manner of Simon VIII Denha as *katholikos,* a group which resented this hereditary succession met at Mosul and elected John Sulaka, who contacted the Franciscan Guardian of the Holy Land and sought the confirmation of Rome, following an ancient Chaldean text that the *katholikos* is to be confirmed by Rome. In 1552 the Franciscans sent him to Rome where he was appointed by Pope Julius III (1550-1555) to be the Patriarch of his rite and given some jurisdiction over the churches in China and India. From him dates the re-established line of Chaldean Patriarchs, as also the use of the word "Chaldean" as distinct from "Nestorian;" his successors all took the name Simon as he himself had done. However, in 1692 Simon XIII apostatized, and from him stems the present line of Nestorian *Katholikoi* who went to live in Kurdistan.

On the other hand, the line of Simon VIII Denha had not continuously remained in schism, for several of his successors, who took the name Elias, had become reconciled with Rome. Diyarbekir became a center of Catholicity,[4] and in 1672 the metropolitan of that city, Mar Joseph, made his profession of faith before Capuchin missionaries. The Holy See, which he visited in 1675-1677, allowed him to have a vague title of patriarch.[5] He was succeeded by other "patriarchs" in that see, so that from 1672 to 1692 (when Simon XIII apostatized) there were two Catholic patriarchs, while from 1692 to 1804 there were two Nestorian patriarchs besides the Catholic one at Diyarbekir. In 1778, when Elias XIII was Nestorian Patriarch, his brother John Hormez, Metropolitan of Mosul, became a Catholic. On July 5, 1830, Pope Pius VIII (1829-1830) initiated in Hormez the present line of Chaldean Patriarchs.

In 1552 Pope Julius III (1550-1555) had given to the reunited

Genuinae Relationes inter Sedem Apostolicam et Assyriorum orientalium seu Chaldaeorum Ecclesiam, pp. xxxii-xlv, 12-395; De Clercq, *Les Églises unies d'Orient,* pp. 111-112.

[4] Cf. Tisserant, "Le habitants de Diarbekir qui etaient foncièrement attachés à l'Église Catholique. . . ."—*DTC,* XI, 230.

[5] The Holy See told him that, since there had been no election as such to make him patriarch, it could not approve him as patriarch, but he was finally given the title, "patriarchatus nationis Chaldaeorum patriarchae regimine destitutus."—Tisserant, *ibid.,* col. 240; Cicognani-Staffa, *Commentarium,* I, 10.

Patriarch the power to dispense in all the degrees of relationship which as impediments to marriage were not forbidden by the divine law.[6] Pope Pius IV (1559-1565), when granting the pallium to Simon Sulaka's successor in 1562, restricted this power of the patriarch by excepting from the previous grant the power over impediments which arise from the first degree of affinity and the first two degrees of consanguinity when this latter relationship derived from the same ancestor.[7] Pope Gregory XIII (1572-1585), in granting the pallium to Patriarch Simon who was elected in 1581, specifically stated that the patriarch could dispense in the third and fourth degrees of consanguinity. Thus, by implication, there is indicated the extent of this impediment among the Chaldeans at that time.

On August 3, 1650, the Sacred Congregation of the Holy Office answered some doubts concerning the Nestorians: (1) A Nestorian priest after the death of his wife, whom he had married before receiving sacred orders, married another from whom he had children, and all were prepared to abjure their heresy if he were permitted to retain his wife and still to exercise his orders. The answer was: "The Holy See does not grant dispensations of this type." [8] (2) A Nestorian priest, who had married after receiving the priesthood and who wished to contract a second marriage after the death of his wife, claimed that he would never have entered the priesthood if he had known that his priestly orders would make it impossible for him to contract marriage. The same answer was given as in the first case.[9] (3) A Nestorian had married a woman who later apostatized to the Turks and married one of them. After his conversion to the Catholic faith the man desired to contract a new marriage. The answer was: "This cannot be permitted." [10]

[6] ". . . nec non super Sacramento Matrimonii in quibusvis gradibus a iure divino non prohibitis dispensare."—Giamil, *op. cit.*, p. 25.

[7] ". . . nec non super Sacramento Matrimonii ex aliquibus honestis causis in quibusvis gradibus a iure divino non prohibitis praeterquam in primo affinitatis ac ex eodem stipite provenientibus p° et 2° consanguinitatis gradibus dispensare."—*Ibid.*, p. 60. Cf. Dauvillier and De Clercq, p. 128, n. 5; cf. also *Fonti*, II, 249.

[8] *Fonti*, I, 35.

[9] *Op. cit.*, II, 31; cf. also Vol. I, p. 63, for a similar case.

[10] *Op. cit.*, I, 287.

Ten years later, on January 29, 1660, the same Congregation was asked: "Could Nestorian priests who became Catholics retain their wives whom they had married after receiving the priesthood?" The answer given was: "Marriages of this kind, contracted after sacred orders were received, are invalid; therefore it must be made known that in no way in the future will anyone be granted a dispensation for entering marriage after having received these orders. However, in the present cast it is expedient to dispense these priests, so that after they have renewed their consent they may remain in their marriage." [11]

On April 29, 1754, the Sacred Congregation for the Propagation of the Faith answered the request of the Carmelite Bishop of Bagdad who sought a dispensation for those Chaldeans who had been ordained as deacons by the heretical patriarch before they acquired the use of reason or reached the age of puberty, and who, after arriving at a maturer age, had married once or twice. The dispensation was sought in order that they could remain in their marriage, the while they were suspended, however, from the exercise of the ministry of the diaconate. The bishop received the faculty to dispense for a period of seven years, at the end of which time he was to have recourse to the Holy See for a renewal of the faculty, and to send in a report on the existing conditions.[12]

Article III. The Antiochene Rite

1. The Syrians [13]

In 1583 Pope Gregory XIII (1572-1585) sent a legate to Aleppo who prepared the way for the establishment of the Capuchins and Jesuits there in 1626; these missionaries were successful in their work and many Jacobites came into the Church. These converts in 1656 elected to the vacant see of Aleppo Andrew Akhidjan, who had been a pupil at the Propaganda College at Rome. He was consecrated

[11] *Op. cit.*, I, 267.

[12] *Op. cit.*, II, 327-331; the answer referred to the Instruction of Pope Benedict XIV, *"Eo quamvis tempore,"* of May 4, 1745—*Fontes*, n. 357.

[13] *Fonti*, VIII, 125-127; Attwater, *The Catholic Eastern Churches*, pp. 161-165; Janin, *Les Églises orientales*, pp. 470-471.

by a Maronite bishop and in 1662, after the death of Patriarch Simeon, he was canonically elected as patriarch. The dissidents became violent, took the Catholic Church at Aleppo with Turkish authority, and inaugurated a methodical plan of persecution of the Catholic Syrians which lasted almost a hundred years. Andrew's successor, Peter of Jerusalem, was opposed by a Jacobite bishop. In 1700, however, the Catholic Syrians received a measure of autonomy and recovered their church at Aleppo, after the ruler of Germany concluded a treaty with the Turks. In 1701 Peter was put into prison together with a Catholic archbishop and ten priests. The two prelates died in their chains in 1706, leaving the Catholic Syrians without a spiritual leader, and until 1783 the severity of the persecutions greatly diminished the number of Catholics.

In 1783 the Jacobite Patriarch of Antioch, Gregory III, nominated as his successor the Archbishop of Aleppo, Michael Jarweh, who had recently became a Catholic, but who had kept this secret for reasons of prudence; while thus secretly a Catholic he was canonically elected as the Patriarch of Antioch by the Jacobite Synod in 1783. He gained the support of four bishops, and sought the confirmation of his election from Rome and the recognition of the election from the civil authority. However, the anti-Catholic party elected a new patriarch, Matthew, who obtained the civil recognition before Jarweh. Matthew had Jarweh put in prison, but Jarweh escaped, first to Bagdad, then to the Lebanon, which was the refuge of persecuted Catholics. He lived in a monastery at Sharfeh, and governed the Catholic Syrians from this town until his death in 1801. In this troubled period there was little opportunity to hold synods, and the contact with the Holy See was infrequent.

2. *The Maronites* [14]

In 1256 Pope Alexander IV (1254-1261) had written to Patriarch Simeon, praising the faith of the Maronites, granting the patriarch the use of the title "Patriarch of Antioch," and recommending to him

[14] Eid, *A l'Ombre des Cèdres ou L'Épopée de Liban*, pp. 61-65; Abraham, *The Maronites of Lebanon*, pp. 80-121; Dib, "Les conciles de l'Église Maronite 1557-1664,"—*Revue des Sciences Religieuses*, IV (1924), 193-220, 421-439.

the care of those Crusaders who had taken refuge in the Lebanon after the Crusades. It was almost two hundred years before another papal letter was sent to the Maronites, for the Mohammedan Sultans of the Mameluke Dynasty in Egypt and Syria ruled at this period and forbade their subjects to have any communication with Europe. Thus the next letter was sent by Pope Eugene IV (1431-1447) in 1439 in praise of the loyal faith of the Maronites. During the fifteenth century a few other Popes sent laudatory letters, all of which were submitted in 1515 to Pope Leo X (1513-1521), who was investigating the previous practice of the Holy See concerning the confirmation of their patriarchs; he then wrote to the patriarch, granting all his requests and likewise praising his subjects for their firmness in the faith.

Pope Pius IV (1559-1565) on September 1, 1562, wrote to Patriarch Moses and referred to the Maronites in these words: "The unbearable yoke of the infidel did not succeed in making them break away from the Christian religion, nor could the proximity of schism and heresy corrupt their faith and separate them from the Catholic Church."[15] Pope Paul V (1605-1621) in a letter to Patriarch Joseph on December 15, 1606, spoke of them as "roses among the thorns of eastern infidelity."[16] Pope Clement XI (1700-1721) wrote to Patriarch Stephen Douihee on February 7, 1702: "Your faith grows brighter in our eyes every time we see it surrounded by the darkness of heresies."[17]

These statements of the Popes furnish a good summary of the position of the Maronites in Syria and the Lebanon in their long subjection to the Moslems and the Turks. Early in the sixteenth century (1515-1517) Syria and the Lebanon passed into the hands

[15] " . . . quos nec infidelium jugum tam grave a Christiana fide deterrere, nec haereticorum aut schismaticorum propinquitas corrumpere et ab Ecclesia Catholica abducere ac separare potuit."—quoted by the Synod of Mt. Lebanon (1736), Pars I, Caput I—*Acta et Decreta Sacrorum Conciliorum Recentiorum, Collectio Lacensis* (7 vols., Friburgi Brisgoviae: Herder, 1870-1890), Vol. II, col. 95 (hereafter cited as *Coll. Lac.*).

[16] " . . . cum vos veluti rosas, gratia Dei, florentes inter orientalis infidelitatis spinas videamus."—*ibid.*, col. 96.

[17] "Fides enim vestra coram oculis nostris effulget, quo magis eam circumseptam undique errorum caligine intuemur"—*ibid.*, col. 97.

of the Ottoman Turks after Sultan Selim I (1512-1520) defeated the forces of the Moslems of the Mameluke Dynasty, which had ruled over its eastern empire from Egypt. The Ottoman Turks never seriously tried to join themselves with the Syriac and Arabic speaking people, but left them to their own social customs and language, so that while the Turkish period of rule in Syria and the Lebanon, which lasted down to the World War of 1914-1918, was marked by many outrages and massacres against their subjects, this rule did not wipe out the customs and language of the people.

In 1860 the European Powers gave the Lebanon a Constitution which brought a measure of liberty to the country, and made the governor accountable to the six European Powers. France especially had taken a special interest in the Christians of the East from the early middle ages, and this guardianship was vigorously renewed at the time of the Crusades when they built Gothic churches in the lands won by the Crusaders. It was King St. Louis IX of France (1226-1270) who proclaimed, at the walls of St. John of Acre, that the French would protect the Christians in this part of the East, in Syria, in Palestine, and in the Lebanon. After Syria and the Lebanon succumbed to the Turks in the early part of the sixteenth century, Francis I of France (1515-1547), in 1535, concluded a treaty with the Turkish Sultan concerning the protection of the French over the Christians. The French kings issued by rescript a promise of protection to the Patriarchs who were confirmed by the Pope; thus, for example, King Louis XIV (1643-1715) sent such a rescript to Patriarch John Safrawy, who had been confirmed in his office by Pope Innocent X (1644-1655) in 1649.

The most important Maronite Council was that which was held at the Monastery of Saidat al-Luaizeh ("Our Lady of the Almond Trees") for a three-day period beginning September 30, 1736. Monsignor Joseph Simeon Assemani (1687-1768) had been sent by Pope Clement XII (1730-1740) with the necessary powers as Papal Legate; he had prepared the agenda for the Council, taking most of the regulations from the Council of Trent, and covering the whole field of Church legislation, and inducing some changes in the Maronite practices for the sake of closer conformity with the Latin Church. The acts of the Council are models of Theology, Canon Law and Church

History. The conciliar acts were confirmed "in specific form" by Pope Benedict XIV on September 1, 1741, thus being enacted with the force of pontifical law, the application of which was restricted however to the limits of the Patriarchate.[18]

This Council was celebrated as the gradual result of several visits by papal legates among the Maronites to restore the old discipline of the rite with certain modifications required by its changing needs. Pope Gregory XIII (1572-1585), who was zealous to procure the diffusion of the decrees of the Council of Trent, sent to them in 1578 Eliano and Raggio, both Jesuits, who inspected the books of the Maronites and visited their churches and monasteries. Unfortunately Eliano was not an expert in their language, and as a result misinterpreted some of their expressions; in 1580 he was sent among them again. It was on his recommendation that Pope Gregory founded the Maronite College in Rome. In 1596 Pope Clement VIII (1592-1605) sent two more Jesuits, Dandini and Bruno, with two men from the Maronite College as interpreters, Anaissi and Elian; during their stay two provincial councils were held, September 18, and November 3, 1596.[19]

In 1768 the Synod of Gusta prescribed the observance of the Council of 1736,[20] and in 1787 Pope Pius VI (1775-1799) refused to confirm a synod of 1786, because its decrees were contrary to those of this Lebanon Council.[21]

The Synod of Mt. Lebanon issued detailed decrees concerning marriage, and thus gave to the Maronites a complete code of mar-

[18] The decrees of this Council and an appendix containing letters of the Popes and decrees of the Sacred Congregations concerning the Maronites constitute a major part (coll. 74-502) of Volume II of the *Collectio Lacensis.* The Brief of confirmation *"Singularis Romanorum,"* issued by Pope Benedict XIV on September 1, 1741, is quoted in coll. 488-492. Cf. *Fonti,* XII, n. 1458, for the decree of the Congregation for the Propagation of the Faith approving the synod and asking the Pope to send a Brief of confirmation. De Clercq, in writing about the Eastern Councils (*Les Églises unies d'Orient,* p. 29) declared: "La legislation des conciles est avant tout territoriale; elle vaut pour le patriarcat ou la province."

[19] Cf. *Coll. Lac.,* II, 413-416, 609-610.

[20] *Fonti,* XII, n. 1461.

[21] *Ibid.,* n. 1457.

riage laws, based on the decrees of the Council of Trent, to obtain uniformity with the marriage laws of the Latin Church.[22]

After two introductory sections which stress the dignity of the sacramental contract and the need of the parties to enter into this contract with purity of intention, the synod urges that the pastors should take care that the old custom of espousals be kept, in order that hasty marriages might be avoided. The minimum age for the espousals is that of seven years if the use of reason is present. The parents can make the arrangements for their children if these give their consent before the parents take action or subsequently ratify their action. Eight broad reasons are listed as causes which suffice for dissolving the espousals, but if no such reason exists, then the impediment of "public propriety" forbids intermarriage between either of the two espoused persons, on the one hand, and their blood relatives within the first degree of the collateral line, on the other; if such intermarriage were attempted, the marriage would be null.[23]

The question of age is mentioned in the next place, among the preliminary investigations the pastor is to make before marriage; the required age is determined as fourteen years for the man and twelve for the woman.[24]

The eighth section concerns the diriment impediments to marriage which may be summarized as follows: [25]

1. *Error.* This factor can exist either in respect to the identity of the person or with regard to the condition, the quality and the fortune of the person known.[26]

[22] Pars II, Caput XI—*Coll. Lac.*, coll. 159-184.

[23] Pars II, XI, 3-5; *Fonti,* Vol. XII, nn. 1418-1422; cf. Korkemaz, *Le Mariage dans L'Église Maronite* (L'Institut catholique de Paris, 1938), pp. 8-26 (hereafter cited as Korkemaz); cf. also Ledit, *Praelectiones de Jure Canonico Orientali* (Quebec: Universitas Lavallensis, 1942), p. 15.

[24] *Fonti,* XII, n. 893; also II, XI, 9, VI (*Fonti,* XII, n. 742); cf. Synod of Patriarch Sergius, September 18, 1596, canon 13 (*Fonti,* XII, n. 874); Korkemaz, pp. 71-72; cf. O'Dea, *The Matrimonial Impediment of Nonage,* The Catholic University of America Canon Law Studies, n. 205 (Washington, D. C.: The Catholic University of America Press, 1944), p. 44.

[25] Cf. Korkemaz, pp. 49-63.

[26] *Fonti,* XII, n. 623.

2. *Solemn vow.* This impediment applies to both men and women whether the vows are expressed publicly or merely tacitly by way of necessary implication.[27]

3. *Relationship.* (a) Natural relationship, or consanguinity. After describing how the various degrees of relationship are computed, the synod mentions that in the Roman Church the contraction of marriage is prohibited between persons related in the fourth degree inclusive, according to the canonical computation, and that in the Oriental Church the marriages were prohibited to persons related in the seventh degree inclusive, according to the civil computation. The synod then quotes the disapproval of Pope Innocent IV in relation to the practices of the Greeks of Cyprus who allowed the contracting of marriage by persons who were related in the eighth degree; the Pope voiced his disapproval since such intermarriage had been barred by the Latin Church in the IV General Council of the Lateran (1215). Thus, apparently, the synod adopted the ruling of this IV General Council as its own.[28]

(b) Spiritual relationship. The impediment exists between the one baptizing on the one hand and the person baptized and his parents on the other; it likewise exists between the godparents on the one hand and the person baptized and his parents on the other.[29] The same spiritual relationship is acquired at confirmation as at baptism. Since among the Maronites confirmation is not given along

[27] *Ibid.*, n. 1525; cf. Pars IV, cap. II, n. 11 (*ibid.*, n. 1270; *Coll. Lac.*, II, 362); Papp-Szilagyi, p. 257.

[28] *Ibid.*, nn. 405-406. This letter of the Pope, "*Sub catholicae,*" of March 6, 1254, is given in the Appendix (coll. 446-448) to the Synod in the *Collectio Lacensis*, Vol. II, but Dib (*art. cit.*, p. 207, n. 4) says that this letter was not promulgated, and so does not have the force of law; cf. also Papp-Szilagyi, p. 265; Mansella, *De Impedimentis*, p. 38. Dauvillier and De Clercq (p. 130) declare that this synod at Mt. Lebanon adopted the Latin extension of the impediment of consanguinity.

[29] *Ibid.*, n. 288; cf. Pars II, cap. II, n. 10 (*ibid.*, n. 286; *Coll. Lac.*, II, 119), which discusses this point in the treatment of the sacrament of baptism; cf. also the Brief of Pope Clement VIII, "*Christifidelium,*" of Aug. 17, 1599 (*ibid.*, n. 284; *Coll. Lac.*, II, 172); cf. canon 4 of synod of Patriarch Sergius, September 18, 1596 (*ibid.*, n. 287; *Coll. Lac.*, II, 414). Cf. Mansella, *De Impedimentis*, pp. 44-45.

with baptism, the synod desires that different godparents be selected when confirmation is to be administered.[80]

(c) Legal relationship arising from adoption. The one adopting must be free from dependence on others, must be twenty-five years old, must be a man, must not be impotent, must be at least eighteen years older than the one adopted, and must be present when the adoption is negotiated. If these conditions are fulfilled, the legal relationship arising from adoption annuls marriage for persons thus related in the direct line whether ascending or descending, to the fourth degree, but in the collateral line to the first degree only. Legal relationship likewise begets a kind of affinity between persons thus related in the first degree of the direct line, so that the adopter cannot marry the widow of the adopted, and the adopted cannot marry the widow of the adopter. This impediment as touching the direct line is perpetual in duration, but if, in a given case, the impediment of legal relationship exists as touching the first degree of the collateral line, it ceases upon the death of the adopter and also upon the emancipation of the adopted.[81]

4. *Affinity.* Effect to this impediment can be given only through carnal intercourse, whether licit or illicit; "according to the civil law an impediment arises also from a valid though not consummated marriage, and then it is called 'public propriety.'" The lines and the degrees are calculated as in the case of consanguinity, and the impediment extends to the eighth degree of inter-relationship. The synod acknowledges that Oriental Law forbids a father's and son's intermarriage with a mother and daughter, and also the intermarriage of two brothers of one family with two sisters of another, but in its desire to follow the custom of the Latins it approves such

[80] Cf. Pars II, cap. III, n. 10 (*Fonti,* XII, n. 285; *Coll. Lac.,* II, 126-127), wherein the synod mentions this relationship in its treatment of Confirmation.

[81] *Fonti,* XII, nn. 280-283; Papp-Szilagyi, pp. 268-269. In a letter of November 15, 1945, to the writer, His Beatitude, Anthony Peter Arida, Maronite Patriarch of Antioch and of all the Orient, gave this summary of this impediment: "Cognatio legalis, ex adoptione certa iuris solemnitate facta, matrimonium dirimit: (a) Inter adoptantem, adoptatum et adoptati liberos ac descendentes (Paternitas legalis); (b) Inter adoptatum et liberos legitimos adoptantis (Fraternitas legalis); (c) Inter adoptantem et uxorem adoptati et vicissim (Affinitas legalis)."

marriages as licit, since "affinity does not arise between those who are blood-relatives of the contracting parties, whereas it does arise between either of the contracting parties and the relatives of the other." The impediment of affinity which arises through an illicit carnal intercourse annuls a marriage between persons thus related within the first or second degree of the collateral line, according to the computation of the Council of Trent, which restricted this particular impediment to these degrees.[82]

5. *Crime.* This diriment impediment exists in the following cases: (a) when one of the spouses after a sin of adultery efficaciously plots the death of his own spouse in order to marry the guilty person who is aware of the murder; (b) when with the consent of both persons one of the spouses is murdered, even if adultery has not been perpetrated; (c) when adultery is committed and there is joined with it both the man's promise to contract marriage after the death of his spouse and the woman's acceptance of that promise by word or sign; and (d) when a spouse enters marriage with another person and consummates it while his or her own legitimate spouse is still alive. In this last case however the impediment is not present if the third party is unaware that the spouses are both alive.[83]

6. *Difference of religion.* Marriages of the Maronites with unbaptized persons are null, with baptized non-Catholics valid but illicit. Marriages of the latter kind become licit if the heretic has promised to become a Catholic, or if he has promised that the children will be Catholic, or at least that he will not interfere with the Catholic faith and practices of his spouse. Espousal with a Jew or a pagan is allowed only if such a one has promised to become a Christian.[84] In support of its position the synod quotes from the early councils of Laodicea and Chalcedon their prohibitions of the contracting of marriage with heretics, Jews or pagans.[85]

[82] *Ibid.*, nn. 54-57.

[83] *Ibid.*, n. 420. Cf. also Pars II, cap. XI, n. 36—*Coll. Lac.*, II, 183; *Fonti*, XII, n. 403. Cf. Donohue, *The Impediment of Crime*, The Catholic University of America Canon Law Studies, n. 69 (Washington, D. C.: The Catholic University of America, 1931), p. 82.

[84] *Ibid.*, n. 478 and n. 1417. Cf. Korkemaz, p. 40; Papp-Szilagyi, p. 258.

[85] The synod of Patriarch Sergius of September 18, 1596, had renewed this traditional prohibition in its 15th canon (*Fonti*, XII, n. 873).

7. *Force or compulsion.* This kind of duress is occasioned when some extrinsic and free agent unjustly interjects grave fear to force a person to contract a marriage.[86]

8. *Sacred Orders.* Priests and deacons cannot marry, whereas subdeacons may, because the Maronites compute subdeaconship among the minor orders.[87]

9. *Abduction.* The seizing of an unwilling woman may be motivated either by a desire of lust or by the intention of contracting marriage. But a valid marriage cannot ensue until the one who was seized has been restored to a place of safety and freedom, and then freely consents to marry her erstwhile abductor.[88]

10. *Public propriety.* This type of relationship arises from espousals or from a valid but nonconsummated marriage. Valid espousals render a marriage with the espoused's relatives in the first degree (Latin computation) null and void; thus a man cannot marry

[86] *Ibid.*, n. 1505.

[87] *Ibid.*, n. 1054; cf. similar decree in Pars II, cap. XI, n. 33 (*ibid.*, nn. 877-878; *Coll. Lac.*, II, 182). A subdeacon could be advanced to higher orders if he had contracted but one marriage and that with a virgin. If he had contracted a marriage with a non-virgin, e.g., a widow, then the marriage was valid, but he was not to be admitted to the further reception of orders (Pars III, cap. II, n. 3—*Coll. Lac.*, II, 269-270; *Fonti*, XII, n. 1440). The synod in another place (Pars II, cap. XIV, n. 35—*Coll. Lac.*, II, 241-242; *Fonti*, XII, n. 184) speaks of the "ancient custom among the Orientals" whereby they could retain their wives whom they had married before sacred orders were received, which custom Rome has approved for them; but if one had married a second time, he was not to be advanced to the diaconate or to the priesthood; if a deacon or a priest presumed to marry, he had to be deposed from his order and completely separated from his illegitimate consort. On April 11, 1628, the Congregation for the Propagation of the Faith transmitted to a Franciscan missionary at Aleppo the decree of the Holy Office of February 3rd of that same year, concerning the following case. A Maronite subdeacon had married a widow as his second wife; the Patriarch had suspended him from his ecclesiastical duties, but had not separated him from his wife. Pope Urban VIII (1623-1644) ordered that he was not only to be suspended, but also to be declared incapable of attaining higher orders, and to be separated from his wife since the marriage was null; he was also with an oath to remove the suspicion of heresy which had attached to his sinful procedure—*Fonti*, I, 63.

[88] *Ibid.*, n. 1219. The phrase "sive fiat ad explendam libidinem" is usually not found in other Oriental legislation concerning the impediment of abduction.

the mother, sister, or daughter of his fiancée. A valid nonconsummated marriage gives rise to a similar effect of invalidity for a marriage attempted between the surviving party and any of the deceased spouse's relatives within the fourth degree (Latin computation) of the collateral line.[39]

11. *Clandestinity.* This element is listed here as an impediment which makes marriage null if the union is contracted in any way but before the pastor, or before a priest who has the permission of the pastor or Ordinary, and simultaneously also before two or three witnesses.[40] In another place [41] the synod amplifies its brief statement regarding this impediment. All who in any way violate this law which the Council of Trent issued are to be punished severely, as the same Council commanded. The marriage is to be celebrated, not simply before *any* pastor, but specifically before the *proper* pastor, namely, "the one in whose parish the contracting parties have remained for the greater part of a year, and in whose parish they still reside at the time of their marriage." A priest who presumptuously assists at the marriage of those who are from another parish is by that very fact suspended. If the man and woman be from different parishes, then the assistance of either of the two pastors suffices, but the pastor of the parish in which the marriage is celebrated should assist at it. Marriage by proxy is allowed. The synod of Patriarch Sergius, of September 18, 1596, had likewise ordered that marriages be celebrated before the proper pastor and witnesses.[42] The mar-

[39] *Ibid.*, n. 727; cf. Brief of Pope Clement VIII, "*Christifidelium,*" August 17, 1599—*Coll. Lac.*, II, 172-173; *Fonti,* XII, n. 726. In this decree, as in many others, the synod pointed to the legislation of the Council of Trent.

[40] *Ibid.*, n. 237; White, *De forma celebrationis matrimonii,* p. 85. This "diriment impediment" of clandestinity received its force not from the publication of the Tridentine form, but from the papal approval of the decrees of the synod. Cf. *S. Romanae Rotae Decisiones,* XXVII (1935), dec. xvii, p. 154. This same decision declared (p. 158) that in the Maronite Church the principles concerning force and fear are identical with those which are employed in the Latin Code.

[41] Pars II, cap. XI, nn. 28 and 29—*Coll. Lac.*, II, 177-178; cf. *Fonti,* XII, nn. 886, 891 and 898.

[42] Canon XIV—*Fonti,* XII, n. 890.

riages should take place in the parish church, not in private homes or any other places.[43]

In the ninth section of the chapter which deals with the legislation of marriage, the synod speaks of the impedient impediments, namely: (a) an interdict placed on a church (but permission for a quiet wedding can be obtained in a case of moral necessity); (b) the "forbidden times," namely, the Advent period from December 5th to the Feast of the Epiphany included, and the time of Lent, from the Monday after *Quinquagesima* Sunday to the octave day of Easter included, during which time not the marriages themselves are forbidden, but only the solemn blessing and extensive festivities which normally accompany the contracting of marriage; (c) espousals (if the marriage takes place outside of the first degree which alone connotes the presence of a diriment impediment after valid espousals are entered); (d) "instructions" connected with the supplying of the ceremonies of baptism; [44] (e) the simple vow of chastity or of religion. "Besides these five prohibiting impediments, some others are mentioned which especially *impede the use of marriage between married people:* (1) incest. . . . Age also, which, as has been mentioned above, in a man should be fourteen and in a girl twelve completed years, for before this time it is not licit to contract marriage, even if the bishop in a case of defect of age could dispense in an urgent necessity, after having taken into consideration the temperament and capacity of the spouses." [45]

[43] Pars II, cap. XI, n. 26—*Coll. Lac.*, II, 176-177; cf. Korkemaz, pp. 74-75.

[44] *Catechismus,* quod impedimentum tunc solum occurrit, quando supplentur caerimoniae baptismi prius sine solemnitate celebrati. Hi enim, qui ad caerimonias supplendas, inter quas est catechismus seu instructio, baptizatum puerum deferunt, impedimentum hoc incurrunt.—Pars II, cap. 11, n. 9 (*Coll. Lac.*, II, 168).

[45] "Praeter haec quinque impedimenta prohibentia nonnulla alia referuntur, quae praesertim matrimonii usum inter conjugatos impediunt: (1) incestus. . . . Aetas etiam, quae, ut supra dictum est, in viro quatuordecim et in muliere duodecim annorum completorum esse debet; nam ante hoc tempus contrahere non licet, etsi Episcopus in aetatis defectu ex urgenti necessitate dispensare possit, attento sponsorum temperamento et capacitate."—*Coll Lac.*, II, 169. Cf. O'Dea, *The Matrimonial Impediment of Nonage,* p. 44. Cf. also Korkemaz, pp. 45-49.

There follows a discussion of the dispensing power of the Church, which is always of course subject to the natural and positive divine law. The causes allowing a dispensation and the conditions under which it can be granted are then listed. Only the Patriarch, through a concession of the Pope, can grant a dispensation from the diriment impediments and from the simple absolute vow of perpetual chastity or of religion, but the Patriarch can also commit this power to others; the bishops under certain conditions can dispense from a diriment impediment in the forum of conscience.[46]

Detailed rules are given concerning the proclamation of the banns of marriage. These rules are practically the same as those which are prescribed by the Latin Code about the time when they are to be made, the method of proceeding if an impediment is discovered, the obligation of the hearers to reveal their knowledge of any impediment, etc.[47]

The synod declares that in the solemnization of marriage only virgins are to be crowned. This is to be done even if a virgin marry a widower. The Council quotes the prohibitions of the early Church about second marriages, but understands them as forbidding only the solemn crowning and the festive banquets. The synod follows "the custom and practice of the Roman Church, the mother and teacher of all churches," and does not condemn second or further marriages.[48]

The synod also cites the teaching of the Fathers and of the general councils that a valid nonconsummated marriage can be dissolved by the solemn religious profession of one of the parties in an approved institute. Finally, after repeating the prohibition which bars marriage to those who are in sacred orders, the synod concludes its treatment on marriage with an intimate exhortation to the married that they should live a pure conjugal life and should seek to fulfill their manifold duties to their children.[49]

[46] *Fonti,* XII, nn. 479-488.

[47] *Ibid.,* nn. 1206-1218. Cf. Korkemaz, pp. 30-43.

[48] *Ibid.,* nn. 897 and 901.

[49] Pars II, cap. XI, nn. 35-37 (*Coll. Lac.,* II, 183-184).

Article IV. The Byzantine Rite

1. The Melkites [50]

The union of the Melkites with Rome after the Council of Florence (1438-1445) was only temporary; during the fifteenth and sixteenth centuries there were some Catholic leaders, but a real lasting union came only in the eighteenth century. At Antioch, Athanasius III Dabbas (1700-1724) and Cyril V Zaim (d. 1720) along with the Archbishop of Tyre, Euthymius (1683-1723), tried to effect a reunion, but their profession of faith was viewed by Rome as inadequate; however, in 1724, a nephew of Euthymius, Seraphim Tanas, who had studied at Rome, was elected by the Latinizing element as patriarch. He immediately submitted to Rome, sent a Catholic profession of faith, and assumed the name of Cyril VI. With him there began the new Catholic Melkite line of patriarchs. His rule, which lasted until 1759, was not an easy one. It was marked by conflicts with the Orthodox, which caused him to flee to the Lebanon.[51] The pallium was sent to him by Pope Benedict XIV in 1744.[52] Nine synods were held during the eighteenth century, but none of them were approved by Rome.[53]

On June 2, 1718, the Sacred Congregation of the Holy Office, in answering some doubts proposed by Patriarch Cyril V, declared

[50] Mansi, XLVI, *passim*. This entire volume of Mansi is devoted to matters of the Melkites from 1716 to 1902. Cf. also *Fonti,* VIII, 282-468, wherein Abela and Coussa present separate historical and analytical studies of the sources of the Melkite Canon Law. Cf. Janin, *Les Églises orientales,* pp. 328-329; Fortescue, *The Uniate Eastern Churches,* pp. 192-202.

[51] It was to this Patriarch and the various Melkite bishops subject to him that Pope Benedict XIV sent his celebrated Encyclical Letter *"Demandatam"* on December 24, 1743, concerning many important questions for the Melkites, such as the jurisdiction of the patriarch and the bishops, the administration of the sacrament of confirmation, the prohibition of missionaries to induce a change to the Latin rite, some rules for the monks and nuns, and other matters. This Encyclical Letter can be found in Mansi, XLVI, 331-338, and in the *Codicis Iuris Canonici Fontes,* n. 338.

[52] *Mansi,* XLVI, 341.

[53] For a synopsis of these synods (held between 1724 and 1797) cf. *Fonti,* VIII, 286-287, 429-439.

that marriages between cousins were not permitted without a dispensation from the Holy See or its empowered delegates, and also that those who had married twice were not to be admitted to sacred orders without a special dispensation.[54]

In March, 1729, the Sacred Congregation for the Propagation of the Faith wrote to Patriarch Cyril VI concerning six doubts which had been submitted by Euthymius, Archbishop of Tyre, in 1716. The latter had changed some customs of the Greek rite. One of these changes was "that he prohibited marriage in the fourth degree." The Congregation declared: "Let the Archbishop be charitably advised concerning all the doubts proposed that he should keep and guard the rites and ceremonies which the Greek Church commonly practices."[55] It is not certain just what degree of consanguinity impeded marriage among the Melkites; they seem never to have known the impediment beyond the sixth degree.[56]

2. *The Ruthenians*[57]

In 1450 most of the Grand Duchy of Lithuania was composed of Ukrainian land, especially Volhynia, east of Galicia; Poland held Galicia and Podolia (south of Volhynia). The entire Ukraine at this period was severely afflicted with internal uprisings (such as those under Hlinsky, Mukha, and Bohdan) and also with constant attacks from Turks and Tatars, who sold whole groups of Ukrainians into slavery. The sixteenth century saw the rise to power of the Cossack Host from the Black Sea steppes to fight the Tatars and the Turks. Many Ukrainians migrated to their lands after Poland, in 1569, annexed from Lithuania the provinces of Volhynia and Kiev and the lands beyond the Dnieper River; Ukrainian Severia was

[54] Mansi, XLVI, 125.

[55] *Ibid.*, col. 90; *Fonti*, XV, 265.

[56] Dauvillier and De Clercq, p. 125.

[57] Hrushevsky, pp. 138-482; Plöchl, "The Church Laws for Orientals of the Austrian Monarchy in the 'Age of the Enlightenment,'"—*Bulletin of the Polish Institute of Arts and Sciences in America*, II (1944), 711-756. Both authors list extensive bibliographies. Cf. also Chamberlin, *The Ukraine* (New York: Macmillan, 1944), pp. 11-28.

seized by Muscovy; Bucovina remained subject to Moldavia (east of Transylvania); Carpathian Ukraine continued under Hungarian rule. Forty years later Poland took Severia, and so ruled most of the Ukraine. Ukrainian migrations continued towards the east, and new towns were opened where previously wild vast steppes had existed.

At the close of 1595 Bishop Terletsky and Bishop Potiy went to Rome, where, before the Cardinals and the Pope, they pledged their loyalty to the Pope and to the Church, and were formally received into the Church, with the understanding that the Ukrainians in their territories would keep their own discipline.[58] This union caused some disturbance, and some bishops then withdrew their support from the reunion movement; different dioceses reacted differently and confusion existed as to the status of the Ukrainian Church. The Ukrainian people were afraid that reunion meant Latinization, which to them meant Polonization, for at that time much of the Ukraine was under Polish rule.

Notable among the Uniate bishops was the Ukrainian hero, Bishop Josaphat Kuncewicz, bishop of Polotsk (1617-1623), who was killed at Vitebsk in a revolt against the reunion (he was canonized by Pope Pius IX in 1867). South of the Carpathian Mountains, Bishop Tarasovitch of Munkács in 1636 acknowledged the Pope to be the head of the Church, and for this he was forced to resign his see. Ten years later, the Bishop of Munkács and the Bishop of Jager (Erlau) at the city of Ungvár (Uzhorod), in a solemn synod attended by sixty-three priests abjured the schism, and professed themselves as "Greek clergy holding the faith of SS. Cyril and Methodius in communion with Rome."

The early seventeenth century was marked by continuous wars among the Cossack Host, Turks, Muscovites, Poles, Ukrainians, Tatars, now on one side and later on another, with a history full of massacres, raids, revolts, treachery, and destruction. In 1654 an alliance was made between the Cossack Host and Muscovy, in accordance with which the Ukraine was supposed to have an autonomous

[58] Cf. Brian-Chaninov, *The Russian Church* (trans. by Warre B. Wells, London: Burns, Oates and Washbourne, 1931), pp. 74-79.

rule, although it was bound to the person of the tsar. But soon Muscovy sent its own officials, and attempted to bring the "Orthodox" Ukrainian Church under the Patriarch of Moscow. At this time Poland and Muscovy engaged in a long war. It ended in 1667 with the treaty of Andrusovo, in which the Ukraine was partitioned between them approximately on a line north and south from Kiev (these boundaries were kept until 1772).

Among the Carpatho-Ukrainians social improvements and religious liberty in Transylvania soon followed the submission of Transylvania to Leopold I of Austria (1657-1705) on May 9, 1688. The able Bishop John Joseph de Camillis consolidated the spiritual and temporal life of the impoverished Ukrainians, who by the express law of the previous Transylvania rulers had practically been made the serfs of the ruling classes. As vicar apostolic, Bishop de Camillis ruled under the jurisdiction of the Congregation for the Propagation of the Faith, while he also served as a vicar under the Latin bishop of Jager (Erlau). Rome favored this position of the Catholic Oriental bishop as a vicar to the Latin bishop, and after the death of Bishop de Camillis in 1704 refused to make the candidate of the government an independent ordinary.

This caused a vacancy in the see until 1716, when another vicar apostolic, Bishop George Bizancy, was appointed. The Empress Maria Theresa (1740-1780) interested herself in the question of an independent ordinary for the Carpatho-Ukrainians, especially after she had received from the Ukrainian clergy a petition which moved her to write directly to Pope Clement XIII (1758-1769) on October 30, 1766. She felt that such an independent ordinary would be of great benefit to the Oriental Church in Podcarpathia. The Pope, however, invoking canon 9 of the IV General Council of the Lateran (1215), which prescribed that only one bishop was to have ordinary jurisdiction in a place, did not grant the request. But his successor, Pope Clement XIV (1769-1774) on September 19, 1771, established the diocese of Munkács and confirmed the Empress's candidate, Brakacs, as its ordinary.

In the eastern part of the Ukraine, Russian [59] generals and min-

[59] Frederiksen, the editor of Hrushevsky's *The History of Ukraine*, wrote (p. 374): "As the tsardom of Muscovy expanded by the conquest of its

isters soon ruled many Ukrainian offices. A real campaign to destroy the traditional forms of government in the Ukraine was undertaken by Catherine II (1762-1796), who sought to replace the Ukrainian rule with that of Russia. Serfdom was legalized by her government, and consequently the condition of the Ukrainian peasants became very wretched, subject to Russian officials. The people became as Russian serfs, and even the estates of the Ukrainian Church became part of the Russian treasury, which allotted salaries for the monks. After the eastern and western parts of the Ukraine were separated by the treaty of 1667 they drifted farther and farther apart; in the east the Ukrainian Church was gradually subjected to the Patriarch of Moscow, while Polish and Ukrainian bishops in the western part spread the reunion with Rome, so that during the first half of the eighteenth century the whole of the western Ukraine became Catholic.

In 1763, after the death of the Polish King Frederick Augustus III (1733-1763), the Russian Empress Catherine II sent an army to put her candidate on the throne, in order that she might rule the country in his name. In the midst of this confusion a Russo-Turkish war broke out in 1768, in which Austria indicated its support of Turkey in order to prevent Russian expansion towards Austria. The King of Prussia, Frederic the Great (1740-1786), suggested a compromise. It led to the treaty of August, 1772, whereby, without a war, Russia took some White Russian land from Poland, Austria annexed Galicia, and Prussia acquired Polish land bordering the Baltic Sea. In 1777 Austria also annexed Bucovina (to the northeast of Transylvania) which in 1786 was united with Galicia. Bucovina retained this status until 1849, when it was made a separate province.

The Empress Maria Theresa took an immediate interest in the Catholic Orientals thus brought under her rule. In 1774 she issued two decrees which stressed the equality of the Latin and the Oriental rites in matters of both ecclesiastical and secular life. The Ruthenian clergy were ordered to be called "Greek-Catholics" instead of "Greek-Uniates." Plans were also advanced to unite the Ruthenians of Galicia, Hungary and Transylvania into one ecclesiastical province

neighbors, it had abandoned its old name and assumed that of 'Russia' which was a Latinization of 'Rus,' the ancient name of Ukraine."

under a metropolitan-archbishop either at Munkács or at Lemberg, but the execution of this plan was deemed inopportune at the time. In the south of Hungary, in 1777, Pius VI (1775-1799) at her request created at Krizevci another independent diocese for Orientals, namely, for the Croats who lived around Sumberak and the Ukrainians who had migrated south from Podcarpathia.

The Emperor Joseph II (1780-1790), called "The Sacristan Emperor" because of his legislation on minute details concerning the Church in her secular and religious spheres, also took a warm interest in the affairs of the Oriental Catholics in his lands. In 1783 he established one major seminary at Lemberg for the Oriental clergy in Galicia, and another in Jager (Erlau) for the Hungarian Oriental clergy, and issued detailed decrees concerning the selection and the education of the seminarians. Leopold II (1790-1792) repeated the decrees of his two predecessors in a Diploma of July 8, 1790, which emphasized the equality of the rites in Galicia; in other decrees too he continued the tradition of the Austrian Emperors of the eighteenth century in enacting detailed and, in the main, beneficial laws for both Catholic and "Orthodox" Orientals.[60]

In the last years of the eighteenth century the Ukraine was taken away from Polish rule entirely. In 1792, when the Russian armies had occupied Warsaw itself, Prussia received more land in Western Poland, while Russia annexed the Ukrainian provinces of Kiev, Podolia, a part of Volhynia, and some parts of White Russia. In 1794 Russian and Prussian armies suppressed another internal insurrection in Poland, again occupying Warsaw, and also Vilna, and in the following year the final partition of Poland took place. Russia took the Ukrainian and White Russian lands above the northeast part of Galicia, while Austria received some provinces to the northwest of Galicia. Warsaw and the province to the north went to Prussia. Thus at the end of the eighteenth century all political distinctions and boundaries marking the Ukraine were abolished, and the Ukrainians thus became completely subjected to two great powers, Russia and Austria.

[60] Hrushevsky attests to the benefits of the Austrian rule in Galicia in saying (p. 468): "The placing of Galicia under Austrian rule was the beginning of the Ukrainian renaissance in western Ukraine."

The various decrees of Ruthenian synods, the Papal Briefs, and the replies of the Roman Congregations, which dealt with the Ruthenian marriage legislation during the period from the Council of Florence to the nineteenth century, can be summarized as follows:

1. *Affinity.* Metropolitan Rutsky of Kiev sought the faculty for granting dispensations from the impediment of affinity when this impediment arose from the third and fourth degrees of relationship, whether constituted in simple or double or also mixed form. The Sacred Congregation for the Propagation of the Faith decided that the Pope was to be asked to grant the faculty for a certain number of cases. The same day, March 23, 1629, Pope Urban VIII approved this decision and ordered a Brief to be drawn, giving the Metropolitan the faculty for twelve marriages, and empowering the Papal Nuncio to grant the same faculty for another certain number of cases to the same Metropolitan.[61] The Brief was issued by the Pope on April 18, 1629.[62] The Synod of Zamost (1720), almost a century later, spoke in general terms of the "prohibited degree" of affinity, showing no change at this time in the law.[63]

2. *Consanguinity.* What has been said about affinity applies in the same documents also to consanguinity, affecting the same degrees.

[61] *Fonti,* I, 279, and XI, n. 307.

[62] *"Ut venerabilis frater,"—Ius Pontificium de Propaganda Fide* (ed. R. de Martinis, *Pars Prima,* 7 vols. in 8 libri, Romae, 1888-1897; *Pars Secunda,* 1 vol., Romae, 1909), *Pars Prima,* I, 110. (Hereafter this collection will be cited as *Ius Pont.* and the citation will be from *Pars Prima,* unless otherwise noted). Cf. also *Fonti,* II, 245-247; XI, n. 305.

[63] Tit. III, § 8—*Coll. Lac.,* II, 43; *Fonti,* XI, n. 406. The first page of Vol. II of the *Collectio Lacensis* contains the confirmation of the synod *"in forma specifica"* by Pope Benedict XIII (1724-1730) in his Brief *"Apostolatus officium,"* of July 19, 1724: ". . . omniaque et singula in ea edita statuta, ordinationes et decreta, auctoritate apostolica tenore praesentium confirmamus et approbamus. . . ." (Cf. *Fonti,* XI, n. 765). In 1807 Pope Pius VII (1800-1823) extended the force of this synod to the districts of Halicz, Lemberg, Chelm and Przemysl in his Bull *"In universalis Ecclesiae regimine,"* which also made Lemberg a Metropolitan See, while not affecting the rights of the Metropolitan See at Kiev. Cf. *Ius Pont.,* IV, 493; *Fonti,* XI, n. 766. For a separate work containing the decrees of this synod and some documents issued in relation to it, cf. *Synodus Provincialis Ruthenorum, habita in civitate Zamosciae anno MDCCXX,* 3. ed., Romae, 1883.

3. *Sacred Orders.* On March 21, 1631, the Holy Office declared that the marriages attempted by Ruthenian priests are null, and that as a consequence the women remained free to marry.[64] On May 21, 1631, the Holy Office declared that Ruthenian priests, if they had married before receiving sacred orders and their wives now had died, and if now they had actually contracted a second union, thinking that such a marriage contracted after the reception of sacred orders would be considered as valid even though it entailed for them a suspension from their ministry, could not validly marry and therefore the women who had attempted marriage with them remained free.[65]

On February 22, 1633, the Sacred Congregation for the Propagation of the Faith denied a request from the bishop of Przemysl for a dispensation for a priest who had married after the death of his first wife. The bishop had sent in the request because he feared that the priest would join the schismatics if the dispensation to allow him to retain his wife were refused.[66] On June 3, 1635, the Holy Office renewed its prohibition against the marriage of priests after their wives had died, and also prohibited deacons, if they contracted marriage, from being ordained as priests if they retained their wives; a priest who had remarried but whose spouse had died could receive a dispensation which allowed him to be readmitted to the ministry. A lay person who had entered a second marriage but who was now again a widower could receive a dispensation which allowed him to be advanced to orders.[67]

On September 2, 1647, the Sacred Congregation for the Propagation of the Faith ordered that the celibate clergy was to be given preference over the married clergy in the matter of their assignment

[64] "Matrimonia contracta inter sacerdotes saeculares Ruthenos post susceptos ordines sacros, sunt nulla; et consequenter mulieres liberae remanent."—*Ius Pont., Pars Secunda,* p. 53, n. LXXXVI; *Fonti,* XI, n. 388. These two sources however contain only this statement and do not give any details of the case in question.

[65] *Ibid.,* p. 54, n. XC; *Fonti,* I, 67; XI, 389.

[66] *Fonti,* XI, n. 392.

[67] *Ius Pont., Pars Secunda,* p. 72, n. CXXIV; *Fonti,* XI, n. 61, n. 335 and n. 390.

to parishes.[68] The Holy Office on May 4, 1660, again refused a request of the bishop of Przemysl to dispense a Uniate priest who had married after ordination; the reason given for the request was that the priest was "very zealous for the holy union." The Holy Office instructed the Papal Nuncio to declare his marriage null and to see to it that the parties be separated.[69]

The Synod of Zamost (1720) declared that if any priest presumed to attempt marriage, or if upon the death of his first wife he presumed to enter a second incestuous union, the bishop was to bar him from communion with the Church, and from the altar; such a priest was to be imprisoned and subjected to other canonical penalties, in order that he might repudiate this transient and spurious union.[70]

4. *Spiritual relationship and public propriety.* Pope Urban VIII confirmed two decrees of the Congregation for the Propagation of the Faith, giving the Metropolitan Rutsky faculties to dispense from these impediments, but the various degrees are not mentioned in the decrees.[71] The Synod of Zamost (1720) declared that valid espousals create an impediment of public propriety between either of the par-

[68] *Fonti,* XI, n. 126.

[69] *Ius Pont., Pars Secunda,* p. 119, n. CCXXXV; *Fonti,* XI, n. 387.

[70] Tit. III, § 8—*Coll. Lac.,* II, 45; *Fonti,* XI, n. 386; Papp-Szilagyi, p. 256; Cappello, n. 908; Mansella, *De Impedimentis,* p. 95. Dauvillier and De Clercq (p. 172) declare: " . . . le concile ruthène de Zamosc (1720) dit que le mariage d'un prêtre est illégitime et que le coupable doit être puni de la prison et d'autres peines; il se réfère au concile *in Trullo.*" The word "illégitime" seems to indicate that in their estimation the marriage was not clearly an invalid union. After discussing this decree of the Synod of Zamost, Bobak (*De caelibatu,* pp. 153-157) asserts that the decree does not point with certainty to the invalidity of such marriages. He takes the phrase "a second incestuous union" in a literal sense, i.e., as indicating that the decree severely forbade a priest to marry a person closely related to him by consanguinity or affinity, e.g., he should not marry the sister of his deceased wife; according to Bobak, it was a common custom for the Ruthenians who were going to take sacred orders, to marry women who were closely related to him, and to do this also after the death of the first wife.

[71] March 23, 1629 (*Fonti,* I, 279 and XI, n. 308) and May 8, 1629 (*Fonti,* I, 281).

ties and the relatives of the other in the second degrees of the direct and collateral lines.[72]

5. *Abduction.* The Synod of Zamost stated that the impediment of abduction was present even if the woman was a willing agent.[73]

6. *Age.* The same synod prescribed fourteen years as the minimum age for the man, and twelve for the woman.[74]

7. *Crime.* Adultery accompanied with the promise of a future marriage, or the murder of a spouse when committed by one but known to the other, or also the murder consented to or aided by the second party, constituted the impediment of crime between the two guilty persons.[75]

8. *Banns.* The same synod decreed that the banns of marriage were to be announced at Mass on three consecutive feast days, in both parishes if the parties were of different parishes; the pastor who assisted at the marriage had to receive previous notice from the other pastor that he had proclaimed the banns and that no impediment was discovered. If the parties lived in a parish to which they had come only recently, and in which therefore they were not well enough known, then the banns were to be proclaimed in the parishes of their previous residence.[76]

9. *The form of marriage.* On October 11, 1619, a synod of Novgorod-Kiev under the Metropolitan of Kiev, Joseph Rutsky,[77] declared that marriages contracted without the blessing of a priest were null, and would be regarded as illicit and impious and as misdeeds punishable with secular and spiritual penalties alike.[78]

[72] Tit. III, § 8—*Coll. Lac.*, II, 43.

[73] *Loc. cit.* Cappello (*De Matrimonio*, n. 914) declares that the phrase, "even if the woman was a willing agent," should be understood as referring to the case wherein the woman indeed gave her consent but in consequence of deceit, or of fraud, or at least because of certain inducements. Cf. also Cappello, "Ius Ecclesiae Latinae cum iure Ecclesiae Orientalis comparatum,"—*Jus Pontificium*, VII (1927), 67.

[74] *Loc. cit.*

[75] *Loc. cit.* Cf. Donohue, *The Impediment of Crime*, p. 83. Cf. also Cappello, n. 916, where he states that the Chaldeans have substantially the same law, concerning this impediment, as the Ruthenians.

[76] *Loc. cit.*

[77] Cf. Hrushevsky, p. 241.

[78] *Fonti*, I, 273.

On August 26, 1626, the Council of Kobryn, under the same Metropolitan, decreed that the "ancient law and holy custom in relation to clandestine marriages" was to be promulgated, so that marriages would be invalid if they were not witnessed by the proper pastor, or by another priest with the proper pastor's permission, and marriages would also be invalid if Uniate priests presumed to assist at the marriages of Latins. Two or three witnesses were required for validity.[79] On December 7, 1626, the Sacred Congregation for the Propagation of the Faith ordered that this decree of the Council on clandestinity be promulgated in each parish[80] In the following month the same Congregation added to the previous decree a further note to explain that the Ukrainian synod of itself did not have the authority to invalidate clandestine marriages, but that only the specific approval of the Holy See could give force to this law.[81]

Two years later, on January 22, 1629, the same Congregation upheld an action of the metropolitan who had declared invalid certain clandestine marriages by invoking the prescriptions of the Council of Kobryn (which of itself could not decree the nullity of clandestine marriages) and by insisting that the Council at least implicitly promulgated the decree of the Council of Trent, because "in it [the Council of Kobryn] it is decreed that there be retained in the parishes the ancient law and the praiseworthy custom by which clandestine marriages were declared nullified and invalid; this ancient law cannot however be verified in the decree of Novgorod-Kiev, since it was issued only six years before [1619-1626] nor from any other constitution of the common law, for besides that of the Council of Trent none exists which nullifies these marriages. Therefore, from necessity, the decree of this very Council of Trent is to be understood, for that decree both nullifies such marriages and, inasmuch as it was enacted sixty-four years ago, can be called 'ancient.' "[82]

[79] This Council was confirmed by Pope Urban VIII in his Brief, *"Militantis ecclesiae regiminis,"* 6 dec. 1629—*Ius Pont.*, I, 116.

[80] *Fonti,* I, 275.

[81] *Ibid.*, p. 277; White, *De forma celebrationis matrimonii,* p. 32.

[82] *Ius Pont., Pars Secunda,* p. 40, n. LXV; cf. Pope Benedict XIV, *De Synodo dioecesana,* Lib. XII, cap. 5, nn. 7-11—*Opera Omnia* (17 vols. in 18, Prati, 1829-1847), XI, 456-457.

On April 18th of the same year Pope Urban VIII ordered the Tridentine form to be observed (the Brief however was concerned directly with consanguinity and affinity).[83] On December 5th he issued a Brief giving Metropolitan Rutsky faculties to allow to live in their second unions those whose clandestine marriages (contracted after the synods of Novgorod-Kiev and Kobryn) had been declared null by him prior to their consummation.[84] On December 14th the same Pope renewed his command that the *"Tametsi"* decree on the form of marriage be promulgated and explained in each parish church as soon as possible, so that marriages not contracted according to this form would be null.[85]

On April 21, 1632, the Pope sent another Brief, decreeing that the banns were to be announced three times for the sake of detecting any impediments, and that marriages would be null if not celebrated in the presence of the pastor or bishop, or of a priest with the permission of either the pastor or the bishop, and of two or three witnesses. This decree was to go into effect in each parish thirty days after its promulgation in the parish, and in the church courts the judges were to act accordingly in settling marriage nullity suits on the ground of a lack of the proper form.[86] This Brief was prepared lest some bishops retain their opinion that it would be sufficient in a provincial council or in diocesan synods alone to promulgate the law concerning the form of marriage, and that it was not necessary to promulgate it in every parish.[87]

With reference to the difficulty of getting the people to comply with this requirement of the Tridentine form, it is to be remembered that in the Ukraine the blessing of the priest was in use only for the marriage of the lords and princes, while the people kept the old forms of marriage without any religious blessing.[88] The actual verbal expression of consent was introduced among the Ukrainian people

[83] Cf. footnote n. 62 *supra* in the discussion of the impediment of affinity.

[84] *"Ut Christifidelium,"—Ius Pont.*, I, 116; *Fonti,* II, 331; XI, n. 393.

[85] Breve *"Licet universorum,"—ibid.*, p. 118; *Fonti,* II, 333.

[86] *"Licet Universorum Christifidelium,"—ibid.*, p. 139; *Fonti,* II, 335; XI, n. 412.

[87] *Fonti,* I, 277.

[88] Dauvillier, p. 425.

only after the "orthodox" Metropolitan Peter Moghila issued his Ritual (*Trebnik*) at Kiev in 1646. Soon after his ritual appeared, a direct interrogation of the spouses about their consent was added to the ceremony of crowning among the Ukrainians. This ritual of Moghila also included the rules for the promulgation of the banns as in force in the Latin Church.[89]

The Synod of Zamost (1720) emphasized that the marriage ceremony in their rite was very similar to that of the Latins when the Synod stated: "Because the rite of administering this sacrament in our Church is practically the same as that in the Latin Church and so needs no correction or change, it will not be licit for pastors to deviate from the received form." [90] This synod prescribed also that, since the church was the proper place for the reception of the sacraments, marriages were not to take place in private houses without the express permission of the ordinary.[91]

3. *The Rumanians* [92]

The Metropolitan Damian signed the reunion decree at the Council of Florence (1438-1445), but the Rumanian "Orthodox"

[89] Dauvillier, "La formation du mariage dans les Églises orientales,"—*Revue des Sciences Religieuses,* XV (1935), 386; Jugie, "Mariage dans l'Église gréco-russe,"—*DTC,* IX (Part 2), 2320; Raes, "Le consentement matrimonial dans les Rites orientaux,"—*Ephemerides Liturgicae,* XLVII (1933), 431; White, *De forma celebrationis matrimonii,* p. 76. Much of Moghila's writing on marriage was inserted in the *Kormtchaia Kniga,* the official canonical collection of the Muscovite Russian Church, published first by Patriarch Joseph in 1650 and by his successor Nikon in 1653; in 1775 a decree of the Holy Synod prescribed it for the entire Russian Church.

[90] Tit. III: "Quoniam ritus administrandi hoc sacramentum in nostra ecclesia idem propemodum est qui in ecclesia Latina, proindeque nulla correctione aut mutatione indiget, non licebit parochis a recepta forma recedere."—*Coll. Lac.,* II, 42; *Fonti,* XI, n. 383.

[91] *Loc. cit.;* cf. *Fonti,* XI, n. 760.

[92] *Fonti,* VIII, 489-504, 538-551, 574-576; Plöchl, "The Church Laws for Orientals of the Austrian Monarchy in the 'Age of the Enlightenment,'"—*Bulletin of the Polish Institute of Arts and Sciences in America,* II (1944), 711-756; *Statistica,* 157-158; Janin, *Les Églises orientales,* pp. 362-364; De Clercq, *Les Églises unies d'Orient,* pp. 86-87; Attwater, *The Catholic Eastern Churches,* pp. 101-102.

Church did not accept his act, and he was thereupon obliged to live in Rome. For almost three centuries there were only very rare attempts of a prince or of a bishop to effect a union with Rome. The Hungarian Calvinists and Saxon Lutherans became powerful in Transylvania, and there was little hope for a Catholic reunion movement. In a law of 1566 the Catholic religion was called idolatry, and every bishop of the Latin rite was expelled from the territories of Moldavia, Wallachia and Transylvania, which composed the Rumania of that time. The law of 1610 permitted only private worship to the Catholics. The contact between Rome and the Rumanians was therefore very greatly hampered. There were only a few papal letters before the end of the seventeenth century, such as the two of Pope Sixtus IV (1471-1484) in 1476, urging the Catholics in Moldavia to help in the fight against the Turks, and that of Pope Alexander VII (1655-1667) in 1658 to John Michael, Prince of Wallachia, on the occasion of his conversion.

After the Council of Florence St. John of Capistrano (1386-1456) brought 30,000 to a reunion, but this movement lasted only twenty-five years. In 1687 the Emperor Leopold I of Austria (1657-1705) drove the Turkish rulers out of Transylvania, and thereupon the Jesuit chaplains sought to effect a reunion. In 1697 the Jesuit Baranyi persuaded the "Orthodox" Metropolitan of Alba Julia, Theophilus Szeremy, to call a synod which signed a reunion act, but the Metropolitan died within a few weeks. His successor in Transylvania, Athanasius Popa, within a few weeks of his arrival at Alba Julia in 1698 signed a profession of faith and a declaration of union.[93] This union was finally confirmed at Vienna in 1701, which brought 200,000 into reunion with Rome.[94]

In 1721 the Latin Bishop of Transylvania invoked the ruling of canon 9 of the IV General Council of the Lateran (1215),[95] in view

[93] Cf. "Declaratio qua ecclesia Valachica ritus graeci unionem ecclesiae Romanae amplexa est."—Mansi, XLII, 617. This declaration is dated October 7, 1698.

[94] Because the Jesuits were so instrumental in securing and maintaining this union, the Primate of Hungary requested from the Pope that they be allowed to offer Mass in the Latin and Rumanian rites, but Pope Clement XI (litt. *"Ubi plurimis,"* 9 maii 1705) did not permit this.

[95] This canon forbade that there be two bishops in one diocese and ordered

of which he claimed that Bishop Pataky, whom Pope Innocent XIII (1721-1724) had allowed to change to the Byzantine rite and had named as bishop for the Rumanians, was only his "ritual vicar." The Pope replied that Bishop Pataky was the proper ordinary for the Rumanians, but that he should reside at Fagaras; the right to present prospective bishops for the Rumanians was given to the Austrian Emperor.[96]

The Emperor Charles VI (1711-1740), who had originally in 1716 presented to Rome his choice of John Pataky, transferred the seat of this new diocese from Fagaras to Blaj in 1738. The Empress Maria Theresa also took a great interest in the Oriental Rumanians; by her decrees of September 9, 1743, and April 5, 1746, she determined the rights of the clergy to the tithes, and also renewed the immunities granted by her predecessors. She favored the erection of a new diocese for them, and in 1748 the Holy See erected a new episcopal vicariate subject to the Latin bishop of Oradea Mare, to serve the Rumanians in Hungary and Transylvania.[97] In 1777 this vicariate of Oradea Mare was raised in its status to that of a diocese with the new Rumanian bishop enjoying ordinary power, under the Primate of Hungary as his Metropolitan, and the crown received the right of presentation to the see.[98]

In the century following the solemn reunion of the Rumanians in 1701 there was very little matrimonial legislation deriving either from their own councils or from the Holy See. The Sacred Congregation for the Propagation of the Faith in a letter of February 5, 1746, to the Vicar General of Fagaras, declared that in no way could a priest be allowed to keep a second wife whom he had married after the reception of sacred orders.[99]

that, if necessary, a vicar be appointed for those of a different rite in the diocese. For the text of the canon, cf. Mansi, XXII, 998.

[96] Litt. ap. *"Rationi congruit,"* 30 iun. 1721—*Appendix ad Bullarium Pontificium S. C. de Propaganda Fide* (8 vols., Romae, 1839-1848), II, 3-6.

[97] This decree, issued by the Sacred Consistorial Congregation on July 12, 1748, at the order of Pope Benedict XIV can be found in his *De Synodo dioecesana,* Lib. II, cap. XII, n. 5—*Opera Omnia,* XI, 49-50.

[98] Pius VI, litt. ap. *"Indefessum personarum,"* 16 iun. 1777. Cf. *Fonti,* VIII, 263.

[99] *Fonti,* X, n. 303.

At Fagaras, which was erected as a diocese in 1721, several synods were held which passed decrees against the marriages of priests and against marriages contracted without the promulgation of the banns; in a synod of 1754 Bishop Peter Paul Aaron declared that a marriage would be null if not contracted before the proper pastor of either party and in the presence of witnesses. The bishop ordered that this rule be promulgated, but did not mention that it was to be promulgated as the Tridentine form. According to a letter of the bishop's successor, Athanasius Rednik, to the Sacred Congregation for the Propagation of the Faith in 1766, the promulgation of this synodal decree caused many of the Rumanians to marry before a schismatic priest. The Holy See did not formally approve this decree, for at that time the diriment impediment of clandestinity was in effect only in those parishes where the decree of the Council of Trent had been promulgated as such.[100]

4. The Italo-Greeks[101]

As seen in the previous chapter, the Albanian chief, George Castriota, called also Scanderbeg, attempted in vain to check the Turkish victories in Albania. In 1465 he came to Rome to ask Pope Pius II (1458-1464), who was trying to organize a crusade, for help against their common enemy; three years later Scanderbeg died fighting at Alessio, and perhaps he died as a Catholic. It is from his time that the history of Italy and Albania became interwoven. In 1478 the Turkish Sultan Mohammed II (1451-1481) subjected all Albania to his rule; thereupon, and throughout the sixteenth century, there was a stream of Albanian refugees spreading throughout the Kingdom of Naples and the Two Sicilies. There was a natural sympathy for these victims of the Turks. Moreover, these Albanians, being industrious and thrifty, were made welcome to reclaim the sparse lands to the south of Italy. There were other Albanian colonists to the north, but they in the course of time adopted the Roman rite.

[100] Cf. *Fonti*, VIII, 543-548.

[101] Fortescue, *The Uniate Eastern Churches*, pp. 116-150; Janin, *Les Églises orientales*, pp. 324-325.

These newly arrived colonists spoke the Albanian language, but their language in their Byzantine ritual was Greek. Unfortunately they had no bishops of their own until the eighteenth century; they were therefore subject to the ordinaries of the places where they settled. This state of affairs created problems. Sometimes a visiting bishop of their own rite began to assume ordinary jurisdiction over his people. Sometimes these people themselves asserted that they were independent of the decrees of the local ordinary, and as a result they were accused of scorning the censures of the Latin bishops. But the Holy See maintained the attitude that, though they were subject to the local ordinary, their own rites and legitimate customs were not to be disturbed.[102]

Despite papal legislation many difficulties continued to exist. The desire of the Holy See that the Latin ordinary appoint a Byzantine vicar general to supervise their affairs did not solve a major problem —that of ordinations. The Byzantine clergy received their ordination at the hands of Latin bishops using the Roman Rite. The Byzantine bishops in Italy prior to the coming of the Albanians had turned Latin. In Rome there was a Byzantine bishop who was attached to the Greek college at the command of Pope Clement VIII since 1595, but this one bishop could not also care for the Italo-Greeks of the south. In the traditional canon law of the time, the decree of the IV General Council of the Lateran (1215) was rigidly followed, namely, that there could not be two bishops in the one diocese.[103]

Pope Clement XII (1730-1740) decided to convert the disused Benedictine monastery of San Benedetto d'Ullano at Bisignano in

[102] Pius IV, const. *"Romanus Pontifex,"* 16 febr. 1564—*Bull. Rom.*, VII, 271-273. The Albanians were ordered to obey the local Latin bishop "in those things which concern the worship of God, the administration of the sacraments, the salvation of souls and the uprooting of heresies." But the Pope expressly stated: "By these decrees however we do not mean that the Greeks themselves are to be taken from their Greek rite, or that they are to be hindered in any way by the Ordinaries or others. *Per haec tamen non intendimus quod ipsi Graeci ab eorum graecanico ritu distrahantur vel alias desuper quoquomodo per locorum Ordinarios aut alios impediantur*"—§ 5 of the cited Constitution.

[103] Cf. footnote n. 95.

the province of Calabria into a Byzantine seminary, and to make the seminary rector an "ordaining bishop," without jurisdiction. In 1784 the Albanians in Sicily obtained from Pope Pius VI (1775-1799) a similar arrangement. These three Italo-Greek bishops assisted the Latin Ordinaries, with delegated jurisdiction over the churches, the clergy and the laity of their rite. The great canonist Pope Benedict XIV (1740-1758), considering the plight of the Italo-Greeks in Italy, Sicily, and the adjacent islands, and wishing to make the papal attitude very clear ("that all are one in Christ"), issued his famous Constitution *"Etsi pastoralis"* on May 26, 1742, which regulated their affairs with the Latin ordinaries and which has been the main source of their legislation.[104]

On August 31, 1595, Pope Clement VIII (1592-1605) issued an Instruction to the Latin bishops in whose cities the Greeks or Albanians of the Greek rite lived.[105] A translation of the decrees concerning marriage in this Instruction is as follows: *20*: "The Ordinaries of places shall provide that the decree of the sacred general Council of Trent about the reformation of marriage be translated into the common Greek language, and then be announced and published in the places and parishes of the Greeks and Al-

[104] *Fontes,* n. 328; *Bullarii Romani Continuatio* (14 vols., Prati, 1861), I, 197-212; *Collectanea,* n. 338; *Coll. Lac.,* II, 507-522. This Constitution is the last legislative document of any length regarding the Italo-Greeks. For a juridical analysis of this decree, cf. *Fonti,* VIII, 257-264. Cf. also King, *Benedict XIV and the Orientals* (Roma: Pontificium Institutum Orientalium Studiorum, 1940), p. 29; Plöchl, "Two Hundred Years—*'Etsi Pastoralis,'* "—*The Jurist,* II (1942), 211-213; Duskie, pp. 26-27.

[105] *"Presbyteri graeci,"*—*Coll. Lac.,* II, 448-450; *Fontes,* n. 179. This Instruction is also cited as *"Sanctissimus"* from its introduction. The Instruction included the following decrees concerning marriage: "20. Curent Ordinarii locorum, ut decretum sacri generalis Concilii Tridentini de reformatione matrimonii vertatur in linguam Graecam vulgarem, et in locis et parochiis Graecorum et Albanensium evulgetur et publicetur. 21. Matrimonia inter conjuges Graecos dirimi seu divortia quoad vinculum fieri nullo modo permittant aut patiantur; et si qua de facto processerunt, nulla et irrita declarent. 22. Maritus Latinus uxoris Graecae ritum non sequatur. 23. Latina uxor non sequatur ritum mariti Graeci. 24. Graeca vero uxor sequatur ritum mariti Latini. 25. Quodsi id fieri non possit, quisque conjugum in suo ritu, catholico tamen, manere permittatur."

banians.[106] *21*: Divorces between Greek spouses cannot in any way be permitted. *22-26*: The Latin husband shall not follow the rite of his Greek wife; the Latin wife shall not follow the rite of her Greek husband; the Greek wife, however, shall follow the rite of her Latin husband; but if this cannot be done, then each spouse should be permitted to remain in his or her own rite, and the children shall follow the rite of the father, unless the Latin mother wields the greater influence."

The eighth section of the Constitution "*Etsi pastoralis*" dealt with marriage: [107]

1. Decree number 20 of Pope Clement VIII, above, is repeated verbatim, but at the end is added, "whenever they [the ordinaries] deem this expedient."

2. This repeats, also verbatim, decree number 21 mentioned above.

3. Second, third and even further marriages are not condemned by the Greeks.

4. However, the priests shall not bless those who marry a second time, nor shall it be licit to advance a twice-married man to sacred orders without a special Apostolic dispensation.

5. Marriages between the persons related in the eighth degree (Greek computation) of consanguinity and affinity shall be invalid. The Pope was aware that the "Greeks" were accustomed to contract marriages when they were related in the eighth degree, but declared that for the future they shall not presume to marry in this degree.

6. The decree of the Council of Trent regarding the impediment of spiritual relationship arising from baptism and confirmation shall also be kept. In baptism the relationship is contracted between the one baptizing on the one hand, and the one baptized and his parents on the other, and also between the sponsor and these same, namely, the one baptized and the parents. In confirmation also a spiritual relationship arises, but it does not extend beyond the one confirming, the one confirmed and the parents, and also between

[106] Cf. Petrani, *De Relatione Iuridica inter Diversos Ritus in Ecclesia Catholica* (Taurini et Romae: Marietti, 1930), p. 98.

[107] *Coll. Lac.*, II, 517; *Fontes*, n. 328.

the sponsor, the one confirmed and the parents. Any other impediments of spiritual relationship are taken away.

7. The Latin husband shall not follow the rite of his Greek wife.

8. The Latin wife shall not follow the rite of her Greek husband.

9. The Greek husband can, if he so wishes, follow the rite of his Latin wife; likewise the Greek wife can follow the rite of her Latin husband, but after his death may not return to the Greek rite.[108]

10. If either husband or wife is unwilling to effect a change, then each shall be permitted to remain in his or her Catholic rite.

11. Marriage between a Latin man and a Greek woman shall be contracted in the Latin way before the Latin pastor; marriage between a Greek man and a Latin woman can be contracted either in the Greek way before the Greek pastor, in the presence of two or three witnesses, or in the Latin way before the Latin pastor, wheresoever the Greek husband desires to contract it.

12. The pastor of the place where the marriage is contracted, who is also the pastor of the rite according to which the ceremony takes place, is the one who shall assist at the marriage.

The preceding section of this Constitution dealt with the sacrament of Holy Orders; the 27th decree of this section declared that any marriage attempted by a subdeacon, deacon or priest would be null and void.

5. *The Russians* [109]

The new Russian state that arose in the middle ages abhorred any thought of union with Rome; it even saw in the fall of Con-

[108] De Clercq ("De ritu et adscriptione ritui apud Orientales Catholicos,"—*Ephemerides Liturgicae*, XLVI [1932], 473-480) declared that the rules allowing a husband to change to the rite of the woman, or preventing a Latin wife from following the rite of her Greek husband, must be viewed as no longer of value, in view of canon 98, § 4, and canon 6, 6°, of the Latin Code; the rule forbidding a Greek woman, who had gone over to the rite of her Latin husband, to return to her former rite after the marriage was dissolved should be considered as still in effect in virtue of the last part of canon 98, § 4: "matrimonio autem soluto, resumendi proprii ritus libera est potestas, nisi iure particulari aliud cautum sit."

[109] Danzas, *The Russian Church*, pp. 21-106; Stanley, *Lectures on the History of the Eastern Church* (London, 1889), pp. 305-390; Brian-Chaninov, *The Russian Church*, pp. 112-140.

stantinople in 1453 at the hands of the Turks a just retribution for the fact that that city had even momentarily considered accepting the decrees of the Council of Florence as promulgated by the Metropolitan Isidor. Moscow began to consider itself the trustee and the heir of the faith of Constantinople. In the late fifteenth century Ivan III (ruled 1462-1505) laid definite claim to this heritage after his marriage with Sofia Paleologus, the last princess of the imperial Byzantine dynasty; he adopted as his coat-of-arms the imperial eagles, and Russia took as its motto, "Two Romes fell; Moscow is the third; there can never be a fourth." In the following century Ivan IV (1534-1584) took the title of *Tsar* (Czar-Caesar), and thus affirmed Russia's succession to the Eastern Empire. In imitation of the old Byzantine system, Church and State became merged, and thus loyalty to the Church and to the State became identical.

In 1589 the Metropolitan Job of Moscow was raised to the rank of patriarch with the sanction of the four Eastern patriarchs who now looked to Moscow as the center of the true faith and to her powerful Tsar as the protector of Eastern Christendom. In consideration, then, of how the Russian national instinct identified itself with its Church, it can be understood that the Union of Brest-Litovsk in 1595 gave rise to both a political and a religious hatred of those who became Uniates. The Catholic Church became associated with Poland as the enemy of Russia, and the Russian-Polish wars of the early seventeenth century only widened the chasm between Russia and the Catholic Church. The accession of the Romanoffs seemed only to consolidate this alliance of Church and State, especially in the figure of Patriarch Philaret (Theodore Romanoff, who had been forced by the Tsar Boris to enter religion) who ruled together with his son, Tsar Michael III (1613-1645), first of the Romanoff rulers, and who was a living symbol of the sacred union of church, state and national feelings, until his death in 1633.

In the seventeenth century enmity against the Catholic Church grew. The Tsars were not unaware that any introduction of the Catholic Church would be but another wedge between Church and State, with the result that a Universal Church could have no standing in Russia. On the death of Patriarch Adrian in 1700, Tsar Peter the Great (1689-1725) cancelled the election of his successor; for twenty years he ruled the Church, and in 1721 instituted the *Most Holy Synod,* a committee of bishops, to replace the rule of a patriarch. Peter desired the complete secularization of the state, and accordingly encouraged skepticism and irreligion. For the next two centuries the Russian Church has no history distinct from that of the State. Because of the official attitude of the State, there was little room for any Catholic missionary work or for any return to Rome on the part of the Russians themselves. After the partitions of Poland (1772-1795) the Russian Emperors gradually "reconverted" to "orthodoxy" the Ukrainian Catholics who were resident in the regions absorbed by Russia.

CHAPTER IV

THE NINETEENTH CENTURY

ARTICLE I. THE ARMENIANS [1]

In 1830 the Turkish government granted a measure of religious liberty, and through the influence of the French the Catholic Armenians were also recognized as a separate "nation." The Armenians were put at first under a civil ruler, besides their own archbishop, but in 1846 these two offices were put in the hands of Msgr. Hassun; in 1867 at Bzommar he was elected patriarch, and in this office united the Armenians of Constantinople and Cilicia. In this year Pope Pius IX (1846-1878) issued the famous apostolic letter concerning the election of Armenian bishops, which restricted the rights of the laity in these elections.[2]

Synods were held at Bzommar in 1851 and at Chalcedon in 1890, but the acts of these synods were not approved by the Holy See. In 1828 Russia had taken possession of part of Armenia; the rest of the Ottoman Empire, the Kurds and the Turks, continued their persecutions of the Armenians. In 1878 at Berlin the protectorate of the Armenian Christians was granted to six European powers, to whom Turkey gave promises of reforms, but these reforms were not forthcoming. The most tragic massacres were those of 1895, which shocked all Europe. In the part controlled by Russia there were not such wholesale massacres, but the Russian government interfered in all their church affairs and controlled their property.

[1] Cf. Fortescue, *The Lesser Eastern Church*, pp. 419-423; Janin, *Les Églises orientales*, pp. 429-430; *Statistica*, pp. 80-81.

[2] Litt. ap. *"Reversurus,"* 19 iul. 1867—*Fontes*, n. 546; *Ius. Pont.*, VI (Pars Prima), 453. This letter united the Armenian Patriarchate at Constantinople with that of Cilicia; the patriarch was to reside at Constantinople. *Collectanea*, n. 1303, gives the first part of this decree. Unfortunately many of the Armenians considered this decree of the Pope an undue restraint on the secular powers, and in the ensuing disturbance several bishops, many monks, and a considerable number of lay people went into schism.

In 1833 the Armenian Archbishop-Primate of Constantinople, Anthony Nurigian, asked that Armenian priests be allowed to marry, but the Sacred Congregation for the Propagation of the Faith refused this request, declaring: "The reason which you give, that Oriental men, and especially women, wish to confess to only married priests, is not proved enough to us, nor is it fitting for this reason or for any other frivolous reason to lessen the praise and the usefulness of sacred celibacy." [3]

Article II. The Chaldeans [4]

The appointment of Hormez in 1830, as seen in the previous chapter,[5] renewed the Catholic succession of the Chaldean Patriarchs. In an attempt to change the custom of handing down the office of patriarch from uncle to nephew, the Holy See gave him a coadjutor with the right of succession. The Pope suppressed the patriarchate of Diyarbekir and created that of Mosul, and gave Hormez the title of "Patriarch of Babylon," a title which was to be thenceforth that of all his successors, who were to reside at Mosul.

The history of the Chaldeans in the nineteenth century is marked with the activities of Patriarch Joseph VI Audo (elected Patriarch in 1847) to restore the ancient jurisdiction of the See of Seleucia-Ctesiphon over the Malabars of India, a branch of their own rite. In 1860, contrary to the wishes of the Apostolic Delegate and the Dominican missionaries, he sent Thomas Rokas as a bishop to the Malabars. Because of this he was called to Rome, where he assured the Holy See that his activities would benefit the Church in India. However, Pope Pius IX, on August 31, 1869,[6] decided that the rules which the Holy See had given to the Armenians two years before concerning the appointments of bishops were to be applied to the

[3] *Fonti*, II, 67.

[4] *Fonti*, VIII, 698-703; Badger, *The Nestorians and their Rituals*, I, *passim;* Tisserant in the *DTC.*, XI, 244-247; Korolevskij, "Audo,"—*Dictionnaire d'histoire et de géographie ecclésiastiques*, V, 324-325, 335-351; Giamil, *Genuinae Relationes inter Sedem Apostolicam et Assyriorum Orientalium seu Chaldaeorum Ecclesiam*, pp. 396-456.

[5] Cf. *supra*, p. 78.

[6] Bulla *"Cum ecclesiastica disciplina,"—Ius Pont.*, VI (Pars Secunda), 32.

Chaldeans. Audo asserted that this was contrary to his traditional rights, and even protested before the Vatican Council. In 1874 he again sent a bishop to the Malabars.[7] Audo was eventually reconciled with the Holy See and highly praised by Pope Leo XIII (1878-1903).

The only modern synod which the Chaldeans held was the one convened at Rabban Hormizd in June, 1853, by the Patriarch Joseph VI Audo with the participation of the Apostolic Delegate, Benedict Plancet. The acts of the synod were sent to Rome, but the Holy See passed no official judgment on them because of the unsettled conditions caused by the troubles with the Church of Malabar.

Because of the general abuses that arose during the controversy between Hormez and Hindi, the Sacred Congregation for the Propagation of the Faith on April 13, 1807, sent a decree which furnished instructions on many matters, such as the avoidance of the books of heretics, the proper care of the churches, the suppression of simony, the suitable administration of ecclesiastical goods, the care to be exercised in granting various dispensations, the function of preaching, etc. As to marriage the decree declared that, if a deacon was ordained by heretics and later married, he could not exercise his ministry unless the Holy See granted a dispensation; also, the bishops and pastors were to watch that not more than a year intervene between espousals and marriage.[8]

Besides this brief official mention of marriage, a factual exposition of some of the rules regarding marriages among the Chaldeans in the nineteenth century can be gathered from the work of Badger,[9]

[7] Cf. *Ius. Pont.*, VI (Pars Secunda), 276-283, for the correspondence between the Holy See and the Patriarch, who assured Rome that his dealings with the Malabars were for the good of the Church there; Pope Pius IX however wrote: "Responsum a te redditum . . . multo nos dolore et moerore affecit; ex eo enim intelleximus, adhuc cor tuum a nobis longe esse etsi verbis honorem nobis redderes"—pp. 276-277. For the letters of Pope Pius IX on November 16, 1872, September 15, 1875, and September 1, 1876, cf. *Analecta Iuris Pontificii*, XVI (1877), 165-183.

[8] *Fonti*, II, 609; *Fonti*, Serie II, Fasc. XVII, pp. 5-6, 13-29; cf. Borgomanero, *Quaestiones practicae Theologiae Moralis ad usum Missionariorum praesertim orientalium regionum* (Romae, 1910), p. 82.

[9] *The Nestorians and Their Rituals.*

who spent some years among them toward the middle of that century. As to the impediment of sacred orders he declared: "The Nestorian priests and deacons marry while their bishops, metropolitans and patriarchs cannot; the Chaldeans do not marry after the priesthood, and a deacon who marries twice or who marries a widow is not allowed to advance to the priesthood." [10] He presented the elaborate ritual of their espousals and marriage,[11] and then added: "The principal changes made in this service by the Chaldeans are the omission of the cup of salvation or blessing and the part which refers to the marriage of priests." Regarding the various prohibited degrees of relationship with reference to marriage as found in the extensive prohibitions of Ebedjesus,[12] which he listed, he asserted that the Chaldeans have "relaxed the enactments of the above table" and have obtained dispensations from Rome in some of the cases, which cases however were not specifically mentioned by him.

The Synod of 1853 declared that the "closed times" in relation to marriage were the periods from December 1 to Epiphany, and from the beginning of Lent to the Sunday after Easter.[13]

Article III. The Antiochene Rite

1. The Syrians

During the nineteenth century several Jacobite bishops became united with Rome, bringing their people with them to Catholicism. An important leader among the Catholic Syrians was the Patriarch Gregory Jarweh (1820-1853), who suffered continuously from dissidents and Mohammedans. In 1843 the Turkish government finally recognized these Catholics as a distinct *millet* (nation), and this

[10] *Op. cit.*, I, 178-181.

[11] *Op. cit.*, I, 244-276. For the same ritual in Latin, cf. Denzinger, *Ritus Orientalium*, II, 420-450.

[12] *Nomocanon*, II, c. 1—Mai, *Scriptorum veterum nova collectio*, X, Pars I, p. 40. This chapter lists the marriages prohibited within 63 very extended degrees of consanguinity and affinity.

[13] Cf. *Fonti*, Serie II, Fasc. XVII, pp. 63-65, 166, for the brief decrees of this Synod concerning marriage. No defined impedient or diriment impediments are listed in the acts of the Synod.

recognition, in accordance with the customs of the times, made their patriarch their civil head.

From July 22 to October 13, 1888, a provincial synod was held at a monastery at Sharfeh in Mount Lebanon by the Syrian Patriarch Ignatius Scelhot under the presidency of the papal legate, Archbishop Louis Piavi. The acts were submitted to the Holy See, and the Sacred Congregation for the Propagation of the Faith, through its commission which dealt with the matters pertaining to the Oirental rites, "recognized" the acts and declared that they could be published; Pope Leo XIII approved this decree on March 28, 1896.[14]

The Synod issued its decrees on the sacraments in the fifth chapter of its acts. The fifteenth article is devoted to marriage, and contains a complete exposition of Catholic dogmatic and moral theology concerning marriage.[15] The detailed decrees compose a complete canonical treatise, and also reveal the Latin influences on this eastern Synod.

In summary form, the following regulations were made:

1. *Espousals.* Betrothal was urged as a praiseworthy custom, though not necessary, and the period of the espousals was to last not less than a week unless the bishops dispensed; however, they could be made validly and licitly at the age of seven, and then at the age of puberty the parties could either marry or rescind the espousals; the pastor of the groom, not of the bride, was to bless the espousals. Many possible reasons for the dissolution of the espousals were listed. Marriage after the espousals was not strictly demanded, for the marriage consent was to be given with entire freedom. However, as will be seen, even after their dissolution valid espousals continued as an obstacle to a marriage between either of the espoused parties and the relatives of the other party.[16]

[14] *"Quo maius Ecclesiae Syriacae bono,"—Analecta Ecclesiastica,* V (1897), 451.

[15] *Synodus Sciarfensis Syrorum in Monte Libano celebrata anno 1888* (Romae: S. C. de Propaganda Fide, 1896), pp. 161-191.

[16] According to Dauvillier ("La formation du mariage dans les Églises Orientales,"—*Revue des Sciences Religieuses,* XV [1935], 386-390) this "choice" of having espousals is very significant, as it showed that the Syrian Church felt the Latin influences and had come to liken its former "first moment of

2. *Vow.* A solemn vow taken in an approved religious institute, or a simple vow taken among the Jesuits, rendered an attempted marriage null. A simple vow of chastity, a vow of entering any religious institute, and a vow of celibacy rendered the marriage illicit though not invalid.

3. *Previous marriage.* The prohibitions of the Councils of Neocaesarea (314-325) and Laodicea (343-381) against second marriages were adverted to, but the Synod declared that these prohibitions were to be understood as meaning that the second marriage ought not to be blessed with the ritual used at a first marriage, but with a particular ritual which is called "the ritual of penance." Though further marriages were not forbidden, the widow was urged to wait nine months before entering into a new marriage.

4. *Affinity.* Affinity did not in turn beget any other affinity. The impediment affected only either spouse and the blood relatives of the other, in all degrees of the direct line and also to the eighth degree of the collateral line (Eastern computation) after the parties consummated the union. Any illicit carnal union gave rise to a diriment impediment likewise in all the degrees of the direct line and in the fourth degree inclusive (Eastern computation) of the collateral line.

5. *Consanguinity.* This impediment affected all blood relatives in the direct line and also blood relatives to the fourth degree of the collateral line according to the Latin computation, or the eighth degree of the Eastern, when the latter corresponded to the fourth degree of the Latin computation.[17]

marriage" to the notion of Latin espousals, which are not an essential part of the marriage contract. It can be added that the impediment to which the espousals give rise, as a type of affinity, recalls the opinion that the marriage consent was really given at the "first" moment of marriage, though the parties could not live as husband and wife until the "second moment," which came in a later ceremony, usually that of a nuptial banquet.

[17] A marriage between persons of whom the one was three degrees, but the other five degrees, removed from the same common ancestor was accordingly not to be considered as an invalid union, for this relationship was not regarded as being a relationship corresponding to the fourth degree of the collateral line in the Latin computation.

6. *Sacred Orders.* A deacon or priest could not marry.[18]

7. *Spiritual Relationship.* This impediment exists between the one baptizing and both the one baptized and his parents; likewise between a sponsor and both the one baptized and his parents. This relationship in the nature of an impediment arose both through baptism and confirmation.

8. *Abduction.* The abductor could not marry the abducted person as long as she remained in his power; if she was given her full liberty and had returned to a safe place, she could give a valid consent to marry her former abductor.

9. *Difference of religion.* A Christian could not validly marry anyone who was not a Christian.

10. *Age.* The age of twelve years for the girl and of fourteen years for the boy was established as the minimum canonical age, but a marriage of parties who were below this age was not to be declared invalid if, in the judgment of the bishop, both parties had actually attained puberty at the time of the marriage.

11. *Public propriety.* A type of affinity, termed public propriety, arose from valid espousals, and bound the betrothed parties even after the espousals were dissolved, so that a valid marriage was excluded between either of the parties and the blood relatives of the other to the second degree (Eastern computation) in the collateral line. This type of affinity arose also from a ratified, non-consummated marriage, and it barred a marriage between the surviving spouse and any blood relative of the other to the eighth degree (Eastern computation) of the collateral line.

12. *Adoption.* If the adoption was "perfect," that is, if it was established through a rescript from the supreme civil ruler or with his permission, then a marriage was to be invalid if attempted between the adopted and the widow of the adopter, or between the

[18] In 1829 the Syrian Patriarch Gregory Jarweh had sought from the Holy See the faculty of dispensing deacons who had been ordained by heretics before the age prescribed by the canons for the ordination of deacons, in order that they might marry validly. The answer given was that each individual case should be referred to Rome. *Ius Pont.*, III, 412, in nota; *Fonti,* I, 129; *Fonti,* Serie II, Fasc. XXVII, p. 97.

adopter and the children of the one adopted as long as these children still remained in their parent's power.

13. *Crime.* Adultery accompanied with the promise of a future marriage or with an actual attempted marriage, adultery together with the murder by one of the adulterers of his or her spouse, or also the murder of a spouse when planned by both of the parties with a view to their later marriage, prevented any marriage between the guilty parties.

14. *The Pauline Privilege.* Marriage between two pagans was acknowledged as valid if no "natural" impediment existed. If both became converted, the marriage acquired the firmness of a Christian marriage. If only one became converted and the other party continued to live with the convert with nothing but scorn for the Christian religion or with a desire to draw the convert into sin, then the convert could leave the pagan partner and marry a Catholic, but only after the pagan party had been properly questioned as to his or her attitude. If these interpellations could not be made, a dispensation from them could be granted by the Pope.

15. *The forbidden times.* The Synod recalls that the prescription of the Council of Laodicea (343-381) against marriage in Lent was observed in ancient times, but in its own decrees it adds to the "forbidden times" for marriage two days before and a week after Lent, and also the fasting period before Christmas together with the subsequent days up to and including the feast of the Epiphany.

16. *The form of marriage.* The synod declared that even though the force of the marriage contract exists in the mutual, free, externally expressed consent of the spouses, and not in the blessing of the crowns, this does not make it right and licit for Christians to contract marriage without this blessing.[19] The synod then declared that the parties were bound to seek the "blessings of the crowns and the prayers of the priest," but it did not expressly say that a marriage would be invalid if these ceremonies were omitted.

Marriage by proxy was valid and licit if the mandate specified a determined person, if all the conditions incorporated in the mandate

[19] C. V, art. XV, n. 12: ". . . Haud significat licitum et fas esse Christianis matrimonium contrahere sine hac benedictione."—*Synodus Sciarfensis Syrorum*, p. 189.

were fulfilled, and if the mandate was not revoked before the celebration of the marriage ceremony.

If a secret marriage was contracted before the bishop or his vicar and two witnesses for urgent reasons, a record of such a marriage was not to be kept in the usual book of marriages, but in a special book which was to remain under the care and seal of the bishop.

In an early article the synod decreed that a Syrian man could not leave his own rite to follow that of his wife even if she be a Latin, and that no one can dispense from this rule except the Holy See. If a Syrian man married a Catholic woman of another rite, Latin or Oriental, the woman was free to pass over to his rite from the very beginning of the marriage or afterwards while the marriage lasted; only after her husband died could she return to her own rite. The same privilege was granted to a Syrian woman who married one of another Catholic rite, even a Latin.[20] In a marriage of Catholics of mixed rite the pastor of the groom was to bestow the nuptial blessing, "in virtue of a custom in force among us and all the Catholic Oriental nations in these regions."[21]

2. *The Maronites*[22]

The Turkish rulers did not govern the Maronites directly, but in the manner of a feudal rule put them under a native emir. The history of the first part of the nineteenth century centers about the turbulent government of the Emir Bechir II (1788-1840), whose

[20] C. III, art. IX, n. 9: "Si vir ex nostris in uxorem duxerit mulierem pertinentem ad alium ritum sive latinum sive orientalem ex catholicis, integrum erit mulieri ad ritum nostrum sive ab ipso principio matrimonii sive postea, durante matrimonio, transire, electionem tamen semel factam non poterit, vivente viro, revocare. Idem valeat de muliere Syra. . . ."—*op. cit.*, p. 54.

[21] C. III, art. IX, n. 11—*op. cit.*, p. 55. Cf. Duskie, *The Canonical Status of the Orientals in the United States*, The Catholic University of America Canon Law Studies, n. 48 (Washington, D. C.: The Catholic University of America, 1928), p. 170 (hereafter cited as Duskie); Petrani, *De Relatione Iuridica inter Diversos Ritus in Ecclesia Catholica*, p. 98.

[22] Cf. Abraham, *The Maronites of Lebanon*, pp. 129-182; Eid, *A l'Ombre des Cèdres ou L'Epopée de Liban*, pp. 68-72; Attwater, *The Catholic Eastern Churches*, pp. 182-185; Janin, *Les Églises orientales*, p. 555.

father had been converted to Christianity by the zealous Patriarch Joseph Stephen in 1768. He first secured the governorship when only twenty-seven years of age, and always hoped for the independence of Syria from the Turkish misrule. In 1822 he went to Egypt and there associated with Mohammed Ali Pasha, who was planning to invade Syria and to attack the Turkish empire directly. This invasion started in 1831, and for a time enjoyed such great military success that even Constantinople was worried lest this invasion would conquer it. However, England, Russia, Austria and Prussia signed a treaty with Turkey on June 15, 1840, against Ali Pasha, and encouraged the Syrians and Maronites to rebel against Abraham Pasha, his son, who was driven out on October 1st of that same year. In the same year Emir Bechir went to Malta in exile.

Civil war soon broke out between the Maronites and the Druses (a sect of the Mohammedans), lasting from 1841-1845. A civil war flared up in 1860 when the Druses were armed and ready, but the Maronites had allowed themselves to be disarmed by the Turkish authorities on the pretense of maintaining order. Thousands of Maronites were massacred, and 100,000 made homeless. In 1860 Napoleon III sent 6,000 soldiers to restore order. After the trouble ceased the European powers drew up an unusual constitution of seventeen articles whereby a Christian "outsider" was to be the governor-general of the Lebanon, which was to remain autonomous though it still was to be linked with the Turkish empire. This system of rule lasted until almost the present day; in 1926 the country was reorganized as the Republic of Lebanon under French mandate.

National figures among the Maronites in the nineteenth century were the patriot Joseph Bey Karam (1825-1888) who, for seven years after the constitution of 1860 had been imposed, labored in vain to restore some of the ancient rights of the Maronites, the Patriarch Paul Massad who ruled from 1854 to 1890, Archbishop Joseph Debs of Beirut (1833-1908), and Archbishop Germanos Chemaly of Aleppo who died in 1895.

There was no change in their marriage laws during the nineteenth century. The synod of 1818, which was concerned principally with the monasteries and the bishops, was approved by the Holy See, but the latest Maronite synod, held at Berkoki in 1856, which was supposed to introduce some modifications in the decrees of the Synod of 1736, was not approved.[23]

Article IV. The Byzantine Rite

1. The Melkites [24]

From 1817 to 1832 the Melkites suffered persecution at the hands of the Turks, and some Melkites are counted as martyrs to the faith. From 1833 to 1855 Maximos III Mazlum ruled as Patriarch, and succeeded in securing civil autonomy for his people as a *millet* under Turkish rule. During the reign of his successor there was a small schism, occasioned by the introduction of the Gregorian Calendar. From 1864 to 1897 another great Patriarch ruled in the person of Gregory II Yusuf, who assisted at the Vatican Council, and who was a leading figure in the International Eucharistic Congress held at Jerusalem in 1893. It was at his suggestion that Cardinal Lavigerie (1825-1892) opened at Jerusalem a Byzantine seminary under the direction of the White Fathers.

A synod was held at Karkafa in 1806, but it was severely condemned by Pope Gregory XVI (1831-1846), who used very emphatic language in pointing out the defects and excesses of the conciliar acts and decrees.[25] In the same year that this condemnation appeared (1835), another synod was held at Ain Traz, and its canons were "recognized" and allowed to be published by the Sacred Congregation for the Propagation of the Faith on August 28, 1841.[26] In 1849 a council was held at Jerusalem, but this was not approved by Rome.

[23] After receiving the acts of this Synod, Pope Pius IX on June 2, 1856, wrote to Patriarch Massad in praise of his zeal in promoting the faith and piety of his people; the Pope said that he referred the acts of the synod to the Sacred Congregation for the Propagation of the Faith. (Breve *"Gratae nobis,"—Ius Pont.*, VI [Pars Prima], 256). The Congregation however failed to approve the acts.

[24] Mansi, XLVI, *passim;* Attwater, *The Catholic Eastern Churches,* pp. 109-114; Charon, *Histoire des Patriarcats Melkites,* Vol. II, Fasc. 1; Janin, *Les Églises orientales,* pp. 329-330.

[25] Breve *"Melchitarum catholicorum synodus,* 16 sept. 1835—Mansi, XLVI, 878.

[26] Mansi, XXXIX, 323; *Fonti,* XV, 832.

The synod of Ain Traz of 1835 issued twenty-five canons, of which the seventh was concerned with marriage.[27] In summary, the synod declared: (a) no espousals or marriages should take place between a Melkite and a non-Catholic; (b) a dispensation was needed for those who married within the forbidden degrees of relationship (the precise degrees are not mentioned in this synod); (c) the minimum age for the espousals was thirteen years for the boy and eleven years for the girl, and the age for the blessing with the nuptial crowning was a year more for each; (d) the essential element of marriage is the consent of the two parties.

As to the form of marriage, the Holy See approved neither the prescription of the synod of Karkafa (1806), namely, that the crowning by the priest was required for validity,[28] nor that of the synod of Jerusalem (1849), which required the presence of the Ordinary, the parish priest or the delegate of either.[29]

[27] A Latin text is found in Mansi, XXXIX, 327, and an Italian text in Mansi, XLVI, 988. Cf. *Fonti,* XV, nn. 261, 317-318, 803-804.

[28] Mansi, XLVI, 764.

[29] *Ibid.,* 1056. Cappello (*De Matrimonio,* n. 924.3) and Dillon (*Common Law Marriage,* The Catholic University of America Canon Law Studies, n. 153 [Washington, D. C.: The Catholic University of America Press, 1942], p. 50) appear to err in citing the councils of 1806 and of 1849, neither of which was approved by Rome, in support of their statement that "among the Melchites marriage is invalid unless it is celebrated with the blessing of the bishop or pastor, or of a priest delegated by either"; cf. also Charon (Korolevskij), *Histoire des Patriarcats Melkites,* III, 692, and White, *De forma celebrationis matrimonii,* pp. 40-41. Canon 6 of this synod of 1849 (Mansi, XLVI, 1055-1057) listed the diriment impediments which were in force among the Melkites as the following: error, the state of absolute slavery, a solemn vow of chastity taken in religion, sacred orders, an existing marriage bond, disparity of cult ("a Christian cannot marry an infidel or a heretic"), force, defect of age, clandestinity, perpetual impotence, abduction (whether of a woman or of a man), consanguinity in all the degrees of the direct line and to the sixth degree of the collateral line, spiritual relationship in the general Byzantine delineation of this impediment, affinity to the sixth degree of the collateral line, public propriety arising from espousals and from a ratified, non-consummated marriage (the degrees to which this impediment extended were not expressly mentioned). In this same canon the synod explicitly declared that the impediment of *crimen* did not exist among the Melkites (cf. Cappello, n. 916).

2. The Ruthenians [80]

In 1795 Poland had been completely partitioned between Russia, Prussia and Austria. In 1815, at the Congress of Vienna, a slight readjustment was made in the partition; White Russia went entirely to Russia, the Ukrainian lands were divided between Russia and Austria (the latter retained only Galicia and the Carpatho-Ukraine), while Poland proper was divided among Austria, Russia and Prussia. This arrangement was not changed until after the World War of 1914-1918.

Among the Ukrainians who became subject to Russia, the nineteenth century witnessed a very intense process of "Russification," which sought to effect in Russia "one law (the Russian Tsar's), one language (the Great Russian), and one religion (the Russian Orthodox)." [81] It began in an important way after the Polish insurrections of 1831 and 1863, but Catherine II (1762-1796) and Alexander I (1801-1825) had already reduced the number of Ukrainian sees to three, closed their monasteries and handed their churches over to the Russian Orthodox sect. Even the language of the Ukrainians was treated as a "dialect," and was prohibited in 1876 in printing, reciting and singing. It may be said, then, that the Ukrainian Catholic Church was put to death in Russia in the nineteenth century. It was in 1905 that Nicholas II (1894-1917) granted religious toleration, and many Ukrainians, especially in the Chelm district which had been ceded to Russia by Austria in 1815, returned to union with Rome. This religious "Russification" was the inevitable result of the notion that every subject of the Russian State must be a member of the Russian Church.

In Bucovina the Ukrainians demanded equal rights with the Rumanians, and they opposed the demands of the Rumanians that Bucovina be united to the neighboring Rumanian provinces in Hungary. In 1848 Austria with the help of Russia crushed a Hungarian revolution in the Carpatho-Ukraine, and then decided to weaken the

[80] Hrushevsky, pp. 483-513; Hayes, *A Generation of Materialism (1871-1900)* (New York: Harper and Brothers, 1941), *passim;* Attwater, *The Dissident Eastern Churches*, pp. 78-79.

[81] Cf. Hayes, *op. cit.*, p. 270.

influence of the Hungarians by supporting the rights of the nationalities over whom these Magyars ruled. This nationalistic movement, however, was hampered by the tendencies of their leaders to favor Russia, which aroused the Hungarians against them. At this period also, intense nationalistic activities appeared among the Ukrainians in Galicia; these movements increased in number, especially after 1860 when Austria granted Galicia some civil autonomy and its own assembly. In 1890 many in Galicia even broke their ties with those in the Russian Ukraine, and tried to make an alliance with the governor-general of Galicia, Count Badeni. In addition to making some political progress, the people before the end of the century tried to free themselves from foreign financial and agricultural institutions, and to found their own credit associations, cooperatives and agricultural associations.

Important events for the Ukrainian Catholic Church at the end of the century include the erection of the Ruthenian College in Rome by Pope Leo XIII (with a generous subsidy provided by the Emperor Francis Joseph) and the celebration of the council held at Lemberg in 1891 under the Metropolitan Sylvester Sembratovitch (who was made a cardinal in 1895). The decrees of this Council were "recognized" by the Sacred Congregation for the Affairs of the Oriental Rite on May 1, 1895. At present these decrees bind only in Lemberg, Przemsyl and Stanislawow, i.e., they do not bind the Ukrainians outside the Lemberg province of Galicia.

The celebrated Constitution of Pope Leo XIII of November 30, 1894, on the dignity of the oriental churches and disciplines,[82] did not apply to the Oriental Catholics residing within the limits of the Empire of Austria-Hungary, according to a decision of the Sacred Congregation for the Propagation of the Faith, transmitted through the Apostolic Delegation at Vienna on December 28, 1898.[83]

Legislation concerning the requisite conditions for and the form of the celebration of mixed marriages was contained in the letter of Pope Gregory XVI to the bishops of Hungary on April 30, 1841.[84]

[82] *"Orientalium dignitas,"—Fontes,* n. 627; *Collectanea,* n. 1883.

[83] *Fonti,* XI, n. 163.

[84] *"Quas vestro,"—Fontes,* n. 497; *Collectanea,* n. 920; *Ius Pont.,* V, 272. These instructions were repeated by the Sacred Congregation for Extraordinary

The conditions to make a mixed marriage licit were to be the removal of all danger of perversion to the Catholic party, the promise guaranteeing the education of all children in the Catholic Faith and the assent of the Catholic party to his obligation to care for the conversion of the non-Catholic party. The Pope realized that sometimes the prescribed promises were not obtainable, in consequence of, for example, the contrary laws of the territory, but that the marriage could not be averted without the danger of greater evil, scandal, and general detriment to religion. In such cases it would be for the good of the Church to allow such a marriage before a Catholic pastor rather than to see it celebrated before a heretical minister. However, when the promises were lacking at such a wedding the Catholic pastor, or the one acting for him, could lend material assistance only "in such manner simply as to play the part of a mere qualified witness, so that after the consent of both was heard, he could then officially record the marriage in the marriage register as a validly contracted union."[85] If the parties of the mixed marriage contracted their union without observing the Tridentine form, then though their act was gravely illicit, the union itself was acknowledged as valid. Pope Pius IX later declared that these conclusions were also to continue as the norms in judging clandestine mixed marriages in Hungary.[86] There is no evidence however that the Tridentine law was binding upon the Ruthenians in Hungary, though it was binding on those in Galicia.[87]

On Dec. 12, 1888, the Sacred Congregation of the Holy Office

Affairs to the archbishops and bishops of Austria in the following month (*Ius Pont.*, V, 367 in nota; *Fonti*, II, 349), and on July 16, 1842, were extended by Pope Gregory XVI to Galicia, where the papal decrees were formally promulgated on January 31, 1843, by Cardinal Lewicki. Cf. Cicognani-Staffa, *Commentarium*, II, p. 572, nota 2.

[85] ". . . perinde ac si partes unice ageret meri testis ut aiunt qualificati seu auctorizabilis, ita scilicet ut utriusque coniugis audito consensu, deinceps pro suo officio actum valide gestum in matrimoniorum librum referre queat."

[86] Litt. ap. *"Obsequentissimis,"* 14 iun. 1850—*Ius Pont.*, VI, (Pars Prima), 317.

[87] Cf. *supra*, pp. 103-104. Cf. Benedetti, *Votum*, n. 11—*ASS*, XLI (1908), 261; Duskie, p. 65.

issued an Instruction on mixed marriages addressed to all Orientals.[38] The Instruction stressed the important distinction between the impediment of mixed religion and that of disparity of cult. The dangers in such marriages, as declared by the canons of the early Councils of Laodicea (343-381) and Chalcedon (451), were cited. It was "illicit and sacrilegious" to marry before a schismatic priest or a heretical minister, but even then, if the pastor heard that one of his flock was going to marry a schismatic or a heretic before a minister of the other party, as long as the parties did not ask him about the licitness of such an act and as long as he foresaw that no good would result from a correction or warning on his part concerning the grave sinfulness of what they intended to do, he could remain silent, provided of course that the danger of scandal was removed and all other conditions and precautions were fulfilled. (Espousals however with a non-Catholic were both illicit and invalid unless a dispensation was first granted).

The Council of Lemberg (1891), which was binding only in the Province of Lemberg and therefore did not bind the Carpatho-Ukrainians, expressly stated that this Instruction of the Holy Office, besides that of Pope Gregory XVI mentioned above, was to be followed.[39] The Council also declared that the marriage laws of the Councils of Trent (1545-1563) and of Zamost (1720) were to be observed, and that grave reasons were required in the petition for a dispensation if the parties desiring to be married were closely related. It then reminded the Ukrainian pastors that they could not validly assist at the marriage of two Latins who had illegitimately passed from the Latin to the Greek rite, since thus their marriage was not celebrated as the Council of Trent prescribed, that is, it was not contracted before their proper pastor.[40]

The same Council declared that it considered the celibate state more perfect than the conjugal state, but that it recognized and would

[38] *Collectanea,* n. 1696; *Fonti,* XI, 394; *Fontes,* n. 1112.

[39] *Fonti,* XI, 416.

[40] ". . . Praeterea caveant ne benedicant matrimonia eorum qui illegitime transierunt a ritu latino ad graecum; . . . matrimonia talia invalida esse sciant, utpote non coram proprio parocho celebrata, prout praescribit Concilium Tridentinum. . . ."—*Fonti,* XI, 399.

not change the liberty which the Church granted to Ukrainian clerics to marry while they were in minor orders, and later to be advanced to the priesthood. However, it urged that the heads of seminaries prudently help and encourage those students who appeared well disposed to remain celibate.[41]

The Sacred Congregation for the Propagation of the Faith on October 6, 1863, issued a decree which contained the rules designating the proper pastor in marriages between Latins and Ukrainians in Galicia. The proper pastor was the pastor of the bride, unless both parties desired to marry before the groom's pastor. The pastor who assisted at such marriages was reminded that he should observe the prohibited times according to the rites of both of the parties, "lest the conscience of either be hurt and lest scandal be given to the other faithful."[42]

3. *The Rumanians*[43]

The Rumanians shared the growing nationalistic tendencies of the nineteenth century. After the Crimean War (1854-1856) the principalities of Wallachia and Moldavia united to form the state of Rumania, which created a center of attraction for the Rumanians in the Austro-Hungarian Empire.

Politically, though Rumania had been accorded autonomy, it lacked sovereignty as late as 1871, and belonged at least legally to the Ottoman Empire. On April 24, 1877, Russia, after making preliminary political compromises with Austria, declared war on the Ottoman Empire. Rumania proclaimed her independence, and formally entered the Russo-Turkish War as an ally of Russia. After the war, at the peace congress at Berlin in July, 1878, Rumania was recognized as an independent sovereign state, but the congress

[41] *Fonti,* XI, 125. For a summary of the discussions among the members of the Council concerning this question, cf. Bobak, *De caelibatu,* pp. 94-106.

[42] *Collectanea,* n. 1243; *Fonti,* XI, 411. This decree is cited in the footnotes arranged by Gasparri under canon 1097, § 2, of the Latin Code—*Fontes,* n. 4859.

[43] *Fonti,* VIII, 507-514, 524-529; Hayes, *A Generation of Materialism (1871-1900)*, *passim.*

disregarded the principle of nationality in depriving Rumania of Bessarabia in favor of Russia, which action took away from Rumania a large number of its own people. Resentment against Russia then grew in Rumania. Under the leadership of Prince Carol who took the title of King in 1881, Rumania on October 30, 1883, concluded an alliance with Austria-Hungary and Germany.

Pope Pius IX gave the Oriental Rumanians their own ecclesiastical province by erecting the archbishopric of "Alba-Julia and Fagaras" in 1853.[44] The increasing need for a unified Catholic Rumanian legislation resulted in two provincial councils held at Blaj May 5-14, 1872,[45] and May 30-June 6, 1882.[46]

The I Provincial Council of Alba-Julia and Fagaras (1872) gave a briefer expression to Rumanian marriage laws[47] than did the II Provincial Council (1882),[48] but in general the prescriptions were the same:[49]

1. *Espousals.* Simple espousals constituted an impedient impediment, while solemn espousals created a type of affinity and public propriety which invalidated intermarriage between either of the betrothed parties and the blood-relatives of the other up to the seventh degree of the collateral line.[50]

[44] Bulla *"Ecclesiam Christi,"* 26 nov. 1853—Mansi, XLII, 620-626.

[45] Cf. Mansi, XLII, 453-614, for the acts of this Council. Pope Pius IX in his letter *"Tuas excepimus"* of September 28, 1872, acknowledged the reception of these acts, and stated that he would hand them over to the Congregation for the Propagation of the Faith for the Affairs of the Oriental Rite, which on March 19, 1881, issued a decree of recognition. (This letter and this decree can be found in Mansi, XLII, 616). This decree was approved by Pope Leo XIII.

[46] Cf. Mansi, XLV, 663-780, for the acts of this Council. It was recognized by the Congregation for the Propagation of the Faith for the Affairs of the Oriental Rite on October 1, 1884 (*ibid.*, 780-782). Cf. *Fonti,* X, 376; Dauvillier and De Clercq, p. 211.

[47] Mansi, XLII, 554-558, 584-585.

[48] Mansi, XLV, 723-734.

[49] For a comparison of the texts of the decrees of these two Councils and for a commentary on each of the impediments, cf. Dib, "La legislation matrimoniale canonique dans l'Orient catholique,"—*Le Canoniste Contemporain,* XLIII (1920), 35-43, 140-152.

[50] *Fonti,* X, nn. 51, 959 and 1105.

2. *Vow.* Solemn vows made in connection with monastic profession created a diriment impediment.[51] The simple vow of chastity was an impedient impediment.

3. *Previous marriage.* No recognition was given to civil divorces. A ratified non-consummated marriage could be dissolved by solemn religious profession.[52] The Pauline Privilege can be invoked under the usual conditions.[53]

4. *Affinity.* Several classes of affinity were listed: (a) the first class, that which existed between one spouse and the blood relatives of the other, invalidated a marriage up to the seventh degree of the collateral line; (b) the second class, that which existed between the relatives of the man and the relatives of the woman, also extended its force as an impediment to the seventh degree; (c) the third class, that which arose from illicit carnal relations, extended as a diriment impediment up to the fourth degree; (d) the fourth class, which arose from a ratified non-consummated marriage, extended to the seventh degree.[54]

5. *Consanguinity.* This impediment extended to all the degrees in the direct line and to the seventh degree of the collateral line inclusive.[55]

6. *Sacred Orders.* The ancient custom of allowing married men to be ordained was kept, but a marriage after the reception of sacred orders was condemned.[56]

[51] *Ibid.,* n. 1233; cf. also *ibid.,* n. 1234, which summarizes an Instruction of the Holy Office of June 20, 1883, that a case involving this impediment is to be sent to the Holy See.

[52] *Ibid.,* n. 761. This decree of the II Provincial Council repeated the declaration of the Sacred Congregation for the Propagation of the Faith in its Instruction of 1858 to the bishops on the indissolubility of marriage—*Collectanea,* I, n. 1152. Pope Pius IX in his letter "*Verbis exprimere*" of August 25, 1859, to the archbishop of Alba-Julia and Fagaras, also declared that such marriages could be dissolved "by solemn profession or by means of a canonical dispensation granted by the Pope alone in rare cases."—*Fonti,* X, n. 759.

[53] *Ibid.,* n. 939.

[54] *Ibid.,* nn. 48-51.

[55] *Ibid.,* n. 314.

[56] *Ibid.,* nn. 296 and 1060. On March 24, 1858, the Sacred Congregation for the Propagation of the Faith sent an Instruction on the celibacy of the

7. *Abduction.* A woman was considered as having been abducted if she was taken away by physical force or if she had been influenced by some deceit to go to a place and then was detained there.[87]

8. *Spiritual relationship.* This impediment was verified in several possible cases: (a) between the one baptizing and the one baptized and also the parents of the baptized; (b) between the sponsors and those baptized; (c) between the sponsors and either a parent or a child of the one baptized; (d) between the child of a sponsor and the one baptized; (e) between the child of a sponsor and the child of the one baptized.[88]

9. *Legal relationship.* In the direct line the adopter could not marry to the fourth degree a descendant of the one adopted if that

clergy, asserting that the early Oriental law, following the Council in Trullo (692), did not allow subdeacons who married to be advanced to higher orders, and so the Pope praised highly the intention of the Archbishop to admit to orders only the one who was a celibate or one who had married before receiving the subdiaconate; the Pope, however, allowed the subdeacons who were already married to be advanced to higher orders and to remain with their wives; those who married after the reception of sacred orders were to be severely punished, so that "if a zeal for keeping the ancient discipline or a love of continence does not move them, fear of penalties would restrain them."—*Collectanea,* I, n. 1158; *Fonti,* X, 294, 304, 1118-1119; II, 67-69; *Analecta Iuris Pontificii,* XVI (1877), 243-246. The same Congregation in a letter of April 30, 1881, ordered that if one in sacred orders were to marry, the whole case was to be referred to the Holy See, and the Congregation of the Holy Office on June 20, 1883, issued a similar decree—*Fonti,* X, 305-306. The earlier Rumanian Council was silent on the question of holy orders. The Holy See asked the reason for this silence. The Archbishop of Fagaras answered that the canons of the Oriental rite severely criticized and punished priests who married (e. g., they were to be deposed), but they did not say positively that such marriages were invalid. The Holy See replied that every case concerning this impediment of holy orders be submitted to its decision. Cf. Souarn, "Impedimentum ordinis in Ecclesia Graeca,"—*Jus Pontificium,* XIII (1933), 48. Cf. also Cicognani-Staffa, *Commentarium,* I, 20; Mansella, *De impedimentis,* p. 95. The documents cited indicate that there was a doubt of law as to whether the priesthood was clearly a diriment impediment to marriage for the Rumanians. Cf. also Bobak, *De caelibatu,* pp. 159-162.

[87] Cf. Dauvillier and De Clercq, p. 187.

[88] *Fonti,* X, n. 315. In a letter of June 25, 1897, the Sacred Congregation for the Propagation of the Faith declared that these last two degrees of spiritual relationship (d and e) were to be retained in the diocese of Gherla—*ibid.,* n. 316.

descendant was under the adopted one's power at the time of the adoption; in the direct line by way of affinity the adopter could not marry the widow of the adopted, nor could the adopted one marry the widow of the adopter; in the collateral line, marriages were forbidden within the first degree.[59]

10. *Difference of religion.* An attempted marriage between one who was baptized and one who was not was ruled as null and void.[60] If one of the parties was a baptized non-Catholic, both Councils declared that a Rumanian Catholic could enter marriage with such a party as long as the usual precautions to safeguard the faith of the Catholic party were properly taken before the marriage.[61]

11. *Age.* The minimum age set as a condition for a valid marriage was that which coincided with the presumed presence of puberty, fourteen years for the boy and twelve years for the girl. Any marriage of a boy or girl below these ages was to be held as valid if investigations revealed that the party concerned had actually attained puberty.[62]

12. *Crime.* Adultery accompanied with the promise of marriage, or with an actual attempt to contract marriage, or the actual murder of a spouse after a common plot while at least one of them intended to marry his or her accomplice, created this diriment impediment.[63]

Among the impedient impediments, the Councils included simple espousals, the simple vow of chastity, the "forbidden times," a lack of sufficient knowledge of the Christian religion, a prohibition of

[59] *Ibid.*, n. 313. Dauvillier and De Clercq (p. 154) feel that in this legislation the Rumanian bishops seem to have imitated the Maronite Council of 1736. Cf. Mansi, XLII, 727-729, for the influences of the Maronite Council on the Rumanian I Provincial Council (1872).

[60] *Ibid.*, n. 477.

[61] *Ibid.*, nn. 766, 769 and 774. Cf. the Instruction of the Congregation for the Propagation of the Faith to the Archbishop of Alba-Julia and Fagaras in 1858 concerning mixed marriages—*Collectanea*, I, n. 1154. Cf. *Fonti*, X, 767, 772-773; Mansi, XLII, 662-688; cf. also the Instruction of the same Congregation to all the Oriental Bishops on December 8, 1888—*Collectanea*, n. 1696; cf. *S. Romanae Rotae Decisiones*, XXVI (1934), dec. lxxi, p. 595.

[62] *Ibid.*, nn. 47 and 647; Dauvillier and De Clercq, p. 159.

[63] *Ibid.*, nn. 45 and 437.

the bishop, and a neglect of three promulgations of the banns.[64] The prescriptions regarding the "forbidden times" were detailed. The season of Advent, the time between Christmas and Epiphany, the entire period of Lent, the time between Easter and "the Sunday of St. Thomas," Pentecost, the vigil of the Feast of the Holy Apostles, the Wednesdays and Fridays of the whole year "as days made sacred by fasting," and Feasts of the Exaltation of the Holy Cross and of the Beheading of St. John the Baptist—all these together constituted the "forbidden times." [65]

As to the form of marriage, the Instruction issued by the Sacred Congregation for the Propagation of the Faith in June, 1858, to the Greek-Rumanian bishops [66] gave many fundamental points to be remembered in a discussion regarding the form of marriage among the Rumanians: (a) only the supreme authority of an Ecumenical Council, or also the Pope by his sole authority, could prescribe a new form for the contracting of marriage and predetermine the nullity of marriages contracted without the required form; (b) the Tridentine form of marriage had to be promulgated *as such* to be binding under pain of nullity; it did not suffice to have a similar form promulgated by some bishop, council or civil law; (c) a mixed marriage contracted before a schismatic priest was to be considered valid, since it could not be admissibly maintained that the Council of Trent had obtained the force of law in the Rumanian parishes; (d) judgment in each case had to be made cautiously and circumspectly; a marriage was not to be immediately declared null for the reason that it was celebrated without the blessing of the priest; (e) no document of the Oriental Church could be revealed which demanded expressly and clearly the blessing of the priest as a condition for the validity of a marriage, for "no statement of any Father of that ancient Church nor any canon of their councils" made such a demand.

An Oriental Commission was formed at the Vatican Council,

[64] *Ibid.*, n. 644. The banns were to be announced in the proper parochial church on three successive Sundays or feast days.

[65] *Ibid.*, n. 1193; Mansi, XLV, 728.

[66] *Collectanea*, n. 1154; *Fontes*, n. 4843; cf. White, *De forma celebrationis matrimonii*, pp. 46-49; Duskie, pp. 153-156.

and it sought to settle the question of clandestinity among the Orientals. In answer to a doubt whether the Tridentine form of marriage was required among the Orientals, one consultor was of the opinion that the Tridentine decree was in force among the Oriental groups in Europe with a few exceptions, such as among the Rumanians, while in the East itself the decree bound only the Maronites (and in India the Oriental Malabars). The Commission decided however that the question of clandestinity among the Orientals could not be settled at that time in view of the many differences of thought on the problem.[67]

The I Provincial Council of 1872 had tried to impose the Tridentine form without expressly mentioning that form by name.[68] The Sacred Congregation for the Propagation of the Faith suspended judgment on this decree which attempted to impose the Tridentine form, and asked the Archbishop of Alba-Julia and Fagaras to inform it as to the existence of the Tridentine form among the Rumanians. On September 7, 1878, Archbishop John Vancsa replied that he had found no document from which it was evident that the decree of the Council of Trent had been published in the parishes of his province, which at the time of the Council of Trent was subject to a lamentable schism. He also declared: "It is undoubtedly clear that the custom of considering clandestine marriages as illicit according to the discipline of both Churches has been in force from the first centuries. . . . But then after the year 1854, when there was published the Instruction for Ecclesiastical Judges of Imperial Austria about matrimonial cases, all the matrimonial courts in this province considered the impediment of clandestinity as diriment." [69]

The Sacred Congregation for the Propagation of the Faith in a reply of April 30, 1881, to Archbishop Vancsa, did not definitely pass on the validity of marriages contracted without the required form, but asked the bishops to draw up a common discipline, and in the meanwhile to deter priests even by means of canonical penalties from crowning those who contracted marriage clandestinely.[70]

[67] Mansi, L, 90.

[68] Mansi, XLII, 814.

[69] Cf. Benedetti, *Votum*, n. 12—*ASS*, XLI (1908), 262.

[70] *Fonti*, X, n. 271. It is to be noted that here a "clandestine marriage"

Thus it happened that the II Provincial Council of 1882 declared that to enter marriage *licitly* the parties had to marry before the proper pastor (or a priest with his delegation) and two or three witnesses; the delegation which an outside priest received had to be not merely a presumptive one, but had to derive from a positive act; a priest who had universal delegation to assist at marriages could subdelegate some other priest in single cases, but if the delegation was received for a single case, then no subdelegation could be made unless the power to do so had been given expressly; the proper pastor was the one in whose parish the spouses had a "true domicile or at least a quasi-domicile." [71]

Concerning the impediments to marriage the two provincial Councils recognized the fact that only the Holy See could create impediments and likewise dispense from them, and that the Rumanian ordinaries could dispense only in virtue of faculties received from the Holy See.[72]

4. *The Italo-Greeks* [73]

The Italo-Albanian seminary for Calabria, which was moved in 1791 from San Benedetto d'Ullano to San Demetrio Corone, slowly dwindled in importance; the Albanian colony near it was turning Latin or emigrating, and the seminarians became fewer. After the revolution of 1860 in Naples the Italian Government sent a commissioner to supervise the affairs of the college, but he soon confiscated much of it. Finally, in 1900, this college was closed.

The Greek College at Rome was closed in the first half of the nineteenth century, but Pope Gregory XVI (1831-1846) reopened it in 1845. In 1897 Pope Leo XIII (1878-1903), taking a deep interest in this college, gave express orders that the use of the Roman Rite there had to be discontinued; in order to secure the

referred to one which was contracted before a priest, but without witnesses or the previous publication of the banns.

[71] Mansi, XLV, 730. Cf. *Fonti,* nn. 453-454 and 752-753.

[72] Cf. *Fonti,* X, nn. 478-481, 641. The letter of June 25, 1897, from the Sacred Congregation for the Propagation of the Faith to the Archbishop of Fagaras repeats this fundamental rule—*Fonti,* X, n. 640.

[73] Fortescue, *The Uniate Eastern Churches,* pp. 150-184.

execution of his orders, he gave the Benedictine superiors there the special faculty of using the Byzantine rite during their stay at the college. The Pope thus desired to furnish the Italo-Greek seminarians the advantage of an exacting training in their own liturgy and Canon Law besides their regular lectures at the Propaganda College.

Pope Leo XIII also took a great interest in their monastery at Grottaferrata in the Alban hills near Rome. In August, 1881, he ordered the restoration of the Byzantine rite in its purest form; the monks are now Albanians from the Italian colonies, and the whole Italo-Greek Basilian Congregation consists of this one great house.

The economic problems to the south of Italy in the Calabria section left the Albanian villages there extremely poor, except that of Lungro. Farther to the south, in Sicily, conditions were better; from their seminary at Palermo missionaries went to Albania. Piana dei Graeci to the south of Palermo remained one of the most important Albanian settlements in the West. In the nineteenth century there were an estimated 60,000 Italo-Albanians in Calabria and Sicily.

5. The Russians [74]

It is said that the Tsar Alexander I (1801-1825) considered some form of reconciliation with Rome; he had come to an agreement with the Pope concerning the establishment of an archbishopric at Warsaw and concerning the religious groups in that city. However, the Holy Synod objected to any compromise, and wanted to make all Ukrainians and Russians subject to itself. Tsar Nicholas I (1825-1855) favored the Orthodox Church, and accordingly supported the reactionaries against the "nonconformists." In 1839 the Ukrainian-Russian Catholic Oriental bishops who had met at Polotsk were forced to "return" to the Russian Orthodox Church. Thus a million

[74] Adeney, *The Greek and Eastern Churches,* pp. 436-458; Danzas, *The Russian Church,* pp. 107-141; Wesseling, "Vladimir Soloviev,"—*The Eastern Churches Quarterly,* II (1937), 12-26, 65-78, 121-137, 185-202; Tondini, *The Future of the Russian Church* (New York, 1876); Brian-Chaninov, *The Russian Church,* pp. 141-155.

and a half Ukrainian Catholics and two thousand churches were forcibly brought within the Russian Church in those parts of the Ukraine and Poland which Russia had taken after the final partition of Poland at the Congress of Vienna in 1815. Attempts of union with Rome became impossible.

The national religion remained one of indefinite mysticism, with an overemphasis on ritual to the neglect of a dogmatic structure; the traditional enmity towards the Catholic Church remained. It is true that in the first part of the century some French Catholic intellectuals who had fled from the French revolution made an impression, as did De Maistre in St. Petersburg, and that the quality of the Jesuit schools was recognized, but apparently nothing could overthrow the age-old opposition to the Church of Rome. A general mental distortion regarding the Church prevailed. One who tried to present a true picture of the Church was the philosopher and theologian Vladimir Soloviev (1853-1900), who made his profession of faith on February 18, 1896, before Fr. Nicholas Tolštoi in the chapel of Our Lady of Lourdes in Moscow, and then devoted himself to an intellectual apostolate, which in reality he had begun some years before actually making the profession of faith. To him is to be traced the origin of a nucleus of Russian Catholics who kept the Byzantine rite.

CHAPTER V

THE STATUS OF THESE RITES IN THE UNITED STATES

ARTICLE 1. THE ARMENIANS [1]

The Turkish massacres of 1895-1896 gave an impetus to the immigration of Catholic Armenians, whose numbers in the United States before these dates were very small. In 1898 the Catholic Patriarch of Cilicia of the Armenians, Patriarch Stephen X, residing at Constantinople, obtained through Cardinal Ledochowski, Prefect of the Congregation for the Propagation of the Faith, the consent of Archbishop Corrigan of New York and of Archbishop Williams of Boston for Armenian priests to serve in their provinces. The first Armenian priest whom the Patriarch sent was the Archpriest Madiros Mighirian, who arrived in 1899. He went first to Boston, then to New York City and Worcester, Massachusetts. He then established his headquarters at St. Stephen's Latin Church in New York, since many Armenians lived in that section.

In 1906 Fr. Manuel Basieganian began his work among the Armenians of New Jersey and Pennsylvania. In 1908 Fr. Joseph Keossajian established a chapel in St. Mary's Church at Lawrence, Massachusetts, to serve the Armenians in the Boston area. In 1909 Fr. Moses Mazarian took charge of the Armenian mission at Cleveland. These few priests tried to serve the 2,000 scattered Catholic Armenians. Today there are four Armenian priests for about 3,000 Catholic Armenians.

An important synod was held in Rome from October 15th to December 8th, 1911, at the Church of St. Nicholas of Tolentino. Pope Pius X (1903-1914) had ordered this Armenian synod to be held at Rome,[2] and the Armenian Patriarch of Cilicia, Paul Peter

[1] *A Memorial of Andrew J. Shipman*, pp. 224-226; Janin, *Les Églises orientales*, pp. 431-434; Malcom, *The Armenians in America* (Boston, 1919), *passim*.

[2] Epist., *"Vobis plane compertum est,"* 30 sextilis 1911—*Acta et Decreta Concilii Nationalis Armenorum*, pp. v-vi.

XIII Terzian, had issued the letter of convocation in September of the same year.[3] The decrees of the Council discuss the essential points of Catholic faith, the Church, the hierarchy, the sacraments, divine worship, education, preaching, missions, orphanages, hospitals, the administration of church goods, various censures and penalties, court processes, etc. These decrees were "recognized" and allowed to be published by the Congregation for the Propagation of the Faith for the Affairs of the Oriental Rite, on September 14, 1913.[4]

The many decrees of the Council concerning espousals and marriage are found in the tenth chapter under the Title III.[5] To have canonical effects, an espousal must be a mutual promise which is to be true, free, deliberate, and entered before the pastor and in a solemn manner; espousals can be made by proxy. Espousals are valid but rescissible if made after the age of reason but before the age of puberty. There must be a just cause to dissolve the espousal and the ordinary or pastor must be informed of such a dissolution. There is no explicit requirement for the pastor to publish the banns in the Latin sense of the term, but the pastor is required to make a thorough investigation of the free state of the parties. Often in the year the pastors are to explain the impediments concerning marriage to the people and to explain to the people their obligation to reveal any impediments that might exist between any parties who desire to contract marriage.

Between two of the faithful the marriage contract and the sacrament are inseparable, and therefore the pastors are urged to teach their people often the dignity and preeminence of the contract they are entering at marriage, a contract which is a source of grace for the parties. Polyandry is opposed to the primary end of marriage, which is the procreation of children; polygyny is opposed to the secondary ends. Even though marriage as an "office of nature" has the qualities of unity and indissolubility, Catholic marriage has the added strength of being a symbol of the union of Christ and the Church, and this is true especially of a consummated marriage.

[3] *"Non latet Vos,"—op. cit.*, p. vii.

[4] *"Paterna sollicitudine motus,"—op. cit.*, p. iii.

[5] *Acta et Decreta*, pp. 264-291, nn. 547-585. These decrees can be presented here only in summary fashion.

The Pauline Privilege can be invoked by a convert from paganism under the usual conditions. Marriage by proxy is allowed if the proxy has the special mandate for a determined person. Conditional marriage consent can be given in the sense that the parties who placed a licit condition cannot act as husband and wife until the condition has been fulfilled. Evil conditions are considered not to have been placed. Conditions when placed in relation to the past or the future leave a marriage valid or invalid according as the proviso has or has not become actualized; impossible conditions, or conditions whose fulfillment is an inevitable accompaniment of the future, are accounted the same as the conditions that have not been placed at all.

A substantial error about the identity of the spouse invalidates the marriage; no error regarding a quality of the person (except an error about his servile condition) makes a marriage to be null, even if the error was the underlying cause for the consent in the marriage. Grave, unjust fear, when brought to bear upon a person by an external free agent for the enforced contracting of marriage, "at least in virtue of the ecclesiastical law" impedes the validity of a marriage so contracted.[6] Impotence, if antecedent and perpetual, i.e., such as cannot be remedied with natural means or only with the commission of sin, by the very law of nature makes the parties incapable of marriage.

After these general rules, which are similar to those of the Latin Code of seven years later, the synod speaks of the various impediments to marriage. The girl must be twelve and the man fourteen, unless "before these years of canonical puberty" they had the mental and physical capacity for marriage. A ratified but non-consummated

[6] Cf. *S. Romanae Rotae Decisiones,* XXVII (1935), dec. xxxix; XXVIII (1936), dec. iv. Two cousin Armenians, after the proper dispensation, married at Alexandria, Egypt, in 1919 before the Procurator of the Armenian Patriarch. In 1929 the woman petitioned for a declaration of nullity on the grounds of grave fear. The Oriental Congregation transmitted the case to the Rota which on May 25, 1935, declared the marriage null on the grounds of force and fear. After an appeal by the defender of the bond, the Rota considered the case as a court of second instance, but on January 23, 1936, the Rota confirmed its previous decision. In both decisions the Rota quoted the decrees of the council of 1911 concerning force and fear.

marriage can be dissolved through solemn religious profession or by means of a dispensation from the Pope. The solemn vow of chastity taken at a solemn religious profession, and likewise the reception of sacred orders, makes an attempted marriage null. The impediment of sacred orders begins to bind after the reception of the subdiaconate.

Consanguinity is computed as in the Latin system. Relationship by consanguinity in the direct line bars marriage between persons related in any degree; in the collateral line, between persons related within the fourth degree. Affinity, when it arises from the marital union itself, bars marriage between persons related within the collateral line to the fourth degree inclusive; if it arises from illicit intercourse, then as an impediment it extends to persons collaterally related within the second degree; affinity as an impediment to marriag exists between persons related in any degree whatsoever of the direct line, regardless of the manner in which the affinity arises. The impediment of public propriety if it arises from valid espousals, bars marriage between persons related in the first degree; if it arises from a contracted marriage (even though an invalid one, unless the invalidity has resulted from a defect of consent) there can be no marriage between persons related within the fourth degree inclusive. This impediment is in its duration perpetual; it does not cease when the espousals have been ended by mutual consent or when one spouse has died.

Legal relationship makes an attempted marriage null if there is a relationship in the direct line to the fourth degree inclusive between the adopter on the one hand, and the adopted and all his descendants on the other hand, if these latter at the time of the adoption came under the power of the adopter. In the collateral line there is a diriment impediment between the adopter's natural legitimate children if these are under his power, and the one adopted, as between legal brothers and sisters, and between the adopter and the widow of the adopted, and between the adopted and the widow of the adopter. The extent of the impediment of spiritual relationship is restricted within the Tridentine rule, so that a spiritual relationship which gives rise to the impediment exists only between the one baptizing or confirming and the subject of the sacrament and his parents, or also between the godparents and the godchildren and their parents. There is no spiritual relationship contracted between the parties and the witnesses at the time of marriage, nor is any spiritual relationship contracted between a boy and a girl who should happen to be baptized at the same baptismal ceremony.

A marriage between a baptized and a non-baptized person is to be accounted invalid, "at least from the general custom of the Church, a custom which many centuries ago was in force and obtained the force of law." [7] If a Catholic marries a heretic, the marriage is illicit but valid. The impediment of crime arises from (a) an act of adultery accompanied with the mutual promise of marriage, whether the promise be made before, along with, or after the act of adultery during the lifetime of the innocent party; (b) an actual murder of a spouse through the mutual planning of two accomplices when at least one of them intends to marry the other; (c) an act of adultery, and then an added act of murder perpetrated by one party with a plan to marry the other. The impediment of abduction arose in the manner indicated by the Tridentine law, i.e., the woman must have been moved from one place to another through either physical or moral force, the abduction must have been intended with a view to marriage, and the woman must have been an entirely unwilling sufferer of this constraint.

As to the form required for a valid marriage, "in the Latin Church the Council of Trent introduced a public form by decreeing the necessary presence of the pastor and two witnesses. Among us, for centuries it has been the practice that marriages contracted before a priest, not necessarily the pastor, are to be considered, and on that score actually are, valid; therefore a marriage entered without the presence of a priest is null and void. From this fact there arises a new impediment of clandestinity." [8]

[7] ". . . saltem ex generali ecclesiae more, qui pluribus abhinc saeculis viget ac vim legis obtinet . . ."—n. 571, § 10.

[8] ". . . quam in ecclesia latina Conc. Trident. introduxit statuens necessariam praesentiam parochi et duorum testium. Apud nos iam a saeculis invaluit, ut valida habeantur et sint matrimonia quae coram sacerdote, non necessario parocho, contrahuntur; quare coniugium sine praesentia sacerdotis initum nullum est et irritum. Unde novum exsurgit impedimentum clandestinitatis."—n. 575. Duskie (p. 158) seems to err in citing this n. 575 in support of his statement, "Apparently the uniate Armenians require that a marriage be celebrated before

There are five impedient impediments which make the marriage illicit, though not invalid. The synod lists them as the sacred times, the interdict placed on a church, espousals, simple vows, and a difference of faith. Not marriage itself, but its solemnization is prohibited during the sacred times. These extend: (a) from the first Sunday in Advent to the Sunday before the Latin Septuagesima Sunday; (b) from the first Sunday of Lent to the Octave of Pentecost inclusive; (c) from any Sunday, if it immediately follows a week of fasting, to the next feast inclusive.[9]

The interdict placed on a church could become a diriment im-

the proper pastor, and two witnesses." Gulovich ("Matrimonial laws of the Catholic Eastern Churches,"—*The Jurist,* IV [1944], 216-217) relies upon Duskie for the following statement: "*The Armenians.* They are said to be bound by the juridical form which consists of the presence of the proper pastor and two witnesses. This is based on the enactments of the latest Plenary Armenian Synod held in Rome in 1911, and approved by the Holy See *in forma communi* on September 14, 1913." And he continues: "We were not given an opportunity to study the Acts of this Synod, but from the fact that it was approved *in forma communi* it can be said that the synodal enactments would have no nullifying effect upon a marriage contracted in contravention of that act, unless it could be proved that the ancient Armenian discipline required the presence of the proper pastor and two witnesses under pain of nullity." He then quotes, by way of an example of the ancient Armenian discipline in this matter, from the encyclical of Nerses in 1166 (cf. *supra,* p. 36), but concludes after the quotation: "The first thing that impresses itself on the mind in reading this paragraph is that by clandestinity is meant a marriage which takes place in the presence of a priest with no other witnesses present. This would seem to imply that a valid marriage requires the presence of a priest (without any further specification) and witnesses." Cf. Cappello, n. 925. However, since this "new impediment of clandestinity" did not receive the specific approval of the Holy See, and since the binding force of the Armenian custom in these matters is doubtful, a definite form of marriage cannot be required for validity. According to Janin (*Les Églises orientales,* p. 390), marriage for the Armenians consists essentially in the contract entered into between the two spouses and therefore, while the blessing of the priest is the official consecration of the contract, it is not the indispensable condition of it. Cf. De Clercq, *Ordre, Mariage, Extreme Onction,* p. 93; *Collectanea,* n. 580 (cf. *supra,* p. 77); De Clercq, *Les Églises unies d'Orient,* p. 99; Dauvillier and De Clercq, p. 28.

[9] Janin (*op. cit.,* p. 392) states that the "closed time" in the strict sense includes 260 days of the year.

pediment only if the Pope included in this interdict an invalidating clause as affecting the very validity of the marriage celebrated in the interdicted church. If there preceded solemn espousals in accord with the ritual, a man cannot licitly marry any person other than the espoused, unless these espousals have been dissolved through a mutual consent or in consequence of a judicial sentence. A simple vow of chastity, of not entering marriage, of embracing the religious life, or of receiving sacred orders, render a marriage illicit, unless the vow for a just cause has been remitted by the power of the Church. Finally, the synod recalls that among the Orientals in the early centuries a marriage between one of the faithful and a baptized heretic was considered null; [10] however, the synod declares that, while now there is no doubt about the validity of such a marriage, the prohibition against it is so universal in the Church that the Pope alone can dispense; a bishop cannot so dispense unless he has the required faculties from the Holy See.

No one can grant a dispensation from impediments which, as deriving from the divine law, whether natural or positive, certainly bar marriage. Only the Pope can dispense from impedient and diriment impediments of ecclesiastical law; patriarchs and bishops can dispense only within the limits of the indult which they have received from the Pope, but they can dispense in a case wherein there is a doubt of fact concerning the existence of an impediment, also in a case wherein the impediment is of an occult character, and finally, in a case of very urgent necessity. When there is danger of death and no time remains for recourse to the Holy See, the patriarch and bishops can dispense, in favor of those who are but civilly married or who live in concubinage, from all impediments except that of the priesthood and also that of affinity in the direct line, when the existence of the latter impediment has resulted from a licit intercourse. This faculty of dispensing the patriarch and the bishops can communicate even habitually to the pastors of their dioceses.

When there is a question of a marriage already contracted, the bishops can dispense from all occult impediments created and

[10] Canon 72 of the Council in Trullo is cited. Cf. *supra*, p. 21.

enacted by purely ecclesiastical law, provided that the following conditions and circumstances be conjointly verified in the case: (1) that with all due solemnities the marriage was contracted *coram Ecclesia;* (2) that the contract was exchanged with good faith on the side of at least one of the parties; (3) that the union has been consummated in the meantime; (4) that a separation cannot be urged without the arising of scandal; and (5) that the Holy See can no longer be approached for a final disposition in the matter with a timely effect.

The last few paragraphs of Chapter X of Title III discuss the mutual obligations of the spouses, the reasons sufficient for a temporary or a permanent separation, and an exhortation to the innocent party to encourage with a full measure of Christian charity the return of the faithless spouse, even though there be no strict and rigid obligation of doing so.

In a later section the Council decreed that in a marriage of mixed rite, the woman is given the option of passing over to the rite of her husband as she enters upon the marriage or while the marriage lasts; after the marriage bond is broken, the woman is free to return to her original rite. In such a marriage of mixed rite the pastor of the man has the right to bless the marriage.[11]

Article II. The Chaldeans [12]

In 1905, Fr. Abdul Messih Andraos from the diocese of Diyarbekir arrived at Yonkers, New York, where he organized a Chaldean community and said Mass in the chapel attached to St. Mary's Church. A few years later Fr. Joseph Ghariba, coming from the diocese of Aleppo, travelled about the country as a missionary for his people. In 1910 Fr. Gabriel Oussani became Professor of Church History, Patrology and Oriental languages in St. Joseph's Seminary, Yonkers, New York (he died in November, 1934).

In the early part of this century the Chaldeans in Chicago were cared for by two visiting priests of their own rite, Fr. Patros Elia

[11] *Acta et Decreta,* n. 622.

[12] Thomay, *A House of Prayer and Worship for the Christians of the Land of Paradise* (Chicago, 1945); *A Memorial of Andrew J. Shipman,* p. 237.

and Fr. Warda Mirza. Their third priest was Fr. Samuel David, who came to Chicago in 1913 after a short stay among the Chaldeans of New Britain, Connecticut. Fr. David celebrated his liturgy in the school hall of the Cathedral of the Holy Name for seventeen years before his death on December 29, 1930. It was during his time that the Chaldeans came to this country in large numbers because of their sufferings during the World War of 1914-1918, during which they were persecuted and massacred by Turks, Kurds, Arabs and Persians, and were forced to journey on foot to the deserts of Mesopotamia, where particularly near Baghdad they lived in tents as exiles; after World War I many of these refugees came to the United States.

In June, 1934, Fr. Simon Joseph came to care for his people in Chicago, but unfortunately he died seven months later. He had been a heroic figure amid the massacres in Persia, and in 1927 he had come to the United States where he became the pastor of the Chaldean community at Yonkers, New York. At the request of the Oriental Congregation, the Chaldean Patriarch, Joseph Emanuel Thomas,[13] appointed his vicar-general of the diocese of Basrah, Fr. Francis Thomay, as the fifth pastor of the Chaldeans in Chicago. After his arrival in August, 1935, Fr. Thomay endeavored to have a separate church for his faithful, and on September 19, 1944, St. Ephraem's Church, the first Chaldean church in the western hemisphere, was solemnly dedicated by the vicar-general of the Archbishop of Chicago. It is planned to replace the temporary chapel with a larger structure built according to their Oriental architecture. Another Chaldean priest, Fr. Sergius Sarmas, lives in Hartford, Connecticut. Besides the places mentioned above, Chaldean families are found in Michigan (Detroit, Flint), Pennsylvania (Philadelphia), and California (San Francisco, Los Angeles, Turlock, Fresno). They number about 1,300 Catholics.[14]

[13] The patriarch was elected on July 10, 1900, and on August 2nd, 1945, was still reigning on his 93rd birthday. Since 1925 he has been by appointment a senator of the Iraqian government.

[14] In general, the Chaldeans of Detroit are from Mesopotamia (Iraq) and speak the Arabic language, while those of the other cities are principally from Persia (Iran) and use the Assyrian language.

No decrees about their marriages in this country are known to exist. The marriage ritual book which they use is the one printed at the Dominican Press in the city of Mosul. The "prohibited times" for marriages are the periods from the first Sunday of Advent to Christmas inclusive, and from the first Sunday of Lent to Easter Sunday inclusive.

Article III. The Antiochene Rite

1. The Syrians [15]

Their poverty in Syria induced some Pure Syrians, neither Maronites nor Melkites, to come to the United States. For the most part they came from the diocese of Aleppo, but were never very numerous in this country. One priest in particular, Fr. Paul Kassar, from the diocese of Aleppo and an alumnus of the Propaganda Unisity in Rome, served these Syrians from 1910 to almost the present day, when they no longer have a definite church of their rite. These Syrians are scattered and now usually attend the Maronite or Melkite churches. They are to be found chiefly in New York City, Paterson, Boston, Columbus, Detroit, Center Falls (Rhode Island), and other cities. They number approximately 4,000.

2. The Maronites [16]

The unbearable restrictions which the Turkish functionaries placed on their various economic activities were some of the reasons which induced the Maronites from the districts of Mount Lebanon and the city of Beirut to leave Syria; thousands of them came to the United States, where at first they were peddlers and small traders before they organized their present well-established businesses. The first

[15] *A Memorial of Andrew J. Shipman*, pp. 238-239; "Chronicle of Events—U. S. A."—*The Eastern Churches Quarterly*, III (1938-1939), 244; Hitti, *The Syrians in America* (New York, 1924), *passim.*

[16] *A Memorial of Andrew J. Shipman*, pp. 234-235; Janin, *Les Églises orientales*, pp. 567-568; *The Separated Christians of the Orient* (*The Year Book*, St. Bonaventure Seminary, St. Bonaventure, N. Y., 1936), pp. 37-38; Hitti, *The Syrians in America*, pp. 47-56, 106, 125-127.

small group of Maronites came to the United States in 1876. This group was without a priest for three years until the arrival of Fr. Joseph Mokarzel, who stayed only a short time; the Very Rev. Louis Kazen, of Port Said, Egypt, came later, but he also remained only a short time.

On August 6, 1890, Fr. Butros Korkemas arrived to establish a permanent mission; after many difficulties he rented a store on Washington Street in New York City, where he opened a chapel. He was accompanied by his nephew, Joseph Yasbek, then in deacon's orders, who later received ordination to the priesthood from Archbishop Corrigan, and then founded the Maronite mission in Boston; in the first decades of this century he became a *Chorepiskopos* among the Maronites and the leader of his people. In May, 1904, Fr. Francis Wakim arrived to care for the Maronites in New York.

Churches were soon established in Philadelphia, Troy, Brooklyn, and also in other cities, so that by 1911 there were fifteen Maronite churches in the United States. Missionary Maronite priests visited their people in the smaller cities. The Maronite clergy in 1911 consisted of two *Chorepiskopoi* (who had certain quasi-episcopal powers) and twenty-three other priests, of whom five were Antonine monks. Today there are forty-four Maronite churches in the United States, and an estimated 40,000 of the faithful.

On January 16, 1936, the Rota issued a decision concerning two Maronites who were allegedly bound by the diriment impediment of consanguinity. The parties were married at Damascus in 1905; in 1914 the man presented the *libellus* to the Ordinary at Damascus, but when the war broke out in the same year the woman went to the United States, and the man became a doctor in the Turkish army. The Oriental Congregation sent the case to the Rota after the Congregation had ordered the securing of further proofs. The Rota affirmed the fact that consanguinity in their eighth degree was diriment, but since in this case not enough proofs were presented to verify the relationship, the Rota decided that the marriage was to be held as valid.[17]

In another case the Rota discussed the impediment of public

[17] *S. Romanae Rotae Decisiones,* XXVIII (1936), dec. ii.

propriety between two Maronites. A man, privately engaged to a certain girl, after her death married her younger 12 year old sister, who had been forced into the marriage by her mother. On April 7, 1934, the Rota considered the impediment of public propriety and quoted the words of the Lebanon Synod on it, which synod however did not declare that a certain formula must be followed to have a valid espousal; there was then a doubt of law whether private espousals among the Maronites created the diriment impediment. The Rota decided that this private espousal, creating at most a doubtful impediment, did not entail the nullity of the marriage, but the Rota declared the marriage null because of the force and fear to which the girl had been subjected.[18]

In 1936 the Rota judged this case again after an appeal had been made. The Rota cited the Synod of Lebanon (1736) in support of the impediment of public propriety, and also declared that the Instruction of the Holy Office to the Patriarchs, Archbishops and Bishops of the Oriental Rites on June 20, 1883, indicated that this impediment was generally in effect among the Orientals. The Rota also mentioned that the doctrine of the Lebanon Synod on force and fear as hindrances to the validity of a marriage was similar to that found in canon 1087 of the Latin Code. The Rota finally affirmed its previous decision, declaring the marriage null because of the force and fear to which the bride had been subjected.[19]

On July 14, 1934, the Rota decided a case between two Maronites which involved several points of Maronite law. The parties had married according to the Tridentine form in their patriarchate after securing a dispensation from the impediment of consangunity in the sixth degree of the Maronite computation. Soon after the wedding it was revealed that the parties were related also in the eighth degree of consanguinity through another common ancestor. Three days after the wedding a dispensation from this other impediment was secured. The marriage proved unhappy, and the woman left within six months. In 1923 she impugned the validity of her marriage on the basis that it had never been convalidated subsequent

[18] *S. Romanae Rotae Decisiones,* XXVI (1934), dec. xv.

[19] *S. Romanae Rotae Decisiones,* XXVIII (1936), dec. lxxiv.

to the dispensation from the impediment which was unknown at the time of the celebration of the marriage. The Synod of Lebanon was quoted by the Rota with reference to the required form of the Maronites, and it was shown that the Synod did not expressly demand that the Tridentine form had to be observed in a case of convalidation after a detected impediment was dispensed. On April 30, 1928, the Oriental Congregation asked the Maronite Patriarch of Antioch whether the Tridentine form must be used in a convalidation; he answered in the affirmative on March 10, 1930. The Rota finally decided that the marriage was null for the reason that the consent had never been renewed in the prescribed form.[20]

On April 30, 1934, the Rota decided another case concerning the impediment of consanguinity. On January 24, 1909, two Maronites had married with a dispensation from the impediment of consanguinity in the eight degree. The man went to America and was never heard of again. In 1929 the woman presented a petition asserting that they were related in the seventh degree of consanguinity, and not in the eighth. The case eventually was sent to the Rota, which quoted the Synod of Lebanon to show that by their law the Maronites were subject to the impediment of consanguinity whether their relationship existed in either the seventh or the eighth degree of the collateral line. The furnished proof, namely, that in the case in question the relationship existed in the seventh degree, was accepted by the Rota as conclusive, and accordingly the marriage was declared null.[21]

On July 28, 1934, the Rota decided a case involving the impediment of affinity among the Maronites. It had been publicly thought that a certain man was carrying on an illicit carnal relationship with a certain woman. When he later wanted to marry this woman's daughter, the case was brought to the attention of their Ordinary, who called on the man and the girl's mother to take an oath regarding the reputed fact of illicit relations. The oath of these parties disavowed the existence of this fact. The contemplated marriage took place in 1917. In 1928 the woman of this marriage decided to

[20] *S. Romanae Rotae Decisiones,* XXVI (1934), dec. lvii.

[21] *Op. cit., ibid.,* dec. xxvii.

go to Persia with a wealthy Egyptian. The husband tried to dissuade her, but the woman presented a petition to the Ordinary to declare the marriage invalid inasmuch as the impediment of affinity had actually arisen in the case. The diocesan tribunal and the tribunal of the Patriarch upheld the validity of the marriage, but the woman obtained a *restitutio in integrum* in her case. She finally appealed to the Oriental Congregation which sent the case to the Rota. The Rota quoted the Synod of Lebanon in relation to the impediment of affinity as arising simply from any carnal union, whether licit or illicit, and in the light of the furnished proof, declared the marriage to be invalid for the reason that the impediment did exist in the case since it had not been removed by any act of dispensation.[22]

In 1934 the Rota likewise declared the invalidity of two marriages between Maronites, since in both instances the woman had been forced into the marriage and had not given valid consent; in both cases the Rota quoted the Synod of Lebanon in its legislation concerning force and fear as factors which invalidate the marriage contract.[23]

In the previous year the Rota considered a case in which it was alleged that the marriage contract was null because neither Maronite party had given valid consent. On April 25th, the Rota decided that the evidence was not sufficiently conclusive to warrant a declaration of nullity, but it approved the concomitant petition that the Pope be requested to grant a dispensation from a ratified, non-consummated marriage. The Pope granted this favor on June 23, 1933.[24]

In 1933 the Rota examined an interesting case concerning clandestinity among the Maronites. The marriage occurred on

[22] *Op. cit., ibid.*, dec. lxiv.

[23] *Op. cit., ibid.*, dec. xxxviii. In this earlier case the girl had been abducted, though later she was rescued. But even after the rescue she went through the marriage ceremony for the sake of avoiding the unjust threat of a jail sentence, planned by the man who had originally abducted her. She soon went to Senegal, and he went to live in the United States. In 1927 she began proceedings to have the marriage declared null. Cf. also *ibid.*, dec. lxxviii. In this later case the witnesses did not give concordant testimony concerning the lack of consent on the part of the girl.

[24] *S. Romanae Rotae Decisiones*, XXV (1933), dec. xxxi.

February 14, 1919, at the monastery church of St. Elias at Antelias (Syria). In 1928 the man impugned the validity of his marriage, claiming that the priest who witnessed the marriage neither was the proper pastor of either spouse, nor was correctly delegated. The diocesan tribunal upheld the validity of the marriage, but the tribunal of the Patriarch declared it invalid. The defender of the bond appealed to the Oriental Congregation, which referred the case to the Rota. The Rota quoted the Synod of Lebanon, which in effect imposed the Tridentine form on the Maronites, who became bound by it, not through the promulgation of the Tridentine decree in the Maronite parishes, but in virtue of the Holy See's specific approval of this Synod. The Rota declared that the legitimate interpretations regarding the Tridentine form had to be applied to the Maronites, and since the evidence in the case revealed that the priest who assisted at the ceremony functioned with a merely *presumed* delegation, the marriage was declared null on April 4, 1933.[25]

On December 19, 1928, in answer to a request from the Bishop of Buffalo, the Oriental Congregation replied to seven questions concerning the Maronites in the United States. The questions that have a bearing on their marriage laws are as follows:

> 1. Whether Maronites, if they have a domicile or quasi-domicile in the United States, are held to the laws of the Code of Canon Law.
>
> 2. Whether two Maronites who have a domicile or quasi-domicile in the United States are able to contract a valid marriage, even though they would be bound by some impediment which has been abrogated by the Code of Canon Law, but which still exists as a diriment impediment for the Maronites.
>
> 3. Whether two Maronites who have a domicile or quasi-domicile in the United States can contract a valid marriage before

[25] *Op. cit., ibid.,* dec. xxii. This opinion, namely, that the Tridentine form was obligatory on the Maronites, not as resulting from the publication of the Tridentine decree in each parish, but in virtue of the specific approval of the Synod by the Holy See, was repeated by the Rota in a decision of March 21, 1935, wherein the Rota declared that the validity of the marriage was to be upheld, since the lack of a properly possessed delegation on the part of the priest was not proved. Cf. *S. Romanae Rotae Decisiones,* XXVII (1935), dec. xvii.

the age of 16 for the groom and 14 for the bride, when it is evident that they have actually reached puberty.

6. Whether Peter, a Maronite, and Rose, a Greek-schismatic, if they have a domicile or quasi-domicile in the Diocese of Buffalo, validly contract marriage, when a schismatic Oriental priest in the presence of two witnesses assists at the marriage and blesses it.

7. Whether James, a Maronite, and Helen, a Greek-schismatic, if they have a domicile or quasi-domicile in the Diocese of Buffalo, contract a valid marriage before a Greek-Catholic priest (who is not a pastor), in the presence of two witnesses.

The Congregation gave the following answers:

To the first question, in the negative, according to the norm of Canon 1 of the same Code, keeping intact however the special Decrees of the Holy See concerning them, and safeguarding the rule given in the Apostolic Letter *"Orientalium dignitas,"* n. IX: "Every Oriental while staying outside his patriarchial territory shall be under the administration of the Latin clergy; but he will continue to belong to his own rite."

To the second, in the negative.
To the third, in the affirmative.
To the sixth, in the affirmative.
To the seventh, in the affirmative.[26]

[26] 1. An Maronitae, habentes in Septentrionalibus Statibus Foederatis Americae domicilium aut quasi-domicilium teneantur legibus Codicis iuris canonici.

2. An duo Maronitae, habentes in Septentrionalibus Statibus Foederatis Americae domicilium aut quasi-domicilium, validum contrahere possint matrimonium, etiamsi ligati uno aliove ex impedimentis, abrogatis quidem a Codice iuris canonici, sed adhuc vigentibus et dirimentibus pro Maronitis.

3. An duo Maronitae, habentes in Septentrionalibus Statibus Foederatis Americae domicilium aut quasi-domicilium, possint validum contrahere matrimonium ante aetatis annum decimum sextum pro sponso, et quartum decimum pro sponsa, quando constet malitiam supplere aetatem.

6. An Petrus, Maronita, et Rosa, graeco-schismatica, habentes domicilium aut quasi-domicilium in Dioecesi Buffalensi, valide contrahant matrimonium assistente et benedicente sacerdote schismatico orientali in praesentia duorum testium.

7. An Jacobus, Maronita, et Helena, graeco-schismatica, habentes domicilium aut quasi-domicilium in Dioecesi Buffalensi, validum contrahant matrimonium coram sacerdote (non parocho) graeco-Catholico, in praesentia duorum testium. Responsum:

It is to be noted that these answers do not specifically consider the case of an intermarriage of two Maronites contracted outside the Church in this country.[27] Some years before these answers were issued by the Holy See, Chelodi had maintained that the decree *"Tametsi"* binds the Maronites only in their patriarchial territory unless they leave the territory purely to elude this law.[28]

Ad Ium negative, ad normam Can. 1 eiusdem Codicis, salvis tamen peculiaribus Decretis Sanctae Sedis eos respicientibus et firmo disposito Litt. Apost. *"Orientalium dignitas"* N. IX: "Quicumque orientalis, extra patriarchale territorium commorans, sub administratione sit cleri latini; ritui tamen suo permanebit adscriptus."

Ad IIum negative.

Ad IIIum affirmative.

Ad VIum affirmative.

Ad VIIum affirmative.

The text of the document is given in *The Jurist,* IV (1944), p. 233, footnote n. 98; cf. also Bouscaren, *The Canon Law Digest* (2 vols., Milwaukee: Bruce, 1934, 1943), I, 4-5 (hereafter cited as Bouscaren, *Digest*). It is to be noted (cf. *The Jurist, ibid.,* footnote 97) that Bouscaren gives an incorrect translation for the 7th question, in referring to the marriage as taking place before a schismatic priest. Cf. *The Ecclesiastical Review,* LXXX (1929), 384-385.

[27] Cf. Fallon, "Syrian Maronites marrying in the United States,"—*The Ecclesiastical Review,* CIII (1940), 480. This author stated: "In these two cases the exemption of the Greek schismatic party from the Tridentine form could well have been communicated to the Maronite party despite the latter's personal subjection to the Tridentine law, whereas in the intermarriage of two Maronites, no such exemption from the decree *Tametsi* would obtain, if indeed the law of the Council of Trent was promulgated for them as a personal law. On the other hand, if a priest of the Latin rite without delegation or permission assists at the marriage of two Maronites, such a marriage cannot be branded as certainly invalid, since it is not beyond all doubt that Maronites are subject to the Tridentine decree whenever they are domiciled in a territory wherein this decree was never promulgated by Latin Ordinaries. It would appear that recourse to the Sacred Congregation for a solution is the one safe policy to adopt."

[28] *Ius Matrimoniale iuxta Codicem* (3. ed., Tridenti, 1921), n. 139: ". . . alii Orientales (Maronitae) ligantur decr. *Tametsi,* quod suam vim localem retinet in eorum territoriis, personalem etiam extra eos qui exeunt in fraudem legis. Secus ipsi quoque possunt valide contrahere sine forma." Later authors indicate that they hold this same opinion. Herman, in speaking of the Council of Mt. Lebanon, declared in part: ". . . formam Tridentinam stabilire valuit tantum pro territorio proprii ritus . . ."—"De 'Ritu' in Iure Canonico,"—*Orientalia*

The mind of the Oriental Congregation concerning the relationship of the Maronites in this country to the Tridentine form of marriage is further revealed in an Instruction issued by the Congregation in 1935.[29] This Instruction specifically mentions the marriage of two Maronites who leave their domicile in the Lebanon and marry outside of it. The Instruction stated:

> I. In a letter of March 31, 1935, followed by another letter dated April 18th, His Excellency Monsignor Cicognani made inquiries at this Sacred Congregation whether the faithful of the Maronite Rite residing in the United States are bound to contract marriage in the presence of the proper pastor *ad validitatem*. It was requested that a response be given independently of the Oriental Code, and that it be given exclusively in regard to Maronites residing outside of their Patriarchate and in regions where they have no diocese of their own Rite.
>
> II. Now, the received doctrine holds that the aforesaid marriages are undoubtedly valid even when not contracted in the presence of the *proper* pastor. Let us summarize the doctrine concerning *clandestinity* in marriages of the Maronites.
>
> 1. At the Lebanon Synod, held in 1736, the Maronites adopted the Tridentine discipline in these precise words: "Nullum est matrimonium clandestinum, id est, quod aliter [contrahitur] quam praesente parocho vel sacerdote de ipsius parochi vel Ordinarii licentia et duobus vel tribus testibus." (II, XI, 8, XII).
>
> 2. This discipline is obligatory for the validity of marriages in the following cases: (1) if two Maronites contract marriage

Christiana, XXXII (1933), 126. Staffa, writing in 1940, also touched this point briefly: "Maronitae in territorio Patriarchali tenentur forma Tridentina, vi Synodi Libanensis a. 1736 in forma specifica approbatae."—"De transitu ad alium Ritum,"—*Apollinaris,* XIII (1940), 185, n. 2. In another article concerning marriages of mixed rites, Herman stated: ". . . Secundum ius Maronitarum matrimonium, intra fines saltem patriarchatus, celebrari debet coram parocho proprio sponsi vel sponsae et duobus saltem testibus."—"Quibus normis matrimonium regatur quod inter fideles diversi ritus contrahitur,"—*Analecta Gregoriana,* Vol. IX, *Miscellanea Vermeersch,* I (Roma: Pontificia Università Gregoriana, 1935), 253. White declared: "Maronitae non tenentur, sub poena nullitatis ad formam Tridentinam: (1) Si relicto domicilio quod habebant in proprio territorio, extra illud contrahant inter se, sive acquisierint domicilium vel quasi-domicilium in loco celebrationis sive non, quia forma Tridentina est localis."—*De forma celebrationis matrimonii,* p. 86.

[29] The Instruction in Italian and in its English translation can be found in *The Jurist,* IV (1944), 234-236. The translation is reproduced here.

in the territory of their own Patriarchate; (2) if two Maronites contract marriage outside of their Patriarchate, but in a place where they have not obtained a domicile or quasi-domicile, but retain it (i.e., domicile or quasi-domicile) in the place of their origin.

3. This discipline is not obligatory for validity (1) if the Maronites contract marriage in or outside of their Patriarchate with faithful of other Oriental Rites (the exemption is communicated); (2) if, leaving their domicile which they had in their proper territory, two Maronites contract marriage outside of their territory, regardless whether they did or did not obtain a new domicile or quasi-domicile; (3) if, after having obtained a legitimate dispensation the Maronites contract marriage in or outside of their Patriarchate with non-baptized or baptized non-Catholics, who were not baptized and were not reared in the Catholic Church.

4. Furthermore, like all other Orientals, the Maronites are bound by the form prescribed by the Latin Code (c. 1094) if they contract marriage with Latins (c. 1099, § 1, 3) or Latin non-Catholics, heretics or schismatics who were baptized and reared in the Catholic Church or were converted to the Church but abandoned her later (c. 1099, § 1, 1).

III. The case proposed by Monsignor Cicognani contemplates Maronites who do not have a domicile or quasi-domicile in the Patriarchate and contract marriage outside of it (cfr. *supra,* II, 2), but rather have a domicile or quasi-domicile in the place where they contract marriage. A marriage contracted in the presence of the local pastor and not in the presence of the Maronite pastor, or his delegate, etc., is valid.

IV. There is no difficulty in declaring that the Maronites, as all the Orientals, for that matter, in places where they have no diocese of their own can contract marriage in accordance with the prescriptions of c. 1094, that is, for validity it is sufficient to celebrate the marriage *coram parocho vel loci ordinario vel sacerdote ab alterutro delegato et duobus saltem testibus.*

On April 20, 1943, the Oriental Congregation, in answer to a doubt proposed by the Archbishop of Chicago about the validity of the marriage of two Maronites before a civil magistrate, declared that "the prescript of the Synod of Lebanon in 1736, inducing the diriment impediment of clandestinity, is not considered to be extended to the Maronites who have left their domicile or quasi-domicile in their patriarchal territory." [30]

[30] Cf. Appendix, p. 264, for a copy of this response.

On March 6, 1945, the Oriental Congregation declared that Maronites are held to the Tridentine form only when they are within the bounds of their own Patriarchate. The Congregation stated this when judging two cases about Maronites proposed to it by the Archbishop of Montreal.[81] In one case the Maronite man with a domicile in Montreal had married a baptized Protestant (who had a domicile in Philadelphia) before a civil official in New York, in the presence of two witnesses. In the other case a Maronite man with a domicile in Montreal had married a Greek-schismatic woman (who had a domicile in Brooklyn) before an Oriental schismatic bishop in Brooklyn. The Congregation declared in favor of the validity of both marriages.

The forbidden times, the "days of abstinence," on which the festivities usually accompanying the celebration of marriage are forbidden, though the marriage itself is not forbidden, are the 12 days before Christmas, the period of Lent, the 8 days before the Feast of the Assumption, and the 4 days before the Feast of Ss. Peter and Paul.

Article IV. The Byzantine Rite

1. The Melkites [82]

In the last decades of the nineteenth century, many immigrants came to the United States from Syria, Palestine, Arabia and Egypt, who were Arabian in culture and language, but Byzantine-Melkite in religion. Many of these Melkites settled in the New York metropolitan area, and also in Lawrence (Massachusetts), Cleveland, Detroit, La Crosse (Wisconsin) and elsewhere. No priests of their own rite came with the first immigrants, and many of these became lost to the faith. Realizing the need for Melkite priests, Patriarch Gregory II Yusof (1864-1897) sent a few priests to care for the Melkites in this country. In 1890 the Archimandrite Abraham

[81] Cf. *infra*, p. 203; Appendix, p. 261.

[82] *A Memorial of Andrew J. Shipman*, pp. 207-209; *The Eastern Observer* (Semi-official organ of the Pittsburgh Greek Rite Catholic Diocese, Homestead, Pennsylvania), issue of April 4, 1943; *Al-Macarrat* (organ of the Greek Melkite Catholic Patriarchate, Harissa, Mt. Lebanon), XXXI (1945), 6; Hitti, *The Syrians in America*, pp. 47-56, 105-106, 128-129.

Bechewaty, a Basilian of the Congregation of the Holy Savior from Saida in Mt. Lebanon, began to celebrate his liturgy in the basement chapel of St. Peter's Church in downtown New York City. Before his death in 1923 Monsignor Bechewaty was able to buy a house near St. Peter's and to use its ground floor as his church. His successor, Monsignor Ghosn, was able to convert the whole building into a church and rectory.

In Boston, the then Archbishop O'Connell applied to the Melkite Patriarch of Antioch for a Melkite priest; Fr. Nicholas Cannam came, and in 1910 opened the Church of Our Lady of the Annunciation. In Brooklyn their liturgy was celebrated for many years in the basement of St. Paul's Church, until in 1922 Fr. Nicholas Araktingi was able to begin the erection of the Church of the Virgin Mary. He had come to this country in 1909, and found that his people were living under great difficulties. The young Melkite men had fled to this country to avoid the payment of the "redemption" of their military service in the Turkish army. The military service in the Turkish army was completely Mohammedan, and Christians were not admitted since their loyalty to the Turkish rule was with good reason doubted; however, they nevertheless had to pay a "redemption" of their military service. Besides those who fled to avoid such payments, there were many who came with an ambition to start a new business and to rise from their poverty. The Chicago Exposition also attracted many to come here.

The number of Melkites in this country can only be approximated. In the Orient the various Melkite bishops had to report to the Patriarch on the number of their faithful in 1945, and the total then listed for the Orient was 176,600. It is estimated that there are 70,550 others in Europe, America, Australia and other countries, and of these it is estimated that 25,000 are in this country.

The Melkite Synod of Ain-Traz, held in 1911, decreed that any marriage contracted without the assistance of the proper pastor or of a priest delegated by the proper pastor, by the bishop or by a vicar who has the faculty to delegate the right to assist, would be invalid. This synod however was not approved by the Holy See.[83]

[83] Cf. Staffa, "De transitu ad alium Ritum,"—*Apollinaris,* XIII (1940), 185, n. 2.

A case concerning the present discipline for the Melkites as regards the form of marriage was submitted to the Sacred Congregation of the Holy Office in 1924 by the Bishop of Helena, Montana.[34]

In June, 1897, Saydeh Najeeb Abo Saad was baptized in the rite of her parents as a Catholic Greek-Melkite in the Melkite Church of St. Elias in Zahleh, Mt. Lebanon. In 1899 her family took her to America, where they began to take her to a Latin church when she was five years old; she received her religious instruction, the Sacraments of Penance, the Holy Eucharist and Confirmation according to Roman rite. She continued to go to Latin churches and moreover expressed her intention to live and die as a Latin.[35] In February, 1912, she married a Greek-schismatic before the Greek-schismatic Bishop Raphael and two assisting schismatic priests in Brooklyn. When the woman sought a declaration of the nullity of this marriage, three questions were proposed to the Holy Office: "1. Is the woman to be considered a Latin or an Oriental? 2. If she belongs to the Latin rite, is the marriage to be considered invalid because of the impediment of clandestinity? 3. If she remains in the Oriental rite, is she bound under pain of nullity for the contraction of a valid marriage to appear before a Catholic Oriental priest?"

The private reply of the Holy Office, upon a previous ascertaining of the fact that the woman had been baptized in the Melkite rite, stated, on May 1, 1925: "The nullity of the marriage is not evident." This reply indicated the mind of the Holy Office, that the only way to change to another rite is with the permission of the Holy See, that the reception of the sacraments in a different rite does not induce a change to that rite, and that a Melkite is not bound to contract marriage before a Catholic Oriental priest.[36]

[34] Cf. Duskie, pp. 174-175; Bouscaren, *Digest,* I, 543. The Latin documents concerning this case can be found in *The Ecclesiastical Review,* LXXIII (1925), 305-308, and in *Periodica,* XIV (1925), 99-101.

[35] "Statuit enim in hac regione, inter fideles ritus Latini, ipsa Latina, vivere et mori."—*The Ecclesiastical Review,* LXXIII (1925), 306.

[36] In referring to this case, Marx (*The Declaration of Nullity of Marriages Contracted Outside the Church,* The Catholic University of America Canon Law Studies, n. 182 [Washington, D. C.: The Catholic University of America Press, 1943], p. 55, note 32) seems to indicate that the Congregation for the Propagation of the Faith issued an annotation about this case concerning the relation-

On January 22, 1941, the Oriental Congregation replied to a case sent by the Bishop of Brooklyn. Two Melkites had attempted a civil marriage in Cuba on September 28, 1928, and never revalidated the union. The Oriental Congregation referred the question of the validity of this civil marriage to a plenary session of the Cardinals. The conclusion reached was that, since there was a doubt of law as to whether the Melkites must for validity receive the blessing of the priest, the marriage must be maintained as valid.[37]

Another case involving a Melkite was sent to the Oriental Congregation by the Archbishop of Los Angeles. A Melkite man was born in New Zealand in 1895 of Melkite parents, who had been born in Zahleh in the Lebanon; in 1919 he came to the United States, and while here always went to the Latin churches. On November 22, 1921, he married a baptized Protestant before a civil magistrate in Oklahoma City, but later sought a declaration of nullity, alleging that his marriage was contracted without the required form. On July 30, 1943, the Oriental Congregation replied that the marriage was not clearly null, without adding any comment.[38]

The Rota has decided some cases involving Melkites, but these decisions concern the factors of force and fear,[39] and of alleged

ship of some Orientals to the decree *"Tametsi"*; the comment was Vermeersch's (*Periodica,* XIV [1925], 102-103): "Nihilo minus caput *Tametsi* est promulgatum inter Ruthenos Galliciae et fortasse etiam in Syria. Ruthenos autem Gallicianae provinciae (non autem alios), *S. C. de Propaganda Fide* pro negotiis ritus Orientalis, decreto 5 maii 1911, legi *Ne temere* obnoxios fecit." It seems also that Marx could leave the impression that Ruthenians were in Syria, for his translation of this annotation is as follows: "Inasmuch as the decree *'Tametsi'* of the Council of Trent had been promulgated among the Ruthenians of Galicia and Syria, the S. Congregation for the Propagation of the Faith ruled that these members of the Oriental rite were bound to observe the prescriptions of the decree *'Ne temere,'* and hence were bound to observe the form of marriage just as the Catholics of the Latin rite." The phrase of Vermeersch, *"non autem alios,"* refers to the Ukrainians outside of the province of Lemberg in Galicia. Also, it seems that the note of causality should not have been introduced into the translation of Marx, for the decree *"Ne temere"* was extended to the Lemberg province of Galicia at the request of the bishops, and not *because* the decree *"Tametsi"* had been in force there.

[37] For this reply, cf. Appendix, p. 263.

[38] For the documents related to this case, cf. Appendix, pp. 262-263.

[39] *S. Romanae Rotae Decisiones,* XXVI (1934), dec. xx. On April 16, 1934,

insanity,[40] rather than any questions regarding impediments or the required juridical form of marriage.

The "forbidden times" for the solemnization of marriage on the part of Melkites are Lent, Advent (December 10th-25th) and the period between the feasts of Christmas and Epiphany.

2. *The Ruthenians* [41]

The earliest immigration of Ruthenians to the United States was in 1879 from the western portion of Galicia, but soon—especially when the reports from America were received—immigration was stimulated on both sides of the Carpathian Mountains; soon thousands of Ruthenians came annually to this country, so that by 1911 there were about 400,000 Ruthenians here. The majority settled in Pennsylvania, and most of them worked in the coal mines there; it was at Shenandoah in that state that Fr. Ivan Volanski of Lemberg built the first Ruthenian church in 1886, after meeting many difficulties occasioned by the Latin authorities in view of the fact that he had married before ordination. Cardinal Sembratovitch of Lemberg interceded for him and had him accepted as a priest in good standing. Within a few years Fr. Volanski had organized congregations in other parts of Pennsylvania, and also in New Jersey and Minnesota.

the Rota in this decision declared that a marriage between a Melkite girl and a schismatic was null because of a deficiency of legitimate consent; however, the case was appealed, and the Rota on August 5, 1936, declared that the previous Rota decision was to be set aside, as the alleged fear and the alleged simulated consent was not such as to make the marriage evidently null—*S. Romanae Rotae Decisiones,* XXVIII (1936), dec. lix. In an earlier case in which the Melkite woman appealed to the Pope, who referred the matter to the Oriental Congregation, which in turn sent it to the Rota, the Rota decided on June 20, 1933, that the marriage was null because of the fear exerted on the girl by her mother—*S. Romanae Rotae Decisiones,* XXV (1933), dec. xliv.

[40] *S. Romanae Rotae Decisiones,* XXIV (1932), dec. xlviii.

[41] Duskie, pp. 30-53; *A Memorial of Andrew J. Shipman,* pp. 127-128, 170-172, 193-203; Janin, *Les Églises orientales,* pp. 353-354; MacKenzie, *The Canonical Status of the Ruthenian Rite in the United States* (Washington: The Catholic University of America, 1919); Heuser, "Greek Catholics and Latin Priests,"—*The Ecclesiastical Review,* IV (1891), 194-204; *Statistica,* pp. 213-216.

However, as other Ruthenian priests arrived with their families, the American bishops sent complaints to the Holy See that a married clergy was causing great scandal here.[42] Thereupon the Congregation for the Propagation of the Faith on October 1, 1890, informed the Ruthenian bishops in Europe that: (1) priests who desire to serve in America must be celibates; (2) the priests should inform the Congregation about the diocese to which they desire to go, so that the local ordinary there may be duly notified about their prospective arrival; (3) faculties must be obtained from the local ordinary; and (4) the priests are to be subject to the jurisdiction of the local ordinary.[43]

These instructions of the Congregation as sent to the European Ruthenian Ordinaries were forwarded to the American bishops in a letter of May 10, 1892, addressed to the Archbishop of Baltimore.[44] These regulations, though they had referred explicitly to the priests of the Greek-Ruthenian rite, were extended in this letter to all the other Oriental priests who desired to labor in the United States.[45]

[42] An example of resentment due to misunderstandings about the presence of married priests was the action of Rev. Alexis Tout who in 1891, apparently because he resented the criticisms of the Latin clergy, led his Russo-Carpathian parish at Minneapolis over to the Russian Orthodox Bishop Vladimir (other Oriental Catholic parishes later joined Bishop Nicholas, the successor to Bishop Vladimir). Cf. *Religious Bodies,* U. S. Census Bureau, 1936, II, 589. For a synopsis of the trouble and schisms caused by this question of celibacy among the Ruthenians, cf. Perhac, *Married Priests in the Catholic Church* (Brooklyn, 1934).

[43] 1. Sacerdotes ritus Graeco-Rutheni, qui in status foederatos Americae Septentrionalis proficisci et commorari cupiunt, debent esse coelibes. 2. Huic S. C. debent in scriptis manifestare quaenam sit dioecesis ad quam pergere exoptant ut res deducatur ad notitiam Ordinarii eiusdem dioeceseos. 3. Sistere se debent coram Ordinario illius dioecesis in qua sacrum ministerium exercere vellent ut ab eo facultates opportunas implorent. 4. Memorati sacerdotes eorumdum Ordinariorum iurisdictioni subesse debent.—*Collectanea,* n. 1966, nota 2; cf. also *Fonti,* XI, n. 620; Duskie, p. 32. For similar instructions of the Congregation to the Oriental Ordinaries on April 12, 1894, cf. *Collectanea,* n. 1866, and *Analecta Ecclesiastica,* VI (1898), 11.

[44] *Decretum de Sacerdotibus Ruthenis,—The Ecclesiastical Review,* VII (1892), 66-67; cf. Arndt, "De rituum relatione iuridica ad invicem,"—*Analecta Ecclesiastica,* III (1895), 272; Duskie, p. 35.

[45] It can be noted here that these regulations still affect all Oriental priests

The letter also mentioned the desire of the Holy See that all married Oriental priests here should return to their own country.

A few years later, the Congregation for the Propagation of the Faith issued another set of instructions,[46] this time for the Oriental laity, allowing them to conform to the Latin rite wherever they would be in this country, without a change in their rite being effected thereby. A special provision was made in this decree for the Ruthenians, that in each ecclesiastical province in which there were many Ruthenians the Archbishop of the province, with the advice of his suffragans, should select a celibate and suitable Ruthenian priest, or a Latin priest acceptable to the Ruthenians, who would exercise vigilance and direction over the Ruthenians, and who would receive special faculties for this work from the Latin Ordinaries.[47] This was the first plan of the Holy See, after it had been petitioned to erect a Vicariate Apostolic for the Ruthenian rite in the United States and to name a Ruthenian Ordinary.[48]

The large number of the Ruthenians, however, continued to present many practical difficulties in the proper care of them; many were lost to the faith. The Holy See appointed the Rt. Rev. Andrew Hodobay of the Ruthenian diocese of Presov (Eperjes) as Apostolic Visitor to the Ruthenians in the United States; he made his investigations from 1902 to 1906. On June 14, 1907, Pope Pius X (1903-

here except the Ruthenians who are now subject to their own ordinaries, that is, all the non-Ruthenian Oriental priests must obtain their faculties from the local ordinary in whatever part of the United States they wish to labor.

[46] *"Romana ecclesia caritate,"* 1 maii 1897—*Collectanea,* n. 1966; *Analecta Ecclesiastica,* V (1897), 383. Cf. *Fonti,* XI, n. 595; Duskie, pp. 38-40.

[47] "In provinciis ecclesiasticis Americae Septentrionalis, in quibus multi sunt fideles Rutheni ritus, Archiepiscopus cuiuscumque provinciae, initis conciliis cum suis suffraganeis, sacerdotem ruthenum coelibatu et idoneitate commendabilem deputet, et, huius defectu, sacerdotem latini ritus ruthenis benevisum, qui super populum et clerum dicti ritus vigilantiam et directionem exerceat, sub omnimoda tamen dependentia Ordinarii loci, qui pro suo arbitrio facultates ei tribuat quas in Domino expedire iudicaverit."

[48] On October 29, 1890, eight Greek-Catholic priests had met at Wilkes-Barre, Pennsylvania, to petition the Holy See to appoint a Vicar General with authority over all the Catholics of the Greek rite in the United States. Cf. Heuser, "Greek Catholics and Latin Priests,"—*The Ecclesiastical Review,* IV (1891), 198.

1914) issued an Apostolic Letter providing for a titular Ruthenian bishop in the United States.[49] He was not to be an Ordinary, as he had to receive delegated jurisdiction from each local Latin Ordinary. The Rt. Rev. Stephen Soter Ortynsky, a Basilian monk, *hegumenos* of the monastery of St. Paul, Michaelovsk, Galicia, was consecrated on May 12, 1907, as titular Bishop of Daulia, and arrived in this country on August 27, 1907. At that time there were about 150 Ruthenian churches, served by 127 Ruthenian priests, of whom 9 were Basilian monks. During 1911 Ruthenian nuns of the Order of St. Basil were introduced into the country.

The canonical position of Bishop Ortynsky as the vicar of the Latin Ordinaries caused widespread dissatisfaction among the Ruthenians; the Ruthenians were told by the "Orthodox" that the Apostolic Letter *"Ea semper"* clearly showed that the Holy See planned a latinization of their rite in the United States. The Holy See, on May 28, 1913, appointed Bishop Ortynsky to be the first Ordinary of the Ruthenians in the United States; he received complete and ordinary jurisdiction over all the clergy, faithful, and over the temporal affairs of the Greek-Ruthenian rite. Because of this important change, the Congregation for the Propagation of the Faith for the Affairs of the Oriental Rite on August 17, 1914, issued a new decree for the Ruthenians to be effective for 10 years (it was renewed on June 21, 1924).[50]

The first part of the decree was concerned with the Ruthenian bishop, and revealed that in most respects the Ruthenian bishop was to have the same powers, obligations and duties as the Latin Ordinaries. The Apostolic Delegate was to represent the Holy See in any controversy between the Ruthenian bishop and a Latin bishop here. The second part deals with the Ruthenian clergy, and urges the establishment of a seminary for them; the procedure of admitting

[49] Litt. apost. "Ea semper,"—*ASS*, XLI (1908), 3-12; *The Ecclesiastical Review*, XXXVII (1907), 513-520.

[50] Decr. *"Cum episcopo,"*—*AAS*, VI (1914), 458-463; *The Ecclesiastical Review*, LI (1914), 586-592. The renewal of the decree in 1924 was made known to the American Ordinaries in a letter from the Apostolic Delegate. For a detailed analysis of the decree, cf. Duskie, pp. 44-53, and Meehan, "The Greek Ruthenian Church in the United States,"—*The Ecclesiastical Review*, LI (1914), 710-717.

priests from Europe is outlined; the priests who come must be of high character; the Ruthenian Ordinary may delegate a Latin priest to care for the Ruthenians in a locality which has no Ruthenian priest. The last two chapters deal with the laity; they may receive the Sacraments and hear Mass in any Catholic church, if there is no Ruthenian church nearby, without any change in their rite being effected thereby; they may observe the feasts and fasts of the place where they live; rules are given for marriages between the faithful of different rites.

Bishop Ortynsky died in 1916, and the see was vacant [51] until 1924, when the Holy See provided for two Ordinaries, Bishop Constantine Bohachevsky for the Ruthenians of Galicia, and Bishop Basil Takach for the Ruthenians of Russian Podcarpathia, of Hungary, of Jugoslavia and of Slovakia. They were both appointed on the same day, May 20, 1924,[52] and were both consecrated on the same day, June 8, 1924, in Rome at the Church of St. Athanasius, attached to the Pontifical Greek College. They were consecrated by the late Assessor of the Sacred Oriental Congregation, Bishop Isaias Papadopoulos.

These newly created Ruthenian bishops received ordinary jurisdiction; they were to appoint a joint vicar in New York to care for the immigrant Ruthenians; they were to decide which Ruthenian parish belonged to the Ruthenians of a certain European geographical location, for the actual European origin of the membership of a parish was to settle the question of their allegiance and subjection to these two bishops; the list of the respective parishes was to be sent to the

[51] After the death of Bishop Ortynsky the Ruthenians were governed by two Administrators, Rev. Gabriel Martyak for the Carpatho-Russians, and Rev. Peter Poniatissin for the Galicians.

[52] *AAS,* XVI (1924), 243. Bishop Bohachevsky was directed to reside at Philadelphia and Bishop Takach at New York. The latter however received the permission of the Holy See to establish his residence at Munhall, near Pittsburgh. The establishment of the Pittsburgh Greek Rite Diocese under Bishop Takach was the occasion for a return of many Catholics who had joined the Russian Orthodox Church. In 1925 Bishop Stephen Dziubay led many of his followers to submit to the jurisdiction of Bishop Takach. Cf. *Historical Records Survey: Inventory of the Church Archives in New York City* (New York, 1941), p. 146.

Apostolic Delegate and to the American bishops. The task of dividing the parishes was a very difficult one in many cases (the status of over 300 parishes had to be determined), and an anomaly existed in a few cases wherein the parish of one European geographical group was allowed to be under the bishop of the other group; and even after the first agreements some parishes were later actually interchanged and the priests transferred to the other Ruthenian diocese. As was to be expected, there were many disputes over the legal ownership of the various parishes; in some cases the bishops encountered a harsh trusteeism.

On March 1, 1929, the Sacred Oriental Congregation issued another decree for the purpose of regulating the status of the Ruthenians in this country.[53] After an introduction, which gives a synopsis of the previous legislation for the Ruthenians here, the first ten articles discuss the canonical position of the two Ruthenian Ordinaries. They were to have full ordinary power over the Ruthenians of their respective European territories, while being dependent on the Apostolic Delegate. A vicar-general was suggested for each to assist in the visiting of the parishes, but a vicar-general is unknown among them, and thus they found this concept strange. The bishops were to make canonical visitations of their parishes and to watch over the temporal administration of them. Article 8 suggested that "for the convenience and advantage both of the clergy and of the Curiae of the two bishoprics, a Ruthenian priest may have a domicile in New York, and act as vicar or delegate of both Ordinaries, giving assistance to the faithful of the Ruthenian rite, but especially to those priests who are just landing in America or sailing away, always under the dependence and according to the wishes of the Ordinaries."[54] The bishops were to send quinquennial reports to the Holy See and to make the *ad limina* visits.

The second chapter of the decree was concerned with the Ruthenian clergy. Both bishops were urged to erect seminaries; until a sufficient number of Ruthenian priests were educated here, the bishops were to ask for Ruthenian European priests through the agency

[53] *"Cum data fuerit,"—AAS,* XXI (1929), 152-159; Bouscaren, *Digest,* I, 6-16; *Periodica,* XVIII (1929), 189-197.

[54] For various reasons this suggestion was not followed.

of the Oriental Congregation. Those priests who were to come here had to be celibates and of blameless life, and those who had come needed the permission of the American Ruthenian bishops to return to or to be called to their own country. During the existing scarcity of Ruthenian priests, article 19 gave the following direction: "The Ruthenian Ordinaries can exercise their jurisdiction only upon the Greek-Ruthenian clergy and people. But if in any place there are faithful of the Greek-Ruthenian rite, but there is no mission established there or no priest of the Greek-Ruthenian rite, the Ordinaries shall communicate their jurisdiction over the faithful of the Greek-Ruthenian rite to a priest of the Latin rite at that place, and notify the Ordinary of what they have done, until such time as there may be a priest of the Greek-Ruthenian rite in the place." Other articles in this chapter discussed clerical retreats, examinations and conferences, and encouraged the priests in the performance of their duties.

The third chapter of the decree discussed questions affecting the Ruthenian laity. If there was no church of their own rite in a place, they were to hear Mass on days of obligation in a Catholic church of another rite. No change of rite was induced by their going to the churches of the Latin rite; Latin priests were not allowed to persuade them to effect a change of rite. Ruthenians could confess their sins to a Latin confessor and *vice versa;* the reserved censures and reserved sins established in one rite could not be absolved by a priest of another rite, unless he possessed the usual delegated powers. Ruthenians could receive the Eucharist consecrated according to any rite; any Oriental could validly and licitly fulfill the precept of Paschal Communion in another rite; Holy Viaticum could be received in any rite. Funerals were to be conducted by the pastor of the rite to which the deceased belonged. Ruthenians could observe the feasts and fasts according to the customs of the place where they were staying. If a holyday of obligation fell on the same day in both rites, Ruthenians were bound to assist at Mass in a church of their rite, if there was one in the place.[55] Finally, the Ruthenians were

[55] The Oriental Congregation on June 11, 1930, changed this declaration, and allowed American Ruthenians to fulfill this obligation in any Catholic church.—*AAS*, XXII (1930), 354.

urged to foster and support their own societies, associations and newspapers.

The fourth chapter presented some regulations concerning questions arising from a consideration of their marriages, as will be shown in the discussion of their marriage laws.

On November 23, 1940, the Oriental Congregation, "after referring with approval to the good results obtained through ten years' experience from the decree *'Cum data fuerit'* of March 1, 1929," confirmed that decree for another ten years, with two changes—one concerning the appointment and removal of Ruthenian rectors (Article 15), and one concerning the marriages celebrated between the faithful of different rites (Article 39).[56]

It can be said that the Ruthenians are the most flourishing of the Eastern Catholics in this country. Bishop Takach, the Ordinary for all Ruthenians from Hungary, Podcarpathia, Slovakia, and Jugoslavia, governs 114 priests, who serve nearly 200 churches. Bishop Bohachevsky, the Ordinary for the Ukrainians from Galicia, governs 118 priests, who serve nearly 150 churches. The latter's Auxiliary, Bishop Senyshyn, was consecrated on October 22, 1942. The number of subjects of each Ordinary is about 300,000.[57]

At the beginning of this century the Tridentine form of marriage was required in the province of Galicia for the validity of the marriage contract; it was not so required among the Ruthenians of Russian Podcarpathia, of Hungary, of Slovakia or of Jugoslavia.[58] On August 2, 1907, the Sacred Congregation of the Council issued the decree *"Ne temere,"* which was to become effective at Easter Sunday, April 19, 1908; a copy of this decree was sent to the bishops of Galicia, who ordered this new form of marriage to be followed in practice.[59] However, on February 1, 1908, the same Congrega-

[56] *AAS,* XXXIII (1941), 27; Bouscaren, *Digest,* II, 6-7.

[57] For the list of priests, parishes and institutions subject to each Ordinariate, cf. *The Catholic Directory* (New York: Kenedy, 1945), pp. 771-779.

[58] Cf. Benedetti, *Votum,* II, A—*ASS,* XLI (1908), 261. For a map revealing the location of the various European Ruthenian dioceses at the beginning of this century, cf. *The Catholic Encyclopedia,* II, 136.

[59] Cf. Gulovich, "Matrimonial laws of the Catholic Eastern Churches,"—*The Jurist,* IV (1944), 213; Dillon, *Common Law Marriage,* p. 39.

tion declared that Catholics of the Oriental rite were not held to the requirements of the *"Ne temere"* law.[60] In the following month the same Congregation decided that an Oriental Catholic, when marrying a Latin Catholic, had to observe the new decree.[61] Soon after this decision, the Metropolitan of the Galician province of Lemberg petitioned the Sacred Congregation for the Propagation of the Faith for the Affairs of the Oriental Rite that the regulations of the decree *"Ne temere"* be extended to that province. This request was explicitly granted by a decree of the same Congregation of May 5, 1911.[62]

Three years later this legislation was extended to the Ruthenians in the United States.[63] Bishop Ortynsky had requested that this be done because of the many difficulties which existed about the required form of marriage, especially since schismatic priests readily assisted

[60] "1. An decreto *'Ne temere'* astringantur etiam catholici ritus orientalis." "Ad I um-Negative."—*ASS,* XLI (1908), 108-109; *Fontes,* n. 4344. Cf. *Analecta Ecclesiastica,* XVI (1908), pp. 5 and 14, wherein this first reply is reported as having been, "Ad I um-Quoad Catholicos ritus orientalis nihil esse immutatum."

[61] S.C.C., 28 mart. 1908: "I. Utrum validum sit matrimonium contractum a catholico ritus latini cum catholico ritus orientalis, non servata forma a decreto *'Ne temere'* statuta." "Ad I um.—Negative."—*ASS,* XLI (1908), 287-288. This answer showed that (unless exceptions were made) there was to be no longer any "communication of exemption" for Latins concerning the required form of marriage. On February 1, 1908, the Holy See had declared that the communication of exemption provided for Germany by the decree *"Provida"* was to remain—*ASS,* XLI (1908), 108-110. Cf. Souarn, *Praxis Missionarii in Oriente servata* (Paris, 1911), n. 181.

[62] Cf. Vermeersch in *Periodica,* XIV (1925), 102-103. This decree was made known in the province of Lemberg on July 6, 1911. Cf. *Archiv für katholisches Kirchenrecht* (Innsbruck, 1857-1861; Mainz, 1862——), XCII (1912), 484. The province of Lemberg, to which the decree *"Ne temere"* was extended, included the archdiocese of Lemberg and the dioceses of Przemysl and Stanislawow. The Congregation on August 2, 1909, had answered the petition of Metropolitan Sheptycky by declaring that temporarily the *"status quo"* was to be observed, implying that the Ukrainians there could continue their practice of following the *"Ne temere"* decree. Cf. Gulovich, *loc. cit.*

[63] Decr. *"Cum episcopo,"* art. 30: "Matrimonia tum inter fideles Graeco-Ruthenos, tum inter fideles mixti ritus, servata forma decreti *Ne temere* contrahi debent . . ."—*AAS,* VI (1914), 463; *The Ecclesiastical Review,* LI (1914), 592. Cf. Duskie, p. 165.

at the marriages of Ruthenians and publicly declared that such marriages were valid. There was much confusion as to the required form for the contracting of marriage until the decree of 1914 definitely gave to the Ruthenians here the same law as the Latins had. The rules of the decree *"Ne temere"* still apply to the Ruthenians in the United States. The decree of 1914 was renewed in 1924 and the decree of 1929 (renewed in 1940) made no change in this regard.[64]

The question relating to the celibacy of the Ruthenian clergy in this country is a complicated one. On the one hand, most of the Ruthenian clergy in Europe were married men, and on the other hand, Catholics in this country (and even bishops) looked askance at a married Ruthenian clergy, even though they realized that a married clergy was a commonplace among the Ruthenians of Europe. No law can be found prohibiting married Ruthenians in Europe from being ordained, and even if they should marry after receiving the priesthood, it is possible that in some Ruthenian dioceses of Europe their marriage would be held as valid, though the priests would become irregular and would have to be dispensed from their irregularity before being allowed to function again as priests.[65]

[64] Decr. *"Cum data fuerit,"* 1 mart. 1929, art. 39: "Matrimonia tum inter fideles Graeco-Ruthenos, tum inter fideles mixti ritus servata forma decreti *'Ne temere'* contrahi debent . . ."—*AAS,* XXI (1929), 159. Cf. Marx, *The Declaration of Nullity of Marriages Contracted Outside the Church,* pp. 55-56; Cappello, n. 925; Dillon, *Common Law Marriage,* pp. 39, 50.

[65] This is a difficult question. Cicognani-Staffa (*Commentarium,* I, 20) state: "Pro Ruthenis et Romenis certo non constat de existentia impedimenti dirimentis ex ordine sacro, sive diaconatus sive presbyteratus." On the other hand, some evidence has been seen (cf. *supra,* pp. 100-101) which favors the invalidity of marriages contracted by Ruthenian priests after their ordination. There has been no general decree from the Holy See declaring that marriages of Oriental clerics in sacred orders would be not only illicit but also invalid. Some rites have particular legislation settling this question for them, but the doubt about the Ruthenians appears to remain. Cf. Cappello, nn. 907-908. He quotes the Synod of Zamost (1720), which seems, however, to speak of second marriages of priests in stronger terms than about first marriages. Also, the decrees of this Synod do not apply to the Ruthenians south of the Carpathian Mountains. However, faculty n. 20 of the Ruthenian Ordinaries in the United States (cf. Appendix, p. 260) does not grant to these Ordinaries the power to dispense from the impediment of priesthood even when there is danger of death, which fact indicates the present force of the impediment among the

The early decree of the Congregation for the Propagation of the Faith on October 1, 1890, to the Ruthenian Ordinaries in Europe, when referring to priests who desired to labor in America, stressed the fact that those who were to come to America had to be celibates. However, as the number of unmarried priests among the Ruthenians in Europe was very small, many married priests came to this country with their wives and children.

The tenth article of the decree *"Ea semper"* of 1907 urged the erection of seminaries for the Ruthenians. Until these seminaries were erected, the Ruthenian young men could go to Latin seminaries, but those who desired to receive Orders had to be celibates.[66] The next article gave the procedure for securing Ruthenian priests from Europe until enough Ruthenians could be educated here; the following article, the twelfth, decreed that those who came had to be celibates, or at most widowers without children.[67]

The decree *"Cum episcopo"* of 1914 in its tenth article omitted mention of the requirement of celibacy.[68] It is disputed whether this silence meant that the Holy See was relaxing this requirement for this country.[69]

Ruthenians. Cf. also Wernz, *Ius Decretalium*, IV, Pars II, pp. 212-214, 229-230; DeSmet, n. 575; Gasparri, *Tractatus Canonicus de Matrimonio* (3. ed., 2 vols., Parisiis, 1904), nn. 680-684. Bobak, who maintains that the priesthood is not a diriment impediment for the Ruthenians, states: "Non tamen negamus ullo modo, aliqua matrimonia post S. Ordines contracta invalida fuisse declarata etiam apud Ruthenos sed unice contendimus probare, haec exempla non esse argumentum sufficiens ad nostram sententiam sua probabilitate frustrandam ut inferius patebit."—*De caelibatu*, p. 158.

[66] Art. 10: ". . . Interim vero clerici rutheni in seminaria latina locorum in quibus nati sunt, vel domicilium acquisiverunt, admittantur. Sed nonnisi caelibes, sive nunc sive in posterum, ad sacros ordines promoveri poterunt."—*ASS*, XLI (1908), 6; *The Ecclesiastical Review*, XXXVII (1907), 515.

[67] Art. 12: "Sacerdos eligendus, sit caelebs, vel saltem viduus et absque liberis . . ."—*loc. cit.* Cf. Cicognani-Staffa, *Commentarium*, I, 20.

[68] *AAS*, VI (1914), 460; *The Ecclesiastical Review*, LI (1914), 589.

[69] Cf. Meehan, "The Greek-Ruthenian Church in the United States,"—*The Ecclesiastical Review*, LI (1914), 713. This author, in giving his paraphrase and commentary on the decree *"Cum episcopo,"* which had appeared in the same year, stated: "The strict regulations of the Propaganda . . . demanding a celibate clergy or at least widowers without children, and determining the formalities to be observed by European bishops in permitting their priests to

Article 11 of the decree of March 1, 1929, *"Cum data fuerit,"* made no explicit mention of celibacy when speaking of the seminaries and vocations for the Ruthenians, but the following article stated: "In the meantime, as has already several times been provided, priests of the Greek-Ruthenian rite who wish to go to the United States of North America, and stay there, must be celibates." [70] The omission of an explicit mention of celibacy as a requirement for admission to the seminary can perhaps be explained by the fact that in this country by 1929 the practice of admitting only celibates to the seminary was well established. It can also be argued *a fortiori* that, if those who come here from a section where custom allows marriage must nevertheless be celibates, those here are surely required to be celibates.[71]

The legislation concerning the marriages contracted between Ruthenians and Catholics of another rite has undergone certain

take up this work in America, are still in force." However, in keeping with their European customs, some Ruthenians married Americans and were later ordained. The silence of the 1914 decree indicates that it was impossible to carry it out in practice, because a sufficient number of celibate priests could not be obtained. The Holy See was informed of this factual condition, and a private instruction was sent to the Apostolic Delegate to the effect that celibates were to be preferred, but that when these could not be obtained, married priests were to be admitted. Cf. MacKenzie, *The Canonical Status of the Ruthenian Rite in the United States,* p. 25.

[70] *AAS,* XXI (1929), 155; Bouscaren, *Digest,* I, 10.

[71] Nine months after issuing this decree in March, 1929, the Oriental Congregation issued a general decree on December 23, 1929, *"Qua sollerti alacritate,"* (*AAS,* XXII [1930], 99-105; Bouscaren, *Digest,* I, 17-24), which applies to "Oriental clerics, secular or religious, who go from an Oriental territory or diocese to North, Central or South America, or to Australia to minister spiritually to the faithful of their own rite in those places." Article 6 of this decree stated: "Secular priests who have a wife shall not be admitted to exercise the sacred ministry in these countries, but only celibate priests or widowers. Widowers may, however, for a just cause, be excluded by this Sacred Congregation from those dioceses and places in which they may have children living or in any way present; and the same is true of adjoining localities." Article 18 stated: "The Ruthenians however who go to the United States of America or Canada to exercise the spiritual ministry under the jurisdiction of Ordinaries of their own rite are to observe the special decrees which have been enacted by this Sacred Congregation. If for the same ministry they go to the other countries above named, they are to observe the provisions of this decree."

changes. The Apostolic Letter *"Ea semper"* of 1907, in Articles 27-31, stated the following concerning the changing of rites in a marriage of mixed rites: "Marriages between Ruthenian and Latin Catholics are not forbidden; but the Latin husband should not follow the rite of his Ruthenian wife, nor should the Latin wife follow the rite of her Ruthenian husband. If indeed a Latin man shall have married a Ruthenian woman, it will be permissible for the woman to go over to the Latin rite, either in the act of marriage or afterwards while the marriage lasts, without being able to revoke her choice, once made, while her husband lives. After the marriage has been dissolved, the Ruthenian woman who had embraced the rite of her husband will be free to resume her own original rite. It will be licit however for a Ruthenian woman who has preferred to remain in her own rite to follow the rite of her husband in the questions of fasts and feasts. The Ruthenian man can, if he would so desire, follow the rite of his Latin wife, and for him it will likewise be licit to conform to the rite of his Latin wife in matters of fasts and feasts. After the marriage has been dissolved, the man will be able to remain in the Latin rite or to resume his Ruthenian rite."[72]

The decree *"Cum episcopo"* of 1914 declared: "Marriages between Greek-Ruthenian Catholics and Latins are not prohibited, but

[72] Art. XXVII: "Matrimonia inter catholicos ruthenos et latinos non prohibentur; sed maritus latinus uxoris ruthenae ritum non sequatur, nec uxor latina ritum mariti rutheni." Art. XXVIII: "Si vero vir latinus in uxorem duxerit mulierem ruthenam, integrum erit mulieri ad ritum latinum, sive in actu matrimonii, sive postea, durante matrimonio, transire, quin electionem semel factam, vivente viro, revocare possit." Art. XXIX: "Soluto matrimonio, mulieri ruthenae, quae ritum mariti amplexa fuerat, resumendi proprii ritus libera erit potestas." Art. XXX: "Uxori ruthenae, quae maluerit in proprio ritu permanere, licebit tamen in ieiuniis et festis suum maritum sequi." Art. XXXI: "Vir ruthenus potest, si velit, ritum uxoris latinae sequi, eique pariter licebit in ieiuniis et festis uxoris latinae sese conformare. Soluto matrimonio, poterit in ritu latino permanere, vel ritum ruthenum resumere."—*ASS,* XLI (1908), 9; *The Ecclesiastical Review,* XXXVII (1907), 517-518. The phrase *"in actu matrimonii"* in Art. XXVIII quoted above, is cited by Staffa ("De transitu ad alium Ritum,"—*Apollinaris,* XIII [1940], 188) to show the meaning of the phrase *"in matrimonio ineundo"* of canon 98, § 4, of the Latin Code. In other words, this change of rite is permitted to the woman immediately after the marriage contract itself, even before the marriage ceremonies are completed, but the change cannot take place before the marriage contract is made.

to avoid inconveniences which usually arise in families because of the difference of rites, the wife, during the marriage, can follow the rite of the man without a change of her native rite being caused thereby. After the marriage has been dissolved, the woman can resume her own original rite." [73] The woman under this legislation could remain in her own rite, and could simply follow the religious practices and customs of her husband, if she decided to do so.

The decree *"Cum data fuerit"* of 1929 is more definite, and embodies the law of the Latin Code, namely, that a woman in a marriage of mixed rite is free to make a real change of her rite after becoming married,[74] when the decree states: "Marriages between Catholics of the Greek-Ruthenian rite and of the Latin rite are not forbidden; but to obviate the inconveniences which usually arise in families from the diversity of rites, it is provided that the wife may on entering the marriage or during its continuance pass over to the rite of her husband. But after the marriage has been dissolved, she is free to return to her own original rite." [75]

The question of the proper rite and proper pastor in marriages between Ruthenians and Catholics of another rite has also undergone changes. The Apostolic Letter *"Ea semper"* stated: "A marriage between a Latin man and a Ruthenian woman should be contracted in the Latin rite before the Latin pastor; a marriage however between a Ruthenian man and a Latin woman can be contracted either in the Ruthenian rite before the Ruthenian pastor, or in the Latin rite

[73] Art. 28: "Matrimonia inter catholicos Graecos-Ruthenos et Latinos non prohibentur; sed ad vitanda incommoda, quae ex rituum diversitate in familiis evenire solent, uxor, durante matrimonio, ritum sequi potest quin ex hoc sui nativi ritus mutatio inducatur." Art. 29: "Soluto matrimonio, mulier proprium ritum originis resumere valet."—*AAS,* VI (1914), 463; *The Ecclesiastical Review,* LI (1914), 592. Cf. Herman, "De ritu mulieris,"—*Periodica,* XXIX (1940), 9.

[74] Canon 98, § 4. As will be seen (cf. *infra,* p. 207), this option of a bride to change her rite does not affect her obligation to follow the form of marriage as required by her native rite.

[75] Art. 38: "Matrimonia inter catholicos graeco-ruthenos et latinos non prohibentur; sed ad evitanda incommoda quae ex rituum diversitate in familiis evenire solent, uxor in ineundo matrimonio aut eo durante, ad ritum viri transire potest. Matrimonio autem soluto, assumendi proprii ritus originis libera est ei potestas."—*AAS,* XXI (1929), 159; Bouscaren, *Digest,* I, 15.

before the pastor of the wife." [76] The decree *"Ne temere"* became effective in the following year, and the decree *"Cum episcopo"* of 1914 extended the *"Ne temere"* to the United States with the result that it ordered that thereafter the marriages between Ruthenians and Catholics of other rites had to be contracted with the observance of the form prescribed by the decree *"Ne temere,"* which meant that such marriages of mixed rite were to be celebrated in the rite of the woman and blessed by the pastor of the woman.[77]

This rule was repeated in the decree *"Cum data fuerit."* [78] When this decree was renewed in 1940 the Sacred Oriental Congregation again stated the rule that marriages in which one party is a Ruthenian and the other party is a Catholic of a different rite should be blessed in the rite of the woman and by the woman's pastor, but the Congregation further added: "But if there is a just reason, such marriages may be celebrated in the rite of the man, according to the judgment and with the consent of the Ordinary of the place." [79] The Chancery Office for the Ruthenians who come from Podcarpathia, and from Slovakia, Hungary and Jugoslavia,[80] has interpreted the phrase, *"Ordinarius loci,"* as meaning "the Ordinary of the bride." [81] On the other hand, it might appear that a literal translation should be given,

[76] Art. XXXII: "Matrimonium inter virum latinum et ruthenam mulierem coram parocho latino contrahatur; inter virum vero ruthenum et mulierem latinam contrahi potest vel ruthene coram parocho rutheno, vel latine coram parocho uxoris."—*ASS,* XLI (1908), 9. Cf. Woywod, *A Brief Explanation of the Decree "Ne temere"* (Philadelphia: The Dolphin Press, 1913), p. 36.

[77] Art. 30: "Matrimonia tum inter fideles Graeco-Ruthenos, tum inter fideles mixti ritus, servata forma decreti *Ne temere* contrahi debent, ac proinde in ritu mulieris a parocho mulieris benedicenda sunt."—*AAS,* VI (1914), 463; *The Ecclesiastical Review,* LI (1914), 592. Cf. Duskie, p. 52; Petrani, *De Relatione Iuridica inter Diversos Ritus,* p. 100.

[78] Art. 39—*AAS,* XXI (1929), 159; Bouscaren, *Digest,* I, 15-16.

[79] S. C. pro Eccl. Or., 23 nov. 1940. Art. 39: ". . . Quod si iusta causa adsit, poterunt nuptiae celebrari in ritu viri, de iudicio et de consensu Ordinarii loci."—*AAS,* XXXIII (1941), 27; Bouscaren, *Digest,* II, 7; Doheny, *Canonical Procedure in Matrimonial Cases,* Vol. II, *Informal Procedure* (Milwaukee: Bruce, 1944), p. 587; Marx, *The Declaration of Nullity of Marriages Contracted Outside the Church,* pp. 55-56; *The Jurist,* I (1941), 267.

[80] This is referred to as the "Pittsburgh Greek Rite Ordinariate" because the Cathedral and Chancery Office are near Pittsburgh, at Munhall, Pennsylvania.

[81] Cf. Gulovich, "Matrimonial Laws of the Catholic Eastern Churches,"—

i.e., "the Ordinary of the place"; as this expression is usually interpreted as referring to the local Latin Ordinary, it might appear that it is only the local Latin Ordinary who should pass a judgment and give his consent in order that a Latin woman may marry a Ruthenian man in a Ruthenian church or that a Latin man may marry a Ruthenian woman in a Latin church. However, the best solution appears to be that the amended article 39 indicates that both the Latin and the Ruthenian Ordinaries are competent to issue the necessary permission. Though it is true that the Ruthenian Ordinaries are not usually referred to as Ordinaries "of a place," their personal jurisdiction is limited to the area of this country and so, in a sense, they could be termed "local Ordinaries" for the Ruthenians in this country. Also, to interpret the phrase *"Ordinarius loci"* as referring to both the Latin and the Ruthenian Ordinaries in this country would help to achieve the purposes of the amendment, namely, to remove any difficulties that may arise in a marriage of mixed rite, to accede to the reasonable requests of the parties and to prevent invalid marriages that might be attempted outside the Church if such permission were denied. A "just cause" for the granting of the required permission would be the indicated desire of the woman that she wishes to change over to the rite of the man after the marriage has been contracted.[82] The

The Jurist, IV (1944), 239; and "Byzantine Slavonic Catholics and the Latin Clergy,"—*The Homiletic and Pastoral Review,* XLV (1945), 594.

[82] Cf. Jaros, "Decretum pro spirituali administratione Ordinariatuum Graeco-Ruthenorum in Foederatis Civitatibus Americae Septemtrionalis,"—*Apollinaris,* XV (1942), 28-32. Jaros considers the phrase *"Ordinarius loci"* as referring to the Ordinary of either rite, "qui potestatem suam singulis parochis delegare valent." He contends that if the legislator wanted to refer to the Ordinary of the bride, he would have used the words "de consensu Ordinarii loci *'mulieris'* vel *'exarchae.'*" He feels that the liberty of going to either Ordinary cannot be regarded as exposing the Ruthenian woman to a latinizing danger, for the Code itself (can. 98, § 4) gives the woman in a marriage of mixed rite the power to change her rite. He also states: "Novam explicitam mentionem traditionalis permissionis, ut nuptias celebrare liceret coram parocho sponsi, uti plurimum latini ritus, exigebat mens quarundam familiarum ruthenarum a longo tempore in Novo mundo degentium proprio ritui usque adeo alienata, ut paratae essent praeferre matrimonium, ut aiunt, civile sollemniis in ecclesia ruthena celebrandis casu, in quo licentia danda parocho latino sponsi, ut matrimonio assisteret, denegaretur."

Latin Code decrees that in a marriage of mixed rite, the marriage is to take place before the pastor of the groom, unless a particular law provides otherwise.[83] At the present time, in this country, the only particular law providing otherwise concerns the Ruthenians who are subject to the decree "*Ne temere*" even now. Therefore, for example, if a Ruthenian man wants to marry a Melkite girl, the marriage should be celebrated before the pastor of the bride, and since there is no longer a "communication of exemption," the form of the decree "*Ne temere*," which involves the assistance of the pastor or Ordinary of the place of marriage, or of a priest delegated by either, and also of two witnesses, must be followed for the validity of the marriage contract. If these two people were to marry in the Ruthenian church, before the Ruthenian pastor, the marriage would of course be valid, but the manner of its celebration would be illicit. A marriage between a Latin girl and a Ruthenian man should take place in the Latin church.

As to the proper Ordinary for matrimonial dispensations, the early decree for the Ruthenians in 1907 did not discuss this point, since Bishop Ortynsky did not receive ordinary power until 1913. The decree of 1914 stated: "Matrimonial dispensations in marriages of mixed rite, if any must be sought or given, must be sought from and given by the bishop of the bride."[84] The decree of 1929

He asserts that the question as to which of the two pastors of different rites is competent to assist licitly at a marriage is a question in some way of public external law, concerning interritual relations, while the conflict of competence between two pastors of the same rite is a question of private law, "Unde benigna interpretatio iuris latini, quo gaudet parochus sponsae, ut in coniugii celebratione praeferatur, nequit undequaque aptari nostrae clausulae articulo 39 adiectae." Cf. Plöchl, "The Change of Rite *in matrimonio ineundo vel eo durante*,"—*The Jurist*, VI (1946), 297-302. In this article, Plöchl strongly asserts that the view of Jaros is correct, namely, that the amended article 39 of the decree "*Cum data fuerit*" empowers the Oriental as well as the Latin Ordinary to exercise his "*iudicium et consensum*" to allow the marriage to take place in the church of the man.

[83] Canon 1097, § 2. Cf. Piontek, "Equitable Practices under Canon 1097, § 2,"—*The Jurist*, III (1943), 469-471.

[84] Decr. "*Cum episcopo*," Art. 31: "Dispensationes matrimoniales in matrimoniis mixti ritus, si quae sint dandae vel petendae, dentur et petantur ab episcopo sponsae."—*AAS*, VI (1914), 463. This regulation is consonant with

repeated this regulation.[85] A violation of this regulation would not, however, affect the validity of the dispensation. Thus, if a Ruthenian woman desires to marry a Latin man, and a dispensation is needed for the valid or the licit contraction of their marriage, the proper Ruthenian bishop in this country should grant the dispensation but if it should happen that the Latin Ordinary grants the dispensation, the granting of the dispensation would be a valid act.[86]

The Ruthenian bishops in this country have received from the Holy See extensive faculties in favor of their subjects, in relation to the administration of the sacrament of matrimony.[87] These faculties were extended for another five year period by the Oriental Congregation on July 10, 1942. The faculties include the faculty to dispense, if there is danger of death, with a view to assuaging the conscience of the spouses and, if need be, to securing the legitimation of the children, not only from the required form of marriage, but also from every impediment of ecclesiastical law, public or occult, even multiple, except the impediments which arise from priesthood and from affinity in the direct line once the marriage has been consummated; the Ordinaries can dispense their own subjects wherever they may be staying and also all persons actually residing in their own territory. In all cases the danger of scandal must be removed and, if a dispensation from the impediment of disparity of cult or of mixed religion be given, the usual promises must be made. In the same circumstances, but only for the cases in which the Ordinary of the place cannot be reached, this same faculty of dispensing is enjoyed by the pastor, by the priest who assists at the marriage, and by the confessor, though the confessor can exercise this faculty only in the act of confession and for the internal forum. The Ordinaries moreover can dispense from impediments, with an

the previous article, which declared that the marriage should follow the rule of the decree *"Ne temere,"* and thus be celebrated in the church of the bride.

[85] *"Cum data fuerit,"* Article 40—*AAS,* XXI (1929), 159; Bouscaren, *Digest,* I, 16.

[86] Plöchl (*art. cit.,* pp. 302-303) says that the Ruthenian Ordinary has *exclusive* jurisdiction to dispense from any impediment that may exist to bar a marriage contemplated between a Latin man and a Ruthenian woman, which exclusive jurisdiction however would give way in a case of emergency.

[87] Cf. Appendix, p. 257.

equal power and to the same extent as they can do when there is danger of death, if the impediment is detected after everything is ready for the marriage which cannot without the probable danger of serious evil be deferred until the dispensation would be obtained from the Holy See. This faculty can also be used when a marriage is to be convalidated and there is present the same danger in delay for a lack of time in which to have recourse to the Holy See.[88] Special faculties are received from the Congregation of the Holy Office by these Ruthenian Ordinaries in order that they may dispense from the impediments of mixed religion and disparity of cult.

As questions may arise concerning the marriages of Ruthenians contracted outside the United States, the extension to the Ruthenians of the laws which were first applied to Latins should be noted here.[89] On May 5, 1911, the decree *"Ne temere"* was extended to the Lemberg province of Galicia. Since the Greek-Catholic parish of St. Barbara in Vienna was under the jurisdiction of this province, the decree was considered as extended to the Byzantines in Vienna. After the Latin Code was issued, this parish in practice followed the Code in this matter, and since the Holy See was aware of this practice, it is considered to have the tacit consent of the Holy See.[90] On March 27, 1916, the Congregation for the Propagation of the Faith extended the decree *"Ne temere"* to the Ruthenians in South America.[91]

In 1917 three Ordinaries of Ruthenian dioceses south of the Carpathian Mountains, Munkács (Mukacevo) and Presov (Eperjes) in Czechoslovakia and Hajdudórög in Hungary, petitioned the Holy See to extend to their dioceses the force of the Latin Code, except

[88] Cf. nn. 20, 21, of the Faculties of the Ruthenian Ordinaries, in the Appendix, pp. 259-260.

[89] The extension of the decree *"Ne temere"* to Canada will be treated in the following chapter.

[90] Cf. Köstler, *Das österreichische Konkordats-Eherecht* (Wien, 1937), pp. 10-12.

[91] Decr. *"Cum sat numerosiores,"* Art. 17,—*AAS,* VIII (1916), 107. This Congregation was entrusted with the extension of this decree to the Orientals. The Congregation of the Council, on February 1, 1908, after declaring that the Orientals were not bound to observe this decree, answered another doubt, "Whether it would be expedient to extend it to them," by stating that this question is to be referred to the Congregation for the Propagation of the Faith—*ASS,* XLI (1908), 108-109.

in the laws which pertained to Latin customs. The rescript of the Pontifical Commission which acceded to this petition first was sent to the bishop of Munkács in 1921, and was later communicated to the bishop of Hajdudórög in 1925, and he, on December 17, 1925, ordered that the marriage laws of the Latin Code be followed in his diocese.[92] The decree *"Ne temere"* was extended to the Ruthenians, as also to all the faithful of the Byzantine Rite, in Jugoslavia on June 4, 1932.[93]

There are four "closed periods" in the Ruthenian discipline: Advent, from November 14th to January 6th inclusive; Lent, from the eighth Monday before Easter to Low Sunday inclusive; from the Sunday after All Saints' Sunday (i.e., the first Sunday after Pentecost) to the feast of SS. Peter and Paul inclusive; and from August 1st to August 18th inclusive. The "forbidden times" also include all fast days, namely, the Wednesdays and Fridays throughout the year, the feast of the Beheading of St. John the Baptist (August 29), and the feast of the Exaltation of the Holy Cross (September 14).[94]

[92] Cf. Coussa, *Epitome Praelectionum de Iure Ecclesiastico Orientali,* I, 17; Sipos, *Enchiridion Iuris Canonici* (3. ed., Pécs: Ex Typographia "Haladas R.T.," 1936), p. 623; Dausend, *Das interrituelle Recht im Codex Iuris Canonici* (Paderborn: Schöningh, 1939), p. 117; Cappello, n. 925.

[93] Staffa, "De transitu ad alium Ritum,"—*Apollinaris,* XIII (1940), 185, n. 2; Cappello, *loc. cit.*

[94] Cf. Gulovich, "Byzantine Slavonic Catholics and the Latin Clergy,"—*The Homiletic and Pastoral Review,* XLV (1945), 591-592. After listing these "forbidden times," he states it however as his opinion that in this country, since the Ruthenians are allowed to follow the feasts and fasts according to the custom of the place where they are staying, and since these feasts and fasts are the basis for the "forbidden times," the Ruthenians are excused from observing these "closed times," if they are living in a community where there is no Ruthenian parish or mission, and thus are subject to the ministrations of the Latin clergy there, and also, they are excused if they marry Latins in Latin churches where the "forbidden times" of the Ruthenians would not obtain. While thus commenting on the marriages of Ruthenians, Gulovich in the same article (p. 591) maintains: "We do not hesitate to say that these canons (1019-1034) as well as those parts of the Instruction of the Congregation of the Sacraments on the investigation of Canon 1020 which are of obligation for the Latin Church, are also binding on the Ruthenians. Hence, a Latin pastor, called upon by Ruthenians to witness their proposed marriage, must scrupulously observe the provisions of Canons 1019-1034."

3. The Rumanians [95]

The first group of Catholic Rumanians arrived here in 1900, and came especially from Transylvania. As many Rumanians gathered around Cleveland, Bishop Horstmann of Cleveland requested the Holy See for a priest of their rite, and accordingly Fr. Epaminondas Lucaciu arrived in 1904. On October 21, 1906, the Church of St. Helena in Cleveland was dedicated as the first Rumanian Catholic Church in America. In 1908, at Scalp Level, Pennsylvania, the second Rumanian church was opened as a center for the missionary work in that state; a third was soon opened at Aurora, Illinois (this church today is a large, thoroughly oriental edifice and has near it its own parochial school); the fourth was built at Youngstown, Ohio. By 1910 there were only six Rumanian priests serving their people, with the natural result that many left the practices of their rite and their faith. Today there are about 7,000 Catholic Rumanians here and eighteen Rumanian churches. There do not appear to be any decrees from the Holy See concerning their marriage legislation in this country, and so the marriage laws of the Rumanians as seen in the previous chapters are to be applied.

4. The Italo-Greeks [96]

At the end of the last century, thousands of Italo-Greeks traveled to the United States from the Calabria, Apulia and Basilicata districts on the mainland of Italy, and from the dioceses of Palermo, Monreale and Messina in Sicily. They settled in New York City, Philadelphia, Chicago and throughout Pennsylvania and Illinois. It has been estimated that one-half of all the Italo-Greeks in Italy and Sicily, that is, about 30,000, had come to the United States by the year 1911.

In 1904 Father Ciro Pinnola came from Mezzojuso (in Sicily, about 25 miles south of Palermo) to serve his Italo-Greek faithful;

[95] *The Eastern Churches Quarterly*, III (1938-1939), 245; Janin, *Les Églises orientales*, p. 367; *A Memorial of Andrew J. Shipman*, pp. 204-207.

[96] *A Memorial of Andrew J. Shipman*, pp. 119-120, 210-212; Janin, *Les Églises orientales*, p. 327; Attwater, "Byzantine Catholics in Italy," *The Eastern Churches Quarterly*, V (1942-1944), 325-330.

at Easter, 1906, he opened a chapel on Broome Street in New York City, but soon opened a larger chapel on Stanton Street, where for 40 years he served his people, and offered for them the Byzantine Liturgy in the Greek language until his death on January 25, 1946. His Church of Our Lady of Grace was the only Italo-Greek church in the United States. It is estimated that in New York City alone there are many thousands of Italian-speaking Italo-Greeks who appear to the Latin priests to be Latins; the same situation is true in other dioceses, as there are about 20,000 Italo-Greeks in this country. The natural tendency of linking such Italian-speaking persons from the south of Italy and Sicily with the Latin rite must be seriously adverted to when an Italian-speaking person from the south of Italy or from Sicily comes to a Chancery Office with a claim that his marriage before a minister or public official was invalid for a lack of the prescribed form. This case must be investigated carefully lest one who is not held to a form here be declared free from a marriage wherein the rules of the Latin Code were not observed.

On February 13, 1919, Pope Benedict XV (1914-1922) erected the Italo-Greek diocese of Lungro in the province of Cosenza, Calabria, in Italy.[97] Since 1930 the faithful of this diocese have been held to observe the same laws regarding marriage as bind those of the Latin Rite according to the various canons in the Code. The Latin Archbishops of Palermo and Monreale had joined the Italo-Greek Bishop Mele of Lungro in an appeal to the Pope on this matter. They stated that since the erection of the diocese of Lungro the marriages of Italo-Greeks had been treated according to the norms of the Latin Code, a practice which had caused some marriages to be invalid; as an example of the differences in the laws they pointed out that the impediment of consanguinity was more extensive under the Constitution *"Etsi pastoralis"* (1742) than under the Code, since that papal enactment, which still bound the Italo-Greeks, proscribed marriages between persons related in the fourth degree of the collateral line. The prelates, therefore, requested that the Pope sanate the invalid marriages of the Italo-Greeks in their territories, and give permission that the norms of the Latin Code on marriage be applied to the Italo-Greeks at least until the promulgation of the Oriental

[97] Const. *"Catholici fideles,"*—*AAS,* XI (1919), 222-226.

Code. On May 26, 1930, the Oriental Congregation prepared the necessary faculties and in an audience of June 22, 1930, the Pope granted the two requests, namely, for the sanation of the invalid marriages of the Italo-Greeks in lower Italy and Sicily and for the use of the norms of the Latin Code in questions of marriages, until the promulgation of the Oriental Code.[98]

In view of this situation in Lungro, it seems imperative for the priests in a Chancery Office, and for the parish priests, who discuss the marriage problems of Catholics from the south of Italy and from Sicily, to determine whether the person is a Latin or an Italo-Greek, and, if he be an Italo-Greek, whether his marriage was affected by the above-mentioned action of the Pope. For a definitive discussion of their marriage problems in connection with marriages contracted in this country, their baptismal record must be examined carefully, and they must be questioned as to the rite of their parents if it is to be determined whether, though they came from Italy, they are Latins or Italo-Greeks.

The majority of the Italo-Greek Catholics live in the Province of Cosenza. It is to be noted that when Pope Benedict XV erected this diocese he assigned to it the following parishes with all their faithful, not only the Italo-Greeks but also the Latins who might be there: (a) S. Demetrio Corone, S. Giorgio Albanese, Vaccarizzo and Macchia (separated from the Archdiocese of Rossano); (b) S. Benedetto d'Ullano and S. Sofia d'Epiro (from the Diocese of Bisignano); (c) Acqua Formosa, Cività, Firmo, Frascineto, Lungro,

[98] This information was secured through a letter of January 24, 1945, from Fr. Emil Herman, S.J., President of the Pontifical Institute for Oriental Studies and Consultor of the Oriental Congregation, to Dr. Willibald Plöchl, Visiting Professor of Oriental Canon Law at the Catholic University of America. Cf. Staffa, "De transitu ad alium Ritum,"—*Apollinaris*, XIII (1940), p. 185, n. 2. It can be noted here that after the Concordat with Italy in 1929 the Sacred Congregation of the Sacraments on July 1, 1929, issued instructions concerning marriages celebrated under the Concordat; one of the provisions declared that the Italo-Greeks would be protected by the State together with the Latins—Capo III, n. 22: "Per ciò che riguarda il tempo, il luogo, la forma canonica e liturgica della celebrazione del matrimonio, anche per gli Italo-Greci nelle parrocchie del Regno, si osservino esattamente le prescrizioni della Chiesa."—*AAS*, XXI (1929), 355.

Plataci, Porcile, and S. Basile (from the Diocese of Cassano all' Ionio); (d) Castroregio, Farneta, S. Costantino Albanese and S. Paolo Albanese (from the Diocese of Anglona); (e) Villa Badessa (from the Diocese of Penne). In the community of S. Cosmo in the Archdiocese of Rossano and in Lecce (in Apulia), where the Latins and the Italo-Greeks are mixed together, the jurisdiction of the Italo-Greek bishop is a personal one, i.e., it extends to only the Italo-Greeks.[99]

The importance of this change for the Italo-Greeks cannot be over-emphasized for, as Charon (Korolevskij) wrote in 1927, it reduced to small importance their previous position under the celebrated Constitution *"Etsi pastoralis"* which regulated their life under Latin Ordinaries.[100]

On October 26, 1937, Pope Pius XI erected the new Italo-Greek Diocese of Piana dei Greci (now known as Piana degli Albanesi) in Sicily, as immediately subject to the Pope.[101] This diocese was erected through the separation of the Italo-Greek parishes from the Latin Archdioceses of Monreale and Palermo; it was decreed that the bishop's residence and cathedral church was to be at Piana dei Greci (in the Latin Archdiocese of Monreale), where the Italo-Greeks had had an ordaining bishop of their own rite; a church in Palermo was named as co-cathedral, and the episcopal Curia of Palermo was to assist the Italo-Greek bishop. To this diocese pertain all parishes, churches, public and semi-public oratories, religious houses of men and women, which have been, or will be, canonically erected in Sicily according to the Byzantine Rite.

There are about 20,000 Italo-Greek faithful of this diocese, in 11 parishes. These parishes are to be found at Palermo, Mezzojuso, Contessa, Entellina, Palazzo Adriano. At the present time the Arch-

[99] *AAS*, XI (1919), 224.

[100] ". . . l'érection de l'éparchie italo-albanaise de Lungro (1919) réduit pratiquement à presque rien ce qui reste de l'*Etsi Pastoralis*, au moins pour la Calabre, en attendant que les circonstances permettent d'en faire autant pour la Sicile."—"L'Uniatisme,"—*Irenikon*, Nos. 5-6 (1927), 53. It can be noted that his prediction about Sicily came true on October 26, 1937, as seen in the text.

[101] Const. *"Apostolica Sedes,"*—*AAS*, XXX (1938), 213-216.

bishop of Palermo is the Apostolic Administrator of this diocese, while his Auxiliary Bishop and Vicar General for the Italo-Greeks is Bishop Giuseppe Perniciaro, who bears the title of Titular Bishop of Arbano and Bishop for the Italo-Albanians in Sicily. It is to be noted that his titular see is located in Tirana in Albania.[102]

When these Italo-Greeks contract marriage in this country, they are not held to follow any definite juridical form. If it be objected that the Constitution *"Etsi pastoralis"* of Pope Benedict XIV on May 26, 1742, imposed the Tridentine form of marriage on all Italo-Greeks, it can be answered that the *"Tametsi"* decree has been abrogated for this country (even before the publication of the decree *"Ne temere,"* the decree *"Tametsi"* was binding on only a part of this country), and even if it be contended that this abrogation would not apply to the Orientals, it appears that the conditions in the mind of the legislators of the decree *"Tametsi"* are not verified in this country, where there is no Italo-Greek "proper pastor" in the Tridentine sense of that term. There was only one Italo-Greek priest who served as a missionary and he governed no specific territory, and thus it cannot be said that he had a parish in the Tridentine sense, as there can be said to be Italo-Greek parishes in Calabria and Sicily.

Secondly, it can be said that Pope Benedict XIV in 1742 imposed the Tridentine form of marriage on only a specific territory of their rite, namely, on Italy, on Sicily and on the neighboring islands.[103]

[102] The writer is indebted to the Rt. Rev. James H. Griffiths, S.T.D., Chancellor of the Military Ordinariate for the United States, for detailed information concerning the two Italo-Greek dioceses. Cf. also Petrani, "Fideles ad ritus orientales pertinentes,"—*Apollinaris,* XII (1939), 97; *A Memorial of Andrew J. Shipman,* pp. 114-115. The Italo-Greek monastery at Grottaferrata near Rome was made an Abbacy *nullius* on May 19, 1929; the Latins there were made subject to this Abbey, which in turn was put directly under the Oriental Congregation and was thus separated from the diocese of Frascati—S. C. pro Eccl. Orientali, decr. *"Quanta Romanorum Pontificum,"* 19 maii 1929—*AAS,* XXII (1930), 134-137.

[103] Cf. Gulovich, "Matrimonial Laws of the Catholic Eastern Churches,"—*The Jurist,* IV (1944), 215, fn. 50. It appears that Gulovich (*ibid.,* p. 216) misunderstood the position of Duskie (*op. cit.,* pp. 162-163) concerning the Italo-Greeks in Italy and Sicily, for Duskie did not assert that the Italo-Greeks in these lands became subject to the decree *"Ne temere"* simply in view of the

Thus, when they have left this territory they appear to be free from the territorial obligation of contracting their marriage before their proper Italo-Greek pastor. When an Oriental leaves the proper territory of his own rite where he had a parochial organization, his contacting of a priest of his own rite often becomes morally impossible. Therefore, as an Instruction of the Oriental Congregation declared: "There is no difficulty in declaring that . . . all the Orientals . . . in places where they have no diocese of their own can contract marriage in accordance with the prescriptions of c. 1094, that is, for validity it is sufficient to celebrate the marriage *coram parocho vel loci Ordinario vel sacerdote ab alterutro delegato et duobus saltem testibus.*"[104]

5. The Russians

Before 1905 the Russian law forbade the withdrawal of any Russian from the State Church, and everyone who followed the Byzantine rite was considered to be a member of the "Orthodox" Church, for the Catholic Byzantine rite had become almost extinct in the Russian Empire.[105] Some, however, became Catholics despite the difficulties and sanctions involved. The slight relaxation of the laws in 1905, which allowed the Russians to return to the religion of their forefathers if they so wished, resulted in further conversions. In 1906 at St. Petersburg the first Russian Catholic Byzantine chapel was opened and there, three years later, the first public church of

fact that they were completely subordinated to the Latin Ordinaries there when the decree *"Ne temere"* became law.

[104] Cf. *The Jurist,* IV (1944), 236. It seems usual for the Holy See to issue laws which require a definite form of marriage for the Orientals, when these have decided to live outside the proper territory of their rite, only after an Oriental diocesan organization of some kind has been established, as was seen in the particular extension of the decree *"Ne temere"* to the Ruthenian dioceses in this country, and as will be seen in the discussion in the subsequent chapter regarding the Ruthenians in Canada.

[105] Cf. Biernacki, *Ius "orthodoxum" Russorum respectu iuris Ecclesiae Romano-catholicae consideratum* (Posnaniae, 1914), p. 8. This work includes (pp. 92-102) a treatment of the marriage laws of the Russian dissidents as these laws existed at the beginning of this century. Cf. also *Fonti,* Serie II, Fasc. VII, caput XIV, for a treatment of these laws, which are substantially the same as the early legislation of the East, as was seen in the first chapter.

the Pure Russian-Byzantine rite (which Pope Pius X accepted in 1905) was opened to the public. In 1910 Pope Pius X entrusted to the Ukrainian Metropolitan of Lemberg, Andrew Sheptycky, the care of the Eastern Rite Catholics in the Russian Empire. However, during World War I, the archbishop was captured by the Russians and sent into exile; freed in 1917 on the overthrow of the Russian regime, he gathered at St. Petersburg all the Catholic priests of the eastern rites at an eparchial synod. In this synod, in virtue of faculties received from Rome, he appointed Leonidas Fedorow as exarch of Russia. In this synod it was decreed that the early Eastern Canon Law was to be observed as taken from the *Canons of the Apostles,* the ecumenical and local councils, those writings of the Fathers which in the modern day were held as obligatory and useful for the entire Eastern Church; but the disciplinary laws of the Roman pontiffs and of the ecumenical councils following the seventh Council (II Nicaea, 787) were considered as binding for the Orientals only when the obligation was clearly indicated.[106]

In 1923 came the Bolshevist religious persecution, which was directed with particular emphasis against these Russian Oriental Catholics; the exarch and all his priests were put into prison and every Eastern Catholic Church was closed. In 1925 Pope Pius XI (1922-1939) instituted the Commission for Russia, which was to have charge of everything pertaining to the Catholic Russians, whether they lived in or out of Russia.[107] This Commission, which was joined to the Oriental Congregation, was made a separate and independent

[106] Cf. Herman, in *Fonti,* Serie II, Fasc. VI, pp. 96-97, for a summary of the 68 decrees of this synod.

[107] *AAS,* XVIII (1926), 62. Pope Pius XI has been called "The Pope of Russia." He founded the Russian College of St. Theresa of the Child Jesus at Rome, and proclaimed the young saint as the special Patroness of Russia. Soon after his accession to the papal throne he sent relief missions throughout Russia.—*AAS,* XIV (1922), 417. He commanded that the prayers after Low Mass be recited for the conversion of Russia.—*AAS,* XXII (1930), 296. At his invitation many Latin priests have become members of the Russian rite to prepare to go into Russia when circumstances permit. In 1926 he founded the Catholic Near East Welfare Association to unite the papal relief efforts in Russia and the Near East.

Commission by the same Pope on April 6, 1930, and at the same time Bishop d'Herbigny was appointed as its president.[108]

Subject to the care of this Commission were all the inhabitants of the Soviet Union whatever their religion or rite, all Catholics who pertained to the Russian hierarchy, all refugees from Russia whatever their religion or rite until they had established themselves in another country, and also all works and institutes which had as their purpose the assistance of Russian subjects.[109] All marriage questions concerning Russians of any religion or rite were referred to this Commission.

Bishop d'Herbigny called a meeting of the Russian Catholic priests to secure uniformity; this meeting was held in October, 1930, under the presidency of Bishop Bucys.[110] Resolutions were passed concerning the conservation of the purity of their rite, the avoidance of any Latinization, the exercises of piety to be carried out by the clergy and the faithful, the various parochial duties, and finally regarding the foundation of a Catholic Russian periodical and press. The rules concerning marriage were not mentioned expressly, but only in a general way, in the sense that they decreed that the Oriental traditions in Canon Law were to be retained.[111]

An important change in the province of the Commission was made by Pope Pius XI by means of a *Motu proprio* issued on December 21, 1934.[112] The Commission for Russia had been entrusted with all matters pertaining to the Russians, whether they lived in or out of Russia. Thenceforth only those matters and cases which pertain

[108] *Motu proprio, "Inde ab inito Pontificatu,"—AAS,* XXII (1930), 153-154.

[109] Cf. the *Animadversiones* of Principi concerning the *Motu proprio "Inde ab inito Pontificatu,"* in *Apollinaris,* III (1930), 354-358.

[110] It can be noted that Bishop Bucys came to the United States in December, 1932, to consider the petition of certain Russian Orthodox priests who desired to submit to the Holy See. On June 4, 1933, at the Chapel of the Holy Ghost at Graymoor, New York, he received into the Church Vladimir Alexandrof (d. 1945), Archbishop of the Russian Orthodox Church on the Pacific Coast; while on his visit here, Bishop Bucys also received other Russian Orthodox priests into the Church.

[111] Cf. *Orientalia Christiana,* XXII (1931), 125-131, for a French version of the rules passed at this meeting.

[112] *"Quam sollicita,"—AAS,* XXVII (1935), 65-67. For a summary of this document, cf. Bouscaren, *Digest,* II, 110.

to Russians who are in their own country were to be reserved to the Commission, without prejudice to the authority and right of the Sacred Oriental Congregation according to canon 257.[113] This revised Commission was annexed to the Sacred Congregation for Extraordinary Ecclesiastical Affairs, whose Secretary was to be the President of the Commission.

Through the same *Motu proprio* a special "Section" was created within the Oriental Congregation to care for all those who, throughout the world, follow the Slavic rite (which is called the Slavic-Byzantine). Therefore this "Section" was thenceforth to have in its charge all those Russians who had left their country, and who had formerly been subject to the care of the "Commission for Russia." [114]

The number of Russian Catholics in the United States has been small.[115] In November, 1935, Fr. Michael Nedtochin was invited by Archbishop Cantwell of Los Angeles to open a Russian Catholic mission in that city. While in Lithuania in 1939, Fr. Nedtochin was caught in the invasion, was later rescued, and in 1945 was in Italy. In his absence Fr. John Ryder, a British Jesuit, who had worked in Esthonia and Rome, was asked to care for this mission, which looks after the spiritual interests of the Ruthenians as well as the Russians, since a Ruthenian church has not as yet been established.

In 1936 Fr. Andrew Rogosh began to use the chapel attached to the former St. Patrick's Cathedral as the Russian Catholic Chapel of St. Michael to serve the Russians Catholics, about fifty in number, in the New York City area.

Dalpiaz points out the difficulties in considering the validity or

[113] "Itaque . . . statuimus . . . ea tantummodo negotia et causas, quae ad Russos pertinent qui in patrio solo degunt, 'Commissioni pro Russia' reservare ac concredere, incolumni tamen Sacrae Congregationis pro Ecclesia Orientali auctoritate ac iure ad norman canonis 257."—*AAS,* XXVII (1935), 66.

[114] "Decernimus itidem ut apud Sacram Congregationem pro Ecclesia Orientali pecularis constituatur 'Sectio' iis quidem omnibus addicta qui, ubicumque terrarum degentes, ritum slavicum (quem slavicum-byzantinum vocant) profiteantur, atque ideo iis quoque a Russiarum gente, qui extorres procul domo versentur, quique adhuc usque 'Commissioni pro Russia' subiiciebantur"—*loc. cit.*

[115] Cf. *The Eastern Churches Quarterly,* III (1938-1939), 244.

invalidity of marriages on the part of Russian schismatics because of the Soviet conception of the temporary nature of marriage.[116] He admits that this is a most difficult question because of the many circumstances involved. In Russia at this time (1933) marriages had merely to be recorded. No one asked the parties for a public expression of their marital consent, and the whole ceremony consisted in the inscribing of the names on the marriage register. It is difficult to grasp the minimum of marital consent on the part of two Russians, as needed for the validity of their marriage contract, for it appears that the Russian attitude on marriage implied much more than a simple error regarding the nature of marriage, which error would not necessarily vitiate the true marital consent.[117]

As marriage was simply the equivalent of an inscription of names, as non-inscribed marriages had no less force civilly than those inscribed, as illegitimate children were of equal status with legitimate children, as the inscription of a marriage served only the social utility of a promised legal aid for securing support from a husband for the children, a large majority of the Russians could easily have succumbed to the influence of this vague type of legislation for marriage, and accordingly have failed to give to one another the perpetual and exclusive marital consent. This difficult question of true marital consent among the Russians would require a decision if one or both Russian dissidents become Catholics, and now desire to convalidate a previous marriage, or contract a new one, for perhaps they successively entered several marriages in Russia, where they had been accustomed to the easy inscription of marriage and the easy formalistic manner of divorce. Dalpiaz also declares that many dissident Russians never received baptism, and thus the question of disparity of cult would likewise call for investigation.

Jelicic considered the following possible case.[118] A dissident

[116] "Quid sentiendum de matrimoniis civilibus contractis in Russia sovietyca ac in regesta publica inscripta?"—*Apollinaris,* VI (1933), 231-234.

[117] Canon 1084. The varying doctrines of the many Russian sects add to the difficulty of judging their attitude in relation to marriage. Cf. Janin, *Les Églises orientales,* pp. 233-240, and *The Separated Eastern Churches,* pp. 101-117.

[118] *"Consultationes,"—Jus Pontificium,* XV (1935), 128.

from Bolshevist Russia flees into Poland, where he is converted and wishes to marry a Catholic woman. However, the dissident left in Russia a dissident wife with whom he had entered only a civil marriage, i.e., before a Bolshevist magistrate, which, however, they did not convalidate before a dissident minister. The Canon Law of the dissident church views the civil marriages of its faithful as invalid, no consideration being given to circumstances that occasioned such a civil marriage. Was this civil marriage valid? Jelicic answered that the Catholic Church has never demanded that marriages contracted in Russia by eastern dissidents must, for validity, be contracted before the minister of their dissident church, and that, on the contrary, it has expressly declared that clandestine marriages celebrated between dissidents in Russia are valid unless some canonical impediment stood in the way. However, after declaring that no special form is required for the validity of a marriage between two Russian dissidents, the same author states: "But it can easily happen that marriages contracted civilly there may be invalid because of some defect in the consent, about which a judgment must be passed in each case."

In a recent article Gulovich discusses two cases affecting Russian dissidents, which cases were reviewed by the Oriental Congregation on April 12, 1945.[119] In one case a Russian dissident woman married an unbaptized Methodist in a civil ceremony, and in the other a Russian dissident woman married a man of unknown religion before a Protestant minister. The Congregation decided that the marriages were to be held as valid from the point of view of the form of marriage, since the non-observance of the traditional Byzantine form does not clearly make the marriage of these dissidents to be invalid. But in both cases the Congregation indicated that Russian dissidents are bound by the law regarding the diriment impediment of disparity of cult.[120]

[119] "The Principle Underlying the Validity of Oriental Marriage Law,"—*The Jurist*, VI (1946), 39-49; in particular pp. 40-41. Cf. Appendix, pp. 264-266.

[120] It may be noted here that in the same article Gulovich reports a third case reviewed by the Congregation at the same time. In this case it was held that the Serbian dissidents were likewise not clearly bound to observe a definite form for the contracting of a valid marriage, but that the diriment impediment of disparity of cult was binding on them. Cf. Appendix, p. 267.

CHAPTER VI

THE STATUS OF THESE RITES IN CANADA

Article I. The Ruthenians

1. A synopsis of their history in Canada[1]

In the last decade of the nineteenth century the first Ukrainians came to Canada. When a railroad was built in the western part of the country Canada sought colonists to open farms throughout the west, and an intensive appeal was made throughout Europe; many thousands of Ukrainians answered the appeal, and most of them went to the three western provinces, Manitoba, Saskatchewan and Alberta. In Manitoba the principal Ukrainian community became located at Winnipeg (where the Ukrainian bishop lives). While those in the west became farmers, in the east they obtained positions in the factories and mines.

These Ukrainians were without their own priests for many years. The schismatic Russians exploited their weakened spiritual condition. There were also some schismatic Ukrainians from Bucovina who asked their hierarchy to send them priests. The reply was that they should contact the dissident Russian Church in America, which was well organized and which by an agreement had been charged with the spiritual needs of the schismatics from Bucovina. The schismatic Russian priests began to proselytize the Catholics of the Greek-Slav rite. The necessary funds for this work came from Russia, the most bitter enemy of any reunion movement. The Holy Synod of Russia, before the Revolution of 1917, had been granting large annual sums for the work of the Russian Church in America. The identity of rite and the appeal of money offered a grave temptation to the Ukrainians who were without their own priests.

[1] Bélanger, *Les Ukrainiens catholiques du rit grec-ruthène au Canada* (Québec: l'Université Laval, 1945), pp. 7-22; Janin, *Les Églises orientales*, p. 354; *Statistica*, pp. 216-219; Bobak, *De Caelibatu*, pp. 128-130.

Protestant groups also tried to compromise the faith of these Ukrainians by exploiting their nationalism, and thus tried to foster the idea of an autocephalous church. The false Bishop Seraphin was a leader in this movement which had such success that one of the Protestants, Carmichael, could boast of "having broken in 1907 from 30,000 to 40,000 from the yoke of Rome." In 1913 the pretence of an autocephalous church was abandoned, and attempts were made to incorporate the new "converts" as a group into the Presbyterian sect. Most of the people by that time realized how they had been misled, and consequently refused to serve the Presbyterian leaders, especially when changes were made in the liturgy, and when their eikon veneration was condemned.

Some internal trouble also divided the Ukrainians even after the Holy See had, in 1912, given them their own Ordinary, in the person of Bishop Budka. In 1916 a difficulty arose between Bishop Budka and a group of the faithful directed by M. Swystun about the ownership of a house of studies situated at Saskatoon; as a result, there was formed in 1918, an Orthodox Ukrainian Church, similar to that which had just been established in the Ukraine after the proclamation of the Ukrainian Republic in 1917. This new church, called "Swystun" from the name of their leader, counted almost 38,000 faithful, but today the number is much smaller.

A hard problem in the first decades was the recruiting of a Ukrainian clergy for Canada. In 1894 the Sacred Congregation for the Propagation of the Faith had decided that the Ukrainian priests who wished to come to North America must be celibates. Though the purpose of the decree was very just, namely, to assure good order and to facilitate amicable relations between the Latin clergy and the Greek-Slav, it made the recruiting of priests very difficult since only 3 per cent of the Ukrainian priests in Galicia were celibates. The Latin bishops in Canada in the meanwhile endeavored to care for the Ukrainian faithful. For example, such men as Bishop Langevin, O.M.I., who governed the vast diocese of St. Boniface in western Canada, sought priests from Galicia, financed their parishes, gave them schools, and defended them against the anti-Catholic laws of the government. Also, Bishop Pascal of Prince Albert went to Galicia in 1898 in order to obtain some priests. As a result Fr. John

Damascene Poliwka came in 1899 to lay the basis of a Ukrainian parish in Winnipeg, where there were already some 40,000 Ukrainians. In 1901 Fr. Albert Lacombe, O.M.I., was sent by the Ordinaries of western Canada to Emperor Francis Joseph of Austria and to the Ukrainian bishops in Europe to engage the help of additional priests.

In 1902 the first Basilian Fathers came to establish themselves at Mundare in east central Alberta. Their coming was the result of the travels of Fr. Jan, O.M.I., through Europe in the same year. Since 1904 the Basilians have had charge of the Ukrainian parish in Winnipeg. Yet the number of priests still was insufficient; Bishop Langevin, accompanied by Fr. Lacombe, went to Emperor Francis Joseph and to the Ukrainian bishops of Europe. Because of the dearth of priests, Fr. Achilles Delaere, a Belgian Redemptorist, with the permission of the Holy See, in 1906 passed over to the Greek-Slav rite for five years to work among the Ukrainians of the west; he established himself at Yorkton, in Saskatchewan. During the next six years, five Latin secular priests followed his example; with the exception of one, all of the latter returned to their original rite when it became easier to secure a national clergy.

On the occasion of the International Eucharistic Congress at Montreal and at the request of the Canadian bishops, Archbishop Andrew Sheptycky of Lemberg, Metropolitan of Galicia, visited Canada in 1910; he traveled among the Ukrainians of the west and submitted to the Holy See his recommendation that a personal bishop be appointed for the Ukrainians of Canada. On July 12, 1912, the Holy See named Msgr. Nicetas Budka, of the seminary at Lemberg, as the Ordinary of the Ukrainians in Canada.[2] On August 18th of the following year, the Holy See promulgated the decree *"Fidelibus Ruthenis,"* which regulated the status of the Ukrainian Ordinariate and its relations with the Latin Catholics.[3] In 1927 Bishop Budka left Canada for reasons of health, and while in Rome the following year he retired and then returned to Galicia.

On May 20, 1929, the Basilian Father Basil-Vladimir Ladyka

[2] *AAS*, IV (1912), 531.

[3] *AAS*, V (1913), 393-399.

was named as Ordinary.[4] In the following year another decree was issued for the Ukrainians because the changing circumstances demanded some modifications.[5] This decree was renewed in 1941.[6] On July 1, 1943, Bishop Nilo N. Savaryn was consecrated as the Auxiliary Bishop to Bishop Ladyka.

There are 57 Ukrainian secular priests serving their people; most of them were born in Galicia, but the number of those born in Canada is increasing. The Basilian Fathers, who had come very early in this century, also have many parishes and missions. Among the Redemptorists, the example of Fr. Delaere in changing his rite influenced his Congregation to found in 1913 some houses in Galicia, to devote themselves to parochial work, and to encourage vocations for their houses in Canada. Today the Redemptorist Fathers of the Vice-Province of Canada are almost all Ukrainians. Many other religious institutes, especially those of women religious, have helped the Ukrainians continue their own rite and practices. Among the laity, there was in 1933 a fusion of the numerous parish societies into one large organization known as the *Confraternity of Ukrainian Catholics,* in order to nourish the spread of Catholic Action among the Ukrainians. At present there are about 300,000 Ukrainians in Canada and the great majority of these come from Galicia; 35 churches and 345 missions are served by both the secular and the regular clergy.[7]

[4] *AAS,* XXI (1929), 320. He is one of the first priests among the Ukrainians to be ordained in either the United States or Canada. He was born in the Western Ukraine in 1884, entered the Basilian Order in 1903, and was sent to Canada by his superiors in 1909 to take his theological courses in Montreal. He was ordained in 1912 by Bishop Soter Ortynsky, the Ukrainian Ordinary in the United States, who was also a Basilian monk.

[5] Decr. *"Graeci-Rutheni Ritus,"* 24 maii, 1930—*AAS,* XXII (1930), 346-354. A translation of the entire decree is given in Bouscaren, *Digest,* I, 29-39.

[6] This renewal was made known in a letter of the Apostolic Delegate in Canada to Bishop Ladyka on March 9, 1941, Prot. 778/41. No changes were made at the time of renewal as were made for the Ruthenians in the United States in 1940.

[7] Cf. *Le Canada Ecclésiastique* (Montreal: Librairie Beauchemin, 1945), pp. 532-537, and *The Catholic Directory* (New York: P. J. Kenedy, 1945), Part III, pp. 138-139, for the list of churches and priests among the Ukrainians in Canada.

2. *Their marriage laws*

In its decree of August 18, 1913, for the Ukrainians in Canada, the Sacred Congregation for the Propagation of the Faith for the Affairs of the Oriental Rite decreed that only those Ruthenian clerics were to be admitted to the seminary "who in the presence of the bishop shall promise to observe perpetual celibacy." [8] This thought was repeated in the decree of the Oriental Congregation of May 24, 1930, which after urging the Ordinary to encourage the work for vocations declared: "But it will not be licit to admit to the seminary any but those who shall promise before the Ordinary to preserve perpetual celibacy; and only celibates may be advanced to sacred orders." [9] Article 15 declared: "As regards priests who come from Europe, let none be admitted to exercise the sacred ministry among the faithful of the Greek-Ruthenian rite, unless they be celibates (or at least widowers with no children), of good life, endowed with zeal and piety, sufficiently learned, and aloof from political factions." [10]

Concerning the possible change of rite on the part of the wife in connection with a marriage to a man of the Latin rite, the decree "*Fidelibus Ruthenis*" stated: "Marriages between Ruthenian and Latin Catholics are not forbidden; but to avoid the inconveniences which usually arise from a difference of rite, the wife, during the marriage, can follow the rite of the man, without a change of her native rite being brought on in consequence of such a practice on her part. After the marriage is dissolved, the woman is able to resume her proper rite of origin." [11]

[8] Decr. "*Fidelibus Ruthenis*," art. 10—*AAS*, V (1913), 395.

[9] "*Graeci-Rutheni Ritus*," art. 12: ". . . Sed non nisi qui se coelibatum perpetuo servaturos coram Ordinario promiserint, in seminarium admittere licebit, et non nisi coelibes ad sacros ordines promoveri poterunt."—*AAS*, XXII (1930), 348.

[10] This article is substantially the same as Article 11 of the decree "*Fidelibus Ruthenis*" of August 18, 1913—*AAS*, V (1913), 395. Cf. Bobak, *De caelibatu*, p. 130.

[11] Article 34: "Matrimonia inter catholicos ruthenos et latinos non prohibentur; sed ad vitanda incommoda quae ex rituum diversitate in familiis evenire solent, uxor, durante matrimonio, ritum viri sequi potest, quin ex hoc sui nativi ritus mutatio inducatur." Article 35: "Soluto matrimonio, mulier proprium ritum originis resumere valet."—*AAS*, V (1913), 398.

However, Article 44 of the decree *"Graeci-Rutheni Ritus"* stated: "Marriages between Greek-Ruthenian and Latin Catholics are not forbidden; but to prevent the inconveniences which usually arise in families from a diversity of rites, the woman may, on entering the marriage or during its continuance, pass over to the rite of her husband. But after the marriage has been dissolved, she is free to return to her own original rite." [12] The words "on entering the marriage" indicate that at the marriage ceremony the woman is free to join the rite of her husband (without any formality being required to effect this change of rite), but not before it, not "in view of a future marriage." [13]

As to the form of marriage, the rite and the proper pastor, Articles 36 and 37 of the decree *"Fidelibus Ruthenis"* declared: "Marriages not only between the faithful of mixed rite, but also between Ruthenians, must be contracted with the observance of the form of the decree *'Ne temere.'* However, marriages of a mixed rite must be blessed in the rite of the man and by his pastor." Article 45 of the decree *"Graeci-Rutheni Ritus"* made an important change when it stated: "Marriages, both between Greek-Ruthenians among themselves and between the faithful of different rites must be contracted with the observance of the form prescribed by the decree *'Ne temere,'* and hence should as a rule be celebrated before the pastor of the bride, unless some just cause excuses therefrom." [14]

The question of the proper Ordinary for a matrimonial dispensation in a marriage of mixed rite was answered by both decrees in the same way—such matrimonial dispensations are to be sought from the Ordinary of the prospective bride.[15]

[12] "Matrimonia inter catholicos graeco-ruthenos et latinos non prohibentur; sed ad vitanda incommoda quae ex rituum diversitate in familiis evenire solent, uxor, in ineundo matrimonio aut eo durante, ad ritum viri transire potest. Matrimonio autem soluto, assumendi proprii ritus originis libera est ei potestas." —*AAS*, XXII (1930), 352. The words of this decree are identical with those of Art. 38 of the decree *"Cum data fuerit"* which was issued for the United States—*AAS*, XXI (1929), 159.

[13] Cf. Bélanger, *op. cit.*, pp. 53-54. Cf. *infra*, p. 207.

[14] *AAS*, XXII (1930), 353. Cf. Bouscaren, *Digest*, I, 38.

[15] Article 38 of the decree *"Fidelibus Ruthenis"* and Article 46 in the decree *"Graeci-Rutheni Ritus."*—*AAS*, V (1913), 398, and *AAS*, XXII (1930), 353.

In the question of dispensations for marriages, the powers of the Ukrainian Ordinary are derived from the present Quinquennial Faculties granted to him by the Oriental Congregation and from the faculties obtained directly from the Holy Office (these faculties were renewed in 1945 for another five year period). In cases of danger of death, or in cases wherein grave harm to souls would result if the parties were made to wait until a dispensation could be obtained in the usual way, the Ukrainian Ordinary and the Ukrainian priests can dispense according to the norms of canons 1043, 1044 and 1045 of the Latin Code (though not in virtue of these canons themselves), since these general favors granted for the good of souls were incorporated into his Quinquennial Faculties (which are the same as those granted to the Ruthenian Ordinaries in the United States).[16]

A Canadian Latin pastor would not act invalidly in assisting, within the limits of his parish, at the marriage of two Ukrainians, for the Ukrainians are ruled by the decree *"Ne temere,"* which refers more to the territorial jurisdiction of a pastor or an Ordinary or of their delegate than to a personal jurisdiction of a proper pastor. In 1913 the decree *"Ne temere"* was extended to the Ukrainians in Canada,[17] two years after it had been extended to the Ukrainians in the province of Lemberg in Galicia.

Article II. Other Orientals

The Church of St. Sauveur in Montreal is in the care of the Melkites under the direction of the Rt. Rev. Maximos Chataoui, who has been in Canada about eight years. There are scattered groups of Melkites in Ottawa, Rimouski, Matane, Lachute, Vancouver, Toronto and Windsor; these Melkites attend the churches of the Latin rite in their vicinity. It is estimated that there are 2,000 Melkites in Canada. The parish of Monsignor Chataoui cares for all the Syrians in Montreal; it has been the plan of the archbishop of that city that a priest of the majority Syrian group be the pastor

[16] Faculties nn. 20 and 21 as quoted in the Appendix. Cf. Cappello, n. 923; Herman, "De 'Ritu' in Iure Canonico,"—*Orientalia Christiana*, XXXII (1933), 137.

[17] *AAS*, V (1913), 398.

of the parish. After Fr. Gabriel Nesher died in 1939, Monsignor Chataoui was asked to care for the Syrians in Montreal.

On March 6, 1945, the Archbishop of Montreal presented the following doubt to the Oriental Congregation: "Whether Tita, a Greek-Melkite Catholic, and Titus, a Greek-schismatic, retaining a domicile in the diocese of Montreal, validly contract marriage before a heretical minister in the city of Montreal, in the presence of two witnesses."

The answer given was in the affirmative, with the note that the answer presupposed the fact that the non-Catholic party was validly baptized, even though not in the Catholic Church; the reason given for the affirmative answer was the fact that the Melkites are not held to the Tridentine form either within or outside their proper Patriarchate.[18]

The Maronites in Canada were never very numerous. In 1911 they had a chapel in New Glasgow in the diocese of Antigonish, and one resident priest.[19] At present there are two Maronite priests serving their people, Fr. Salwanos Jowdy at Windsor in the diocese of London (Ontario), and Fr. Louis Souaib at Sydney in the diocese of Antigonish (Nova Scotia). Fr. Stephen Auad served at Long Branch in the Archdiocese of Toronto, but he died on December 26, 1944. The Maronites in Montreal attend the Church of St. Sauveur, under the care of the Basilians of St. Sauveur.[20]

The recent decision from the Oriental Congregation in answer to questions submitted to it by the Archbishop of Montreal on March 6, 1945, reveals also the mind of the Congregation concerning the form of marriage for Maronites who are outside the limits of their patriarchate. The Congregation was asked to solve the following questions:

[18] For the text of the doubt and of the reply cf. Appendix, pp. 261-262.

[19] *A Memorial of Andrew J. Shipman*, p. 235; Janin, *Les Églises orientales*, p. 568.

[20] It may be noted here that there are three kinds of "Basilians" in Canada; the Ukrainian Basilians of St. Josaphat, who have their provincial house at Mundare in Alberta; the Basilians of St. Sauveur, Syrian by race, Greek-Melkites by rite; and the Congregation of St. Basil of Toronto, belonging to the Latin rite and having their central house in Toronto.

I. Whether Peter, a Maronite, who keeps his domicile in the diocese of Montreal, and Mary, who was baptized in a heretical sect and who has a domicile in the diocese of Philadelphia in the United States, validly contract marriage when the marriage is witnessed by a civil official in New York, in the presence of two witnesses.

II. Whether Peter, a Maronite, who keeps his domicile in the diocese of Montreal, and Catherine, a Greek-schismatic, who has a domicile in the diocese of Brooklyn in the United States, validly contract marriage when the marriage is witnessed and blessed by an Oriental schismatic bishop in the city of Brooklyn: (1) in the presence of only one witness: (2) in the presence of at least two witnesses.

The Oriental Congregation on April 12, 1945, answered that it is to be noted that the Tridentine form for the celebration of marriage is in force among the Maronites not precisely as the law of the Council of Trent, which does actually affect the Maronites, but in the sense that the Tridentine law was received by them and adopted with the consent of the Holy See, in such a way that their marriage must be celebrated, under pain of nullity, "before the pastor and at least two witnesses"; this form of marriage however obliges only those Maronites who are within the confines of their proper patriarchate, and not those outside it. The Congregation then decided in favor of the validity of the marriage, but added that this answer presumed that the Protestant party was validly baptized.[21]

There do not appear to be any other Oriental Catholic churches in Canada, nor are there priests of the other rites known to be serving the scattered families of Armenians, Chaldeans, Rumanians, Italo-Greeks and Russians.

[21] For the text of the questions and of the reply cf. Appendix, pp. 261-262.

CHAPTER VII

SOME MARRIAGE QUESTIONS COMMON TO ALL THE RITES

Article I. Marriages Between Catholics of Mixed Rite in the United States and in Canada

As there is no "communication of exemption" in a marriage which involves those who are held to the use of the Latin form for the contracting of a valid marriage, the various canons of the Latin Code concerning the marriage ceremony itself and the recording of it must be followed if an Oriental desires to marry a Latin.[1] Every Latin Catholic who is held to the canonical form of marriage must marry before the pastor or ordinary of the place in which the marriage is contracted, or before a priest delegated by either, and at least two witnesses. The Ruthenians also, in this country and in Canada, must observe this essential form, since the decree *"Ne temere"* which requires this canonical form has been extended to them, as was shown in the two previous chapters. There is likewise no "communication of exemption" under the decree *"Ne temere."*[2] Thus, any person wishing to marry either a Latin or a Ruthenian in this country or in Canada must, for the validity of the marriage contract, express the matrimonial consent before the pastor or ordinary of the place where the marriage is contracted, or before a priest delegated by either, and at least two witnesses.

[1] Lib. III, Caput VI, *De forma celebrationis matrimonii*, canons 1094-1103. Herman ("Quibus normis matrimonium regatur quod inter fideles diversi ritus contrahitur,"—*Analecta Gregoriana*, Vol. IX, *Miscellanea Vermeersch*, I, 248) stated: Matrimonium quod contrahitur inter latinum et orientalem, secundum ius hodie vigens subicitur normis Codicis Iuris Canonici."

[2] Cf. the reply of the Congregation of the Council on March 28, 1908, ad I um—*ASS*, XLI (1908), 287-288. For a summary of the canonical discussions, which arose soon after the *"Ne temere"* was issued on August 2, 1907, as to whether Orientals who were exempt from any certain form of marriage communicated this exemption to a Latin, cf. Boudinhon, *Le Mariage et les Fiançailles* (Paris, 1912), nn. 107-108.

The Latin Code expressly mentions Orientals in relation to the form of marriage, but merely states that they are bound by the canonical form of marriage "if they contract with Latins who are bound by this form." [3] The Latin Code does not consider Orientals who marry among themselves, since the question of their form of marriage belongs to their own discipline.[4] The Latin Code also does not mention Orientals in connection with a marriage which they might contract with those who are *"ab acatholicis nati,"* [5] but according to a private reply received by the Apostolic Delegate to the United States from the Oriental Congregation on July 9, 1942, those who are *"ab acatholicis nati"* are not bound by the Latin form of marriage when they contract a marriage with Orientals who likewise are not bound by any prescribed form for the contracting of a valid marriage.[6]

Besides these main principles which affect the validity of a marriage, there remain for consideration the questions of the licit assistance at marriage when an Oriental person contracts marriage with a Latin person. The Latin Code provides that "marriages of Catholics of mixed rite shall be celebrated in the rite of the man and before his pastor, unless a particular law provides otherwise." [7] Particular prescriptions have been issued by the Holy See for the Ruthenians in this country and in Canada, as has been shown in the two previous chapters, whereby the marriage which involves a Ruthenian is to take place before the pastor of the bride and in his rite.[8] Thus in this country and in Canada a marriage between

[3] Canon 1099, § 1, 3°.

[4] Thus Noldin (*Summa Theologiae Moralis,* recognitum et emendatum a A. Schmitt [25. ed., 3 vols., Oeniponte, 1938], III, *De Sacramentis,* n. 644, 2, A) seems inaccurate in stating: "Non tenentur, seu sine ulla forma valide contrahunt: Catholici rituum orientalium sive inter se sive cum acatholico quocunque (orientali vel latino) matrimonium ineunt."

[5] Cf. canon 1099, § 2.

[6] Bouscaren, *Digest,* II, 338; *The Jurist,* II (1942), 399. Cf. Wouters, *Manuale Theologiae Moralis* (2 vols., Brugis: Beyaert, 1933), II, p. 584, nota 6; Rossi, *De Matrimonii Celebratione* (Romae, 1924), n. 45.

[7] Canon 1097, § 2.

[8] Cf. *supra,* p. 178, for the legislation affecting the Ruthenians in the United States, and p. 200 for that affecting them in Canada.

a Latin or Oriental man (whether Ruthenian or not) and a Ruthenian woman is to take place in her church. A marriage between a Ruthenian man and a Latin woman is to take place in the Latin church. A marriage between a non-Ruthenian Oriental man and a Latin woman is to take place in the church of the man.

If a Latin woman desires to marry a man of a non-Ruthenian Oriental rite, e.g., an Armenian, it is clear that the marriage must be contracted according to the juridical form prescribed for the Latins in virtue of canon 1099, § 1, 3°, but this possible marriage gives rise to the question as to what ritual and what liturgical ceremonies are to be followed. As there is no particular law providing otherwise for this country and Canada, a marriage between a Latin woman and an Armenian man should be celebrated before the pastor of the man and in the rite of the man. The ritual and liturgy of the Armenian pastor can be used as long as the canonical minimum is observed at the ceremony, namely, that the priest ask and receive the parties' consent before two witnesses. However, if an Armenian man desired to marry a Ruthenian woman, the marriage is to be celebrated before the pastor of the woman and in the Ruthenian rite. If the man is the Ruthenian and the woman is the Armenian, the marriage is to be celebrated before the Armenian pastor and according to his rite.[9] Also, lest the rite of one party be disregarded, and for the purpose of precluding all possible conflict between diverse customs, the "forbidden times" of each party should be carefully observed.

Another important question in marriages of mixed rite is the possible change of rite on the part of the woman in connection with the marriage, for the Latin Code declares that she has the option to change over to the rite of her husband as she enters the marriage or while the marriage lasts.[10] Two questions can be asked in this matter. Does this option of changing her rite affect the obligation of the woman to follow the canonical form of marriage as prescribed

[9] The priest must likewise ask and receive the consent of those who are subject to the decree *Ne temere,* for Article IV, 3, of the decree declared, concerning the officiating priests: ". . . dummodo invitati ac rogati . . . requirant excipiantque contrahentium consensum."—*ASS,* XL (1907), 528; *Fonti,* XI, n. 506.

[10] Canon 98, § 4.

for her in her native rite? Can she change her rite before the marriage, or must the change take place only after she is actually married? In answer to the first question, on April 29, 1940, the Commission for the Interpretation of the Code answered in the affirmative to the following doubt: "Whether a woman of the Latin rite who, in virtue of canon 98, § 4, declares that she wishes to transfer *"in matrimonio ineundo"* to the Oriental rite of the man, is still bound by the form for the celebration of marriage as mentioned in canon 1099, § 1, 3°." [11]

Staffa, in discussing this response,[12] answers the second question by declaring that the woman before the ceremony can manifest her intention of changing over to the rite of her husband, and then the transfer to his rite would follow the marriage as an immediate effect of the actual marriage contract, even before all the ceremonies connected with the marriage are completed. Thus he interprets the words *"in matrimonio ineundo"* as indicating that there would be hardly a moment when the wife would not pertain to the rite of her husband.[13] The woman can go over to the rite of the man at any time until the marriage is dissolved; after the marriage is dissolved she may return to her former rite, unless a particular law provides otherwise.[14]

[11] *AAS,* XXXII (1940), 212; Bouscaren, *Digest,* II, 49.

[12] "De transitu ad alium Ritum,"—*Apollinaris,* XIII (1940), 182-189.

[13] "Nullum aut fere adest momentum in quo uxor ad ritum viri non pertineat."—*art. cit.,* p. 188. In other words, as the *"mulier"* becomes the *"uxor"* she passes over to the rite of her husband, but not before. Herman stated: ". . . transitus si non tempore, ordine saltem sequitur matrimonium, cum ex canone 98 permittatur transitus non sponsae quae matrimonium initura sit, sed uxori, uxor autem non sit nisi contracto matrimonio. Accedit quod in hac quoque sententia can. 98, § 4 optimam habet explicationem. Transitus enim 'in ineundo matrimonio' fieri dicitur propterea quod a primo momento matrimonii uxor mariti ritui adscripta, ita, ut nullo temporis momento hunc ritum non sequatur."—"De ritu mulieris,"—*Periodica,* XXIX (1940), 12. Cf. the words "sive ab ipso principio matrimonii sive postea" used by the Syrian Synod of 1888 (cf. *supra,* p. 123) to show that the change of rite on the part of the woman can be effected only when married life begins or thereafter.

[14] Canon 98, § 4. Cf. *supra,* p. 112, the discussion regarding the Italo-Greeks, where mention was made of the article by De Clercq, "De ritu et adscriptione ritui apud Orientales Catholicos,"—*Ephemerides Liturgicae,* XLVI (1932), 473-480. De Clercq shows that the provision in the Constitution *"Etsi pastoralis"* against the return to her native rite on the part of an Italo-Greek woman who

In a marriage between persons of different rites, if one party is bound by an impediment which in the rite of the other does not exist, a dispensation must nevertheless be secured to prevent an invalid or illicit marriage, depending on whether the impediment is a diriment or impedient one. For example, if a Latin desires to marry an Oriental, and they are related in a degree of consanguinity which in its nature as an impediment to marriage has been abolished by the Latin Code, but which in the rite of the Oriental is a diriment impediment, the dispensation from the impediment must be secured for the validity of the marriage.[15]

had transferred to the rite of her Latin husband (VIII, § 9: ". . . Graeca uxor potest, si velit, sequi ritum mariti Latini, post cuius obitum ad ritum Graecum redire nequeat") is still in effect. The *"Concordia"* for the Ruthenian and the Latin clergy in Galicia, issued by the Congregation for the Propagation of the Faith on October 6, 1863 (*Fontes*, n. 4859), did not encourage any change of rite in a marriage between a Latin and a Ruthenian. The Syrian Synod of 1888 expressly forbade the woman to return to her former rite while the husband lived; after his death, however, she was free to do so (cf. *supra*, p. 123). The Armenian Council in 1911 declared (Decree n. 622): "In casu matrimonii ritus promiscui, mulieri integrum erit ut ad ritum viri, vel ineundo matrimonium, vel durante matrimonio, transeat; matrimonio autem soluto, resumendi proprii ritus libera erit potestas."

[15] Herman ("Quibus normis matrimonium regatur quod inter fideles diversi ritus contrahitur,"—*Analecta Gregoriana*, Vol. IX, *Miscellanea Vermeersch*, I, 243) gives the example of a Ruthenian man who is related in the fourth degree touching the third of the collateral line (Latin computation) to a Latin woman whom he desires to marry. This degree constitutes a diriment impediment for him, though not for her, that is, not according to her rite, though she becomes bound *"ratione contractus"* in her desire to marry the Ruthenian man. Herman first presents the view of those who argue that the exemption of the woman from this impediment, in virtue of the Latin Code, is communicated to the man because of the "individuality" of the marriage contract. The proponents of this view present the analogy of the communication of the exemption which one party would derive, under the common interpretation of the decree *"Tametsi,"* from the other party. If one party is exempt from the form decreed by the *"Tametsi,"* the other would not be held. Herman declares however: "Verum haec sententia non videtur admittenda." He says that, if one considers the nature of the case, "potius communicatio impedimenti, non libertatis, consequitur." He asserts that the capacity (*habilitas*) of one party cannot cancel out the incapacity (*inhabilitas*) of the other party, for if one party to a contract is unable to make that contract, the ability of the other party to do so does not make him to share the same ability. No rite

If two Orientals, or one Oriental and a non-Catholic, approach a local Latin pastor in this country or in Canada and request that he assist at their marriage, may he proceed to witness this marriage? He should persuade them to go to their own Oriental priest, if such a priest is not a considerable distance removed from their homes. But if in their refusal to go to their own priest they appear to have a reasonable cause for wanting to celebrate the marriage in the Latin church, may he validily assist at their marriage? It appears that he can validly witness their marriage, for the Latin Code simply declares that the local pastor can validly assist at the marriages of non-subjects if he stays within the limits of his own territory.[16] Also, in an Instruction of 1935 in answer to a question from the Apostolic Delegate to the United States the Oriental Congregation declared in part: "There is no difficulty in declaring that the Maronites, as all Orientals for that matter, in places where they have no diocese of their own can contract marriage in accordance with the prescriptions of c. 1094, that is, for validity it is sufficient to celebrate the marriage *coram parocho vel loci ordinario vel sacerdote ab alterutro delegato et duobus saltem testibus.*"[17]

If the two Orientals are Ruthenians, then simply for the validity of the marriage contract the Latin pastor could proceed to the marriage, inasmuch as the Ruthenians in this country and in Canada have been put under the general prescriptions of the decree *"Ne temere,"* and that decree makes no demand that constrains the parties to seek their *proper* pastor for the validity of the marriage contract, while at

in the Church, he declares, can exempt a person of another rite from the laws of that other rite (though of course the supreme authority of the Church could enact legislation to that effect). He adds that the principle of the communication of liberty was unknown in the East except in those regions where it was admitted in relation to the Tridentine form of marriage when the latter became binding on the Orientals, and that even in questions of the form of marriage this communication has been abolished in virtue of canon 1099 if a Latin Catholic is involved in the marriage. He asserts also that in the past any communication of exemption was verified only in relation to the "impediment" of clandestinity, and not for the strictly canonical impediments to marriage.

[16] Canon 1095, § 1, 2°.

[17] *The Jurist*, IV (1944), 235-236.

the same time the Latin pastor may validly marry non-subjects if he remains within his own parochial territory. The main change in the decree *"Ne temere"* from the decree *"Tametsi"* was its elimination of the absolute need of going to a particular pastor for the validity of the contracted marriage. The Latin pastor should persuade the Ruthenians to go to a church of their own rite, but if the circumstances will not permit this, and especially if there appears to be danger that the marriage will be contracted outside the Church if he refuses to assist at it, the Latin pastor may proceed to assist validly at the wedding. In an emergency, if there is not sufficient time for obtaining the permission of the bride's pastor, or of the groom's pastor, the permission can be presumed. But usually the parties will not have their records of baptism and the adequate proofs of their free status. Hence, while the parties are procuring these records (or while the priest obtains these for them), there will normally be sufficient time for obtaining the requisite permission.[18]

In brief, to require that persons who are subject to the decree *"Ne temere"* (as are the Ruthenians in this country and in Canada) must, for the validity of their marriage contract, exchange their con-

[18] Cf. the *Votum* of Aloysius a Tabia—*ASS,* XLI (1908), 521-523. He states that if the faithful who have a personal pastor cannot validly marry before a territorial pastor, they are put into a position inferior to that of the other faithful, and also the element of "territoriality" which attaches to the power possessed by the local pastors would suffer some diminution. He shows that the innovations of the decree *"Ne temere"* in relation to the decree *"Tametsi"* were introduced by the Holy See to remove the essential obligation of appearing before a definite pastor for safeguarding the validity of the marriage contract. He emphasizes, however, that he is dealing solely with the question of validity and that one would seriously have to weigh the circumstances in any given case before one could at the same time rightfully conclude that it was licit on the part of the local pastor to assist at the marriage. De Becker (*De Matrimonio Praelectiones Canonicae,* p. 135) stated: " . . . Hic habemus maximam legi Tridentinae modificationem allatam: personali, siquidem, competentiae, substituta est, *quoad validitatem,* territorialis seu localis competentia. Et iure merito." The decree *"Ne temere"* declared in Article IV, 2: "Parochus et loci ordinarius valide matrimonio adsistunt . . . intra limites dumtaxat sui territorii, in quo matrimoniis nedum suorum subditorum, sed etiam non subditorum valide adsistunt."—*ASS,* XL (1907), 528. Cf. also Gulovich, "Byzantine Slavonic Catholics and the Latin Clergy,"—*The Homiletic and Pastoral Review,* XLV (1945), 593-594.

sent before a particular pastor would be to return to the decree *"Tametsi."*

Herman presents the following case.[19] An Oriental man who is held to the decree *"Tametsi"* concerning the prescribed form for the contracting of marriage desires to marry a Latin woman. There is no doubt, so Herman declares, that the Latin pastor of the territory where the marriage takes place assists validly at this wedding.[20] Herman however insists that one should not minimize the power of the personal pastor. He cites three of the replies issued by the Congregation of the Council on February 1, 1908 (Nos. VII, VIII, IX), as leaving intact the powers of personal pastors.[21] He states that Oriental pastors are not merely personal pastors, but that they must rather be considered to be pastors who rule over a certain territory cumulatively with one or more other pastors, and who, therefore, according to these replies of the Congregation of the Council,[22] can validly assist at all marriages within their territory, even the marriages of non-subjects. He admits however that a strong objection can be made against his opinion in view of the consideration that these replies were meant as interpretations for Latin pastors, and not for Orientals (the first of the replies concerning the decree *"Ne temere"* declared under the date of February 1, 1908, that the decree was not binding upon the Orientals). He states that this objection can be admitted, but that it does not affect the force of his argument, for at least these replies revealed that the decree *"Ne temere"* did not, in the matter of a valid assistance at marriage, circumscribe personal pastors to the subjects entrusted to them in a given territory.

Herman next discusses the canonical form required in a marriage between two Orientals of whom one is not held to any required form. If one of them is held to the observance of the decree *"Ne temere"*

[19] *Art. cit.—Analecta Gregoriana,* Vol. IX, *Miscellanea Vermeersch,* I, 248.

[20] "Nullum dubium est quin parochus latinus territorii, in quo nuptiae celebrantur, valide assistat."—*art. cit.—ibid.,* p. 249.

[21] *ASS,* XLI (1908), 109-111; *Fontes,* n. 4344.

[22] N. VIII: "Ubinam et quomodo parochi, qui territorium exclusive proprium non habentes, cumulative territorium cum alio vel aliis parochis retinent, matrimoniis adsistere valeant. Ad VIII: Affirmative in territorio cumulative habito."

(e.g., a Ruthenian in this country or in Canada), he would have to observe this decree also when marrying some Oriental not similarly held to its observance. If, however, one is held to a form other than that of the decree "*Ne temere*" and the other Oriental is not held to any required form of marriage, is there a communication of exemption in this matter in a marriage between two Orientals? Herman admits the difficulties in this question,[23] inasmuch as the laws of one rite would declare invalid a form which in another Catholic Oriental rite would be declared valid, but a marriage cannot be valid in one rite and invalid in another. After stating that the law which requires that a marriage be celebrated before the bride's pastor or before the groom's pastor implies a question of licitness, he declares that, since no certain norms have been issued on this matter, it must be presumed that the Church, which permits the celebration of marriage in a certain rite, permits also that the rules of this particular rite regarding the validity of the ceremony be applied in practice. Therefore he concludes that a marriage between two Orientals (except with regard to those who are bound by the decree "*Ne temere*") is valid as long as it can juridically be considered as valid according to the rules of at least one of the rites involved.

In comment on this it should be stated that it is the position of the present writer that there are only two forms required for the validity of a marriage of Orientals, namely, those forms which are required by the decree "*Tametsi*" and the decree "*Ne temere.*" Apart from these two forms, there is, as may be judged from the evidence seen in the previous chapters, a doubt of law as to the absolute need for the blessing of the priest or the coronation, the consequence of that doubt being that a marriage entered in contravention of these customs should not be held as invalid. Communication of exemption is allowed in the decree "*Tametsi,*" but not in the decree "*Ne temere.*" Any Oriental who marries another Oriental who is held to the observance of the latter decree must observe the form prescribed in that decree. In a marriage between two Orientals of whom one is held to the observance of the decree "*Tametsi*" while the other is

[23] "Cum res neque gravitate neque difficultatibus careat, dicam quid mihi in hac re videatur quin sententiam meam aliis imponere velim."—*art. cit.—ibid.*, p. 253.

not held to any form there exists, according to the common interpretation, the possible communication of exemption which is allowed under that decree, the consequence being that the exemption of the latter Oriental is communicated to the former. In this last case the position of Herman appears certain.

If two Latins desire to marry before an Oriental pastor, can he validly assist at their marriage without previous delegation from the local Latin pastor in whose territory his church is located? Sipos, writing in 1939, declared that he found no author who discussed this problem.[24] After referring to canon 1094 of the Latin Code, which requires that the consent of the contracting parties be manifested in the presence of the pastor or Ordinary of the place of marriage, or a priest delegated by either, and also two witnesses (apart from the case envisioned in canon 1098), Sipos mentions that the canon does not expressly mention the rite of the pastor, but that it appears that the pastor of the Latin rite is meant, in virtue of canon 1, which limits the Latin Code to the Latin Church except in certain cases. He is of the opinion, however, that the most exacting requirement of canon 1094 is that the pastor actually be a true pastor, or at least a vicar with full parochial power. He maintains that the Oriental pastors are true pastors. While admitting that the Oriental pastors have no jurisdiction over Latins, Sipos asserts that such jurisdiction is not at all required. He argues, by analogy, from canon 1095, § 2, which states that a pastor can assist at marriages only in his own territory, but that in this territory he can validly assist at the marriages of non-subjects also.[25]

He states that very often the Oriental pastor is the territorial pastor of a place with definite and known parochial lines, and that within the limits of this territory it is exclusively he who exercises the parochial power. He states that there are also territorial Oriental pastors who do not have an exclusive proper territory, but govern a territory cumulatively with other pastors. He points to the Greek-

[24] "Possintne Latini coram parocho orientali matrimonium celebrare?"—*Jus Pontificium,* XIX (1939), 97-99.

[25] *Art. cit.*: "Iurisdictionem in latinos non habent, sed id minime requiritur. Parochus loci intra fines sui territorii matrimoniis nedum suorum subditorum sed etiam non subditorum valide assistit."

Catholic parish in Budapest, which has as its parish the whole territory of the city cumulatively with all the Latin pastors. Sipos asserts that this Oriental pastor is the territorial pastor of the Oriental faithful who are dispersed throughout the whole city, and that therefore he can validly assist in this whole territory at marriages contracted either by his subjects, or also by non-subjects. He states: "We deduce this from the declaration of the Congregation of the Council on February 1, 1908, to the ninth doubt proposed." It appears however that this ninth response referred simply to the subjects of a personal pastor, and has no reference to non-subjects.[26] Perhaps he intended here to refer to the eighth doubt, which does refer to his case of an Oriental pastor and non-subjects of that pastor.[27]

Sipos also states that in a marriage between a Latin woman and an Oriental man the Latin Code in canon 1097, § 2, prescribes that the marriage should take place before the pastor of the man and in his rite (unless particular law provides otherwise). Sipos argues that, if an Oriental pastor may assist at the marriage of a mixed rite, he should also be able to assist at the marriage of two Latins. He points also to the decree *"Cum data fuerit,"* issued in favor of the Ruthenians in the United States in 1929, which declared that a marriage between a Ruthenian and a Catholic of another rite should take place before the pastor of the bride, and from this he argues that similarly the Ruthenian pastor should be able to assist at the marriage of two Latins. He admits that writers on canonical matters do not discuss this problem, but he feels that they do speak of it indirectly when they speak of pastors who hold a certain territory cumulatively, that is, there may be parishes in a territory where none of the parishes has any parochial lines, but where the whole territory is entrusted to these parishes, e.g., to one parish which is to care for all the Germans, to another which is to minister to all the Italians, etc. In this connection he refers to the eighth doubt answered by the

[26] "Ubinam et quomodo parochus, qui in territorio aliis parochis assignato nonnullas personas vel familias sibi subditas habet, matrimoniis adsistere valeat."—Affirmative, quoad suos subditos tantum, ubique in dicto territorio, facto verbo cum SSmo."—*ASS*, XLI (1908), 109-111; *Fontes*, n. 4344.

[27] "Ubinam et quomodo parochi, qui territorium exclusive proprium non habentes, cumulative territorium cum alio vel aliis parochis retinent, matrimoniis adsistere valeant.—Affirmative in territorio cumulative habito."—*loc. cit.*

Congregation of the Council on February 1, 1908,[28] as the basis for the opinion of those authors who give to all the pastors in this territory competence to assist at the marriages of non-subjects, provided that they remain in the territory over which their rule cumulatively extends. He concludes from this that these pastors can assist validly at the marriage of people of another rite, and consequently an Oriental pastor can validly assist at a marriage contracted between two Latins.

Sipos then states that where however the Oriental pastors are strictly personal pastors, having no territory either absolutely or cumulatively with another pastor, and where thus they exercise jurisdiction directly over persons or families, the Oriental pastors cannot assist at the marriages of non-subjects, and hence neither at the marriages contracted between Latins.[29]

What is to be concluded? First of all, as Herman himself mentioned in the article cited above, the replies of the Congregation of the Council on February 1, 1908, were interpretations of the decree "*Ne temere.*" The first reply was that the decree "*Ne temere*" —at that time—did not apply to the Orientals.[30] The subsequent replies of the Congregation in the same session concerning this decree ought therefore not to be applied to Oriental pastors. Secondly, the status of the Oriental parishes varies throughout the world. Sipos mentions the Greek-Catholic parish in Budapest as having cumulative jurisdiction throughout the whole city of Budapest. In Syria and the Lebanon, the Pure Syrian, Melkite and Maronite parishes are without doubt territorial parishes. In lower Italy and Sicily there are territorial parishes for the Italo-Greeks (in many cases there the Latin Catholics are subject to the Italo-Greek pastor). Other examples could be cited. In the judgment of this question, however, as it applies to the United States and to

[28] *Loc. cit.*

[29] "Sicubi parochi orientales stricte personales sunt, nullum absolute territorium nec cumulative cum alio parocho habentes, sed iurisdictionem directe exercent in personas aut familias, ita ut has personas sequantur quocumque se conferant, non subditorum ac ideo latinorum matrimonio nullibi assistere possunt."

[30] Cf. *supra*, p. 172, in the discussion of the marriage laws of the Ruthenians.

Canada, with which this dissertation is primarily concerned, the last thought of Sipos seems verified—in a place where the Oriental pastors are strictly personal pastors, they cannot assist at the marriages of non-subjects. It seems that the Ruthenian pastors in this country and in Canada, since they have definite territories assigned to them by their respective Ruthenian Ordinaries, can be called "pastors of the place" besides being the personal pastors for the Ruthenians located in the territory. Other Oriental pastors in this country and in Canada seem to be only personal pastors without a defined territory, unless in a certain case, in which the Orientals of a certain rite almost exclusively occupy a certain territory, the Latin Ordinary appointed the Oriental pastor as the "pastor of the place" to minister to the needs of all Catholics, inclusive of Latins, in that territory. Outside of such a particular case, the position is here taken that, while the Ruthenian local pastor does not appear to need delegation to assist validly at a marriage contracted between two Latins in his church, a non-Ruthenian Oriental pastor in this country and in Canada cannot, without delegation, assist validly at a marriage contracted between two Latins. It should be added, however, that even though an Oriental pastor could secure the delegation of a Latin pastor and then assist validly at a marriage contracted between two Latins (who, for example, may be personal friends of this Oriental priest), such a "mixture of rites" should not be favored outside of exceptional circumstances.

Article II. The Power of the Latin Ordinary in This Country and in Canada to Dispense Orientals from Their Impediments to Marriage

A distinction should be drawn between the power of the Latin Ordinary to legislate for the Oriental Catholics in his diocese and the power to dispense them from the impediments to marriage. An Oriental Catholic, no matter how long he stays in a place outside his own patriarchate, remains enrolled in his own rite and retains his own disciplinary laws.[81] At the same time the Oriental Catholic who is outside

[81] Cicognani-Staffa (*Commentarium,* I, 31) state: "Unusquisque fidelis per totam vitam proprio ritui manet adscriptus, nec ipsum absque venia Sanctae

the patriarchal territory of his rite, if he has acquired a domicile or quasi-domicile in a Latin diocese, or if he is only a visitor there, falls under the administration of the Latin Ordinary. As Pope Leo XIII (1878-1903) stated: "Every Oriental, staying outside his patriarchal territory, is to be under the administration of the Latin clergy, but he will nevertheless remain enrolled in his own rite; this is so true that, despite the length of time that he is away from his territory or despite any other reason, he returns to the jurisdiction of his Patriarch immediately upon his return to his territory." [82] Coussa, though he is discussing the possible situation in the East where a Latin missionary may be called upon to care for Orientals who are bereft of their own ordinaries rather than the situation in this country, asserts that according to this declaration of Pope Leo XIII the Latin Ordinary acquires true jurisdiction over the Orientals.[83]

According to Cicognani-Staffa [84] and Rodrigo,[85] if an Oriental

Sedis relinquere potest ut alium acquirat, etiam si extra territorium proprii ritus transeunter aut permanenter egrediatur. Ubicumque se conferat, sicut proprium ritum ita et leges tam liturgicas quam disciplinares omnis fidelis retinet. Ius ergo orientale pro orientalibus, sicut ius latinum pro latinis, non est tantum ius territoriale sed *personale.* Hoc principium tamen quasdam limitationes admittit quae possunt esse maioris vel minoris momenti si agatur de orientalibus qui in territorio latino domicilium acquirunt, vel per latinum territorium transeunt."

[82] Litt. ap. *"Orientalium dignitas,"* 30 nov. 1894, n. IX: "Quicumque orientalis, extra patriarchale territorium commorans, sub administratione sit cleri latini, ritui tamen suo permanebit adscriptus; ita ut, nihil diuturnitate aliave causa ulla suffragante, recidat in ditionem Patriarchae, simul ac in eius territorium revenerit."—*Fontes,* n. 627.

[83] "Latini clerici Orientales, Ordinario et parocho orbatos, administrant: 'Quicumque Orientalis . . . [as quoted above].' Quo in casu Ordinarius loci latini ritus veram de proprie dictam iurisdictionis potestatem—excepto tamen ritu—in Orientales obtinet. Hinc eosmet regere, ac causas quaslibet—etiam matrimoniales—iudicare ipsis latini ritus Ordinariis loci competit."—*Epitome Praelectionum de Iure Ecclesiastico Orientali,* I, 52. Cf. also Herman, "De 'Ritu' in Iure Canonico,"—*Orientalia Christiana,* XXXII (1933), 153-158; Arndt, "De rituum relatione iuridica ad invicem,"—*Analecta Ecclesiastica,* III (1895), 184.

[84] *Commentarium,* I, 31-33: "Orientales qui in territorio latino domicilium acquisiverunt: (I) *Administrationi et curae ordinarii latini subiacent ipsiusque subditi fiunt* ita ut et pro orientalibus valeant omnes leges ab Ordinario datae in quibus distinctio ritus momentum non habet, et catholicos ut catholicos obligant: ita omnia praescripta quae iurisdictionem vel administrationem, curam

Catholic has acquired a domicile in a Latin diocese he is held to observe all the laws promulgated by the local Ordinary, if in relation to these laws a difference of rite does not affect their binding force inasmuch as these laws bind the Catholics as Catholics, such as all diocesan laws governing the care of souls, the obligations of pastors and of other priests, the administration of ecclesiastical property, the payment of diocesan assessments, and also the laws enacting penalties for any future violations of these ordinances. The Latin Ordinary, however, cannot bind his Oriental subjects to things which are not befitting the Oriental rite such as the public recitation of certain prayers during their liturgical functions. Oriental Catholics likewise would be bound by the rules of the diocesan tribunals, by the regulations about processions and funerals, by statutes the violation of which would cause public scandal, and by interdicts, and by laws governing the solemnities of acts.[86]

et gubernationem animarum respiciunt; quae regulant obligationes parochorum et sacerdotum, administrationem bonorum ecclesiasticorum, taxas dioecesanas etc. et poenae quae contra transgressores istarum legum statuuntur. Ordinarii latini tamen subditis orientalibus imponere nequeunt quae ritui orientali non conveniunt: e. g. preces quae in liturgia orientali non habentur; praescribere tamen possunt preces aequivalentes iuxta normas ritus orientalis. (II) *Obstringuntur omnibus legibus tam generalibus quam particularibus quae ordini publico consulunt in ipso territorio in quo resident. . . .* (III) *Tenentur legibus quae actuum sollemnia determinant. . . .* (IV) *Adstringuntur denique legibus stricte territorialibus. . . .*"

[85] *Praelectiones Theologico-Morales Comillenses,* Series I, *Theologia Moralis Fundamentalis,* Tomus II, *Tractatus de legibus* (Santander: Sal Terrae, 1944), p. 144, n. 192. In discussing the subjection to the local Latin Ordinaries of Orientals who have a domicile or quasi-domicile in a Latin territory, Rodrigo states: "DOMICILIATI AUT QUASI-DOMICILIATI in latino territorio extra proprium Patriarchatum, subiacent tamquam veri subditi administrationi et curae Ordinarii latini in cuius territorio domicilium vel quasi-domicilium adquisierunt. (a) *Id ad minimum eruitur,* ut videtur, ex Litt. LEONIS XIII, 30 nov. 1894: *'Orientalium dignitas,'* n. 9: 'Quicumque. . . .' Idque tenet etiam quoad vagos, et quoad divertentes ad territoria alieni Patriarchatus orientalis. (b) *Adstringunt igitur hos Orientales* leges omnes et dispositiones Ordinarii etiam latini in cuius territorio sunt incolae, advenae aut vagi, quae cum proprio ritu sint compatibiles."

[86] For the subjection of an Oriental priest to the Latin Ordinary in this country and in Canada, cf. the decree *"Qua sollerti alacritate,"* issued by the

If an Oriental Catholic does not acquire a domicile, he is bound as is any traveler in a diocese by the laws which affect the public order, which govern the solemnities of acts, and those which are strictly territorial laws, such as the laws in the Code concerning the choice of a place of burial.[37] The Oriental Catholics retain their own laws which concern their state in life and their personal juridical position; thus, their obligations arising from their religious state, or, on the other hand, their impediments to marriage, if they desire to marry, must be determined according to their own rite.[38] Rodrigo points out that there is no contradiction in the fact that the Orientals retain their own rites and general laws wherever they may be, that they have been exempted from the general laws of the Latin Code as is determined by canon 1, and that at the same time they are subject to the laws which insure good order in a Latin diocese, since "the

Oriental Congregation on December 23, 1929, nn. 11, 12: "The priest shall be subject to the jurisdiction of the Ordinary of the place. Hence, always without prejudice to his own rite, he must obey the orders of the Ordinary of the place, both as regards the spiritual care of his faithful in the church and place assigned to him, and as regards going to any other church, parish, or place within the diocese to exercise his ministry, or to visit the faithful of his rite in the course of his sacred ministry. . . ."—*AAS,* XXII (1930), 104. The translation is taken from Bouscaren, *Digest,* I, 22. The Ruthenian priests are to observe the special decrees for them. Cf. n. 18 of this same decree.

[37] Canons 14, 1203-1242; Cicognani-Staffa, *Commentarium,* I, 33; Duskie, p. 64; Van Hove, *Commentarium Lovaniense,* Vol. I, Tom. II, *De Legibus Ecclesiasticis* (Mechliniae-Romae: Dessain, 1930), p. 9. Rodrigo (*op. cit.,* n. 193) declares: "Peregrinantes per territorium latinum tenentur tantum illis Ordinarii loci legibus et praescriptis quae ordini publico consulunt in illo territorio; itemque illis legibus quae aut actuum sollemnia determinant, exceptis normis pro celebrandis sponsalibus et matrimonio, aut sunt plenissime territoriales, ut circa electionem sepulturae in ecclesia latina. CONCLUDITUR EXINDE: *in primis,* Orientales in latino territorio aequiparantur latinis quoad subiectionem Ordinariis locorum latinis. salvis propriis ritibus et disciplina generali Orientalium: et inde plene subsunt si sint incolae aut advenae in latino territorio aut etiam vagi; non plene, si fuerint peregrini. Profecto, si plenam subiectionem extenderemus ad quamlibet etiam per modum actus commorationem, fierent Orientales peioris condicionis quam ipsi Latini."

[38] Cicognani-Staffa, *ibid.,* nota 1. Cf. Pius XII, Pont. Max. (E. Pacelli), "La personnalité et la territorialité des lois particulièrement dans le droit canon," —*Ephemerides Canonicae,* I (1945), 20.

proximate and more particular government of the faithful happens through the ordinaries." [39]

The laws of each rite concerning the matrimonial impediments are personal laws which follow the person wherever he may go.[40] The rules concerning the form of marriage are often affected by the place where the Oriental Catholic is staying. This results in view of the difficulties which would accompany a demand for a certain prescribed juridical form to be observed by Orientals of a particular rite every place in the world. A marriage impediment, on the other hand, is something intimately connected with the individual person, such as blood-relationship or affinity with the intended spouse, the personal desire to marry an infidel, the perpetration of adultery with which there has been joined the reciprocal promise of marriage, etc. The Latin Ordinary, either through his own knowledge, or in reliance on the opinion of the nearest pastor of the particular rite in question, must consider the impediment in the light of the laws for that rite, and not act merely according to the norms for Latins.

It should be noted here that this present discussion prescinds from the ample powers of the various Eastern Rite patriarchs who can dispense their subjects in most cases in their own territory. Likewise this article foregoes a discussion of the various powers of the Oriental bishops, either the powers belonging to them in accordance with their own rite, and as approved by the Holy See, or the powers granted to them through the faculties communicated directly by the Holy See. In this country and in Canada the Ruthenian Ordi-

[39] "Deinde, Orientales huiusmodi subsunt tantum iurisdictioni et legibus particularibus Ordinarii latini, non autem legibus generalibus Ecclesiae latinae, ne pessumdemus can. 1 Codicis IC. Ratio huius disparitatis est, quia proxima et magis particularis gubernatio fidelium fit per Ordinarios; ergo recte horum legibus subici possunt, dum eximuntur a iure communi Ecclesiae latinae."—*loc. cit.*

[40] Cf. Coussa, *Epitome*, I, 44-45, where he declares: "In legibus enim ecclesiasticis—sicut et apud Occidentales (vide can. 13, 14, C.I.C.)—distinguendae sunt leges ritum praecipue respicientes a coeteris mere disciplinaribus: illae respectivi ritus fideles tenent ubique (ita v.g. de impedimentis matrimonii, de irregularitatibus et impedimentis ad sacram Ordinationem, de festis *de praecepto*, etc.). . . ."

naries have received extensive faculties to be exercised on behalf of their subjects.[41]

The quinquennial faculties issued to the Latin Ordinaries of the United States contain delegated powers over matrimonial impediments, which powers are communicated to them by the Holy Office, the Sacred Congregation of the Sacraments, and from the Sacred Penitentiary.[42] The question then arises: "Can the Latin Ordinaries in the United States use these faculties to dispense Oriental Catholics who are present in their dioceses?" The same problem arises for the Latin Ordinaries in Canada.

Duskie claims, with merit, that these quinquennial faculties come from Congregations which have no jurisdiction over the Orientals (save the Holy Office) and therefore the Latin Ordinaries cannot use them for Orientals unless these Ordinaries received special authorization from the Oriental Congregation to make these faculties operative in favor of the Orientals.[43] While affirming the present exclusive competency of the Holy Office in regard to the Pauline Privilege and the impediments of mixed religion and disparity of cult, Duskie refers to the fact that the section of the Congregation for the Propagation of the Faith that dealt with the affairs of the Oriental Church had, up until the time of the Code, power to dispense from these two impediments.[44] He requires therefore that Latin Ordinaries apply

[41] Cf. the Appendix, p. 257. Though the position is here taken that in an emergency the local Latin Ordinary may use his quinquennial faculties for Ruthenians, this article is concerned primarily with non-Ruthenian Orientals.

[42] Cf. Bouscaren, *Digest,* II, 30-34, 40.

[43] *The Canonical Status of the Orientals in the United States,* pp. 178-180.

[44] Pope Gregory XV (1621-1623) on June 22, 1622, established the Congregation for the Propagation of the Faith. It was to have two sections, one for the missions in general, and the other for the affairs of the Eastern Rites. Pope Pius IX (1846-1878) on January 6, 1862, made the section for the Orientals a distinct Congregation in itself, but without its proper Prefect, and left it still connected with the Congregation for the Propagation of the Faith. When Pope Pius X (1903-1914) on June 29, 1908, rearranged the spheres of competence of the various congregations, this condition remained. In the same year a doubt arose about the competence of this Congregation for the Affairs of the Oriental Rite, whether namely it could continue to grant dispensations from the impediments of mixed religion and of disparity of cult. The Sacred Consistorial Congregation on November 12, 1908, answered in the affirmative, but repeated the

to the Oriental Congregation for faculties to dispense Orientals from their matrimonial impediments, and that "even for dispensations reserved to the Holy Office, proper procedure seems to demand the intervention of the Oriental Congregation which will obtain the required faculty from the Holy Office or the concession of the requested dispensation." [45]

In 1944 Gulovich was of the opinion that Duskie placed too strict an interpretation on canon 257, which describes the competency of the Oriental Congregation.[46] He admitted that the Latin Ordinaries receive their quinquennial faculties from other Congregations, but, so he argued, the fundamental purpose of these faculties—to permit impeded marriages under certain conditions—would be frustrated if the Latin Ordinaries were powerless to use the faculties on behalf of Orientals in their dioceses. Gulovich stated: "It must be remem-

exclusive jurisdiction of the Holy Office in any question concerning the Pauline Privilege: "VI. Se la Congregazione per gli Affari di rito orientale possa continuare a concedere dispense matrimoniali di mista religione e di disparità di culto. Al VI. Affermativamente, fatta eccezione del solo privilegio Paolino, il quale è di competenza del S. Officio."—*AAS,* I (1909), 149-151; cf. Duskie, p. 179. On May 1, 1917, Pope Benedict XV (1914-1922) created for the Oriental Churches a special Congregation of which the Pope himself was to be the Prefect. The Code however (canon 257, § 2) withdrew from its competence the matters that pertain to the Holy Office. Cf. also Ayrinhac, *Constitution of the Church* (New York: Longmans, Green & Co., 1930), n. 55, and Villien, "La nouvelle Congregation pour l'Église orientale,"—*Le Canoniste Contemporain,* XL (1917), 497-502. For details of the historical development of the Oriental Congregation, cf. Dziob, *The Sacred Oriental Congregation,* The Catholic University of America Canon Law Studies, n. 214 (Washington, D. C.: The Catholic University of America Press, 1945).

[45] *Loc. cit.*

[46] "Matrimonial Laws of the Catholic Eastern Churches,"—*The Jurist,* IV (1944), 242-245. Canon 257 states: "§ 1. Congregationi pro Ecclesia Orientali praeest ipse Romanus Pontifex. Huic Congregationi reservantur omnia cuiusque generis negotia quae sive ad personas, sive ad disciplinam, sive ad ritus Ecclesiarum orientalium referuntur, etiamsi sint mixta, quae scilicet sive rei sive personarum ratione latinos quoque attingant. § 2. Quare pro Ecclesiis ritus orientalis haec Congregatio omnibus facultatibus potitur, quas aliae Congregationes pro Ecclesiis ritus latini obtinent, incolumni tamen iure Congregationis S. Officii ad normam can. 247. § 3. Haec Congregatio controversias dirimit via disciplinari; quas vero ordine iudiciario dirimendas iudicaverit, ad tribunal remittet quod ipsa Congregatio designaverit."

bered that the Holy See commissioned the Latin Ordinaries to exercise full jurisdiction over the Oriental faithful. They were to administer to these faithful within the limits of their faculties, be they ordinary or delegated. If the exercise of these faculties was to be curtailed or limited, the Sacred Congregation for the Oriental Church should have made this clear. Would we be out of order if in this case we applied the well known juridical principle: *"In favorabilibus lex late est interpretanda."* Gulovich added that though only the Oriental Congregation is directly competent in matters affecting Oriental Catholics, other Congregations may have an "accidental" competence.

Even though, as will be mentioned, Gulovich revised this opinion, two years later, it is the opinion of the present writer that the above mentioned arguments of Gulovich are cogent enough to be followed in actual practice. There is no explicit statement in the Code, nor any official statement of the Holy See since the Code, which puts an absolute demand on the Latin Ordinaries to secure special faculties if they wish to dispense Orientals living in their dioceses according to the norms expressed in their quinquennial faculties. The Oriental Congregation must be aware of the practice on the part of Latin Ordinaries in this country to dispense Orientals, and yet no Instruction on this important point has been issued from any Congregation. In this country and in Canada many Latin Ordinaries have been using their quinquennial faculties in favor of Orientals in virtue of the "Official Note" after the list of faculties granted by the Sacred Congregation of the Sacraments which states: "The Ordinary may use these faculties . . . in the case of his own subjects wherever they may be, and of all other persons within his territory . . . ," and inasmuch as the faculty granted by the Holy Office allows them to dispense from the impediments of mixed religion and disparity of cult "their own subjects even outside their territory, and other persons within it."[47] These Latin Ordinaries, who can

[47] Cf. Bouscaren, *Digest,* II, 30, 34. Cf. however, McCormick, "The Ministration of Sacraments by a Latin priest to Catholics of the Oriental rite,"—*Conference Bulletin of the Archdiocese of New York,* VI (1928), 37-38. He maintained that outside the cases of emergency (cf. canons 81, 1043-1045), "applications for dispensations for Orientals or in marriages of mixed rites

validly assist at the marriages of Orientals in their dioceses, consider the Orientals also capable of receiving a dispensation from them, as such a dispensation would be a necessary accessory to the principal act of assisting at the marriage. This does not mean that the Latin Ordinaries can dispense Orientals without a grave cause, since the quinquennial faculties themselves limit the use of the faculties to only "emergency cases." For example, the Latin Ordinary, in the opinion of the writer, may dispense two Orientals in his diocese, who are blood relatives in the second degree of the collateral line, who have grave and urgent reasons to seek a dispensation, who would encounter danger in any delay of the marriage, and whose marriage cannot be postponed until a dispensation can be obtained from the Holy See.

Such a use of their faculties in a case of emergency is allied to the use by Latin Ordinaries of the powers granted to them in the Latin Code in canons 81, 1043, 1045, §§ 1-2. In an emergency the Latin Ordinaries can use in favor of the Orientals the exceptional faculties delineated in canons 81, 1043 and 1045, §§ 1-2; most probably Latin pastors and confessors can likewise in favor of the Orientals who ask their aid use the faculties which are granted in canons 1044 and 1045, §3, for extraordinary use.[48] The basic reason for the use of these exceptional faculties is that they are based on general principles of law which have been designed for the spiritual good of souls who are in a state of spiritual emergency.[49] If the conditions

should be sent to the Congregation for the Oriental Church, whose powers are defined in canon 257, or to an Oriental local Ordinary who has the required faculty." In this article McCormick did not mention explicitly the quinquennial faculties, and consequently did not discuss his opinion in the light of such quinquennial faculties. As will be noted in the text, the present writer is of the opinion that the quinquennial faculties received from the Congregation of the Sacraments can be used to dispense Orientals from matrimonial impediments, as the conditions for the use of these faculties are substantially equivalent to the conditions mentioned in the "emergency" canon 1045, §§ 1-2.

[48] Cf. Cicognani-Staffa, *Commentarium*, I, 29; Herman, "De 'Ritu' in Iure Canonico,"—*Orientalia Christiana*, XXXII (1933), 136; Duskie, p. 178. Oriental bishops, pastors and confessors can probably also use the favorable faculties described in canons 1043-1045 as norms for dispensing their Oriental subjects. Cf. Cappello, n. 923.

[49] Cf. *S. Romanae Rotae Decisiones*, XVII (1925), dec. xxv, p. 198. The

limiting the use of the quinquennial faculties are followed carefully by the Latin Ordinaries, these faculties will not be exercised except in a case of emergency, and such a use of the faculties, in the opinion of the writer, will be valid without the intervention of the Oriental Congregation, in this country or in Canada.

Even though the Orientals, strictly considered, are not the subjects of the Latin Ordinaries in the same sense as the Latins are, the Orientals are under the supervision of these Ordinaries. On May 29, 1925, the Oriental Congregation sent a letter to the Apostolic Delegate to the United States, affirming the fact that the Oriental clergy and laity, in places where they do not have a proper Ordinary of their own rite, are subject in all matters to the local Latin Ordinary. The occasion for this letter was the request received by the Oriental Congregation to extend the *celebret* of a certain Syrian priest serving in the diocese of Brooklyn. The Congregation granted this favor with certain modifications, and took the occasion to declare that the priest concerned, as well as other Orientals who have not their own Ordinary in America, are subject in everything and for everything to the Ordinary of the place; also, the Oriental Patriarchs and Ordinaries do not have jurisdiction over their clergy and faithful outside their respective territories, save in the cases provided in the common law.[50] The Orientals in this country and in

Rota, in discussing the case of a Latin Ordinary dispensing a *peregrinus*, declared: " . . . legislator voluit Episcopcs vi Codicis tanta munitos esse potestate, ut, quoties utilitas Ecclesiae et animarum salus id requirat, communis legis rigorem temperare et iustas dispensationes largiri aeque opportuneque valeant." It seems that the same can be said if an Oriental in this country or in Canada would find himself in the situation described in canons 1043 and 1045, §§ 1-2. Rodrigo, however, doubts that these faculties can be used. In discussing the application of the "favorable participation of the Orientals in certain favor-granting laws in the Latin Code," he states: "Ex benigna allegata sententia, extendenda est ulterius memorata iuris favorabilis participatio, non solum ad facultates in periculo mortis circa reservata cuivis sacerdoti concessas, de quibus c. 882 . . . quod libenter admittimus . . . sed ulterius, quod valde dubium nobis est, ad quaslibet facultates dispensandi vel absolvendi in periculo mortis vel in gravi necessitate concessas, ut quae conceduntur in can. 990, § 2, quoad irregularitates, in can. 1043 ad 1045, quoad impedimenta matrimonialia. . . ."—*op. cit.*, p. 439, n. 601, c.

[50] " . . . Quindi egli come tutti gli altri Orientali che non abbiano un proprio

Canada are considered by the local Latin Ordinaries, as, in a sense, *peregrini* in their dioceses; the Orientals retain their own laws and customs but at the same time they are not independent of the Ordinaries, as they are subject to them insofar as the differences of rite will allow. The Latin Ordinaries of course cannot view the Orientals as though they were Latins.[51]

It is fairly certain that the faculties issued by the Holy Office to the Latin Ordinaries in this country and in Canada can be used in favor of the Orientals in their dioceses, for the Code emphasizes the exclusive jurisdiction of the Holy Office. Canon 257, § 2, which speaks of the competence of the Oriental Congregation declares: "The right of the Congregation of the Holy Office however is to be kept intact, according to the norm of canon 247," and canon 247, § 3, declares that the Holy Office "*alone* has jurisdiction in matters which concern the Pauline Privilege and the matrimonial impediments of disparity of cult and of mixed religion; and to it pertains the faculty of dispensing from these impediments." Therefore, the Latin Ordinaries can use their faculties over these impediments in cases involving Orientals.[52] The faculties received from the Sacred Penitentiary for the internal forum may also be extended to Orientals by Latin Ordinaries.[53]

Ordinario in America deve in tutto e per tutto stare soggetto all' Ordinario del luogo nel quale risiede, ne potra ivi o altrove esercitare facoltà eventualmente accordate dal suo Patriarca o Ordinario, i quali fuori del rispettivo territorio non hanno alcuna giurisdizione sul Clero e sui fedeli salva nei casi provvisti dal Diritto Comune . . . "—quoted by Duskie, p. 106.

[51] For an extreme view on the position of Orientals in Latin dioceses, which view would advise that they be treated as Latins in order to have a unity of rule, and inasmuch as laws are presumed territorial rather than personal, cf. Terzariol, "An fideles Orientales extra proprium Patriarchatum adstringantur impedimentis matrimonialibus quae C.I.C. abrogavit pro fidelibus latinis?"—*Apollinaris,* VII (1934), 487-489. Terzariol himself of course rejects this opinion; he does not mention the names of those who defended the opinion.

[52] Cf. Arendt, "De exclusiva S. Officii competentia circa matrimonium mixtum,"—*Jus Pontificium,* VII (1927), 120-137; cf. Cappello, n. 313.

[53] Cf. "Dubium de competentia Sacrae Poenitentiariae Apostolicae circa negotia fori interni orientalium": "Cum postulatum fuerit 'utrum ad ea quae forum internum, etiam non sacramentale, respiciunt, de quibus in Can. 258 Codicis Iuris Canonici, fideles ad Ecclesias rituum orientalium pertinentes recur-

On November 15, 1945, His Beatitude, Anthony Peter Arida, the Maronite Patriarch of Antioch and of all the Orient, in answer to a query sent to him by the writer, declared: "As to what concerns a dispensation from the diriment and impedient impediments, the Maronites, as the other Orientals, dwelling outside their patriarchal territory, are subject to the Latin ordinaries of the places, according to the Apostolic letter of Pope Leo XIII, *'Orientalium dignitas Ecclesiarum.'* "[54]

In a recent article Dr. Plöchl presents private information obtained through Fr. Herman. The pertinent reply was as follows: "The third question, to what extent the faculties of the Latin Ordinaries can be applied to the Orientals was answered as follows: 'The Oriental Congregation readily extends the faculties of Latin Ordinaries also to the Orientals, but such an "extension" is necessary that the Latin Ordinary can use the faculties for Orientals.' "[55]

rere debeant ad Sacram Poenitentiariam Apostolicam,' Sacra haec Congregatio, collatis consiliis cum Emo D. Card. Poenitentiario Maiore, respondendum censuit *Affirmative.* Quam resolutionem SSmus D.N. Pius div. Prov. Pp. XI, in Audientia die 10 maii 1930, adprobare ac ratam habere dignatus est."—*AAS,* XXII (1930), 394; *Periodica,* XIX (1930), 339; cf. Bouscaren, *Digest,* I, 174. Cf. Cance, *Le Code de Droit canonique* (7. ed., 3 vols., Paris: Lecoffre, 1933, 1934), I, n. 260; II, n. 283; Beste, *Introductio in Codicem* (ed. altera, Collegeville: St. John's Abbey Press, 1944), p. 247; Vermeersch-Creusen, *Epitome Iuris Canonici* (3 vols., Vol. I, ed. sexta, 1937; Vol. II, ed. sexta, 1940; Vol. III, ed. quinta, 1936, Mechliniae-Romae: Dessain), I, 375; Cappello, *Summa Iuris Canonici* (3 vols., Vol. I, 3. ed., 1938; Vol. II, 3. ed., 1939; Vol. III, ed. altera, 1940, Romae: Apud Aedes Universitatis Gregorianae), I, n. 335.

[54] "Ad dispensationem ab impedimentis dirimentibus et impedientibus quoad spectat, Maronitae, sicut caeteri Orientales, commorantes extra Territorium Patriarchale, subduntur, iuxta litteram Apostolicam P. P. Leonis XIII *'Orientalium dignitas Ecclesiarum'* locorum Ordinariis latinis."

[55] "Quinquennial faculties extended by the S. Congregation for the Oriental Church to Latin Ordinaries,"—*The Jurist,* VI (1946), 75. The text of the answer quoted is: "Die Orientalische Kongregation dehnt bereitwillig die Fakultäten der lateinischen Ordinarien auch auf die Orientalen aus, aber eine solche 'extensio' ist notwendig, damit der lateinische Ordinarius die Fakultäten den Orientalen gegenüber gebrauchen kann." Plöchl adds the comment of Fr. Herman that by "faculties" are meant the quinquennial faculties received from the various Congregations by the Latin Ordinaries. In a private letter written soon after this reply was published in *The Jurist,* Gulovich changed the opinion which he had presented in 1944 (as summarized above).

Plöchl therefore concludes: "Attention is called to the fact that the Latin Ordinary *has to ask* the S. Congregation for the Oriental Church for the extension of the faculties he received from the several Roman Congregations (exclusive of the Holy Office), in order to be authorized to exercise these faculties in cases involving his Oriental subjects. Thus, actual extension granted by the S. Congregation for the Oriental Church is an essential and necessary requirement for the application of such faculties to Oriental Catholics under the jurisdiction of Latin Ordinaries."

In summary, what conclusions can be drawn from these various considerations concerning the quinquennial faculties enjoyed by the local Latin Ordinaries in the United States and in Canada? The dispensations granted by these local Latin Ordinaries for Orientals from the matrimonial impediments of mixed religion and disparity of cult will be valid inasmuch as these faculties are received from the Congregation of the Holy Office which has exclusive jurisdiction over these impediments. Likewise, the faculties received from the Sacred Penitentiary for the internal forum can be used in favor of the Orientals. As to those impediments which are mentioned in the quinquennial faculties received from the Congregation for the Discipline of the Sacraments, it is the opinion of the writer that the grants of dispensation would be held as valid, until the contrary interpretation is received from the Holy See, if the local Latin Ordinaries, both in this country and in Canada, where they have been entrusted with the care of the Orientals, comply with all the conditions mentioned in the grant of these faculties, since such conditions describe a state of urgency in which a delay would occasion harm to souls; for those other impediments which are different in the Oriental discipline from those affecting the Latins, recourse must be made to the Holy See to secure a dispensation. Opposed to this view of the writer is the opinion that such faculties cannot be used without the intervention of the Oriental Congregation which must extend these faculties in favor of the Orientals, as indicated in the private information received by Dr. Plöchl from Fr. Herman, as noted above. Finally, though not all authors agree on this point, it seems certain that if the conditions mentioned in canons 81 and 1043-1045 are fulfilled, the local Latin Ordinaries, pastors and confessors respectively may exercise these special faculties on behalf of Orientals.

Article III. The Competence of the Latin Tribunals Over Orientals

All cases involving two Catholic Ruthenians, or a Catholic Ruthenian as the petitioner in the marriage case, are to be referred to the proper Ruthenian Ordinary in this country or in Canada.[56] The Ruthenian Ordinaries in a particular case which involves the taking of testimony of Ruthenians who live far from their own Ordinaries, and of testimony of Latins who also live far from the Curias of the Ruthenian Bishops, if the deposition of these persons is needed in a case before the Ruthenian matrimonial tribunal, will send a rogatory commission to the Latin tribunal.

The discussion here about the competence of Latin tribunals in this country and in Canada over Orientals concerns then the Latin tribunals and non-Ruthenian Orientals. In this country and in Canada, since these people have been placed under the administration and care of the Latin Ordinaries, their juridic ability to present a marriage case to the Latin Ordinary should be judged by the same norms as for Latins; these laws insure the common good and proper order.[57] If an Oriental were to assert that his marriage was null because of a defect of the substantial canonical form, and the Ordinary has a doubt whether this non-Ruthenian was held to a definite form, the case should be submitted to the Holy See for decision. If an Oriental was married in the diocese, or if the defendant (or the Catholic party, if one of the spouses is not a Catholic) has a domicile or quasi-domicile there, the Oriental can present a petition to the Latin Ordinary to institute a formal trial to examine and pronounce on the alleged nullity of the marriage.

If a formal trial involving a Catholic Oriental has been tried in the Latin courts of first and second instance, and an appeal is then made to the Holy See, the case is to be sent to the Oriental Congre-

[56] Cf. *The Jurist,* V (1945), 295.

[57] The competent forum in general is treated in canons 1556-1568, and in marriage cases in particular in canons 1960-1965.

gation, which will, if the case warrants it, designate a tribunal to try the case.[58] According to Cappello the Oriental Congregation has the authority to settle in a disciplinary manner matrimonial cases which have been appealed to it in first, second or third instance, even though these cases have been tried according to the rules for strictly judicial procedure in the lower courts, but still the Congregation could send the cases to a tribunal such as that of the Sacred Roman Rota, and in fact the Congregation should do so if it judges that the case should be completed in a strictly judicial manner.[59] If the case is to be presented immediately to the Holy See, or if an appeal is made directly to the Holy See after the decision of the court of first instance, then the Latin Ordinary is to refer the case directly to the Oriental Congregation.[60]

[58] Cf. canon 257, § 3. The position taken here is that formal marriage trials involving Oriental Catholics are reserved to the Oriental Congregation only when there is question of an appeal to the Holy See. Cf. Beste, *Introductio in Codicem*, p. 837. It may be noted here that according to Bernardini ("De alterius appellationis instantia in causa nullitatis matrimonii fidelium ritus Orientalis,"—*Apollinaris*, VIII [1935], 287-290), in the law of the Oriental Church the parties can, after a second contrary sentence, appeal the case to the court of third instance without exhibiting new arguments or documents.

[59] "S. C. pro Ecclesia orientali competens est circa causas matrimoniales Orientalium, easque in linea disciplinari dirimit in prima vel secunda aut tertia instantia, licet ordine stricte iudiciali apud tribunalia inferiora actae ac definitae sint. Potest tamen eas remittere ad tribunalia, v.g. ad S. R. Rotam; imo *debet* remittere, si causa ordine stricte iudiciali pertractanda videatur."—*Summa Iuris Canonici*, III, n. 337. Canon 257, § 3 states: "Haec Congregatio controversias dirimit via disciplinari; quas vero ordine iudiciario dirimendas iudicaverit, ad tribunal remittet quod ipsa Congregatio designaverit."

[60] For an example of a case sent in first instance to the Oriental Congregation, which referred it to the Rota, cf. *S. Romanae Rotae Decisiones*, XXVII (1935), dec. xxix. This case was considered again by the Rota, sitting as a court of second instance, after the first Rota decision was appealed by the defender of the bond—*op. cit.*, XXVIII (1936), dec. iv. For other cases sent to the Oriental Congregation and then forwarded to the Rota, cf. *S. Romanae Rotae Decisiones*, XXV (1933), dec. xxii, xxxi; XXVI (1934), dec. xv, xxvii, xxxviii, lvii, lxiv, lxxviii; XXVII (1935), dec. xvii; XXVIII (1936), dec. ii, lxxiv. For a marriage case which was introduced at the behest of the Pontifical Commission for Russia, cf. *S. Romanae Rotae Decisiones*, XXI (1929), dec. xiii. Two Russian schismatics had married, and eventually one of them petitioned the Pontifical Commission to allow a trial to show the nullity of her marriage.

If a schismatic Oriental, or any other non-Catholic, is to act as a plaintiff in a formal trial, permission to institute the trial must be sought from the Holy Office.[61] If an Oriental Catholic has become an apostate from the faith and desires to begin a judicial trial, permission must likewise be sought from the Holy Office.[62] If a dissident Oriental is a party to a petition for a dispensation from a ratified, non-consummated marriage, the permission to draw up the process is to be requested from the Holy Office, which will examine the merits of the petition, and will, if the case warrants it, refer the petition to the Congregation of the Sacraments, which will then proceed to act in the name of the Holy Office.[63] If a dissident

The Commission granted the request, and sent the case to the Oriental Congregation, which referred the question to the Rota for decision; the Rota finally declared that the validity of the marriage was to be upheld.

[61] Consult the celebrated reply of the Holy Office on January 27, 1928, concerning questions of its competence: "I. Utrum in causis matrimonialibus *acatholicus,* sive baptizatus sive non baptizatus *actoris* partis agere possit. II. Utrum in quibuslibet causis matrimonialibus inter partem catholicam et partem acatholicam sive baptizatam sive non baptizatam, quocumque modo ad Sanctam Sedem delatis, Suprema Sacra Congregatio Sancti Officii exclusivam habeat competentiam. Ad I. *Negative,* seu standum Codici I.C., praesertim can. 87. Siquidem autem speciales occurrant rationes ad admittendos acatholicos ut actores in huiusmodi causis, recurrendum ad Supremam Sacram Congregationem Sancti Officii in singulis casibus. Ad II. *Affirmative,* habita praesertim ratione can. 247, § 3, et salvo praescripto can. 1557, § 1, 1°."—*AAS,* XX (1928), 75. For precedents concerning the topic of this reply, cf. *Periodica,* V (1913), 100, and XIV (1925), 166. For a case involving a schismatic since this reply, cf. *S. Romanae Rotae Decisiones,* XXVI (1934), dec. xx. The case was sent to the Oriental Congregation, which referred it to the Holy Office.

[62] Cf. the general reply concerning apostates by the Holy Office on January 15, 1940—*AAS,* XXXII (1940), 52; Bouscaren, *Digest,* II, 534. Cf. also the comments of Roberti on this reply in *Apollinaris,* XIII (1940), 7-10; cf. *Jus Pontificium,* XX (1940), 43-44; *Periodica,* XXIX (1940), 149.

[63] Cf. Kay, *Competence in Matrimonial Procedure,* The Catholic University of America Canon Law Studies, n. 53 (Washington, D. C.: The Catholic University of America, 1929), pp. 74-81. Even though a *case* of a petition for a dispensation from a ratified, non-consummated marriage is not a matrimonial *cause,* the words of the question to the Holy Office: " . . . in quibuslibet causis matrimonialibus . . . quocumque modo ad Sanctam Sedem delatis . . . " appear to include these cases (the word *"causa"* usually refers to a judicial trial, while *"casus"* usually refers to an administrative process). Cf. also Hannan, "Non-

Oriental denounces his marriage as null, the promoter of justice can then impugn the validity of the marriage if the public good, in the judgment of the Ordinary, demands it.[64]

If a non-Ruthenian Oriental Catholic desires to petition the Pope for a dispensation from a ratified, non-consummated marriage, contracted with another Catholic party, it seems that in this country and in Canada the Latin Ordinary can request the necessary permission from the Sacred Congregation of the Sacraments,[65] and, after the permission has been received, draw up the acts of the case as he would for Latins. On June 10, 1935, the Oriental Congregation issued an Instruction concerning the rules to be observed in drawing up the process in the cases of ratified, non-consummated marriages,[66] but as it was addressed to Oriental Ordinaries for their subjects, and as it contains no contrary provision, it does not appear to bind the Latin Ordinaries in the cases of Orientals who are under their care and administration, though it does bind the Ruthenian Ordinaries in this country and in Canada.[67] Cappello however de-

Catholic Petitioners and Plaintiffs,"—*The Jurist,* IV (1944), 623-626; Vermeersch, in *Periodica,* XVIII (1929), 54-56; Roberti, in *Apollinaris,* I (1928), 215-219.

[64] Cf. the reply of the Holy Office on March 22, 1939—*AAS,* XXXI (1939), 131; Bouscaren, *Digest,* II, 547.

[65] Cf. *Regula 8* of the Instruction of 1923, *"Catholica doctrina,"* concerning these cases of non-consummation—*AAS,* XV (1923), 393. This rule reveals that the regulations dealing with the question of the Ordinary's competence in cases of ratified, non-consummated marriages, are not as strict as are the rules which govern this same consideration in formal trials. The nature of the process is an informative one, and the Ordinary issues no decision and does not grant any dispensation; he simply gathers all the information and sends his findings to the Holy See, so that the Pope may decide whether the favor is to be granted.

[66] *AAS,* XXVII (1935), 333-340. Previous to this Instruction the Orientals had followed the Instruction of the Holy Office for the Orientals in 1883.—Cf. *S. Romanae Rotae Decisiones,* XXV (1933), dec. xxx, p. 257.

[67] The preface to the Instruction declares: "Quo facilius Revmi Ordinarii Orientalium Rituum conficere possint processus super matrimonio rato et non consummato, necessarium Sacrae huic Congregationi pro Ecclesia Orientali visum est, pro hisce processibus normas praescribere quas praefati Revmi Ordinarii observare teneantur." For a comparison of this Instruction with the Instruction *"Catholica doctrina,"* issued in 1923 by the Sacred Congregation of

clares that if both parties or even only one party in such a case be of an Oriental rite, the Oriental Congregation is the competent Congregation, and that the process should be drawn up according to this Instruction of June 10, 1935.[68]

If there has been a marriage between two schismatics, and then, after both have become Latin Catholics, they desire to impugn the validity of their marriage which was contracted in schism, the case can be taken by the Latin diocesan tribunals in the ordinary procedure, and later be appealed directly to the Rota without the intervention of the Oriental Congregation or of the Holy Office.[69]

Article IV. Oriental Schismatics and the Marriage Laws of the Latin Code

The proposal of the following possible marriage case in 1935 aroused the interest of canonists. If two Oriental schismatics who contracted marriage before a schismatic minister were bound by a diriment impediment of affinity or of consanguinity, e.g., in second, third, or fourth degree of the collateral line, i.e., a degree which according to the canon law of the schismatics implied a diriment impediment, and if they secured a dispensation from the impediment from their schismatic bishop, then, after one or both of the parties became converted, is the marriage to be viewed as valid, or must it be convalidated after a dispensation from the diriment impediment

the Sacraments, cf. Bernardini in *Apollinaris*, VIII (1935), 501-549; he presents (p. 505, nota 3) the background and sources of this Instruction in 1935, which is shorter because there are no canons of an Oriental Code to repeat, while the 1923 Instruction repeats many canons of the Latin Code. Bernardini does not treat the question of the proper procedure if a Latin Ordinary is asked by an Oriental, who is under the care of the Latin Ordinary, to present a petition of this nature.

[68] *De Matrimonio*, nn. 764, 871; *Summa Iuris Canonici*, III, n. 337.

[69] Cf. *S. Romanae Rotae Decisiones*, XVIII (1926), dec. xxxix, pp. 315-316. An objection was made against the competence of the Rota to try the case of a marriage contracted in schism; the Rota, after declaring that the parties were now Latins, answered in part: " . . . Proinde non nimis urgenda videtur privativa competentia Congregationis pro Ecclesia Orientali quae proprie Catholicos huius ritus concernit."

has been duly secured.[70] After proposing the case, Jelicic answered that the marriage was valid on the question of form, since the parties were not held to a definite juridical form, but that it was invalid for the reason that the schismatic bishop had no power to dispense them from the diriment impediment; the marriage had to be convalidated, though no dispensation was any longer necessary if the parties had become Latin Catholics and the degree of their relationship constituted no impediment in the law of the Latin Code. He commented that the Code's restrictions of the extent of the impediments of consanguinity and of affinity did not affect any of the Orientals, Catholic or dissident, as such, since the Code did not induce any changes in the laws which were binding on them.

Haring, in 1936, changed the case slightly to consider the parties as actually related in the fourth degree of the collateral line of consanguinity. He likewise maintained that as schismatics they were not held to any form, and that their bishop lacked the power of dispensing them, so that the marriage had to be convalidated after their conversion to the Latin Church, though no dispensation was necessary since that degree of relationship in its nature of a matrimonial impediment was abrogated for Latins.[71]

Dalpiaz took exception to this view,[72] and held that canon 1 of the Latin Code does not exclude all Orientals from the ambit of its laws, but only Catholic Orientals. He pointed to: (a) the Index of the Code (while admitting that the Index is not an official part of the Code) which says, concerning the word "Orientals": "The Code does not in general consider Orientals, i.e., Catholics of the Oriental Rite"; [73] and (b) the authority of Gasparri (1852-1934), who stated that not only does the Church not exempt from any of her laws those Catholics who have lapsed into heresy or schism, but she actually wishes to bind as subject to her marriage laws those

[70] Jelicic, "Consultationes,"—*Jus Pontificium,* XV (1935), 127.

[71] "Konvalidation einer orthodoxen Ehe,"—*Theologisch-praktische Quartalschrift,* LXXXIX (1936), 145.

[72] "An Orientales schismatici legibus matrimonialibus Ecclesiae latinae teneantur,"—*Apollinaris,* X (1937), 457-459.

[73] "*Orientales* seu catholicos ritus orientalis generatim Codex non respicit, etc., 1. . . ."

who were simply born in heresy or schism, except with regard to the impediment of disparity of cult, and the requirements for a valid form of marriage, even though she possibly intends to exempt them in other matters.[74]

Dalpiaz asserted that in the documents adduced to show that non-Catholics are generally held to the marriage laws of the Church there never was any distinction drawn between heretics and schismatics, and that they are treated in the same way; he pointed to canon 1070, § 1,[75] and canon 1099, § 1, 1°,[76] where converts from heresy and schism are treated identically. He also adverted to the affirmative reply of the Sacred Congregation of the Council on March 28, 1908, to the question, "Whether in Article XI, § 2, of the decree '*Ne temere*' under the word 'non-Catholic' are embraced also schismatics and heretics of the Oriental Rites." [77] Dalpiaz concluded that

[74] " . . . Sed etiam illos, qui in haeresi et schismate nati sunt, si aliis fortasse legibus Ecclesia ob rationem commiserationis ligare non intendit, vult tamen eos impedimentis matrimonialibus adstringere, excepta forma canonica et impedimento *disparitatis cultus.* Id certissimum est, ac illi AA. catholici qui de hoc dubitant, nesciunt quid dicant."—*Tractatus Canonicus de Matrimonio* (ed. nova, 2 vols. in 1, Romae: Typis Polyglottis Vaticanis, 1932), I, n. 257. In his edition of 1904 (I, n. 308) Gasparri had made the same statement, except for the added clause, "excepta forma canonica et impedimento *disparitatis cultus,*" which he inserted into his former text after the promulgation of the Code. Cf. also Payen, *De Matrimonio in Missionibus* (2. ed., 3 vols., Zi-ka-wei, 1935, 1936), I, n. 1094.

[75] "Nullum est matrimonium contractum a persona non baptizata cum persona baptizata in Ecclesia catholica vel ad eandem ex haeresi aut schismate conversa."

[76] "Ad statutam superius formam servandam tenentur: Omnes in catholica Ecclesia baptizati et ad eam ex haeresi aut schismate conversi, licet sive hi sive illi ab eadem postea defecerint, quoties inter se matrimonium ineunt."

[77] "II. An in art. XI, § 2 eiusdem decreti sub nomine acatholicorum comprehendantur etiam schismatici et haeretici rituum orientalium. Ad II. Affirmative."—*ASS,* XLI (1908), 288; *Fontes,* n. 4349. The phrase "etiam schismatici et *haeretici rituum orientalium*" suggests that there was still a controversy whether it would be possible to have some dissident Orientals termed "schismatics" and some termed "heretics." Article XI, § 2 had declared: "Vigent quoque pro iisdem de quibus supra catholicis, si cum acatholicis sive baptizatis sive non baptizatis, etiam post obtentam dispensationem ab impedimentis mixtae religionis vel disparitatis cultus, sponsalia vel matrimonium contrahunt, nisi pro aliquo particulari loco aut regione aliter a Sancta Sede sit statutum."—*ASS,* XL

the marriage was valid because, even though their bishop lacked jurisdiction, this degree of consanguinity as a matrimonial impediment had been abrogated by the Code prior to the marriage, and also because the parties were exempt from the required form of marriage in accordance with the law of the Code.

An anonymous writer in *Apollinaris* agreed that the marriage was contracted validly, but he advanced as his reason for this the fact that the impediment of consanguinity did not exist among the schismatics before the schism, and that the impediments enacted after the schism by a dissident hierarchy were of doubtful force.[78] He cited the opinion of Maroto (1875-1937),[79] who asserted that in the question of heretics and schismatics the following points are certain: (a) until the contrary is clearly and expressly evident, the Church always intends to oblige them to laws which are ordained for the common good such as invalidating laws (e.g., laws about marriage impediments), disqualifying laws, general laws about delicts and penalties, and preceptive universal laws about human actions; (b) those who leave the Church to embrace heresy or schism are bound by the laws dealing with the matter of personal sanctification; (c) but those who were born in heresy or schism are probably not bound by the laws which concern the matter of personal sanctification, such as the laws about the observance of feasts, and the laws about fasting.

Referring to the celebrated reply of the Sacred Congregation for the Propagation of the Faith on July 15, 1876, to the Apostolic Delegate of Mesopotamia,[80] wherein this Congregation decreed that dissident Orientals who embraced Western Protestantism were not thereafter to be considered as belonging to the Latin rite inasmuch as they remained in their original rite, the same anonymous writer states that in like manner schismatics today in no way pertain to

(1907), 530. Cf. *S. Romanae Rotae Decisiones*, XVIII (1926), dec. xxxix, p. 315.

[78] "An orientales schismatici legibus matrimonialibus Ecclesiae latinae teneantur,"—XI (1938), 121-125. (Cicognani-Staffa [*Commentarium*, I, p. 25, n. 1] indicate that Coussa was the author of this article.)

[79] *Institutiones Iuris Canonici ad normam Novi Codicis* (2 vols., Romae, 1919), I, n. 196.

[80] *Collectanea*, n. 1458.

the Latin rite, and therefore are not bound by the matrimonial impediments enacted for Latins. He adds that it is wrong to argue, against his position, from the above-mentioned reply of the Sacred Congregation of the Council concerning the word "non-Catholics" as employed in the decree *"Ne temere,"* since the Article in question concerned only the form of marriage and in effect declared that there was no longer to exist any possibility of a communication of exemption in the form of marriage required by this decree. He asserts, as his opinion, that if any impediment in the Code is to be extended to the dissidents it must be shown that the impediment was decreed for the universal Church, Latin and Oriental, and since the impediment of consanguinity is not of such a nature, the dissidents are not held to this impediment; therefore, in the case at hand, the marriage was valid, since the impediment which elsewhere arose from this degree of consanguinity did not exist in the East before the schism.[81]

Herman[82] admits that the Church could bind dissidents if she wished, but he asserts that it is entirely another question whether she wishes to bind them to the laws of the Latin Code. There is, he says, no document of the Holy See which answers this question; but the Popes have often declared that they have no intention of changing the laws of schismatics when these become united to the Holy See. Herman furthermore cites the "Pamphilian" decision

[81] Cf. Coussa, *Epitome,* I, 48. After quoting part of the above-mentioned reply of July 15, 1876, he states: "Haec aperte docent Sacram Congregationem habere dissidentes adscriptos ritui in cuius caeremoniis baptizati sunt; atque ideo ipsis in sinum Ecclesiae redeuntibus optionem concedit inter diversos ritus orientales. Hoc posito, iure deducitur dissidentes teneri legibus omnibus quae in respectivo ritu *ante* haeresim vel schisma obtinebant, cum haeresis professio leges, in catholica Ecclesia datas, minime solvat. Id prae oculis habendum quoties agendum de validate praesertim actuum. Dicimus *"ante* haeresim" cum saltem in dubio sit num Hierarchae dissidentes valide, sacra ordinatione aucti, potestatem habeant iurisdictionis in foro externo. Ideo, leges ab ipsis datas, in iudicandis redeuntium in sinum Ecclesiae actis pro non existentibus habentur."

[82] "Reguntурne Orientales dissidentes legibus matrimonialibus Ecclesiae latinae?"—*Periodica,* XXVII (1938), 7-20. Cf. Vermeersch-Creusen, *Epitome Iuris Canonici,* II, p. 194, nota 2: "Orientales dissidentes iure ritus sui non iure latino regi nobis videntur. Sic Aem. Herman, S. I. in *Per.,* XXVII, 7 ss., sententiam plurium canonistarum bene refellens."

of the Sacred Congregation for the Propagation of the Faith of June 4, 1631, wherein the Cardinals were of the opinion that Papal Constitutions did not bind schismatics unless (a) there was question of matters of faith; (b) the Pope explicitly mentioned them; and (c) the Pope mentioned them implicitly, as in the question of an appeal to a future council.[83]

He also asserts that the Popes have not passed on the validity of the marriages of schismatics in sacred orders, which would be an easy matter if they were subject to the Latin Code, that it would be incongruous for the Catholic Oriental bishops and priests to judge the marriages of dissident converts according to the Latin laws, and that canon 1070, § 1, concerning the impediment of disparity of cult, has no reference whatsoever to the Oriental discipline. He refers to Vermeersch (1858-1936) [84] and Cappello [85] as expressly teaching

[83] *Collectanea,* I, p. 252 (where this decision is quoted in note 1 to par. 44 of n. 395, the Constitution *"Allatae sunt"* of Pope Benedict XIV); *Fontes,* n. 4449; *Fonti,* II, 279-281. Cf. Goodwine, *The Reception of Converts,* The Catholic University of America Canon Law Studies, n. 198 (Washington, D. C.: The Catholic University of America Press, 1944), pp. 164-165, where that writer follows the opinion of Herman. This decision is called the "Pamphilian decision" since the Cardinals met at the home of Cardinal Pamphili. Cf. Cicognani-Staffa, *Commentarium,* I, 24; Duskie, p. 24; Dib, "La legislation matrimoniale canonique dans l'Orient catholique,"—*Le Canoniste Contemporain,* XXXIX (1916), 394; *Analecta Ecclesiastica,* V (1897), 270. Cf. also Herman, "De conceptu 'Ritus,'"—*The Jurist,* II (1942), 337. Herman there comments concerning this "Pamphilian decision": "Quae norma quamquam numquam authentice confirmata est, de facto tam ab Orientalibus servata est, quam a S. Sede. . . ."

[84] "De disparitate cultus,"—*Periodica,* XXIV (1935), 41-42. In this article he stated that canon 1070, § 1, does not pertain to the Orientals as "they are not held to the Code except in questions of faith or morals." In 1928, however, Vermeersch had written: "Exceptio qua personae natae et perseverantes in schismate aut haeresi ab impedimento disparitatis cultus eximuntur prorsus nova est in iure."—"De canone 1070.1 eiusque opportunitate,"—*Periodica,* XVII (1928), 53-55. In this article however he did not define what he meant by the term "schismatic." Cf. *infra,* p. 245.

[85] *De Matrimonio,* n. 906. This view, as expressed in the section dealing specifically with Orientals, was held by Cappello in his edition of 1927 (also n. 906). Duskie (*op. cit.,* p. 172), following this opinion of Cappello, wrote: "According to the Oriental Church, the diriment impediment of disparity of cult obtains between any baptized person whether Catholic or non-Catholic and

that Oriental dissidents are held by the impediment of disparity of cult. Herman claims that the word "schismatic" is used in the Code in a juridical sense rather than in a historical sense, and points to the juridical definition of a schismatic in canon 1325, § 2: ". . . if, finally, one refuses to be subject to the Pope, or refuses to communicate with the members of the Church subject to him, he is a schismatic." [86]

Herman states, as expressing his position: "Only Western dissidents are held by the Latin laws, while Eastern dissidents are held by Eastern laws." [87] He feels that the historical dissidents, that is, the schismatics who usually are called "orthodox," are really included under the term "heretics" in the Code, and that the juridic schismatic as mentioned in the Code must be identified with the unusual person who admits completely the position of the Pope but refuses to be subject to him. Yet, though asserting that those dissidents who are popularly termed "schismatics" are really included under the term "heretics" in the Code, Herman does not admit that therefore the dissidents are held to the marriage laws of the Code as are the heretics (with the exception of the laws regarding the required juridical form, and subjection to the impediment of disparity of cult).

But this pure, juridical schism as explained by Herman could be verified when a diocese, province, region or parish refused to be subject to the Pope, while claiming to retain all their Catholic beliefs, for it is difficult to conceive of an individual person as being a schismatic in the sense of the Code without at the same time being a heretic. It may happen, however, that an individual Catholic would

any non-baptized person." Cappello, however, when treating the impediment of disparity of cult in the regular place among the Latin impediments, has stated, in many editions, when discussing the change in legislation concerning disparity of cult: "Ratio immutatae disciplinae est, quia valor baptismi in pluribus sectis collati valde dubius est; quare ne innumera matrimonia essent invalida, Ecclesia noluit haereticos et schismaticos sua lege ligare."—n. 414 in the editions of 1923, 1927, 1933, and n. 415 in the edition of 1939.

86 " . . . si denique subesse renuit Summo Pontifici aut cum membris Ecclesiae ei subiectis communicare recusat, schismaticus est."

87 "Tantummodo dissidentes occidentales latinis legibus, orientalibus legibus orientales teneri affirmamus."—*art. cit.*, p. 18.

admit the position of the Pope, but refuse at the same time to acknowledge his authority, and thus would continue to attend, e.g., an individual Oriental Church which has withdrawn from the authority of the Holy See because of some local difficulty.[88]

McCloskey holds that not only those who are formally guilty either of pure schism or of schism which involves heresy, but also those who are material schismatics are bound actually to all ecclesiastical laws unless they are expressly exempted, for they are still subjects of the Church by reason of their baptism, which causes them to be bound fundamentally and actually to the legislation of the Church.[89]

Noldin (1838-1922) maintained that it is beyond doubt that heretics and schismatics are held to the marriage laws of the Code,[90] and also stated expressly that those born in heresy and schism are not held to the impediment of disparity of cult.[91]

[88] Coronata, *Institutiones Iuris Canonici* (5 vols., Vols. I-II, 2. ed., 1939; Vol. III, 2. ed., 1941; Vol. IV, 2. ed., 1945; Vol. V, 1936, Taurini, Romae: Marietti, 1936-1945), II, n. 911. Cf. also Hervé, *Manuale Theologiae Dogmaticae* (17. ed., 3 vols., Parisiis, 1934), Vol. I (*De Revelatione Christiana, De Ecclesia Christi, De Fontibus Revelationis*), p. 456. Hervé states the following concerning a few types of schismatics: "*Schismatici.*—Schismatici enim, qui *pertinaciter* et *publice* 'subesse renuunt Summo Pontifici aut cum membris Ecclesiae eidem subiectis communicare recusant' (Cod. c. 1325.2), certo certius ad Ecclesiae corpus non pertinent, non secus ac haeretici notorii.—Schismatici vero *occulti* communius reputantur non esse simpliciter extra Ecclesiam. Si qui autem sint qui sine haeresi fiant schismatici, v.g. propter meram denegationem obedientiae Summo Pontifici vel simplicem recessum a communione catholicae Ecclesiae, hi ad Ecclesiae corpus adhuc pertinerent; hodie autem vix dari potest schisma *purum,* scilicet quod non sit cum aliqua haeresi conjunctum." In this connection may be mentioned the definition of a schismatic by St. Basil in the fourth century: " . . . schismata autem qui propter aliquas ecclesiasticas causas et medicabiles quaestiones inter se dissident."—*Fonti,* IX, p. 573, n. 809 (for the Greek text, cf. Pitra, I, 577).

[89] *The Subject of Ecclesiastical Law According to Canon 12,* The Catholic University of America Canon Law Studies, n. 165 (Washington, D. C.: The Catholic University of America Press, 1942), pp. 155-156.

[90] "Haereticos et schismaticos quoque legibus ecclesiasticis quoad matrimonia teneri, ex codice non est dubium. . . ."—*De Sacramentis,* n. 556. For a similar statement, cf. Wernz-Vidal, *Ius Canonicum,* Tom. V, *Ius Matrimoniale* (ed. altera, Romae, 1928), n. 58.

[91] "Haeretici et schismatici (nati) hoc impedimento non tenentur. Matri-

Vermeersch likewise asserted the subjection of schismatics to the marriage laws of the Church, with the same two exceptions.[92]

In the particular question of disparity of cult, Gasparri in 1932 wrote that the reason for the impediment does not exist in the case of heretics and schismatics, that is, in their marriages with infidels there is no question of protecting the Catholic Faith.[93]

Michiels also exempts schismatics from this impediment, after stating that they are not held to the form of marriage.[94]

According to Cicognani-Staffa, not only Catholic Orientals but also dissident Orientals are excluded from the scope of the Latin Code.[95] In the list which they present of the impediments in force

monium ergo inter haereticum vel schismaticum valide baptizatum et infidelem nunc validum est."—*op. cit.*, n. 574.3.

[92] "Aliae leges ecclesiasticae ad ordinem publicum et commune societatis christianae bonum tutandum directe constitutae sunt: tales sunt leges de matrimonii forma et condicionibus. Istis legibus haeretici et schismatici per se obnoxii sunt. Attamen, positiva concessione, quae decreto *Ne temere,* 2 aug. 1907, primum facta est generalis, et nunc c. 1099 Codicis confirmatur, acatholici qui inter se contrahunt, nullibi ad catholicam matrimonii formam servandam tenentur. Impedimentis vero ecclesiasticis, excepta cultus disparitate ex c. 1070, subiacere dicendi sunt."—*Theologiae Moralis Principia-Responsa-Consilia* (3. ed., 4 vols., Romae, 1933-1937), Tom. I, n. 253. Two years later, in the above-mentioned article in *Periodica* for 1935, he held without hesitation that schismatics were held to the impediment of disparity of cult. In 1937, Vermeersch-Creusen (*Epitome Iuris Canonici,* I, 106) declared: " . . . Impedimentis autem matrimonii nullo iuris textu [acatholici] liberantur." It is beyond dispute that heretical Protestant non-Catholics are free from the impediment of disparity of cult, and so this statement of Vermeersch-Creusen seems inaccurate, and should not be cited on either side of the discussion.

[93] " . . . Ratio praecipua impedimenti disparitatis cultus, tuendae scilicet fidei partis catholicae, non verificatur si pars est quidem baptizata, sed extra ecclesiam catholicam, scilicet in haeresi praesertim vel schismate vivit. Praeterea non est ratio reddendi nulla tot matrimonia, quae ab haereticis et schismaticis baptizatis contrahuntur cum infidelibus. . . ."—*op. cit.*, I, n. 587.

[94] "Non desunt leges, a quibus acatholici expresse eximuntur; ita can. 1099, § 2, quoad formam in matrimonii celebratione servandam . . . item can. 1070, vi cuius ab impedimento disparitatis cultus eximuntur haeretici et schismatici, extra Ecclesiam catholicam baptizati et ad eandem nondum conversi."—*Normae Generales Iuris Canonici* (2 vols., Lublin: Universitas Catholica, 1929), I, 288.

[95] *Commentarium,* I, p. 25, n. 1.

among the Catholic Orientals, they speak of "disparity of cult according to the norm of the old law," which implies that the impediment exists between any person and an Oriental, Catholic or dissident, if one of the parties is not baptized.[96]

In a recent article Gulovich presents the replies of the Oriental Congregation on April 12, 1945, concerning three marriage cases presented to it by Bishop Takach.[97] In two of the cases the dissident party was a Russian, and in the third the dissident party was a Serbian. In all three cases the Oriental Congregation declared that these dissidents were not clearly held to any required form of marriage, but that such parties were held to the impediment of disparity of cult if they married persons who were not baptized. Gulovich declares: ". . . it should be noted that the decision of the Sacred Congregation with regard to the binding force of the impediment of disparity of worship so far as the Dissidents of the Byzantine rite are concerned evidently intends to nullify that portion of the well known *private* response of the Commission for the Authentic Interpretation of the Code in which it is stated that the impediment of disparity of worship is not binding on schismatics.[98] It is, however, possible that the same nullification should be extended to all Eastern Dissidents." [99]

To comment on this, a possible reconciliation may be suggested

[96] "XI. *Disparitas cultus* ad normam antiqui iuris."—*op. cit.*, p. 21.

[97] "The Principle Underlying the Validity of Oriental Marriage Law,"—*The Jurist,* VI (1946), 40-41. For the texts of the replies, cf. the Appendix, pp. 264-267.

[98] Gulovich refers in his footnote to the private response of the President of the Commission for the Interpretation of the Code on December 3, 1919, in answer to some questions proposed by the Vicar Apostolic of Natal. In answering in the affirmative to the following question: "Whether canon 1099, § 2, is so to be understood that the words *acatholici non baptizati* include also a pagan, in other words, whether baptized Protestants contracting with pagans contract validly," the President of the Commission commented: " . . . Protestants or schismatics who were baptized, even validly, in heresy or schism, and have not been converted to the Church from heresy or schism when they contract marriage with pagans, contract validly under the new Code, because they are bound neither by the impediment of disparity of cult nor to the observance of the canonical form of marriage."—Bouscaren, *Digest,* II, 337.

[99] *Art. cit.,* p. 43.

between these two apparently contradictory replies. The President of the Code Commission was considering dissidents only in relation to the Latin Code, and in relation to the impediment of disparity of cult as described in the Latin Code, and so he declared that schismatics were not bound to this impediment. The replies of the Oriental Congregation, on the other hand, consider the dissidents in the light of their own legal position and, in one of the replies, pointed to the 14th canon of the Council of Chalcedon (451) as the "sanction" of this impediment. In summary, on the one hand the impediment of disparity of cult was in force among the Orientals before the schism in the East, and on the other hand the Latin Code in its first canon declares that it does not legislate for the Oriental Church, but for only the Latin Church. Thus the Latin Code leaves the impediments of the East intact, and therefore a dissident Oriental needs a dispensation to marry validly one who is not baptized.

Rodrigo declares that the dissidents share "at least probably" in the exemption of the Catholic Orientals from the disciplinary laws of the Latin Church as established in canon 1. For his reasons he states that no papal document is known which declares that dissidents are subject to the Latin laws and, in addition, Pope Leo XIII (1878-1903) promised the dissidents that the Church would respect their laws. Rodrigo also states that such a subjection to the Latin laws would estrange them from the Church and from the Oriental Catholics whose rites they will follow after their conversion.[100]

[100] "ORIENTALES SCHISMATICI participant saltem probabiliter de exemtione catholicorum orientalium a iure disciplinari Ecclesiae Latinae quae in can. 1 statuitur. (a) *Ratio est,* quia praeter quam quod nullibi de eorum subiectione legibus latinis documenta pontificia statuisse videntur aut eam generaliter supposuisse, potius e contra dissidentes alloquens v. c. Leo XIII, Epist. *'Praeclara,'* 29 iun. 1894, n. 7, FIC 3,444 ait: 'Neque est cur dubitetis, quidquam propterea vel Nos vel successores Nostros de iure vestro, de patriarchalibus privilegiis, de rituali cuiusque Ecclesiae consuetudine detracturos.' Atqui si ante reconciliationem essent tractandi ut subiecti iuri Latinorum, idipsum potius eos arceret a reconciliatione et occasio esset fidei denegandae promissis huiusmodi de disciplina orientali penes ipsos semel reconciliatos retinenda. (b) *Confirmatur,* quia incongruum esset urgere in ipsis disciplinam latinam, quam reconciliati non retinebunt, quaeque ante reconciliationem eos potius seiungeret a catholicis

In the question of the validity of the marriage of dissident priests after their ordination to the diaconate or the priesthood, the Holy See has not issued any official decree concerning the validity of such marriages. If a convert dissident priest desires to know the status of his marriage which was contracted after his ordination, the whole case must be submitted to the Holy See.[101]

The Latin Code exempts non-Catholics, when marrying among themselves, from the canonical form of marriage; likewise exempt are those children of non-Catholics who, though they were actually baptized as Catholics, grew up from childhood in heresy, schism or infidelity or without any religion, whenever they contract marriage with a non-Catholic,[102] or with an Oriental Catholic who is also not bound to any form for the contracting of a valid marriage.[103]

Converts to the Latin Church from heresy or schism are held to the canonical form of marriage.[104] No explicit provision is made in the Code for the children of converts from heresy or schism, and thus it appears that they are not held to the canonical form unless they themselves, independently of the action of their parents, make some juridical act of conversion to the Church. Thus a child who is

orientalibus, quibus semel ad unitatem Ecclesiae conversi essent incorporandi."—*Tractatus de legibus*, p. 437, n. 599.

[101] Cf. Dauvillier and De Clercq, *Le Mariage en Droit canonique Oriental*, p. 173; Herman, "De impedimentis matrimonialibus secundum codificationes iuris ecclesiastici recentes 'orthodoxorum,'"—*Orientalia Christiana Periodica*, III (1937), 251-253; Souarn, "Impedimentum ordinis in Ecclesia Graeca,"—*Jus Pontificium*, XIII (1933), 48-51; *Fonti*, Serie II, Fasc. XXVII, p. 97; Vlaming, *Praelectiones Iuris Matrimonii* (3. ed., 2 vols., Bussum in Hollandia, 1919-1921), n. 300. Cf. the Instruction of Pope Benedict XIV on May 4, 1745, to the missionaries of Egypt, *"Eo quamvis semper,"* which instructed the missionaries to refer all cases concerning the marriages of the Coptic dissident priests to the Holy See—*Fontes*, n. 357. Cf. *supra*, p. 17, fn. 72.

[102] Canon 1099, § 2. For the celebrated replies of the Commission for the Interpretation of the Code concerning the meaning of the phrase *"ab acatholicis nati"* which appears in this canon, cf. Bouscaren, *Digest*, I, 534-544. On April 29, 1940, the Commission for the Interpretation of the Code declared that these persons (*"ab acatholicis nati"*) are held to the impediment of disparity of cult if they desire to marry a person who is not baptized—*AAS*, XXXII (1940), 212; Bouscaren, *Digest*, II, 290-291.

[103] Cf. *supra*, p. 205.

[104] Canon 1099, § 1, 1°.

baptized as a member of a schismatic church is not affected by the conversion of his parents in regard to his own obligation to the canonical form, even though the converted parents instructed him in the teachings of the Church and brought him to church with them for a time. The child, after reaching the age of reason, would have to perform some act indicative of his own personal conversion.[105] Opposed to this opinion is that of Petrovits, who maintains that infants who are below the age of seven years, and who had been validly baptized in a schismatic church, should be considered as converts upon the conversion of their parents.[106] According to Augustine, "if children, when they commence to realize the difference between religions, object to embracing the Catholic religion, which the parents would impose upon them, there is no conversion to the Catholic faith." [107]

In a discussion of the relationship of "schismatics" to the marriage laws of the Latin Code, it is important to emphasize that the word "schismatic" may refer to Oriental schismatics or to Latin schismatics. Therefore, unless the authors mentioned in these pages qualified their use of the word "schismatic" it is difficult to grasp their exact meaning when they state that "schismatics" are, or in some cases are not, held to the marriage laws of the Latin Code. Cicognani-Staffa, in their canonical study of the First Book of the Code, do make the proper distinction. In their commentary on canon 1 they declare that not only Catholic Orientals but also dissident Orientals are excluded from the scope of the Latin Code.[108] In their analysis of canon 12, which enumerates those who are not held to the laws of the Church,[109] before they begin the discussion of the question whether the Church wishes to bind apostates, heretics and schismatics to her laws, they refer the reader to their comments

[105] Cf. *S. Romanae Rotae Decisiones,* XVIII (1926), dec. xxxix, p. 314.

[106] *The New Church Law on Matrimony,* n. 228.

[107] *A Commentary on the New Code of Canon Law,* V (4. ed., St. Louis: Herder, 1929), 299.

[108] Cf. *supra,* footnote n. 95.

[109] "Legibus mere ecclesiasticis non tenentur qui baptismum non receperunt, nec baptizati qui sufficienti rationis usu non gaudent, nec qui, licet rationis usum assecuti, septimum aetatis annum nondum expleverunt, nisi aliud iure expresse caveatur."

concerning Orientals in the discussion of canon 1. Thus, while these authors assert that material heretics and schismatics are held to the marriage laws of the Code, except in the questions of the canonical form of marriage and of the impediment of disparity of cult,[110] it is clear that they are not speaking about Oriental schismatics.

The words "heresy" and "schism" in canon 1070, § 1, can be referred to Latins alone, and thus reference to Orientals, Catholic or schismatic, need not be found in this canon. In virtue of canon 1, which declares that the Code is concerned principally with the Latin Church and does not oblige the Oriental Church unless the Oriental Church is expressly mentioned or unless the Code treats a topic which of its very nature affects the Orientals, the legislation of the Church concerning the impediments to marriage which are listed in the Latin Code should be considered without any reference to Oriental law. Although the impediment of disparity of cult, as delineated in canon 1070, § 1, does not bind non-Catholics,[111] it does not affect the legislation which binds the dissident Orientals.

The words of canon 1070, § 1: ". . . with a person . . . converted from schism" appear to refer to those who were born of parents who withdraw into schism from the Latin Church, and thus it seems that no allusion is made to Oriental schismatics in this canon. An indication of the mind of the legislator in support of this interpretation can be drawn from canon 751, which explicitly mentions such children when it states: "As to the baptism of the infants of two heretics or schismatics, or of two Catholics who have lapsed into apostasy or heresy or schism, there should be observed, in general, the norms which have been established in the previous canon." [112] The norms

[110] *Op. cit.*, pp. 203-204.

[111] Cf. the private reply of the Holy Office on December 21, 1924, to the Archbishop of Freiburg, who had asked whether canon 1070, § 1, is restricted to the marriages of Catholics with non-Catholics or whether it also extends to the marriages of baptized non-Catholics with those who are not baptized. The Holy Office answered: " . . . impedimentum hoc ad normam ipsius can. 1070 tenere catholicos, non autem acatholicos nisi hi fuerint baptizati in Ecclesia catholica aut ad eam conversi. Res adeo clara est, ut nullum de ea dubium habere liceat." —*Archiv für katholisches Kirchenrecht*, CV (1925), 202. Cf. Bouscaren, *Digest*, I, 512.

[112] "Circa baptismum infantium duorum haereticorum aut schismaticorum,

of action which are decreed in the previous canon provide rules governing the various possible cases in which it is licit to baptize the children of infidel parents. In canon 751 there is an explicit reference to the possibility that a priest, or lay person, may be called upon to baptize the child of two Catholic Latin parents who have lapsed into schism. It would seem that it is to such a child that the words of canon 1070, § 1: *"cum persona . . . ex schismate conversa"* refer. In other words, a child of Latin schismatic parents who have the child baptized outside the Church, while they are in their schism, would not be held to the impediment of disparity of cult until he became converted to the Church.

Petrovits, in his commentary on canon 1070, § 1, declares that the words "Catholic baptism" do not refer to the baptism administered by the Catholic Oriental Churches for, he states, their baptism "makes one a member of the Catholic Church, but not subject to this legislation." [113]

Schenk, who made a special study of the impediments of mixed religion and of disparity of cult, stated: "The restriction of the Code to baptism in the Catholic Church or conversion thereto from heresy or schism, does not, however, affect the Oriental Churches, whether they be united to Rome, or separated through schism or heresy." [114] He also expressed this important opinion: "When, therefore, the Code in canon 1070, § 1, speaks of conversion from heresy or schism, it seems to regard primarily a conversion from heretical or schismatic sects which represent separations from the Latin Church." [115]

In conclusion, any statement concerning the extent of the impediment of disparity of cult should be properly qualified. The impediment of disparity of cult, as it is delineated in the Latin Code in canon 1070, § 1, binds only Latin Catholics, those who were baptized in the Latin Church or converted to it. No defection from the Catholic faith would excuse one from this impediment. The word

aut duorum catholicorum qui in apostasism vel haeresim vel schisma prolapsi sint, generatim serventur normae in superiore canone constitutae."

[113] *Op. cit.*, n. 223.

[114] *The Matrimonial Impediments of Mixed Religion and Disparity of Cult*, n. 156.

[115] *Op. cit.*, n. 157.

"schism" as used in the canon refers to a schism from the ranks of the Latin Church. The canon prescinds from any interpretation of the impediment in the Oriental Churches, Catholic or dissident. The Latin Code makes no reference to the relationship of the Oriental schismatics to the marriage laws of the Code nor has the Holy See issued any decree on this question, and thus cases involving their marriage impediments should be sent to the Holy See. It is fairly certain, however, that a marriage contracted by a validly baptized Oriental schismatic with an unbaptized person is invalid because of the impediment of disparity of cult, if the needed dispensation was not previously obtained.

Conclusions

1. As each Oriental rite is a distinct legal entity, the laws of one rite cannot be applied to the members of another rite.

2. It cannot be demonstrated conclusively from the documents of the Oriental Churches in the early centuries that marriages contracted without religious rites were contracted invalidly. Clear distinctions were not made between invalid and illicit marriages, nor between diriment and impedient impediments.

3. It cannot be demonstrated conclusively that the usage among the Oriental Churches, namely, of considering the blessing of the priest, or the crowning of the parties, as indispensable for a valid first marriage, contains all the conditions required for a juridical custom, that is, one which operates as a customary law. The Holy See at various times has indicated that there is a doubt of law as to whether this usage really acquired the force of binding customary law.

4. An example of a usage in the East which obtained the force of law was the custom of considering disparity of cult as a diriment impediment. This impediment of disparity of cult binds all Orientals, Catholics and dissidents. Canon 1070, § 1, of the Latin Code prescinds from the Oriental discipline concerning this impediment.

5. It is maintained that the Oriental Catholics, in this country and in Canada, are bound by the impediments which are listed at the end of these conclusions. These lists are not absolutely comprehensive, since some impediments, such as impotence and an existing marriage bond, about which there is no dispute, are not mentioned.

6. The Latin Code prescribes that a marriage of mixed rite is to be contracted before the pastor of the groom unless a particular law provides otherwise. In this country and in Canada particular laws prescribe that marriages involving a Ruthenian are to be celebrated before the pastor of the bride and in that pastor's rite. If the parties to a contemplated marriage of mixed rite, of which one party is a

Ruthenian, allege that they have a just cause in their desire to marry in the church of the groom and according to his rite, permission is to be sought from either the local Latin Ordinary of the place of marriage or the proper Ruthenian Ordinary of the bride; the ordinary who is asked to give his permission must pass a serious judgment concerning the alleged just cause before he gives his consent.

7. A change of rite before a marriage ceremony can take place only by means of a particular indult from the Holy See. If a woman in a marriage of mixed rite wishes to pass over to the rite of her husband, she can do so at the very marriage ceremony itself, but not before the actual ceremony of the marriage. She can also pass over to the rite of her husband at any time during the continuance of the marriage. This option to change her rite in connection with her marriage does not in any way affect the laws for the form, place and liturgical ceremony of the marriage.

8. Marriages celebrated in the United States or in Canada, if they involve either a Latin or a Ruthenian, must, for their validity, be celebrated before the local pastor or ordinary, assisting within their respective territories, or before a priest delegated by either of these, if such a priest assists within the territory of the one who delegated him for the marriage.

9. Though marriages without religious rites are abhorred by the Church in view of the sacred character of marriage, nevertheless, since there is a doubt of law as to whether the marriages of non-Ruthenian Orientals, when contracted in the United States or in Canada among themselves or with non-Catholics, must for their validity receive the blessing of the priest or have the ceremony of coronation, the marriages of these persons when contracted in a civil ceremony or before a schismatic priest or a non-Catholic minister, cannot be declared invalid because of a defect of the proper form, as long as this doubt has not been resolved by the Holy See.

10. In marriages between Catholics of mixed rite in the United States or in Canada, the following norms concern the proper place and rite for the ceremony. While certain letters in the list actually overlap through mutual identification (A and K; B and L; C and F; D and E; G and J; H and I), yet the consideration of convenient reference suggests the following exhaustive listing:

A. Latin man—non-Ruthenian Oriental woman of any rite: the church of the man.
B. Latin woman—non-Ruthenian Oriental man of any rite: the church of the man.
C. Latin man—Ruthenian woman: the church of the woman.
D. Latin woman—Ruthenian man: the church of the woman.
E. Ruthenian man—Latin woman: the church of the woman.
F. Ruthenian woman—Latin man: the church of the woman.
G. Ruthenian man—non-Ruthenian Oriental woman of any rite: the church of the woman.
H. Ruthenian woman—non-Ruthenian Oriental man of any rite: the church of the woman.
I. Non-Ruthenian Oriental man of any rite—Ruthenian woman: the church of the woman.
J. Non-Ruthenian Oriental woman of any rite—Ruthenian man: the church of the woman.
K. Non-Ruthenian Oriental woman of any rite—Latin man: the church of the man.
L. Non-Ruthenian Oriental man of any rite—Latin woman: the church of the man.
M. Non-Ruthenian Oriental man of any rite—non-Ruthenian Oriental woman of any rite: the church of the man.

11. If the juridic form of marriage as enacted in the Latin Code is followed, then, here in the United States or also in Canada, a Latin pastor in his own parish assists validly, with reference to the canonically required juridical form, at the marriages of any persons—two Latin Catholics, two Ruthenian Catholics, two non-Ruthenian Oriental Catholics, a Latin Catholic and an Oriental Catholic of any rite, a Latin Catholic, or any Oriental Catholic, who desires to marry a non-Catholic, whether heretic, schismatic, infidel—when such couples have presented themselves before him. The Latin pastor must however give serious consideration to the rules for licitness as outlined in conclusion n. 10.

12. The Latin diocesan tribunals, in this country and in Canada, may conduct the matrimonial trials of non-Ruthenian Oriental plaintiffs according to the procedure which is followed in the trials of Latins. If the two parties are Ruthenians, or if the plaintiff alone is a Ruthenian, the case is to be judged by the tribunal of the proper Ruthenian Ordinary. Latin tribunals can consider the cases presented by dissident Oriental plaintiffs after the permission of the Con-

gregation of the Holy Office has been sought and obtained. It appears that the Latin Ordinary in this country and in Canada can draw up the process concerning a ratified, non-consummated marriage according to the Instruction issued in 1923 by the Congregation of the Sacraments, in a case presented by a non-Ruthenian Oriental; if a dissident Oriental is involved in such a petition, the permission of the Holy Office is to be secured. Formal trials involving Orientals, if an appeal is made to the Holy See, are to be sent to the Oriental Congregation.

13. Even though the Oriental Catholics in this country and in Canada are not the subjects of the Latin Ordinaries in the same sense as the Latins are, those Oriental Catholics who have acquired a domicile in a Latin diocese are held to observe all the laws promulgated by the local Ordinary, if in relation to these laws a difference of rite does not affect their binding force inasmuch as these laws bind the Catholics as Catholics. Examples of such laws are the diocesan laws governing the care of souls, the obligation of pastors and of other priests, the administration of church property, the payments of diocesan assessments, and also the laws enacting penalties for any future violations of these ordinances. If an Oriental Catholic does not acquire a domicile, he is bound as is any traveler in a diocese by the laws which affect the public order, which govern the solemnities of acts, and those which are strictly territorial laws. The Latin Code suggests that the Latin Ordinary appoint a Vicar General to care for the Orientals in his diocese, if there are many Orientals in the diocese. There are an estimated 700,000 Oriental Catholics in the United States, and over 300,000 in Canada.

14. If the conditions described in canons 1043-1045 of the Latin Code are fulfilled, the Latin Ordinary can use these extraordinary faculties for the Orientals in his diocese, and Latin and Oriental pastors and confessors can probably also dispense Orientals in such a state of emergency.

15. The Ruthenian Ordinaries in the United States and in Canada have received ample faculties for the granting of matrimonial dispensations to their Ruthenian subjects. In a marriage between a Ruthenian and a Latin, the request for the dispensation is to be sent to the bishop of the bride. In a case of emergency, the bishop of the

groom may licitly dispense, whether the Latin Ordinary or the Ruthenian Ordinary be the bishop of the groom; if no emergency exists the bishop of the groom can validly, but not licitly, grant the dispensation.

16. It is here maintained that the Latin Ordinary in the United States and in Canada can dispense the Oriental Catholics who are in his diocese from those certain impediments which are mentioned in his quinquennial faculties. The Latin Ordinary cannot dispense from the Oriental rite impediments which are not found among the Latins, and which are not mentioned in any faculty possessed by a Latin Ordinary; the petition for such a dispensation is to be forwarded to the Holy See.

17. If dissident Orientals impugn the validity of their marriage, alleging that they were bound by an impediment of ecclesiastical law, from which impediment they did not secure a dispensation, the case should be submitted to the judgment of the Holy See. However, it does not appear necessary to consult the Holy See if it is proved that no dispensation was ever granted for the impediment of disparity of cult, which binds the dissident Oriental in his marriage with a non-baptized person.

IMPEDIENT IMPEDIMENTS [1]

	Armenians	*Chaldeans*	*Syrians*	*Maronites*	*Melkites*	*Ruthenians*	*Rumanians*	*Italo-Greeks*	*Russians*
Espousals (outside the degrees of the diriment impediment)	x	x	x	x	x	x	x	x	x
Prohibited times [2]	x	x	x	x	x	x	x	x	x
Simple vow	x	x	x	x	x	x	x	x	x
Mixed religion	x	x	x	x	x	x	x	x	x
Temporary prohibition of a bishop [2]		x	x		x	x	x		
Interdict placed on a church [2]	x			x				x	
"Catechismus"—part of the ritual in supplying the ceremonies of baptism [3]				x					
Nonage (impeding rather the use of marriage than the licitness of the marriage)				x					

[1] These two outlines concern those Catholic Orientals who are considered in this dissertation, in their juridic status in the United States and in Canada. Cf. McCormick, in *The Conference Bulletin of the Archdiocese of New York,* VI (1928), 6-7; 18-19, for similar outlines with some incidental differences; cf. also Cappello, *De Matrimonio,* nn. 895-901; *idem,* "Ius Ecclesiae Latinae cum iure Ecclesiae Orientalis comparatum,"—*Jus Pontificium,* VII (1927), 55-71.

[2] These are "impediments" only in the wide sense of the term.

[3] Cf. *supra,* p. 91.

DIRIMENT IMPEDIMENTS

	Armenians	*Chaldeans*	*Syrians*	*Maronites*	*Melkites*	*Ruthenians*	*Rumanians*	*Italo-Greeks*	*Russians*
Sacred Orders—									
(a) priesthood	x	x	x	x	x	?	?	x	x
(b) diaconate	x	x	x	x	x	?	?	x	x
(c) subdiaconate	x							x	
Solemn Religious Profession	x	x	x	x	x	x	x	x	x
Abduction	x	x	x	x	x	x	x	x	x
Crimen	x	x	x	x		x	x	x	
Consanguinity—collateral line[1]	4[2]	8	8	8	6	8	7	8	7
Affinity—coll. line[1]—*ex copula licita*	4	8	8	8	6	8	7	8	7
Affinity—coll. line—*ex copula illicita*	2	4	4	4		4	4	4	4
Public propriety — *ex sponsalibus*, both direct and coll. lines	1	2	2	2	3	2	7	2	2
Public propriety — from a ratified, non-consummated marriage—coll. line[1]	4	8	8	8	6	8	7	8	7
Disparity of cult	x	x	x	x	x	x	x	x	x
Nonage—14 (man), 12 (girl)—*nisi malitia aetatem supplet*	x	x	x		x	x	x	x	x
Spiritual relationship—Byzantine[3]					x	x	x		x
Spiritual relationship—Tridentine[4]	x	x	x	x				x	
Legal relationship[5]	x		x	x			x		

[1] Consanguinity, affinity, and the public propriety which arises from a ratified, non-consummated marriage, in the direct line bar any marriage.

[2] The degrees of consanguinity, affinity and public propriety are computed in the fashion of Roman Law, except in the case of the Armenians, who declared in their Council of 1911 that they would follow the Latin manner of computation. The numbers indicate the degrees within which a valid marriage cannot be contracted apart from a dispensation.

[3] The Byzantine spiritual relationship barred marriage between the minister of the sacrament, the sponsors, and the children of the sponsors on one side, and anyone of the following: (a) the subject, (b) his parents, or (c) his children on the other side. Cf. Cappello, *De Matrimonio*, n. 920.

[4] The Council of Trent (Sess. XXIV, *de ref. matrim.*, c. 2) decreed: "Experience teaches that by reason of the large number of prohibitions, marriages are often unknowingly contracted in prohibited cases in which either the parties continue to live, not without great sin, or the marriages are dissolved, not without great scandal. Wherefore, the holy Council wishing to provide against this condition, and beginning with the impediment arising from spiritual relationship, decrees that in accordance with the prescriptions of the holy canons, one person only, whether man or woman, or at most one man and one woman, shall act as sponsors in baptism for the one baptized, and spiritual relationship shall be contracted between these only and the one baptized, and his father and mother, and also between the one baptizing and the one baptized and the father and mother of the one baptized."—Schroeder, *Canons and Decrees of the Council of Trent,* Original Text with English Translation (St. Louis: Herder, 1941), p. 185. As the Maronite and Chaldean priests do not administer the Sacrament of Confirmation immediately after the conferral of Baptism (Armenian priests do not confirm the adults whom they baptize), and as in their rite was adopted the Tridentine legislation concerning the impediment arising from spiritual relationship, the following words of the Council apply to these Orientals: "That relationship also which is contracted in confirmation is not to be extended beyond him who confirms, the one confirmed, his father and mother, and the sponsor; all impediments of this spiritual relationship between other persons being completely removed."—*op. cit.*, p. 186.

[5] The discipline of these rites concerning this impediment varies. Cf. Index, *Legal Relationship.*

APPENDIX I

1. Faculties of the Ruthenian Ordinaries in the United States and in Canada in questions concerning marriage.[1]

Caput II

Facultates circa matrimonii sacramentum

9. Dispensandi ab impedimento cognationis spiritualis praeter quam inter levantem et levatum, baptizantem et baptizatum.

10. Dispensandi super impedimento publicae honestatis, iustis ex sponsalibus proveniente.

11. Dispensandi super criminis impedimento, neutro tamen coniugum machinante, tam in matrimoniis contractis, renovato secreto a partibus consensu, quam in contrahendis, iniuncta in utroque casu gravi poenitentia salutari; nec non restituendi ius amissum petendi debitum.

12. Dispensandi in tertio et quarto consanguinitatis et affinitatis gradu simplici et mixto tantum, et in secundo, tertio et quarto mixtis, tam in contractis quam in contrahendis: et etiam, quoad contracta, in secundo solo, dummodo non attingat primum, cum iis qui ab haeresi, vel schismate, vel infidelitate convertuntur ad fidem catholicam, datis, si una pars tantum convertatur, cautionibus ab Ecclesia praescriptis, et in praefatis casibus prolem susceptam declarandi legitimam.

13. Hae vero dispensationes matrimoniales, videlicet n. 9, 10, 11, 12, non concedantur nisi cum clausula: "dummodo mulier rapta non fuerit, vel si rapta fuerit, in potestate raptoris amplius non existat," et in dispensatione tenor huiusmodi facultatis inseratur, cum expressione temporis ad quod fuerint concessae.

14. Dispensandi Catholicos sibi subiectos super impedimento primi gradus simplicis vel etiam mixti cum secundo affinitatis ex copula licita provenientis in linea collaterali, dummodo iusta ac legitima causa concurrat, in matrimoniis tam contractis quam contrahendis.

[1] These faculties were renewed by the Oriental Congregation on July 10, 1942, for another five-year period, for the Ruthenian Ordinaries in the United States. These faculties were renewed for Bishop Ladyka in Canada on May 30, 1945. Faculties to grant dispensations from the impediments of mixed religion and disparity of cult come from special grants from the Holy Office.

15. Dispensandi, iusta tamen ac legitima concurrente causa, catholicos sibi subditos super primo et secundo gradu simplici et mixto affinitatis ex copula illicita, sive occulta sive publica provenientis, in linea sive collaterali sive recta, dummodo si de linea recta agatur, nullum sit dubium quod coniux possit esse proles ab altero contrahentium genita, in matrimoniis tam contractis quam contrahendis.

16. Dispensandi—ad effectum tantum matrimonii contrahendi—super voto simplici virginitatis, castitatis perfectae, non nubendi, suscipiendi ordines sacros, et amplectendi statum religiosum.

17. Cumulandi dispensationes super impedimentis matrimonialibus circa quae eidem Ordinario facultas datur, ita ut, uti etiam possit in casibus in quibus duo vel plura simul concurrant ex praedictis impedimentis; nec non concurrente quoque impedimento mixtae religionis, si pro huius dispensatione concedenda facultatem iam obtinuerit; accedentibus tamen iustis iisque gravibus causis, et in urgentioribus casibus pro quibus tempus non suppetat recurrendi ad Sanctam Sedem, et dummodo singulae facultates, sive primitus ab Ordinario obtentae sive ei renovatae, adhuc perdurent, et si agatur de facultatibus pro certo casuum numero taxative eidem concessis, hunc numerum non excedant.

18. Sanandi et convalidandi in radice per se vel per ecclesiasticum virum ad hoc expresse deputandum, matrimonia ob aliquod impedimentum invalide contracta, dummodo utraque pars in consensu de praesenti perseveret.

Ipse vero dispensans, in hoc munere explendo, declaret se agere nomine Sanctitatis Suae, et tanquam ab Apostolica Sede specialiter delegatum; serio moneat, si matrimonium sit criminose invalidum, de gravissimo patrato scelere, salutares poenitentias imponat, et a censuris aliisque ecclesiasticis poenis ob praemissa quomodolibet incursis absolvat; simulque declaret ob hanc dispensationem sic concessam et acceptam matrimonium fieri validum ac legitimum, et indissolubile evadere iure divino, prolemque sive susceptam sive suscipiendam exinde legitimam habendam esse. Cum autem de matrimonii validitate in foro externo constare debeat, Ordinarius nomina, cum reliquis personarum consuetis indicationibus, in regestis matrimoniorum secretorum describi iubeat, simulque autographum documentum concessionis, communicationis, acceptationis, absolutionis et declarationum ut supra factarum, servetur in Curia Episcopali, et exemplar authenticum sedulo custodiendum tradatur parti cui interest.

In concedenda autem convalidatione vel sanatione in radice, et quod attinet ad prolis legitimationem prae oculis habeat normas quae in appendice referuntur, pag. 21-22.[2]

[2] On pages 21 and 22 of these faculties are 8 canons taken from the Latin

19. Sanandi in radice matrimonia invalide inita inter catholicum et acatholicum, pro suo prudenti iudicio et conscientia, dummodo utriusque partis consensus perseveret, et moraliter certum sit partem acatholicam universae prolis *tam natae quam* [8] nasciturae baptismum catholicum et catholicam educationem non esse impedituram, sive per se sive per alium ecclesiasticum virum ab ipso Ordinario specialiter deputandum, praevia dispensatione super impedimentis iuris ecclesiastici quae forte exoritura sint.

Ipse vero dispensans serio moneat partem catholicam de gravissimo patrato scelere, salutares ei poenitentias imponat, et a censuris absolvat, si matrimonium contractum fuit coram ministro acatholico; simulque ipsi declaret, ob hanc dispensationem ab ea acceptam, matrimonium fieri validum et legitimum, et indissolubile evadere iure divino, et prolem, sive susceptam sive suscipiendam, legitimam habendam esse.

Eidem insuper parti catholicae imponat atque declaret obligationem, qua semper tenetur, implendi conditiones ab Ecclesia praescriptas: videlicet de conversione coniugis ad fidem catholicam pro viribus curanda, ac de universa utriusque sexus prole in catholicae religionis sanctitate baptizanda et educanda, non obstante, si forte adsit, legum civilium oppositione.

Cum autem de matrimonii validitate in foro externo constare debeat, Ordinarius nomina, cum reliquis personarum consuetis indicationibus, in regestis matrimoniorum secretorum describi iubeat, simulque autographum documentum concessionis, communicationis, acceptationis, absolutionis, et declarationum a parte catholica ut supra factarum, servetur in Curia Episcopali, et exemplar authenticum eidem parti catholicae sedulo custodiendum tradatur.

Ordinarius, in hac sibi concessa facultate explenda, expressam faciat mentionem Apostolicae delegationis.

20. Urgente mortis periculo, locorum Ordinarii, ad consulendum conscientiae et, si casus ferat, legitimationi prolis, possunt tum super forma in matrimonii celebratione servanda, tum super omnibus et

Code, canons 1133-1140, which are quoted in full as norms to be followed in questions of convalidations and sanations.

[8] When these quinquennial faculties were renewed for Bishop Ladyka in Canada on May 30, 1945, the following instruction was given: "On No. 19, the words *'tam natae quam'* must be suppressed, as the requirement of moral certitude that the non-Catholic party will not impede the baptism and the Catholic education of the offspring is limited to the offspring yet unborn. Instead, however, a serious promise must be obtained from the Catholic party, to the effect that the latter will do whatever possible for the baptism and the Catholic education also of the children who have already been born."

singulis impedimentis iuris ecclesiastici, sive publicis sive occultis, etiam multiplicibus, exceptis impedimentis provenientibus ex sacro presbyteratus ordine et ex affinitate in linea recta, consummato matrimonio, dispensare proprios subditos ubique commorantes et omnes in proprio territorio actu degentes, remoto scandalo, et, si dispensatio concedatur super cultus disparitate aut mixta religione, praestitis consuetis cautionibus.[4]

21. Possunt quoque Ordinarii locorum, sub clausulis in praecedenti numero expressis, dispensationem concedere super omnibus impedimentis quae in praecedenti numero memorata sunt, quoties impedimentum detegatur cum iam omnia sunt parata ad nuptias, nec matrimonium, sine probabili gravis mali periculo, differri possit usque dum a Sancta Sede dispensatio obtineatur.

Haec facultas valet quoque pro convalidatione matrimonii iam contracti, si idem periculum sit in mora nec tempus suppetat recurrendi ad Sanctam Sedem.

Caput V

Facultates pro foro interno

(Ex Sacra Poenitentiaria Apostolica)

49. Dispensandi super occulto criminis impedimento, neutro tamen coniugum machinante, tum in matrimoniis contractis, renovato secreto a partibus consensu, tum in contrahendis, iniuncta in utroque casu gravi poenitentia salutari—restituendi ius amissum petendi debitum.

Caput VII

Animadversiones

54. Facultates caracterem episcopalem non requirentes, Ordinarius suis sacerdotibus subdelegare potest, pro sua prudentia et iudicio.

55. Facultatibus omnibus supradictis Ordinarius sive per se sive per alios uti tantum valet infra limites suae iurisdictionis.

Eas gratis et sine ulla mercede exerceat, factaque semper mentione Apostolicae delegationis.

[4] The faculties add this footnote: "In eisdem rerum adiunctis et solum pro casibus in quibus nec loci quidem Ordinarius adiri possit, eadem dispensandi facultate pollet tum parochus, tum sacerdos qui matrimonio assistit, tum confessarius, sed hic pro foro interno, in actu sacramentalis confessionis tantum."

57. Quod si forte, ex oblivione vel inadvertentia, ultra tempus praefinitum his facultatibus Ordinarium uti contingat, absolutiones, dispensationes, concessiones omnes exinde impertitae uti ratae atque validae habeantur. Insuper datis ab Ordinario precibus pro renovatione seu prorogatione earum facultatum, ipsae in suo robore perseverare censeantur, usque dum responsum huius Sacrae Congregationis ad eumdem Ordinarium pervenerit.

---

2. Questions concerning the form of marriage of Maronites and Melkites in the United States and Canada, submitted by the Archbishop of Montreal.[5]

Quaeritur:

I. Utrum Petrus, maronita, domicilium retinens in dioecesi Marianopolitana, et Maria, baptizata in secta haeretica et domicilium habens in dioecesi Philadelphiensi (in Statibus Foederatis Americae Septentrionalis), valide contrahant matrimonium assistente officiali civili in civitate Neo-Eboracensi (S.F.A.S.) in praesentia duorum testium.

II. Utrum Petrus, maronita, domicilium retinens in dioecesi Marianopolitana, et Catharina, graeco-schismatica, domicilium habens in dioecesi Brookliniensi (S.F.A.S.), valide contrahant matrimonium assistente et benedicente episcopo schismatico orientali in civitate Brookliniensi
 1° in praesentia unius tantum testis
 2° in praesentia duorum saltem testium.

III. Utrum Tita, graeco-melchita catholica, et Titus, graeco-schismaticus, domicilium retinentes in dioecesi Marianopolitana, valide contrahant matrimonium assistente ministro haeretico in civitate Marianopolitana in praesentia duorum testium.

Archevêché de Montréal, le 6 mars 1945.

Roma, 12 Aprile 1945.

SACRA CONGREGAZIONE
"PRO ECCLESIA ORIENTALI"
Prot. N. 112/45

Eccellenza Reverendissima,

Mi reco a premura di significare alla E. V. Rev.ma che questa S. Congregazione ha preso in esame i tre dubbi matrimoniali esposti con lettera in data 6 marzo u.s.

[5] Cf. *Semaine Religieuse de Montréal,* issue of October 17, 1945.

A tal proposito è bene ricordare che la forma tridentina della celebrazione del matrimonio è in vigore presso i Maroniti non in quanto legge tridentina che rigardi anche i Maroniti o la Chiesa Maronita; ma nel senso che la legge tridentina fu da essi ricevuta e adottata col consenso della S. Sede, in maniera che il loro matrimonio deve essere celebrato, sotto pena di nullità, "coram parocho et saltem duobus testibus."

Questa forma di celebrazione del matrimonio obbliga però soltanto i Maroniti che sono entro i confini del proprio Patriarcato e non quelli che sono al difuori.

I Melchiti e i Greci poi non sono tenuti affato alla forma suddetta nè entro nè fuori i confini dei loro rispettivi Patriarcati.

Ciò posto, ai tre dubbi sottopositi da V. E. questa S. Congregazione risponde in senso affermativo, cioè in favore della validità del matrimonio, sempre che la parte protestante sia validamente battezzata, non però nella Chiesa Cattolica. (Cfr. can. 1099.)

Profitto volentieri dell' occasione per esprimerLe i sensi del mio profondo ossequio, con cui mi professo

della Eccellenza Vostra Rev.ma
aff.mo come fratello
Eugène Card. Tisserant
segr.

---

3. A case submitted to the Oriental Congregation by Archbishop Cantwell of Los Angeles concerning a marriage contracted by a Melkite man with a Presbyterian woman before a civil judge.

Eminentissime ac Reverendissime Domine:

Casum expono quo N. N. ex parentibus N. N. et N. N., natus in Wellington, N. Zealand, die 2a Martii 1895, baptizatus in ecclesia S. S. Cordis, Wellington, a sacerdote Catholico Romano, Thoma G. Dawson, die 5a Maii 1895. Scholam Catholicam (Marist Brothers) in Auckland, N. Z., frequentavit ubi sacramenta Sfñi Eucharistiae et Confirmationis recepit. Tandem mense Julii anno 1919 ad Status Foederatos Amer. Sept. cum parentibus venit.

Parentes ejus in Zahle, Lebanon nati—ambo in ritu Greco-Melchito baptizati fuerunt et plusquam 30 annos habentes anno 1892 in N. Zealand venerunt.

N. nunquam ecclesiam ritus latini frequentare destitit, sed die 22a Novembris 1921 cum quadam N. N., baptizata in secta Presbyteriana coram judice civili matrimonium contraxit in civitate Oklahoma, Status Oklahoma, S. F. A. Ab hoc autem matrimonio neque prolis neque felicitas evenit, et multis abhinc annis —die 30a Julii 1926—per divortium civile partes separatae sunt, nec ulla remanet possibilitas vitam conjugalem restaurandi.

Quaeritur: Utrum praedictum matrimonium censendum sit invalidum ob defectum formae juridicae?

Et Deus, . . .

Addictissimus in Domino
Joannes J. Cantwell,
Ordinarius Angelorum.

Romae, die 30 Julii anno 1943.

SACRA CONGREGAZIONE
"PRO ECCLESIA ORIENTALI"
Prot. N. 348/43

Exc.me Domine:

Litteris quibus casum exponebas cuiusdam N. N., melchitae, qui matrimonium iniit cum N. N., presbyteriana, coram magistratu civili, S. haec Congregatio respondendum censuit: "non constare de nullitate matrimonii in casu."

Interim, Tibi omnia a Deo fausta adprecans, eo quo par est obsequio sum et permanere gaudeo

Excellentiae Tuae Rev.mae
Addictissimus uti frater
Eugenius Card. Tisserant.
a secretis.

---

4. A reply of the Oriental Congregation on January 22, 1941, to the Bishop of Brooklyn. Two Melkites had married civilly in Cuba and had never convalidated the marriage. A doubt arose as to the validity of the marriage. The pertinent paragraphs of the reply are as follows:

Città del Vaticano, 22 Genn. 1941.

SACRA CONGREGATIO
"PRO ECCLESIA ORIENTALI"
Prot. N. 690/32

Eccellenza Revm̃a,

Con foglio n. 833/31 in data 20 agosto 1932 il Revm̃o Cancelliere di codesta Curia Vescovile esponeva a questa S. Dicasterio il caso matrimoniale di N. N. con N. N., i quali avevano contratto matrimonio in Cuba soltanto civilmente, e poco dopo si separavano, senza aver fatto prima benedire la loro unione da un sacerdote.

Questo S. Dicastero ha esaminato con lungo studio il dubbio al quale ha dato origine il predetto caso matrimoniale, se cioè il matrimonio contratto da due fedeli di rito greco-melchito (che è lo stesso che dire bizantino) senza la benedizione del sacerdote o "Incoronatio" sia valido o no; e poichè su questo dubbio vi è opposta conclusione tra i dotti, la S. Congregazione dopo aver sottoposta la questione anche ad una Plenaria degli Em̃i Cardinali deve conchiudere che, essendo il diritto incerto, prevale il principio "standum esse pro validitate matrimonii" e pertanto, nel caso N-N non consta della invalidità del loro matrimonio ex defectu formae.

---

5. A reply received by the Archbishop of Chicago concerning a marriage entered by two Maronites before a civil magistrate.

Romae, 20 Aprilis, a. 1943.

SACRA CONGREGAZIONE
"PRO ECCLESIA ORIENTALI"
Prot. N. 178/43

Excellentissime Domine,

Litteris Tuis d. 30 Novembris a. 1942, quae tantum d. 19 mensis currentis ad me pervenerint, haec S. Congregatio prout sequitur respondere decrevit: "Praescriptum Synodi Libanenensis a. 1736 impedimentum dirimens clandestinitatis inducens, ad Maronitas qui tum domicilium cum quasi-domicilium in territorio Patriarchali amiserunt, non censetur extendi. De matrimonii igitur contracti ab N. N. cum N. N., coram magistratu civili, saltem iuxta ea quae refers, nullitate non constat. Si vero partes in bona fide versentur, prudentiae Tuae committitur iudicium, omnibus circumstantiis diligenter perpensis, praesertim vero periculo scandali si casus notus sit aut fiat, de opportunitate responsum huius Sacrae Congregationis significandi sive praefatis coniugibus sive viro cum quo N. N. nunc vivit."

Interim cuncta fausta a Deo Tibi adprecans, sum et remaneo

Tibi addictissimus uti frater
Eugenius Card. Tisserant
a secretis
Ant. Arata, Archiepiscopus Sardicensis
Adsessor

---

6. A case involving the marriage of a Russian schismatic with an unbaptized Methodist before a civil magistrate, as submitted to the Holy See by Bishop Takach.

SACRA CONGREGATIO
"PRO ECCLESIA ORIENTALI"
Città del Vaticano.

Beatissime Pater,

Infrascriptus Episcopus Basilius Takach, Ordinarius Ordinariatus Pittsburgensis ritus byzantino-slavi in Statibus Foederatis Americae septentrionalis, ad pedes Sanctitatis Vestrae humillime provolutus responsa altissima quaerit ad dubia hic proposita.

Die 22 Augusti, anno 1937, quaedam Helena, catholica ritus byzantino-slavi. matrimonium attentavit coram ministello acatholico cum quodam Roberto. methodista nonbaptizato. Poenitentia mota, supradicta Helena petit dispensationem in ordine ad matrimonium convalidandum. Ex investigatione autem apparuit quod supradictus Robertus iam prius matrimonium civile contraxit cum quadam Patricia. Ipsa Patricia vero baptizata et educata fuit in ecclesia Russica dissidentium, et pro quanto scitur, ambo parentes fuerant russiacae nationis et adhaerebant ecclesiae russiacae dissidentium. Hinc quaeritur:

(1) An Patricia, baptizata et educata in ecclesia russiaca dissidentium, validum iniit matrimonium cum Roberto, methodista nonbaptizato, contrahendo matrimonium coram auctoritate civilis tantum juris, contra praescripta antiquae disciplinae byzantinae?

(2) An Patricia, baptizata et educata in ecclesia russiaca dissidentium, volens inire matrimonium cum Roberto, methodista nonbaptizato, tenetur, sub poena nullitatis, petere et obtinere dispensationem super impedimento disparitatis cultus, vel etiam super impedimentum mixtae religionis et disparitatis cultus ad cautelam?

(3) Si affirmative ad secundum, quinam potest valide dispensare in casu? Et Deus etc.

Datum in civitate Munhall, Pa., die 23 novembris, 1943.

Basilius Takach, Ordinarius
episcopus tit. Zelensis.

Romae, die 12 Apr. a. 1945.
Via della Conciliazione 34.

SACRA CONGREGAZIONE
"PRO ECCLESIA ORIENTALI"
Prot. N. 93/45

Exc.me ac Rev.me Domine,

Ad quaesita proposita ab E. T. Rev.ma in litteris d. 23 novembris a. 1943 circa matrimonium Patriciae cum Roberto, audito voto cuiusdam Rev.mi Consultoris, S. Congregatio pro Ecclesia Orientali haec respondendum censuit:

ad 1. um: non constare de nullitate ex hoc capite;

ad 2. um: matrimonium Patriciae cum Roberto ex impedimento disparitatis cultus invalidum est;

ad 3. um: ad dispensandum ab impedimento disparitatis cultus obtinenda est facultas a S.S.C.S. Officii, nisi Delegatus Apostolicus eam concedere valeat.

Haec dum communico Tecum, omni qua par est obsequio sum ac permanere gaudeo

Excellentiae Tuae Rev.mae addictissimus uti frater
Eugenius Card. Tisserant, m.p.
a secretis
Ant. Arata, archiep. Sardicensis,
Adsessor

Exc.mo ac Rev.mo Domino
D. Basilio Takacs
Exarchae Apostolico Ruthen. Subcarpat. in S. F. A.
Homestead

7. The reply of the Oriental Congregation concerning a marriage contracted before a Protestant minister by a Russian dissident woman with a man whose religion was unknown.

12 Aprile 1945.

SACRA CONGREGAZIONE
"PRO ECCLESIA ORIENTALI"
Prot. N. 85/45

Eccellenza Rev.ma,

Riferendomi alla lettera della E.V.Rev.ma in data 2 febbraio u.s. n. 375/45, mi pregio significare alla E.V. che questa S. Congregazione ha preso in esame il dubbio presentato dall'Ecc.mo Mons. Takach a riguardo del matrimonio contratto da Maria, battezzata ed educata nella chiesa russa dissidente, con un certo Guglielmo, di religione ignota, davanti al ministro protestante.

Siccome non risulta che i dissidenti russi siano tenuti ad una qualsiasi forma religiosa nella celebrazione del matrimonio, ne deriva che il matrimonio contratto da Maria con Guglielmo sia da ritenersi valido. Tuttavia si potrebbe esaminare meglio la circostanza della religione ignota del Guglielmo, perchè se risultasse con certezza che egli non è stato battezzato validamente, allora il suo matrimonio con Maria sarebbe nullo ex capite disparitatis cultus, poichè questo impedimento vale anche per i dissidenti russi, essendo stato sancito nel can. 14 del Concilio di Calcedonia; così pure se risultasse con certezza che Guglielmo è cattolico latino, il suo matrimonio con Maria sarebbe nullo per difetto di forma.

V.E. avrà la bontà di comunicare quanto sopra all'Ecc.mo Mons. Takach per sua opportuna intelligenza e norma.

RingraziandoLa in anticipo, con sensi di profondo ossequio mi è grato confermarmi

dell'Eccellenza Vostra Rev.ma
aff.mo come fratello
Eugenio Card. Tisserant
Segr.
Ant. Arata, archiep. Sardicensis
Adsessor

A Sua Eccellenza Rev.ma
Mons. AMLETO GIOVANNI CICOGNANI
Delegato Apostolico,
Washington

8. The reply of the Oriental Congregation concerning a marriage contracted before a Protestant minister by a Serbian dissident man with a Protestant woman.

12 Aprile 1945.

SACRA CONGREGAZIONE
"PRO ECCLESIA ORIENTALI"
Prot. N. 90/1945

Eccellenza Reverendissima,

Riferendomi alla lettera del 2 febbraio u.s. n. 375/45 circa il caso matrimoniale B-V, rispettivamente battezzato ed educato nella Chiesa Serba Dissidente e battezzata ed educata nella setta protestante, i quali hanno contratto matrimonio davanti al ministro protestante, mi pregio far noto all'Eccellenza Vostra Rev.ma che per i serbi non appartenenti al rito latino non è certo che la presenza del sacerdote sia necessaria alla validità del contratto matrimoniale e perciò non consta che il matrimonio contratto dai predetti sia nullo.

Trattandosi, nel caso, di una protestante si potrebbe indagare maggiormente sulla circostanza del suo battesimo, perchè se risultasse con certezza che essa non è stata validamente battezzata, il suo matrimonio con il serbo dissidente sarebbe nullo ex capite disparitatis cultus, da cui sono tenuti anche i serbi dissidenti.

Quanto sopra Vostra Eccellenza avrà la bontà di comunicare allo Eccellentissimo Mons. Takach.

RingraziandoLa fin da ora, mi valgo dell'incontro per confermarmi con sensi di profondo ossequio

dell'Eccellenza Vostra Rev.ma
aff.mo come fratello
Eugenio Card. Tisserant
Segr.
Ant. Arata, archiep. Sardicensis
Adsessor

A Sua Eccellenza Rev.ma
Mons. AMLETO CICOGNANI
Delegato Apostolico
Washington

APPENDIX II

A. Oriental Catholic Churches, Chapels, and Missions in the United States

ARMENIAN

St. Stephen's Chapel,
Very Rev. Pascal Maljian,
Res. 303 Elizabeth Street,
New York, N. Y.

Holy Cross Church,
Rev. Lorenz Kogy, Mechitarist,
27 Hillside Road,
Watertown, Mass.

St. Mark's Church,
Rev. Stephen Stepanian,
Res. 140 N. Robinson Street,
Philadelphia, Pa.

Sacred Heart Church,
Rev. Paul Kouchakji,
Res. 44 Mary Street,
Paterson, N. J.

CHALDEAN

St. Ephraem's Church,
Rev. Francis Thomay,
1054 Oakdale Avenue,
Chicago, Ill.

Chaldean Mission,
Rev. Sergius Sarmas, Adm.,
Res. St. Francis Hospital,
Hartford, Conn.

MARONITE

ALABAMA:
St. Elias' Church,
Rev. Joseph F. AbiChedid,
2007 6th Avenue,
Birmingham.

CALIFORNIA:
Our Lady of Mount Lebanon Church,
Rev. Philip Nagem,
1307 Warren Avenue,
Los Angeles.

CONNECTICUT:
St. Anthony's Church,
Rt. Rev. George Zouain, C.B.,[6]
Rt. Rev. Louis Zouain,
34 New Street,
Danbury.

St. Maron's Church,
Rt. Rev. Paul A. Rezk, C.B.,
613 Main Street,
Torrington.

GEORGIA:
St. Joseph's Church,
Rev. Paul Risk, Adm.,
291 Hunter Street S. E.,
Atlanta.

INDIANA:
Sacred Heart Church,
Rt. Rev. Michael Abraham, C.B.,
1001 West 8th Street,
Michigan City.

[6] C. B. refers to the title of Chor-Bishop (*Chorepiskopos*).

MAINE:
St. Joseph's Church,
Rev. Joseph E. Awad,
1 Appleton Street,
Waterville.

MASSACHUSETTS:
Our Lady of the Cedars of Lebanon Church,
Rt. Rev. Stephen el-Douaihy,
457 Shawmut Avenue,
Boston.

St. Anthony's Church,
Rt. Rev. Joseph David,
258 Elm Street,
Lawrence.

St. Theresa's Church,
Rt. Rev. Paul Merab,
106 No. Montello Street,
Brockton.

St. Anthony's Church,
Rev. Michael Abi Saab,
50 Charles Street,
Springfield.

Our Lady of Mercy Church,
Rev. J. M. Reardon, Adm.,[7]
70 Mulberry Street,
Worcester.

Church of St. Anthony of the Desert,
Rev. Joseph Eid, D.D., Ph.D.,
359 Quequechan Street,
Fall River.

Our Lady of Purgatory Church,
Rev. Joseph Eid, D.D., Ph.D.,
11 Franklin Street,
New Bedford.

MICHIGAN:
St. Maron's Church,
Rev. Michael G. Abdoo,
1555 E. Congress Street,
Detroit.

MINNESOTA:
St. Maron's Church,
Rt. Rev. Peter Assemani, C.B.,
602 University Avenue,
Minneapolis.

Holy Family Church,
Rt. Rev. Peter Aschkar, C.B.,
201 East Robie Street,
St. Paul.

MISSOURI:
St. Raymond's Church,
Rev. John M. Marren, Adm.,
Rev. Joakim Stephen,
925 La Salle Street,
St. Louis.

Church of St. Anthony the Hermit,
Rev. Joakim Stephen,
209 Walnut Street,
St. Louis.

NEW HAMPSHIRE:
St. George's Church,
Dover.

NEW YORK:
St. Joseph's Church,
Rt. Rev. Francis Wakim, C.B.,
57 Washington Street,
New York.

Our Lady of Lebanon Church
Rt. Rev. Mansour Stephen, C.B.,
113 Remsen Street,
Brooklyn.

[7] A Latin diocesan priest.

St. John Maron's Church,
Rt. Rev. Francis Shemalie,
41 Cedar Street,
Buffalo.

Church of St. Louis Gonzaga,
Rev. Francis Lahoud,
519 Rutger Street,
Utica.

St. Joseph's Church,
Rev. Nemat Allah Chemaly,
331 No. 4th Street,
Olean.

St. Anne's Church,
Rt. Rev. Stephen Corkemaz, C.B.,
190 4th Street,
Troy.

Our Lady of Lebanon Church,
(Attended by Latin priests from Niagara University),
327 Elizabeth Street,
Niagara Falls.

OHIO:
St. Maron's Church,
Rev. Joseph Komaid,
2214 East 14th Street,
Cleveland.

St. Maron's Church,
Rev. Peter Eid,
120 S. Forest Avenue,
Youngstown.

Church of St. Anthony of Padua,
Rev. Charles L. Moore, Adm.,[7]
429 East 3rd Street,
Cincinnati.

Our Lady of the Cedars of Lebanon Church,
Rev. Paul Corkemaz,
281 Codding Street,
Akron.

PENNSYLVANIA:
St. Maron's Church,
Rev. John Nehme,
1005 Ellsworth Street,
Philadelphia.

Our Lady of Lebanon Church,
Rev. William J. Magee, Adm.,[7]
321 Lehigh Street,
Easton.

St. Ann's Church,
Rev. Joseph Solomon,
1320 Price Street,
Scranton.

St. Anthony's Church,
Rev. John Khoury,
253 Dana Street,
Wilkes-Barre.

St. George's Church,
Rev. David Mouallem,
79 Loomis Street,
Wilkes-Barre.

St. George's Church,
Rev. Nematallah Hayek,
124 Lincoln Street,
Uniontown.

Church of St. John the Baptist,
Rev. Elias G. Nader,
2 West Reynolds Street,
New Castle.

St. Anne's Church,
Rt. Rev. Elias Basil, C.B.,
33 Fullerton Street,
Pittsburgh.

RHODE ISLAND:
St. George's Church,
Rev. Nematallah Gedeon,
85 America Street,
Providence.

TEXAS:
St. George's Church,
Rev. Anthony Dahdah,
426 No. Pecos Street,
San Antonio.

VIRGINIA:
St. Anthony's Church,
Rev. Anthony Korkemaz, J.C.D.,
2501-A East Broad Street,
Richmond.

St. Elias' Church,
Rt. Rev. Peter Rabil, C.B.,
701 Salem Avenue, S.W.,
Roanoke.

WEST VIRGINIA:
Our Lady of Mount Lebanon Church,
Rev. Paul Abraham,
2216 Eoff Street,
Wheeling.

MELKITE

ALABAMA:
St. George's Church,
Rt. Rev. Andrew Hallak,
1224 9th Avenue, S.,
Birmingham.

CALIFORNIA:
St. Ann's Church,
Rt. Rev. Clement Salman,
812½ N. Hoover Street,
Los Angeles.

CONNECTICUT:
St. Ann's Church,
Rt. Rev. Philip Salmone,
51 William Street,
Danbury.

St. Ann's Church,
Rev. Basil Shaheen, B.S., Adm.,
7 Connecticut Avenue,
New London.

ILLINOIS:
Church of St. John the Baptist,
Rev. Raphael Riashi, O.S.B.M.,
1249 S. Washtenaw Avenue,
Chicago.

MASSACHUSETTS:
St. Joseph's Church,
Rt. Rev. Peter Abouzeid,
298 Oak Street,
Lawrence.

Our Lady of Annunciation Church,
Warren Avenue and W. Canton Street,
Boston.

Our Lady of Perpetual Help Church,
Archimandrite Polycarpe Warde,
13½ Houghton Street,
Worcester.

MICHIGAN:
Our Lady of Redemption Church,
Rt. Rev. Agabios Riashi,
2731 McDougall Street,
Detroit.

NEW JERSEY:
St. Ann's Church,
Rev. Cyril Anid,
235 Mill Street,
Paterson.

NEW YORK:
St. George's Church,
Archimandrite Bernard Ghosn,
103 Washington Street,
New York.

Church of the Virgin Mary,
Rev. Nicholas Araktingi,
134 Amity Street,
Brooklyn.

St. Basil's Church,
Rt. Rev. Benedictus Abdelnour,
527 Lansing Street,
Utica.

NEBRASKA:
St. Saviour's Church,
Rev. Marcel T. Keliher, Adm.,[7]
1468 So. 13th Street,
Omaha.

OHIO:
St. Elias' Church,
Archimandrite Malatios Mufleh,
1216 Webster Avenue,
Cleveland.

St. Joseph's Church,
Archimandrite Paul K. Malouf, Adm.,
W. Exchange Street at Rhodes Avenue,
Akron.

PENNSYLVANIA:
Our Lady of Mercy Church,
Rev. Philip K. Sayegh,
9 So. West Street,
Shenandoah.

St. Joseph's Church,
Rev. Joseph A. McGowan,[7]
130 Chestnut Street,
Scranton.

RHODE ISLAND:
St. Basil's Church,
Rev. Timothy Jock,
445 Broad Street,
Central Falls.

St. Elias' Church,
Hamilton and Jackson Streets,
Woonsocket.

WISCONSIN:
St. George's Church,
Rev. Raphael Gedah,
1617 W. State Street,
Milwaukee.

RUTHENIAN

(Cf. *The Catholic Directory*, 1945, pp. 771-779.)

RUMANIAN

ILLINOIS:
St. Michael's Church,
Very Rev. Basil Marchis,
609 No. Lincoln Avenue,
Aurora.

INDIANA:
St. Nicholas' Church,
Rev. George Muresan,
4310 Olcott Avenue,
East Chicago.

St. Demetrius' Church,
Rev. Anthony Dunca,
3801 Butternut Avenue,
East Chicago (Indiana Harbor).

St. Mary's Church,
Rev. Anthony Dunca,
15th Avenue and Lincoln Street,
Gary.

MICHIGAN:
Church of St. John the Baptist,
Rev. George Pop,
13594 Orleans Street,
Detroit.

St. Mary's Church,
Rev. George Pop,
2640 Holly Street,
Dearborn.

NEW JERSEY:
St. Basil's Church,
Rev. Gabriel Ivascu,
238 Adeline Street,
Trenton.

St. Mary's Church,
Rev. Gabriel Ivascu,
26 Alden Avenue,
Roebling.

OHIO:
St. Helena's Church,
Rev. George Babutiu,
1367 W. 65th Street,
Cleveland.

Most Holy Trinity Church,
Rev. George Babutiu,
2650 E. 93rd Street,
Cleveland.

St. Basil's Church,
Rev. George Babutiu,
Gary Avenue and 31st Street,
Lorain.

St. George's Church,
Rev. Elie Crihalmean,
1835 7th Street N. E.,
Canton.

St. Theodore's Church,
Rev. Elie Crihalmean,
520 N. Freedom Street,
Alliance.

St. Mary's Church,
Rev. John Spatariu,
73 So. Prospect Street,
Youngstown.

PENNSYLVANIA:
Church of St. John the Baptist,
Rev. Louis Puscas,
1119 Market Avenue,
Farrell.

St. George's Church,
Rev. Louis Puscas,
1711 Plum Street,
Erie.

St. Mary's Church,
Scalp Level.

St. Mary's Church,
Rev. John Spatariu,
318 26th Street,
McKeesport.

RUSSIAN

St. Andrew's Church,
Rev. John H. Ryder, S.J.,
453 So. Cummings Street,
Los Angeles, Calif.

St. Michael's Chapel,
Rev. Andrew Rogosh,
266 Mulberry Street,
New York, N. Y.

B. Oriental Catholic Churches in Canada

MARONITE

St. Peter's Church,
Rev. Salwanos Jowdy,
686 Marentette Avenue,
Windsor, Ontario.

Rev. Louis Souaib,
Sydney, Cape Breton,
Nova Scotia.

MELKITE

Church of St. Sauveur,
Rt. Rev. Maximos Chataoui,
329 Avenue Viger,
Montreal, Canada.

RUTHENIAN

Cf. *Le Canada Ecclésiastique,* 1945, pp. 532-537; *The Catholic Directory,* 1945, Part III, pp. 138-139.

BIBLIOGRAPHY

Sources

Acta Apostolicae Sedis, Commentarium Officiale, Romae, 1909—

Acta et Decreta Concilii Nationis Armenorum Romae habiti ad Sancti Nicolai Tolentinatis anno MDCCCCXI, Romae: Typis Polyglottis Vaticanis, 1913.

Acta et Decreta Sacrorum Conciliorum Recentiorum, Collectio Lacensis, 7 vols., Friburgi Brisgoviae: Herder, 1870-1890.

Acta Sanctae Sedis, 41 vols., Romae, 1865-1908.

Anaissi, Tobias, *Bullarium Maronitarum,* Romae, 1911.

Bouscaren, T. Lincoln, *The Canon Law Digest,* 2 vols., Milwaukee: Bruce, 1934, 1943.

Bruns, Hermann T., *Canones Apostolorum et Conciliorum Saeculorum, IV, V, VI, VII,* 2 vols., Berolini, 1839.

Bullarii Romani Continuatio, 14 vols., Prati, 1861.

Bullarum Diplomatum et Privilegiorum Sanctorum Pontificum Taurinensis editio, 24 vols. in 25, Augustae Taurinorum, 1857-1872.

Bullarium Pontificium Sacrae Congregationis de Propaganda Fide, 8 vols., Romae, 1839-1848.

Chabot, J. B., *Syndicon Orientale,* Paris, 1902.

Codex Iuris Canonici Pii X Pontificis Maximi iussu digestus Benedicti Papae XV auctoritate promulgatus, Romae: Typis Polyglottis Vaticanis, 1917.

Codex Theodosianus, ed. Paulus Krueger, Berolini: Apud Weidmannos, 1928.

Codicis Iuris Canonici Fontes cura Emi Petri Card. Gasparri editi, 9 vols., Romae (postea Civitate Vaticana): Typis Polyglottis Vaticanis, 1923-1939. (Vols. VII, VIII et IX ed. *cura et studio Emi Iustiniani Card. Serédi.*)

Codificazione Canonica Orientale, Fonti, Parte I, 16 vols., Parte II, 3 Serii, Città del Vaticano: Tipografia Polyglotta Vaticana, 1930—.

Collectanea S. Congregationis de Propaganda Fide, 2 vols., Romae: Typographia Polyglotta, S. C. de Propaganda Fide, 1907.

Corpus Iuris Canonici, editio Lipsiensis secunda, post Aemilii Richteri curas instruxit Aemilius Friedberg, 2 vols., Lipsiae, 1879-1881.

Corpus Iuris Civilis, 3 vols., Vol. I., *Institutiones* recognovit Paulus Kreuger, *Digesta* recognovit Theodorus Mommsen, retractavit Paulus Kreuger, 15. ed.; Vol. II, *Codex Iustinianus* recognovit et retractavit Paulus Kreuger, 10. ed.; Vol. III, *Novellae* recognovit Rudolfus Schoell, absolvit Gulielmus Kroll, 5. ed., Berolini: Apud Weidmannos, 1928-1929.

Ecloga, The, A Manual of Roman Law, trans. by Edwin Freshfield, Cambridge: The University Press, 1926.

Fontes Iuris Romani Antejustiniani, ed. Ioannes Baviera, Florentiae, 1909.

Funk, Franz X., *Didascalia et Constitutiones Apostolorum,* 2 vols. in 1, Paderbornae, 1905.

Funk, F. X.-Bihlmeyer, K., *Die Apostolischen Väter,* Tubingen, 1924.

Galante, Andreas, *Fontes Iuris Canonici Selecti,* Oeniponte, 1906.

Ius Graecoromanum, Vol. I, *Novellae et Aureae Bullae Imperatorum post Iustinianum,* ed. Zacharias von Lingenthal, Athenis, 1930.

Ius Pontificium de Propaganda Fide, ed. R. de Martinis, *Pars Prima,* 7 vols. in 8 (Vol. VIII, Supplementum et Index), Romae, 1888-1897; *Pars Secunda,* 1 vol., Romae, 1909.

Jaffé, Phillipus, *Regesta Pontificum Romanorum ab condita Ecclesia ad annum post Christum natum MCXCVIII,* 2. ed., correctam et auctam auspiciis Gulielmi Wattenbach curaverunt F. Kaltenbrunner, P. Ewald, S. Löwenfeld, 2 tomes in 1 vol., Lipsiae, 1885-1888.

Lauchert, Friedrich, *Die Kanones der wichtigsten altkirchlichen Concilien nebst den apostolischen Kanones,* Leipzig, 1896.

Mai, A., *Scriptorum Veterum Nova Collectio,* e vaticanis codicibus edita, Vol. X, Romae, 1838.

Mansi, Ioannes, *Sacrorum Conciliorum Nova et Amplissima Collectio,* 53 vols. in 60, Parisiis, Arnhem, Lipsiae, 1901-1927.

Monumenta Germaniae Historica, Epistolae, Tom. VI, pars 2, fasc. 1: *Epistolae Karolini Aevi,* ed. E. Perels, Berolini, 1912.

Pitra, Joannes B., *Iuris Ecclesiastici Graecorum Historia et Monumenta,* 2 vols., Romae, 1864, 1868.

Potthast, Augustus, *Regesta Pontificum Romanorum inde ab anno post Christum natum MCXCVIII ad annum MCCCIV,* 2 vols., Berolini, 1874-1875.

Sacrae Romanae Rotae Decisiones seu Sententiae, Romae, 1912—.

Synodus Gangrensis evangelicae promulgationis anno circiter trecentesimo congregata, Parisiis, 1560.

Synodus Provincialis Ruthenorum, habita in civitate Zamosciae anno MDCCXX, 3. ed., Romae, 1883.

Synodus Sciarfensis Syrorum in Monte Libano celebrata anno 1888, Romae: S. C. de Propaganda Fide, 1896.

Schroeder, H. J., *Canons and Decrees of the Council of Trent,* Original Text with English Translation, St. Louis: Herder, 1941.

Authors

Abraham, Paul, *The Maronites of Lebanon,* Wheeling, 1931.

Acta Congressus Iuridici Internationalis, 5 vols., Romae, 1935-1937.

Adeney, Walter, *The Greek and Eastern Churches,* New York, 1908.

Assemani, Joseph Simon, *Bibliotheca Iuris Orientalis (Clementino-Vaticana),* 3 vols. in 4, Romae, 1719-1728.

Attwater, Donald, *The Catholic Eastern Churches,* 2. ed., Milwaukee: Bruce, 1937.

———, *The Dissident Eastern Churches,* Milwaukee: Bruce, 1937.

Ayrinhac, H. A., *Constitution of the Church,* New York: Longmans, Green, 1930.

[Bachofen], Charles Augustine, *A Commentary on the New Code of Canon Law,* Vol. V, 4. ed., St. Louis: Herder, 1929.

Badger, G. P., *The Nestorians and Their Rituals,* ed. by J. M. Neale, 2 vols., London, 1852.

Baronius, Caesar, *Annales Ecclesiastici,* 37 vols., ed. Theiner, Vols. I-XXVIII, Barri-Ducis, 1864-1875; Vols. XXIX-XXXVII, Parisiis, 1876-1883.

Bélanger, Louis-E., *Les Ukrainiens catholiques du rit grec-ruthène au Canada,* Québec: l'Université Laval, 1945.

Benedictus XIV, *Opera Omnia,* 17 vols. in 18, Prati, 1829-1847.

Beneševic, Vladimir, *Iohannis Scholastici Synagoga L titulorum, Abhandungen der Bayerischen Akademie der Wissenschaften,* N. F. Heft 14, München, 1937.

Beste, Uldalricus, *Introductio in Codicem,* ed. altera, Collegeville: St. John's Abbey Press, 1944.

Biernacki, Nicolaus, *Ius "orthodoxum" Russorum respectu iuris Ecclesiae Romano-catholicae consideratum,* Posnaniae, 1914.

Bingham, Joseph, *The Antiquities of the Christian Church,* 2 vols., London, 1845.

Bobak, Joannes, *De caelibatu ecclesiastico deque impedimento Ordinis Sacri apud Orientales et praesertim apud Ruthenos,* Urbaniana, Series II, Num. 3, Romae: Officium Libri Catholici, 1941.

Borgomanero, J., *Quaestiones practicae Theologicae Moralis ad usum Missionariorum praesertim orientalium regionum,* Romae, 1910.

Boudinhon, A., *Le Mariage et les Fiançailles,* Paris, 1912.

Brian-Chaninov, Nicholas, *The Russian Church,* trans. by Warre B. Wells, London: Burns, Oates & Washbourne, 1931.

Cance, Adrien, *Le Code de Droit canonique,* 7. ed., 3 vols., Paris: Lecoffre, 1933-1934.

Cappello, Felix, *Tractatus Canonico-Moralis de Sacramentis,* 3 vols. in 6, Romae: Marietti, 1932-1939. Vol. III, Partes I et II, *De Matrimonio,* 4. ed., 1939.

———, *Summa Iuris Canonici,* 3 vols., Romae: Apud Aedes Universitatis Gregorianae, Vol. I, 3. ed., 1938; Vol. II, 3. ed., 1939; Vol. III, ed. altera, 1940.

Carberry, John J., *The Juridical Form of Marriage,* The Catholic University of America Canon Law Studies, n. 84, Washington, D. C.: The Catholic University of America, 1934.

Cayré, F., *Manual of Patrology,* trans. by H. Howitt, 2 vols., Paris: Desclée, 1936, 1940.

Chabot, J. B., *Littérature Syriaque,* Bibliothèque Catholique des Sciences Religieuses, n. 66, Paris: Bloud et Gay, 1934.

Chamberlin, William H., *The Ukraine,* New York: Macmillan, 1944.

Charon, Cyril (Korolevskij), *Histoire des Patriarcats Melkites,* Vol. II, fasc. 1, and Vol. III, Rome, 1910, 1911.

Chelodi, Ioannes, *Ius Matrimoniale iuxta Codicem,* 3. ed., Tridenti, 1921.

Cicognani, Amleto, *Ius Canonicum,* Romae, 1925.

———, *Canon Law,* trans. by J. O'Hara and F. Brennan, Philadelphia: The Dolphin Press, 1935.

———, *Commentarium ad Librum Primum Codicis Iuris Canonici,* recognitum et auctum a Dino Staffa, 2 vols., Romae, 1939, 1942.

Cimetier, F., *Les Sources du Droit Ecclésiastique,* Paris: Bloud et Gay, 1930.

Corbett, Percy, *The Roman Law of Marriage,* Oxford: The Clarendon Press, 1930.

Coronata, Matthaeus Conte a, *Institutiones Iuris Canonici,* 5 vols., Vols. I-II, 2. ed., 1939; Vol. III, 2. ed., 1941; Vol. IV, 2. ed., 1945; Vol. V, 1936, Taurini, Romae: Marietti, 1936-1945.

Coussa, Acacius, *Epitome Praelectionum de Iure Ecclesiastico Orientali,* 2 vols., Vol. I, Città del Vaticano: Typis Polyglottis Vaticanis, 1940; Vol. II, Venetiis: Typis Polyglottis Insulae S. Lazari, 1941.

Danzas, J. N., *The Russian Church,* trans. by Countess Olga Bennigsen, London: Sheed & Ward, 1936.

Dausend, Hugo, *Das interrituelle Recht im Codex Iuris Canonici,* Paderborn: Schöningh, 1939.

Dauvillier, Jean, *Le Mariage dans le Droit classique de L'Église,* Paris: Recueil Sirey, 1933.

———, et De Clercq, Carlo, *Le Mariage en Droit canonique Oriental,* Paris: Recueil Sirey, 1936.

Dawson, Christopher, *The Making of Europe,* New York: Sheed & Ward, 1945.

De Angelis, Philippus, *Praelectiones Iuris Canonici,* 5 vols. in 9 (Vols. 4, 5 prosequi curavit Nazarenus Gentilini, 1881-1891), Romae, 1877-1891.

De Becker, Julius, *De Matrimonio Praelectiones Canonicae,* ed. nova, Lovanii, 1931.

De Clercq, Carlo, *Les Églises Unies d'Orient,* Bibliothèque Catholique des Sciences Religieuses, n. 65, Paris: Bloud et Gay, 1934.

———, *Ordre, Mariage, Extrême-Onction,* Bibliothèque Catholique des Sciences Religieuses, n. 83, Paris: Bloud et Gay, 1939.

Denzinger, Henricus, *Ritus Orientalium, Coptorum, Syrorum et Armenorum in Administrandis Sacramentis,* 2 vols., Wirceburgi, 1863.

De Smet, Aloysius, *De Sponsalibus et Matrimonio,* 4. ed., Brugis: Charles Bayaert, 1927.

Dictionnaire d'histoire et de géographie ecclésiastique, Paris, 1909—.

Dictionnaire de théologie catholique, Paris, 1903—.

Dillon, Robert E., *Common Law Marriage,* The Catholic University of America Canon Law Studies, n. 153, Washington, D. C.: The Catholic University of America Press, 1942.

Doheny, William, *Canonical Procedure in Matrimonial Cases,* Vol. I, *Formal Procedure,* Vol. II, *Informal Procedure,* Milwaukee: Bruce, 1938, 1944.

Donohue, John F., *The Impediment of Crime,* The Catholic University of America Canon Law Studies, n. 69, Washington, D. C.: The Catholic University of America, 1931.

Donovan, James J., *The Pastor's Obligation in Pre-Nuptial Investigation,* The Catholic University of America Canon Law Studies, n. 115, Washington, D. C.: The Catholic University of America, 1938.

Duchesne, Louis, *Christian Worship,* 3. ed., trans. by M. McClure, London, 1903.

———, *The Churches Separated from Rome,* trans. by D. Mathew, New York: Benziger Bros., 1907.

Duskie, John A., *The Canonical Status of Orientals in the United States,* The Catholic University of America Canon Law Studies, n. 48, Washington, D. C.: The Catholic University of America, 1928.

Duval, Rubens, *Anciennes Littératures Chrétiennes, II, La Littérature Syriaque,* Paris, 1907.

Dziob, Michael, *The Sacred Oriental Congregation,* The Catholic University of America Canon Law Studies, n. 214, Washington, D. C.: The Catholic University of America Press, 1945.

Eastern Branches of the Catholic Church, The, Six Studies on the Oriental Rites, New York: Longmans, Green & Co., 1938.

Eid, Joseph, *A l'Ombre des Cèdres ou L'Épopée de Liban,* Fall River, Mass., 1940.

Esmein, A.-Genestal, R.-Dauvillier, J., *Le Mariage en Droit Canonique,* 2. ed., 2 vols., Paris: Sirey, 1929-1935.

Ferraris, Lucius, *Prompta Bibliotheca, Canonica, Iuridica, Moralis, Theologica necnon Ascetica, Polemica, Rubricistica, Historica,* 9 vols., ed. novissima, Romae, 1885-1899.

Fleury, Jean, *Recherches Historiques sur les Empêchements de Parenté dans le Mariage Canonique,* Paris: R. Sirey, 1933.

Fortescue, Adrian, *The Orthodox Eastern Church,* London, 1907.

———, *The Lesser Eastern Churches,* London, 1913.

———, *The Uniate Eastern Churches,* ed. G. Smith, London: Burns, Oates & Washbourne, 1923.

Gasparri, Petrus, *Tractatus Canonicus de Matrimonio,* 3. ed., 2 vols., Paris, 1904.

———, *Tractatus Canonicus de Matrimonio,* ed. nova ad mentem Codicis Iuris Canonici, 2 vols. in 1, Romae, 1932.

Giamil, Samuel, *Genuinae Relationes inter Sedem Apostolicam et Assyriorum Orientalium seu Chaldaeorum Ecclesiam,* Romae, 1902.

Gilbert, Maurice, *Le Mariage des Prêtres,* Paris: A. Rousseau, 1904.

Goodwine, Joseph, *The Reception of Converts,* The Catholic University of America Canon Law Studies, n. 198, Washington, D. C.: The Catholic University of America Press, 1944.

Gregory, Donald J., *The Pauline Privilege*, The Catholic University of America Canon Law Studies, n. 68, Washington, D. C.: The Catholic University of America, 1931.

Halich, Wasyl, *Ukrainians in the United States*, Chicago: The University of Chicago Press, 1937.

Hayes, Carlton J. H., *A Generation of Materialism (1871-1900)*, New York: Harper & Brothers, 1941.

Hefele, Karl, and Le Clercq, Henri, *Histoire des Conciles*, 10 vols. in 19, Paris: Letouzey and Ané, 1907-1938.

Hervé, J. M.: *Manuale Theologiae Dogmaticae*, 17. ed., 3 vols., Parisiis, 1934.

Historical Records Survey, Inventory of the Church Archives in New York City, Vol. II, The Archdiocese of New York, New York: Community Service Projects, 1941.

Hitti, Philip, *The Syrians in America*, New York, 1924.

Hrushevsky, Michael, *A History of Ukraine*, ed. by O. Frederiksen, New Haven: Yale University Press, 1941.

Janin, Raymond, *Les Églises orientales et les Rites orientaux*, 3. ed., Paris: La Bonne Press, 1926.

———, *The Separated Eastern Churches*, trans. by P. Boylan, St. Louis: B. Herder, 1933.

Joyce, George, *Christian Marriage*, New York: Sheed & Ward, 1933.

Kay, Thomas, *Competence in Matrimonial Procedure*, The Catholic University of America Canon Law Studies, n. 53, Washington, D. C.: The Catholic University of America, 1929.

Kidd, Beresford, *The Churches of Eastern Christendom*, London: The Faith Press, 1927.

King, William F., *Benedict XIV and the Orientals*, Fascicle I, Documents, Roma: Pontificium Institutum Orientalium Studiorum, 1940.

Koncevicius, Joseph, *Russia's Attitude Towards Union with Rome (9th-16th centuries)*, Washington, D. C.: The Catholic University, 1927.

Korkemaz, Antoine, *Le Mariage dans L'Église Maronite*, Paris: L'Institut Catholique, 1938.

Köstler, Rudolf, *Das österreichische Konkordats-Eherecht*, Wien, 1937.

Leage, R. W., *Roman Private Law*, 2. ed. by C. Ziegler, London: Macmillan, 1942.

Ledit, Joseph, *Praelectiones de Theologia Orientali*, Quebec: Universitas Lavallensis, 1942.

———, *Praelectiones de Iure Canonico Orientali*, Quebec: Universitas Lavallensis, 1943.

MacKenzie, Eric, *The Canonical Status of the Ruthenian Rite in the United States*, Washington, D. C.: The Catholic University of America, 1919.

Malcom, M. Vartan, *The Armenians in America*, Boston, 1919.

Mansella, Joseph, *De Impedimentis Matrimonium dirimentibus ac de Processu iudiciali in Causis Matrimonialibus*, Romae, 1881.

Maroto, Philippus, *Institutiones Iuris Canonici ad normam Novi Codicis,* 2 vols., Romae, 1919.

Marx, Adolph, *The Declaration of Nullity of Marriages Contracted Outside the Church,* The Catholic University of America Canon Law Studies, n. 182, Washington, D. C.: The Catholic University of America Press, 1943.

McCloskey, Joseph, *The Subject of Ecclesiastical Law According to Canon 12,* The Catholic University of America Canon Law Studies, n. 165, Washington, D. C.: The Catholic University of America Press, 1942.

Michiels, Gommarus, *Normae Generales Iuris Canonici,* 2 vols., Lublin: Universitas Catholica, 1929.

Migne, Jacques P., *Patrologiae Cursus Completus,* Series Graeca, 161 vols., Parisiis, 1856-1866.

———, *Patrologiae Cursus Completus,* Series Latina, 221 vols., Parisiis, 1844-1864.

Moyle, J. B., *Imperatoris Justiniani Institutiones,* Oxford: Clarendon Press, 1923.

Nau, F., *Les Canons et les Resolutions canoniques de Rabboula, Jean de Tella, Cyriaque d'Amid, Jacques d'Edesse, George des Arabes, Cyriaque d'Antioche, Jean III, Theodose d'Antioches et des Perses,* Paris, 1906.

Noldin, H., *Summa Theologiae Moralis,* recognitum et emendatum a A. Schmitt, 25. ed., 3 vols., Oeniponte, 1938.

O'Dea, John, *The Matrimonial Impediment of Nonage,* The Catholic University of America Canon Law Studies, n. 205, Washington, D. C.: The Catholic University of America Press, 1944.

Papp-Szilagyi, Joseph, *Enchiridion Iuris Ecclesiae Orientalis Catholicae,* 2. ed., Magno-Varadini, 1880.

Pargoire, J., *L'Église Byzantine de 527 à 847,* Paris, 1905.

Payen, G., *De Matrimonio in Missionibus,* 2. ed., 3 vols., Zi-ka-wei, 1935-1936.

Petrovits, Joseph J. C., *The New Church Law on Matrimony,* 2. ed., Philadelphia: John Joseph McVey, 1926.

Perhac, George, *Married Priests in the Catholic Church,* Brooklyn, 1934.

Petrani, Alexius, *De Relatione Iuridica inter Diversos Ritus in Ecclesia Catholica,* Taurini et Romae: Marietti, 1930.

Pitzipios, Jacques, *L'Église Orientale,* Rome: Propaganda, 1855.

Prümmer, D. M., *Manuale Iuris Canonici,* 3. ed., Friburgi Brisgoviae, 1922.

Raab, Clement, *The Twenty Ecumenical Councils of the Catholic Church,* New York: Longmans, Green, 1937.

Rodrigo, Lucius, *Praelectiones Theologico-Moralis Comillenses,* Series I, *Theologia Moralis Fundamentalis,* Tom. II, *Tractatus de legibus,* Santander: Sal Terrae, 1944.

Rossi, Joseph, *De Matrimonii Celebratione,* Romae, 1924.

Schenk, Francis J., *The Matrimonial Impediments of Mixed Religion and Disparity of Cult,* The Catholic University of America Canon Law Studies, n. 51, Washington, D. C.: The Catholic University of America, 1929.

Schroeder, H. J., *Disciplinary Decrees of the General Councils,* St. Louis: Herder, 1937.

Scott, S. P., *The Civil Law,* 17 vols. in 7, Cincinnati: The Central Trust Co., 1932.

Separated Christians of the Orient, The, The Year Book, Vol. XX, St. Bonaventure Seminary, St. Bonaventure, N. Y., 1936.

Shipman, Andrew J., A Memorial of, ed. by Condé B. Pallen, New York: Encyclopedia Press, 1916.

Sipos, Stephanus, *Enchiridion Iuris Canonici,* 3. ed., Pécs: Ex Typographia "Haladás R. T.," 1936.

Souarn, Romualdus, *Praxis Missionarii in Oriente servata,* Paris, 1911.

Stanley, Arthur, *Lectures on the History of the Eastern Church,* London, 1889.

Statistica, con cenni storici della Gerarchia e dei Fedeli di Rito Orientale, Sacra Congregazione Orientale, Roma: Typografia Poliglotta Vaticana, 1932.

Thomay, Francis, *A House of Prayer and Worship for the Christians of the Land of Paradise,* Chicago, 1945.

Tondini, Caesarius, *The Future of the Russian Church,* New York, 1876.

Van Hove, A., *Commentarium Lovaniense in Codicem Iuris Canonici,* Vol. I, Tom. I (*Prolegomena*), 2. ed., Mechliniae-Romae: Dessain, 1945; Tom. II, *De Legibus Ecclesiasticis,* Mechliniae-Romae: Dessain, 1930.

Vermeersch, Arthurus, *Theologiae Moralis, Principia-Responsa-Consilia,* 3. ed., 4 vols., Romae, 1933-1937.

Vermeersch, Arthurus-Creusen, Josephus, *Epitome Iuris Canonici,* 3 vols., Vol. I, ed. sexta, 1937, Vol. II, ed. sexta, 1940, Vol. III, ed. quinta, 1936, Mechliniae-Romae: Dessain.

Vlaming, Th. M., *Praelectiones Iuris Matrimonii,* 3. ed., 2 vols., Bussum in Hollandia, 1919, 1921.

Wernz, F.-Vidal, P., *Ius Canonicum,* 7 vols. in 8, Romae: Universitas Gregoriana, 1923-1938.

Wernz, Franciscus X, *Ius Decretalium,* 2. ed., 6 vols., Romae et Prati, 1906-1913.

White, Leo F., *De Forma Celebrationis Matrimonii seu de Clandestinitate apud Byzantinos Catholicos,* Romae: Pontificium Institutum Utriusque Juris, 1935.

Wouters, Ludovicus, *Manuale Theologiae Moralis,* 2 vols., Brugis: Beyaert, 1933.

Woywod, Stanislaus, *A Brief Explanation of the Decree "Ne temere,"* Philadelphia, The Dolphin Press, 1913.

Articles

Pius XII, Pont. Max. (Eugène Pacelli), "La personnalité et la territorialité des lois particulièrement dans le droit canon,"—*Ephemerides Canonicae,* I (1945), 5-27.

Arendt, G., "De exclusiva S. Officii competentia circa matrimonium mixtum (can. 247),"—*Jus Pontificium,* VII (1927), 120-137.

Arndt, A., "De rituum relatione iuridica ad invicem,"—*Analecta Ecclesiastica,* II (1894), 416-421, 499-504; III (1895), 41-45, 86-89, 181-188, 222-227, 268-273.

Attwater, D., "Byzantine Catholics in Italy,"—*The Eastern Churches Quarterly,* V (1942-1944), 325-330.

Ayrout, H., "The Melkites and the Mohammedans,"—*The Eastern Churches Quarterly,* IV (1940-1941), 64-67.

Bernardini, C., "De alterius appellationis instantia in causa nullitatis matrimonii fidelium ritus orientalis,"—*Apollinaris,* VIII (1935), 287-290.

Cappello, F. M., "Ius Ecclesiae Latinae cum iure Ecclesiae Orientalis comparatum,"—*Jus Pontificium,* VII (1927), 55-71.

Charon (Korolevskij), C., "L'Uniatisme,"—*Irenikon,* II (1927), Nos. 5-6.

Cheiko, L., "Catalogue Raisonné des Manuscrits de la Bibliothèque Orientale,"—*Mélanges de l'Université Saint Joseph de Beyrouth,* XI (1926), 216-225.

Coussa, A., "An Orientales schismatici legibus matrimonialibus Ecclesiae Latinae teneantur,"—*Apollinaris,* XI (1938), 121-125.

Dalpiaz, V., "An Orientales schismatici legibus matrimonialibus Ecclesiae latinae teneantur,"—*Apollinaris,* X (1937), 457-459.

———, "Quid sentiendum de matrimoniis civilibus contractis in Russia sovietyca ac in regesta publica inscripta?"—*Apollinaris,* VI (1933), 231-234.

Darblade, J. B., "La collection canonique Melkite d'après les manuscrits arabes des XIIIe-XVIIe siècles,"—*Orientalia Christiana Periodica,* IV (1938), 85-119.

Dauvillier, J., "La formation du mariage dans les Églises Orientales,"—*Revue des Sciences Religieuses,* XV (1935), 386-395.

De Baumgarten, N., "Aux origines de la Russie," *Orientalia Christiana Analecta,* No. 119 (1939).

De Clercq, C., "De ritu et adscriptione ritui apud Orientales Catholicos,"—*Ephemerides Liturgicae,* XLVI (1932), 473-480.

———, "Notae historicae circa fontes iuris particularis Orientalium Catholicorum,"—*Apollinaris,* IV (1931), 409-427.

Deslandes, J., "Le mariage clandestin des Orientaux est-il valide?"—*Echos d'Orient,* XXVIII (1929), 5-19.

Dib, P., "La legislation matrimoniale canonique dans l'Orient catholique,"—*Le Canoniste Contemporain,* XXXIX (1916), 385-399; XL (1917), 6-19; XLIII (1920), 35-43, 140-152.

———, "Les Maronites et leur liturgie,"—*Le Canoniste Contemporain,* XL (1917), 302-314, 401-418.

———, "Les conciles de l'Église Maronite, 1557-1664,"—*Revue des Sciences Religieuses,* IV (1924), 193-220, 421-439.

Doens, I., "Armenian Canon Law,"—*The Eastern Churches Quarterly,* III (1938-1939), 419-429, 460-473.

Dvornik, E., "National Churches and the Church Universal,"—*The Eastern Churches Quarterly,* V (1942-1944), 172-219.

Englert, C. C., "Orientals and the Parish Priest,"—*The Homiletic and Pastoral Review,* XLII (1941), 35-39.

Fallon, M. J., "Syrian Maronites Marrying in the United States,"—*The Ecclesiastical Review,* CIII (1940), 477-480.

Fedotov, C. G., "Le baptême de saint Vladimir et la conversion de la Russie,"—*Irenikon,* XV (1938), 417-436.

Gulovich, S., "Matrimonial Laws of the Catholic Eastern Churches,"—*The Jurist,* IV (1944), 200-245.

———, "Byzantine Slavonic Catholics and the Latin Clergy,"—*The Homiletic and Pastoral Review,* XLV (1945), 517-527, 586-596.

———, "The Principle Underlying the Validity of Oriental Marriage Law,"—*The Jurist,* VI (1946), 39-49.

Hannan, J., "Non-Catholic Petitioners and Plaintiffs,"—*The Jurist,* IV (1944), 623-626.

Haring, J., "Konvalidation einer orthodoxen Ehe,"—*Theologisch-praktische Quartalschrift,* LXXXIX (1936), 145.

Herman, E., "De 'Ritu' in Iure Canonico,"—*Orientalia Christiana,* XXXII (1933), 96-158.

———, "Ius Iustinianeum qua ratione conservatum sit in iure ecclesiastico orientali,"—*Acta Congressus Iuridici Internationalis,* II (1935), 147-155.

———, "Quibus normis matrimonium regatur quod inter fideles diversi ritus contrahitur,"—*Analecta Gregoriana,* Vol. IX, *Miscellanea Vermeersch,* I (Roma: Pontificia Università Gregoriana, 1935), 241-255.

———, "De impedimentis matrimonialibus secundum codificationes iuris ecclesiastici recentes 'orthodoxorum,'"—*Orientalia Christiana Periodica,* III (1937), 251-253.

———, "Reguntume Orientales dissidentes legibus matrimonialibus Ecclesiae latinae?"—*Periodica,* XXVII (1938), 7-20.

———, "De benedictione nuptiali quid statuerit ius byzantinum sive ecclesiasticum sive civile,"—*Orientalia Christiana Periodica,* IV (1938), 189-234.

———, "De ritu mulieris,"—*Periodica,* XXIX (1940), 5-16.

———, "De conceptu 'Ritus,'"—*The Jurist,* II (1942), 333-345.

Heuser, T., "Greek Catholics and Latin Priests,"—*The Ecclesiastical Review,* IV (1891), 194-204.

———, "The Jurisdiction of Latin Bishops over Catholics of the Greek Rite," —*The Ecclesiastical Review,* XIV (1896), 338-345.

Jaros, J., "Decretum pro spirituali administratione Ordinatuum Graeco-Ruthenorum in Foederatis Civitatibus Americae Septemtrionalis,"—*Apollinaris,* XV (1942), 28-32.

Jelicic, V., "Consultationes,"—*Jus Pontificium,* XV (1935), 126-128.

Jugie, M., "Joseph de Maistre et le Schisme Gréco-Russe,"—*Echos d'Orient,* XXI (1922), 129-161.

Maroto, P., "De regendis fidelibus diversorum rituum permixtim in eodem territorio degentibus,"—*Apollinaris,* VI (1933), 179-184.

McCormick, R., "The Ministration of the Sacraments by a Latin Priest to Catholics of the Oriental Rite,"—*Conference Bulletin of the Archdiocese of New York,* V (1927), 104-119; VI (1928), 6-40.

Meehan, A. B., "The Greek Ruthenian Church in the United States,"—*The Ecclesiastical Review,* LI (1914), 710-717.

Petrani, A., "Fideles ad ritus orientales pertinentes,"—*Apollinaris,* XII (1939), 94-102.

Petrides, S., "Chrysobulle de l'imperatrice Theodora (1283),"—*Echos d'Orient,* XIV (1911), 25-29.

Piontek, Cyril, "Equitable Practices under Canon 1097, § 2,"—*The Jurist,* III (1943), 456-474.

Plöchl, W., "Two Hundred Years—'*Etsi Pastoralis,*'"—*The Jurist,* II (1942), 211-213.

———, "The Church Laws for Orientals of the Austrian Monarchy in the 'Age of the Enlightenment,'"—*Bulletin of the Polish Institute of Arts and Sciences in America,* II (1944), 711-756.

———, "Quinquennial faculties extended by the S. Congregation for the Oriental Church to Latin Ordinaries,"—*The Jurist,* VI (1946), 73-76.

———, "The Change of Rite '*in matrimonio ineundo vel eo durante,*'"—*The Jurist,* VI (1946), 275-304.

Principi, P., "Animadversiones,"—*Apollinaris,* III (1930), 354-358.

Raes, A., "Le consentemente matrimonial dans les rites orientaux,"—*Ephemerides Liturgicae* XLVII (1933), 34-37; 126-140; 249-259; 431-445; XLVIII (1934), 80-94; 310-318.

Sandalgi, P., "The Uniate Oriental Churches,"—*The Ecclesiastical Review,* LXXIII (1918), 113-130.

Schrijnen, J. P., "La courrone nuptiale dans l'antiquité chrétienne,"—*Mélanges d'archéologie et histoire,* XXI (1911), 309-319.

Sipos, S., "Possintne Latini coram parocho orientali matrimonium celebrare?"—*Jus Pontificium,* XIX (1939), 97-99.

Souarn, R., "Impedimentum Ordinis in Ecclesia Graeca,"—*Jus Pontificium,* XIII (1933), 42-51.

———, "L'ordre, empêchement canonique du mariage chez les Grecs,"—*Echos d'Orient,* IV (1900-1901), 65-71.

———, "Un cadre oriental pour le droit canon oriental,"—*Ephemerides Canonicae,* I (1945), 35-40.

Spácil, Th., "Commentarium de theologia dogmatica,"—*Orientalia Christiana,* XVIII (1930), 169-202.

Staffa, D., "De transitu ad alium Ritum,"—*Apollinaris,* XIII (1940), 182-189.

Terzariol, A., "An fideles orientales extra proprium Patriarchatum adstringantur impedimentis matrimonialibus quae C. I. C. abrogavit pro fidelibus latinis?" —*Apollinaris,* VII (1934), 487-489.

Vernadsky, G., "The status of the Russian Church during the first half-century following Vladimir's conversion,"—*The Slavonic and East European Review,* XX (1941), 294-314.

———, "Byzantium and Southern Russia,"—*Byzantion: International Journal of Byzantine Studies,* XV (1940-1941), 67-86.

Villien, A., "La nouvelle Congregation pour l'Église orientale,"—*Le Canoniste Contemporain,* XL (1917), 497-502.

Wesseling, T., "Vladimir Soloviev,"—*The Eastern Churches Quarterly,* II (1937), 12-26; 65-78; 121-137; 185-202.

Tournebize, F., "Les cent dix-sept accusations présentées à Benoît XII contre les Arméniens,"—*Revue de l'Orient Chrétien,* XI (1906), 163-181; 274-301; 352-370.

Vermeersch, A., "De canone 1070.1 eiusque opportunitate,"—*Periodica,* XVII (1928), 53-55.

———, "De disparitate cultus,"—*Periodica,* XXIV (1935), 41-42.

Periodicals

American Ecclesiastical Review, Vols. I-XXXII, Philadelphia, 1889-1905; from 1905: *The Ecclesiastical Review,* Vols. XXXIII-CIX, Philadelphia, 1905-1943; from 1944: *The American Ecclesiastical Review,* Washington, D. C., Vol. CX, 1944—.

Analecta Ecclesiastica, Romae, 1893-1911.

Analecta Iuris Pontificii, Romae, 1855-1869; Parisiis, 1872-1891.

Apollinaris, Romae, 1928—.

Archiv für katholisches Kirchenrecht, Innsbruck, 1857-1861; Mainz, 1862—.

Bulletin of the Polish Institute of Arts and Sciences in America, New York, 1942—.

Byzantion: International Journal of Byzantine Studies, Vols. I-XIV, Paris, 1924-1939; American Series, Vols. XV—, Boston, 1942—.

Canoniste, Le, Paris, 1924-1926 (originally *Le Canoniste Contemporain,* Paris, 45 vols., 1878-1922).

Conference Bulletin of the Archdiocese of New York, New York, 1923—.

Eastern Churches Quarterly, The, London, 1936—.

Echos d'Orient, Paris, 1889—.

Ephemerides Canonicae, Romae, 1945—.

Ephemerides Liturgicae, Romae, 1887—.

Ephemerides Theologicae Lovaniensis, Brugis, 1924—.

Homiletic and Pastoral Review, The, New York, 1900—.

Irenikon, Amay, 1926—.

Jurist, The, Washington, 1941—.

Jus Pontificium, Romae, 1920—.

Mélanges d'Archéologie et Histoire, Paris, 1881—.

Mélanges de l'Université Saint Joseph de Beyrouth, Beyrouth, 1906—.

Orientalia Christiana, Romae, 1922-1935; ab anno 1935: *Orientalia Christiana Analecta*, Romae, 1935—.
Orientalia Christiana Periodica, Romae, 1935—.
Revue de l'Orient Chrétien, Paris, 1896—.
Revue des Sciences Religieuses, Paris, 1921—.
Theologisch-praktische Quartalschrift, Linz, 1832—.
Slavonic and East European Review, The, London, 1922—.
Periodica de Religiosis et Missionariis, 8 vols., Brugis, 1905-1919; from 1920: *Periodica de Re Canonica et Morali utilia praesertim Religiosis et Missionariis*, 7 vols., Brugis, 1920-1927; from 1927: *Periodica de Re Morali, Canonica, Liturgica*, Brugis (1927-1936) et Romae (1937—), Vol. XVI, 1927—.

ABBREVIATIONS

AAS—*Acta Apostolicae Sedis.*
ASS—*Acta Sanctae Sedis.*
C.—Codex Iustinianus.
C. Th.—Codex Theodosianus.
Collectanea—*Collectanea S. C. de Propaganda Fide.*
Coll. Lac.—*Collectio Lacensis.*
D.—Digesta Imperatoris Iustiniani.
DTC—*Dictionnaire de théologie catholique.*
Fontes—*Codicis Iuris Canonici Fontes cura . . . Gasparri editi.*
Fonti—*Codificazione Canonica Orientale, Fonti.*
Inst.—Institutiones Iustinianae.
Ius Pont.—*Ius Pontificium de Propaganda Fide.*
Jaffé—*Regesta Pontificum Romanorum*, etc.
Mansi—*Sacrorum Conciliorum Nova et Amplissima Collectio.*
MGH—*Monumenta Germaniae Historica.*
MPG—Migne, *Patrologia, Series Graeca.*
MPL—Migne, *Patrologia, Series Latina.*
Periodica—*Periodica de Re Morali, Canonica, Liturgica.*
S. C. Pro Eccl. Or.—Sacra Congregatio pro Ecclesia Orientali.
S.S.C.S. Off.—Suprema Sacra Congregatio Sancti Officii.

INDEX OF PERSONS

INDEX OF PLACES

INDEX OF TOPICS

BIOGRAPHICAL NOTE

JOSEPH FRANCIS MARBACH was born in Newark, N. J., on July 30, 1917. He attended Sacred Heart School in Newark, but completed his primary education at St. John's School in White Plains, N. Y. After graduating from Regis High School in New York City in 1934, he attended the College of the Holy Cross in Worcester, Mass., where he received the degree of Bachelor of Arts in June, 1938. In September of that year he entered St. Joseph's Seminary in Yonkers, N. Y. He was ordained to the holy priesthood on May 1, 1943, and in the fall of that year he enrolled in the School of Canon Law of the Catholic University of America, Washington, D. C., where he received the degree of the Baccalaureate in Canon Law in May, 1944, and the degree of the Licentiate in Canon Law in May, 1945.

CANON LAW STUDIES *

1. Freriks, Rev. Celestine A., C.PP.S., J.C.D., Religious Congregations in Their External Relations, 121 pp., 1916.
2. Galliher, Rev. Daniel M., O.P., J.C.D., Canonical Elections, 117 pp., 1917.
3. Borkowski, Rev. Aurelius L., O.F.M., J.C.D., De Confraternitatibus Ecclesiasticis, 136 pp., 1918.
4. Castillo, Rev. Cayo, J.C.D., Disertacion Historico-Canonica sobre la Potestad del Cabildo en Sede Vacante o Impedida del Vicario Capitular, 99 pp., 1919 (1918).
5. Kubelbeck, Rev. William J., S.T.B., J.C.D., The Sacred Penitentiaria and Its Relation to Faculties of Ordinaries and Priests, 129 pp., 1918.
6. Petrovits, Rev. Joseph, J.C., S.T.D., J.C.D., The New Church Law on Matrimony, X-461 pp., 1919.
7. Hickey, Rev. John J., S.T.B., J.C.D., Irregularities and Simple Impediments in the New Code of Canon Law, 100 pp., 1920.
8. Klekotka, Rev. Peter J., S.T.B., J.C.D., Diocesan Consultors, 179 pp., 1920.
9. Wanenmacher, Rev. Francis, J.C.D., The Evidence in Ecclesiastical Procedure Affecting the Marriage Bond, 1920 (Printed 1935).
10. Golden, Rev. Henry Francis, J.C.D., Parochial Benefices in the New Code, IV-119 pp., 1921 (Printed 1925).
11. Koudelka, Rev. Charles J., J.C.D., Pastors, Their Rights and Duties According to the New Code of Canon Law, 211 pp., 1921.
12. Melo, Rev. Antonius, O.F.M., J.C.D., De Exemptione Regularium, X-188 pp., 1921.
13. Schaaf, Rev. Valentine Theodore, O.F.M., S.T.B., J.C.D., The Cloister. X-180 pp., 1921.
14. Burke, Rev. Thomas Joseph, S.T.D., J.C.D., Competence in Ecclesiastical Tribunals, IV-117 pp., 1922.
15. Leech, Rev. George Leo, J.C.D., A Comparative Study of the Constitution "Apostolicae Sedis" and the "Codex Juris Canonici," 179 pp., 1922.
16. Motry, Rev. Hubert Louis, S.T.D., J.C.D., Diocesan Faculties According to the Code of Canon Law, II-167 pp., 1922.
17. Murphy, Rev. George Lawrence, J.C.D., Delinquencies and Penalties in the Administration and the Reception of the Sacraments, IV-121 pp., 1923.
18. O'Reilly, Rev. John Anthony, S.T.B., J.C.D., Ecclesiastical Sepulture in the New Code of Canon Law, II-129 pp., 1923.

* From nn. 1-100 inclusive only nn. 25 and 57 are still obtainable.
From n. 101 onward all numbers are available except the following: nn. 101-118 inclusive, and also n. 122.

19. Michalicka, Rev. Wenceslas Cyrill, O.S.B., J.C.D., Judicial Procedure in Dismissal of Clerical Exempt Religious, 107 pp., 1923.

20. Dargin, Rev. Edward Vincent, S.T.B., J.C.D., Reserved Cases According to the Code of Canon Law, IV-103 pp., 1924.

21. Godfrey, Rev. John A., S.T.B., J.C.D., The Right of Patronage According to the Code of Canon Law, 153 pp., 1924.

22. Hagedorn, Rev. Francis Edward, J.C.D., General Legislation on Indulgences, II-154 pp., 1924.

23. King, Rev. James Ignatius, J.C.D., The Administration of the Sacraments to Dying Non-Catholics, V-141 pp., 1924.

24. Winslow, Rev. Francis Joseph, O.F.M., J.C.D., Vicars and Prefects Apostolic, IV-149 pp., 1924.

25. Correa, Rev. Jose Servelion, S.T.L., J.C.D., La Potestad Legislativa de la Iglesia Catolica, IV-127 pp., 1925.

26. Dugan, Rev. Henry Francis, A.M., J.C.D., The Judiciary Department of the Diocesan Curia, 87 pp., 1925.

27. Keller, Rev. Charles Frederick, S.T.B., J.C.D., Mass Stipends, 167 pp., 1925.

28. Paschang, Rev. John Linus, J.C.D., The Sacramentals According to the Code of Canon Law, 129 pp., 1925.

29. Piontek, Rev. Cyrillus, O.F.M., S.T.B., J.C.D., De Indulto Exclaustrationis necnon Saecularizationis, XIII-289 pp., 1925.

30. Kearney, Rev. Richard Joseph, S.T.B., J.C.D., Sponsors at Baptism According to the Code of Canon Law, IV-127 pp., 1925.

31. Bartlett, Rev. Chester Joseph, A.M., LL.B., J.C.D., The Tenure of Parochial Property in the United States of America, V-108 pp., 1926.

32. Kilker, Rev. Adrian Jerome, J.C.D., Extreme Unction, V-425 pp., 1926.

33. McCormick, Rev. Robert Emmett, J.C.D., Confessors of Religious, VIII-266 pp., 1926.

34. Miller, Rev. Newton Thomas, J.C.D., Founded Masses According to the Code of Canon Law, VII-93 pp., 1926.

35. Roelker, Rev. Edward G., S.T.D., J.C.D., Principles of Privilege According to the Code of Canon Law, XI-166 pp., 1926.

36. Bakalarczyk, Rev. Richardus, M.I.C., J.U.D., De Novitiatu, VIII-208 pp., 1927.

37. Pizzuti, Rev. Lawrence, O.F.M., J.U.L., De Parochis Religiosis, 1927. (Not Printed.)

38. Bliley, Rev. Nicholas Martin, O.S.B., J.C.D., Altars According to the Code of Canon Law, XIX-132 pp., 1927.

39. Brown, Mr. Brendan Francis, A.B., LL.M., J.U.D., The Canonical Juristic Personality with Special Reference to its Status in the United States of America, V-212 pp., 1927.

40. Cavanaugh, Rev. William Thomas, C.P., J.U.D., The Reservation of the Blessed Sacrament, VIII-101 pp., 1927.

41. Doheny, Rev. William J., C.S.C., A.B., J.U.D., Church Property: Modes of Acquisition, X-118 pp., 1927.
42. Feldhaus, Rev. Aloysius H., C.PP.S., J.C.D., Oratories, IX-141 pp., 1927
43. Kelly, Rev. James Patrick, A.B., J.C.D., The Jurisdiction of the Simple Confessor, X-208 pp., 1927.
44. Neuberger, Rev. Nicholas J., J.C.D., Canon 6 or the Relation of the Codex Juris Canonici to the Preceding Legislation, V-95 pp., 1927.
45. O'Keefe, Rev. Gerald Michael, J.C.D., Matrimonial Dispensations Powers of Bishops, Priests, and Confessors, VIII-232 pp., 1927.
46. Quigley, Rev. Joseph A. M., A.B., J.C.D., Condemned Societies, 139 pp. 1927.
47. Zaplotnik, Rev. Johannes Leo, J.C.D., De Vicariis Foraneis, X-142 pp., 1927.
48. Duskie, Rev. John Aloysius, A.B., J.C.D., The Canonical Status of the Orientals in the United States, VIII-196 pp., 1928.
49. Hyland, Rev. Francis Edward, J.C.D., Excommunication, Its Nature, Historical Development and Effects, VIII-181 pp., 1928.
50. Reinmann, Rev. Gerald Joseph, O.M.C., J.C.D., The Third Order Secular of Saint Francis, 201 pp., 1928.
51. Schenk, Rev. Francis J., J.C.D., The Matrimonial Impediments of Mixed Religion and Disparity of Cult, XVI-318 pp., 1929.
52. Coady, Rev. John Joseph, S.T.D., J.U.D., A.M., The Appointment of Pastors, VIII-150 pp., 1929.
53. Kay, Rev. Thomas Henry, J.C.D., Competence in Matrimonial Procedure, VIII-164 pp., 1929.
54. Turner, Rev. Sidney Joseph, C.P., J.U.D., The Vow of Poverty, XLIX-217 pp., 1929.
55. Kearney, Rev. Raymond A., A.B., S.T.D., J.C.D., The Principles of Delegation, VII-149 pp., 1929.
56. Conran, Rev. Edward James, A.B., J.C.D., The Interdict, V-163 pp., 1930.
57. O'Neill, Rev. William H., J.C.D., Papal Rescripts of Favor, VII-218 pp., 1930.
58. Bastnagel, Rev. Clement Vincent, J.U.D., The Appointment of Parochial Adjutants and Assistants, XV-257 pp., 1930.
59. Ferry, Rev. William A., A.B., J.C.D., Stole Fees, V-136 pp., 1930.
60. Costello, Rev. John Michael, A.B., J.C.D., Domicile and Quasi-Domicile, VII-201 pp., 1930.
61. Kremer, Rev. Michael Nicholas, A.B., S.T.B., J.C.D., Church Support in the United States, VI-136 pp., 1930.
62. Angulo, Rev. Luis, C.M., J.C.D., Legislation de la Iglesia sobre la intencion en la application de la Santa Misa, VII-104 pp., 1931.
63. Frey, Rev. Wolfgang Norbert, O.S.B., A.B., J.C.D., The Act of Religious Profession, VIII-174 pp., 1931.

64. Roberts, Rev. James Brendan, A.B., J.C.D., The Banns of Marriage, XIV-140 pp., 1931.
65. Ryder, Rev. Raymond Aloysius, A.B., J.C.D., Simony, IX-151 pp., 1931.
66. Campagna, Rev. Angelo, Ph.D., J.U.D., Il Vicario Generale del Vescovo, VII-205 pp., 1931.
67. Cox, Rev. Joseph Godfrey, A.B., J.C.D., The Administration of Seminaries, VI-124 pp., 1931.
68. Gregory, Rev. Donald J., J.U.D., The Pauline Privilege, XV-165 pp., 1931.
69. Donohue, Rev. John F., J.C.D., The Impediment of Crime, VII-110 pp., 1931.
70. Dooley, Rev. Eugene A., O.M.I., J.C.D., Church Law on Sacred Relics, IX-143 pp., 1931.
71. Orth, Rev. Clement Raymond, O.M.C., J.C.D., The Approbation of Religious Institutes, 171 pp., 1931.
72. Pernicone, Rev. Joseph M., A.B., J.C.D., The Ecclesiastical Prohibition of Books, XII-267 pp., 1932.
73. Clinton, Rev. Connell, A.B., J.C.D., The Paschal Precept, IX-108 pp., 1932.
74. Donnelly, Rev. Francis B., A.M., S.T.L., J.C.D., The Diocesan Synod, VIII-125 pp., 1932.
75. Torrente, Rev. Camilo, C.M.F., J.C.D., Las Procesiones Sagradas, V-145 pp., 1932.
76. Murphy, Rev. Edwin J., C.PP.S., J.C.D., Suspension Ex Informata Conscientia, XI-122 pp., 1932.
77. MacKenzie, Rev. Eric F., A.M., S.T.L., J.C.D., The Delict of Heresy in its Commission, Penalization, Absolution, VII-124 pp., 1932.
78. Lyons, Rev. Avitus E., S.T.B., J.C.D., The Collegiate Tribunal of First Instance, XI-147 pp., 1932.
79. Connolly, Rev. Thomas A., J.C.D., Appeals, XI-195, pp., 1932.
80. Sangmeister, Rev. Joseph V., A.B., J.C.D., Force and Fear as Precluding Matrimonial Consent, V-211 pp., 1932.
81. Jaeger, Rev. Leo A., A.B., J.C.D., The Administration of Vacant and Quasi-Vacant Episcopal Sees in the United States, IX-229 pp., 1932.
82. Rimlinger, Rev. Herbert T., J.C.D., Error Invalidating Matrimonial Consent, VII-79 pp., 1932.
83. Barrett, Rev. John D. M., S.S., J.C.D., A Comparative Study of the Third Plenary Council of Baltimore and the Code, IX-221 pp., 1932.
84. Carberry, Rev. John J., Ph.D., S.T.D., J.C.D., The Juridical Form of Marriage, X-177 pp., 1934.
85. Dolan, Rev. John L., A.B., J.C.D., The Defensor Vinculi, XII-157 pp., 1934.
86. Hannan, Rev. Jerome D., A.M., S.T.D., LL.B., J.C.D., The Canon Law of Wills, IX-517 pp., 1934.

87. LEMIEUX, REV. DELISE A., A.M., J.C.D., The Sentence in Ecclesiastical Procedure, IX-131 pp., 1934.
88. O'ROURKE, REV. JAMES J., A.B., J.C.D., Parish Registers, VII-109 pp., 1934.
89. TIMLIN, REV. BARTHOLOMEW, O.F.M., A.M., J.C.D., Conditional Matrimonial Consent, X-381 pp., 1934.
90. WAHL, REV. FRANCIS X., A.B., J.C.D., The Matrimonial Impediments of Consanguinity and Affinity, VI-125 pp., 1934.
91. WHITE, REV. ROBERT J., A.B., LL.B., S.T.B., J.C.D., Canonical Ante-Nuptial Promises and the Civil Law, VI-152 pp., 1934.
92. HERRERA, REV. ANTONIO PARRA, O.C.D., J.C.D., Legislacion Ecclesiastica sobra el Ayuno y la Abstinencia, XI-191 pp., 1935.
93. KENNEDY, REV. EDWIN J., J.C.D., The Special Matrimonial Process in Cases of Evident Nullity, X-165 pp., 1935.
94. MANNING, REV. JOHN J., A.B., J.C.D., Presumption of Law in Matrimonial Procedure, XI-111 pp., 1935.
95. MOEDER, REV. JOHN M., J.C.D., The Proper Bishop for Ordination and Dismissorial Letters, VII-135 pp., 1935.
96. O'MARA, REV. WILLIAM A., A.B., J.C.D., Canonical Causes for Matrimonial Dispensations, IX-155 pp., 1935.
97. REILLY, REV. PETER, J.C.D., Residence of Pastors, IX-81 pp., 1935.
98. SMITH, REV. MARINER T., O.P., S.T.Lr., J.C.D., The Penal Law for Religious, VIII-169 pp., 1935.
99. WHALEN, REV. DONALD W., A.M., J.C.D., The Value of Testimonial Evidence in Matrimonial Procedure, XIII-297 pp., 1935.
100. CLEARY, REV. JOSEPH F., J.C.D., Canonical Limitations on the Alienation of Church Property, VIII-141 pp., 1936.
101. GLYNN, REV. JOHN C., J.C.D., The Promoter of Justice, XX-337 pp., 1936.
102. BRENNAN, REV. JAMES H., S.S., M.A., S.T.B., J.C.D., The Simple Convalidation of Marriage, VI-135 pp., 1937.
103. BRUNINI, REV. JOSEPH BERNARD, J.C.D., The Clerical Obligations of Canons 139 and 142, X-121 pp., 1937.
104. CONNOR, REV. MAURICE, A.B., J.C.D., The Administrative Removal of Pastors, VIII-159 pp., 1937.
105. GUILFOYLE, REV. MERLIN JOSEPH, J.C.D., Custom, XI-144 pp., 1937.
106. HUGHES, REV. JAMES AUSTIN, A.B., A.M., J.C.D., Witnesses in Criminal Trials of Clerics, IX-140 pp., 1937.
107. JANSEN, REV. RAYMOND J., A.B., S.T.L., J.C.D., Canonical Provisions for Catechetical Instruction, VII-153 pp., 1937.
108. KEALY, REV. JOHN JAMES, A.B., J.C.D., The Introductory Libellus in Church Court Procedure, XI-121 pp., 1937.
109. McMANUS, REV. JAMES EDWARD, C.SS.R., J.C.D., The Administration of Temporal Goods in Religious Institutes, XVI-196 pp., 1937.

110. Moriarty, Rev. Eugene James, J.C.D., Oaths in Ecclesiastical Courts, X-115 pp., 1937.

111. Rainer, Rev. Eligius George, C.SS.R., J.C.D., Suspension of Clerics, XVII-249 pp., 1937.

112. Reilly, Rev. Thomas F., C.SS.R., J.C.D., Visitation of Religious, VI-195 pp., 1938.

113. Moriarty, Rev. Francis E., C.SS.R., J.C.D., The Extraordinary Absolution from Censures, XV-334 pp., 1938.

114. Connolly, Rev. Nicholas P., J.C.D., The Canonical Erection of Parishes, X-132 pp., 1938.

115. Donovan, Rev. James Joseph, J.C.D., The Pastor's Obligation in Prenuptial Investigation, XII-322 pp., 1938.

116. Harrigan, Rev. Robert J., M.A., S.T.B., J.C.D., The Radical Sanation of Invalid Marriages, VIII-208 pp., 1938.

117. Boffa, Rev. Conrad Humbert, J.C.D., Canonical Provisions for Catholic Schools, VII-211 pp., 1939.

118. Parsons, Rev. Anscar John, O.M.Cap., J.C.D., Canonical Elections, XII-236 pp., 1939.

119. Reilly, Rev. Edward Michael, A.B., J.C.D., The General Norms of Dispensation, XII-156 pp., 1939.

120. Ryan, Rev. Gerald Aloysius, A.B., J.C.D., Principles of Episcopal Jurisdiction, XII-172 pp., 1939.

121. Burton, Rev. Francis James, C.S.C., A.B., J.C.D., A Commentary on Canon 1125, X-222 pp., 1940.

122. Miaskiewicz, Rev. Francis Sigismund, J.C.D., Supplied Jurisdiction According to Canon 209, XII-340 pp., 1940.

123. Rice, Rev. Patrick William, A.B., J.C.D., Proof of Death in Prenuptial Investigation, VIII-156 pp., 1940.

124. Anglin, Rev. Thomas Francis, M.S., J.C.D., The Eucharistic Fast, VIII-183 pp., 1941.

125. Coleman, Rev. John Jerome, J.C.D., The Minister of Confirmation, VI-153 pp., 1941.

126. Downs, Rev. John Emmanuel, A.B., J.C.D., The Concept of Clerical Immunity, XI-163 pp., 1941.

127. Esswein, Rev. Anthony Albert, J.C.D., Extrajudicial Penal Powers of Ecclesiastical Superiors, X-144 pp., 1941.

128. Farrell, Rev. Benjamin Francis, M.A., S.T.L., J.C.D., The Rights and Duties of the Local Ordinary Regarding Congregations of Women Religious of Pontifical Approval, V-195 pp., 1941.

129. Feeney, Rev. Thomas John, A.B., S.T.L., J.C.D., Restitutio in Integrum, VI-169 pp., 1941.

130. Findlay, Rev. Stephen William, O.S.B., A.B., J.C.D., Canonical Norms Governing the Deposition and Degradation of Clerics, XVII-279 pp., 1941.

131. GOODWINE, REV. JOHN, A.B., S.T.L., J.C.D., The Right of the Church to Acquire Property, VIII-119 pp., 1941.
132. HESTON, REV. EDWARD LOUIS, C.S.C., Ph.D., S.T.D., J.C.D., The Alienation of Church Property in the United States, XII-222 pp., 1941.
133. HOGAN, REV. JAMES JOHN, A.B., S.T.L., J.C.D., Judicial Advocates and Procurators, XIII-200 pp., 1941.
134. KEALY, REV. THOMAS M., A.B., Litt.B., J.C.D., Dowry of Women Religious, IX-152 pp., 1941.
135. KEENE, REV. MICHAEL JAMES, O.S.B., J.C.D., Religious Ordinaries and Canon 198, V-164 pp., 1942.
136. KERIN, REV. CHARLES A., S.S., M.A., S.T.B., J.C.D., The Privation of Christian Burial, XVI-279 pp., 1941.
137. LOUIS, REV. WILLIAM FRANCIS, M.A., J.C.D., Diocesan Archives, X-101 pp., 1941.
138. MCDEVITT, REV. GILBERT JOSEPH, A.B., J.C.D., Legitimacy and Legitimation, X-247 pp., 1941.
139. MCDONOUGH, REV. THOMAS JOSEPH, A.B., J.C.D., Apostolic Administrators, X-217 pp., 1941.
140. MEIER, REV. CARL ANTHONY, A.B., J.C.D., Penal Administrative Procedure Against Negligent Pastors, XI-240 pp., 1941.
141. SCHMIDT, REV. JOHN ROGG, A.B., J.C.D., The Principles of Authentic Interpretation in Canon 17 of the Code of Canon Law, XII-331 pp., 1941.
142. SLAFKOSKY, REV. ANDREW LEONARD, A.B., J.C.D., The Canonical Episcopal Visitation of the Diocese, X-197 pp., 1941.
143. SWOBODA, REV. INNOCENT ROBERT, O.F.M., J.C.D., Ignorance in Relation to the Imputability of Delicts, IX-271 pp., 1941.
144. DUBÉ, REV. ARTHUR JOSEPH, A.B., J.C.D., The General Principles for the Reckoning of Time in Canon Law, VIII-299 pp., 1941.
145. MCBRIDE, REV. JAMES T., A.B., J.C.D., Incardination and Excardination of Seculars, XX-585 pp., 1941.
146. KRÓL, REV. JOHN T., J.C.D., The Defendant in Ecclesiastical Trials, XII-207 pp., 1942.
147. COMYNS, REV. JOSEPH J., C.SS.R., A.B., J.C.D., Papal and Episcopal Administration of Church Property, XIV-155 pp., 1942.
148. BARRY, REV. GARRETT FRANCIS, O.M.I., J.C.D., Violation of the Cloister, XII-260 pp., 1942.
149. BOLDUC, REV. GATIEN, C.S.V., A.B., S.T.L., J.C.D., Les Études dans les Religions Cléricales, VIII-155 pp., 1942.
150. BOYLE, REV. DAVID JOHN, M.A., J.C.D., The Juridic Effects of Moral Certitude on Pre-Nuptial Guarantees, XII-188 pp., 1942.
151. CANAVAN, REV. WALTER JOSEPH, M.A., Litt.D., J.C.D., The Profession of Faith, XII-143 pp., 1942.
152. DESROCHERS, REV. BRUNO, A.B., Ph.L., S.T.B., J.C.D., Le Premier Concile Plénier de Québec et le Code de Droit Canonique, XIV-186 pp., 1942.

153. DILLON, REV. ROBERT EDWARD, A.B., J.C.D., Common Law Marriage, X-148 pp., 1942.

154. DODWELL, REV. EDWARD JOHN, Ph.D., S.T.B., J.C.D., The Time and Place for the Celebration of Marriage, X-156 pp., 1942.

155. DONNELLAN, REV. THOMAS ANDREW, A.B., J.C.D., The Obligation of the Missa pro Populo, VII-131 pp., 1942.

156. ELTZ, REV. LOUIS ANTHONY, A.B., J.C.D., Cooperation in Crime, XII-208 pp., 1942.

157. GASS, REV. SYLVESTER FRANCIS, M.A., J.C.D., Ecclesiastical Pensions, XI-206 pp., 1942.

158. GUINIVEN, REV. JOHN JOSEPH, C.SS.R., J.C.D., The Precept of Hearing Mass, XIV-188 pp., 1942.

159. GULCZYNSKI, REV. JOHN THEOPHILUS, J.C.D., The Desecration and Violation of Churches, X-126 pp., 1942.

160. HAMMILL, REV. JOHN LEO, M.A., J.C.D., The Obligations of the Traveler According to Canon 14, VIII-204 pp., 1942.

161. HAYDT, REV. JOHN JOSEPH, A.B., J.C.D., Reserved Benefices, XI-148 pp., 1942.

162. HUSER, REV. ROGER JOHN, O.F.M., A.B., J.C.D., The Crime of Abortion in Canon Law, XII-187 pp., 1942.

163. KEARNEY, REV. FRANCIS PATRICK, A.B., S.T.L., J.C.D., The Principles of Canon 1127, X-162 pp., 1942.

164. LINAHEN, REV. LEO JAMES, S.T.L., J.C.D., De Absolutione Complicis in Peccato Turpi, V-114 pp., 1942.

165. MCCLOSKEY, REV. JOSEPH ALOYSIUS, A.B., J.C.D., The Subject of Ecclesiastical Law According to Canon 12, XVII-246 pp., 1942.

166. O'NEILL, REV. FRANCIS JOSEPH, C.SS.R., J.C.D., The Dismissal of Religious in Temporary Vows, XIII-220 pp., 1942.

167. PRINCE, REV. JOHN EDWARD, A.B., S.T.B., J.C.D., The Diocesan Chancellor, X-136 pp., 1942.

168. RIESNER, REV. ALBERT JOSEPH, C.SS.R., J.C.D., Apostates and Fugitives from Religious Institutes, IX-168 pp., 1942.

169. STENGER, REV. JOSEPH BERNARD, J.C.D., The Mortgaging of Church Property, 186 pp., 1942.

170. WALDRON, REV. JOSEPH FRANCIS, A.B., J.C.D., The Minister of Baptism, XII-197 pp., 1942.

171. WILLETT, REV. ROBERT ALBERT, J.C.D., The Probative Value of Documents in Ecclesiastical Trials, X-124 pp., 1942.

172. WOEBER, REV. EDWARD MARTIN, M.A., J.C.D., The Interpellations, XII-161 pp., 1942.

173. BENKO, REV. MATTHEW ALOYSIUS, O.S.B., M.A., J.C.D., The Abbot *Nullius*, XVI-148 pp., 1943.

174. CHRIST, REV. JOSEPH JAMES, M.A., S.T.L., J.C.D., Dispensation from Vindicative Penalties, XIV-285 pp., 1943.

175. CLANCY, REV. PATRICK M. J., O.P., A.B., S.T.Lr., J.C.D., The Local Religious Superior, X-229 pp., 1943.
176. CLARKE, REV. THOMAS JAMES, J.C.D., Parish Societies, XII-147 pp., 1943.
177. CONNOLLY, REV. JOHN PATRICK, S.T.L., J.C.D., Synodal Examiners and Parish Priest Consultors, X-223 pp., 1943.
178. DRUMM, REV. WILLIAM MARTIN, A.B., J.C.D., Hospital Chaplains, XII-175 pp., 1943.
179. FLANAGAN, REV. BERNARD JOSEPH, A.B., S.T.L., J.C.D., The Canonical Erection of Religious Houses, X-147 pp., 1943.
180. KELLEHER, REV. STEPHEN JOSEPH, A.B., S.T.B., J.C.D., Discussions with Non-Catholics: Canonical Legislation, X-93 pp., 1943.
181. LEWIS, REV. GORDIAN, C.P., J.C.D., Chapters in Religious Institutes, XII-169 pp., 1943.
182. MARX, REV. ADOLPH, J.C.D., The Declaration of Nullity of Marriages Contracted Outside the Church, X-151 pp., 1943.
183. MATULENAS, REV. RAYMOND ANTHONY, O.S.B., A.B., J.C.D., Communication, a Source of Privileges, XII-225 pp., 1943.
184. O'LEARY, REV. CHARLES GERARD, C.SS.R., J.C.D., Religious Dismissed After Perpetual Profession, X-213 pp., 1943.
185. POWER, REV. CORNELIUS MICHAEL, J.C.D., The Blessing of Cemeteries, XII-231 pp., 1943.
186. SHUHLER, REV. RALPH VINCENT, O.S.A., J.C.D., Privileges of Religious to Absolve and Dispense, XII-195 pp., 1943.
187. ZIOLKOWSKI, REV. THADDEUS STANISLAUS, A.B., J.C.D., The Consecration and Blessing of Churches, XII-151 pp., 1943.
188. HENEGHAN, REV. JOHN JOSEPH, S.T.D., J.C.D., The Marriages of Unworthy Catholics: Canons 1065 and 1066, XVI-213 pp., 1944.
189. CARROLL, REV. COLEMAN FRANCIS, M.A., S.T.L., J.C.L., Charitable Institutions.
190. CIESLUK, REV. JOSEPH EDWARD, PH.B., S.T.L., J.C.L., National Parishes in the United States.
191. COBURN, REV. VINCENT PAUL, A.B., J.C.D., Marriages of Conscience, XII-172 pp., 1944.
192. CONNORS, REV. CHARLES PAUL, C.S.SP., A.B., J.C.D., Extra-Judicial Procurators in the Code of Canon Law, X-94 pp., 1944.
193. COYLE, REV. PAUL RAYMOND, A.B., J.C.D., Judicial Exceptions, X-142 pp., 1944.
194. FAIR, REV. BARTHOLOMEW FRANCIS, A.B., S.T.L., J.C.L., The Impediment of Abduction.
195. GALLAGHER, REV. THOMAS RAPHAEL, O.P., A.B., S.T.LR., J.C.D., The Examination of the Qualities of the Ordinand, X-166 pp., 1944.
196. GANNON, REV. JOHN MARK, S.T.L., J.C.D., The Interstices Required for the Promotion to Orders, XII-100 pp., 1944.

197. Goldsmith, Rev. J. William, B.C.S., S.T.L., J.C.D., The Competence of Church and State Over Marriages—Disputed Points, X-128 pp., 1944.

198. Goodwine, Rev. Joseph Gerard, A.B., S.T.B., J.C.D., The Reception of Converts, XIV-326 pp., 1944.

199. Kowalski, Rev. Romuald Eugene, O.F.M., A.B., J.C.D., Sustenance of Religious Houses of Regulars, X-174 pp., 1944.

200. McCoy, Rev. Alan Edward, O.F.M., J.C.D., Force and Fear in Relation to Delictual Imputability and Penal Responsibility, XII-160 pp., 1944.

201. McDevitt, Rev. Vincent John, Ph.B., S.T.L., J.C.L., Perjury.

202. Martin, Rev. Thomas Owen, Ph.D., S.T.D., J.C.D., Adverse Possession, Prescription and Limitation of Actions: The Canonical "Praescriptio," XX-208 pp., 1944.

203. Miklosovic, Rev. Paul John, A.B., J.C.L., Attempted Marriages and Their Consequent Juridic Effects.

204. Mundy, Rev. Thomas Maurice, A.B., S.T.L., J.C.D., The Union of Parishes, X-164 pp., 1944.

205. O'Dea, Rev. John Coyle, A.B., J.C.D., The Matrimonial Impediment of Nonage, VIII-126 pp., 1944.

206. Olalia, Rev. Alexander Ayson, S.T.L., J.C.D., A Comparative Study of the Christian Constitution of States and the Constitution of the Philippine Commonwealth, XII-136 pp., 1944.

207. Poisson, Rev. Pierre-Marie, C.S.C., A.B., Ph.L., Th.L., J.C.L., Droits Patrimoniaux des Maisons et des Eglises Religieuses.

208. Stadalnikas, Rev. Casimir Joseph, M.I.C., J.C.D., Reservation of Censures, X-141 pp., 1944.

209. Sullivan, Rev. Eugene Henry, S.T.L., J.C.D., Proof of the Reception of the Sacraments, X-165 pp., 1944.

210. Vaughan, Rev. William Edward, J.C.D., Constitutions for Diocesan Courts, X-210 pp., 1944.

211. Paro, Rev. Gino, S.T.D., J.C.L., The Right of Apostolic Legation.

212. Balzer, Rev. Ralph Francis, C.P., J.C.L., The Computation of Time in a Canonical Novitiate.

213. Dougherty, Rev. John Whelan, A.B., S.T.L., J.C.L., De Inquisitione Speciali.

214. Dziob, Rev. Michael Walter, J.C.L., The Sacred Congregation for the Oriental Church.

215. Eidenschink, Rev. John Albert, O.S.B., B.A., J.C.L., The Election of Bishops in the Letters of Pope Gregory the Great.

216. Gill, Rev. Nicholas, C.P., J.C.L., The Spiritual Prefect in Clerical Religious Houses of Study.

217. Hynes, Rev. Harry Gerard, S.T.L., J.C.D., The Privileges of Cardinals, XII-183 pp., 1945.

218. McDevitt, Rev. Gerald Vincent, S.T.L., J.C.D., The Renunciation of an Ecclesiastical Office, XIV-179 pp., 1945.
219. Manning, Rev. Joseph Leroy, J.C.L., The Free Conferral of Offices.
220. Meyer, Rev. Louis G., O.S.B., A.B., S.T.B., J.C.D., Alms-gathering by Religious, XII-163 pp., 1945.
221. O'Donnell, Rev. Cletus Francis, M.A., J.C.L., The Marriage of Minors.
222. Prunskis, Rev. Joseph, J.C.D., Comparative Law, Ecclesiastical and Civil, in Lithuanian Concordat, X-161 pp., 1945.
223. Sweeney, Rev. Francis Patrick, C.SS.R., J.C.D., The Reduction of Clerics to the Lay State, X-199 pp., 1945.
224. Vogelpohl, Rev. Henry John, J.C.L., The Simple Impediments to Holy Orders.
225. Brockhaus, Rev. Thomas Aquinas, O.S.B., J.C.L., Religious who are known as *Conversi*.
226. Griese, Rev. Orville Nicholas, S.T.D., J.C.L., Marriage and the Procreation of Offspring.
227. Boudreaux, Rev. Warren Louis, J.C.L., The *"ab acatholicis nati"* of Canon 1099, § 2.
228. Bowe, Rev. Thomas Joseph, A.B., J.C.L., Superioresses in Communities of Women Religious.
229. Diederichs, Rev. Michael Ferdinand, S.C.J., J.C.L., The Jurisdiction of the Latin Ordinaries over their Oriental Subjects.
230. Dingman, Rev. Maurice John, A.B., S.T.L., J.C.L., The Plaintiff in Contentious Trials.
231. Frison, Rev. Basil, C.M.F., M.Mus., J.C.L., The Retroactivity of Law.
232. Galvin, Rev. William Anthony, M.A., J.C.L., The Administrative Transfer of Pastors.
233. Goracy, Rev. Joseph C., J.C.L., The Diriment Impediment of Major Orders.
234. Hale, Rev. Joseph Francis, M.A., S.T.L., J.C.L., The Pastor of Burial.
235. Henry, Rev. Joseph Arthur, A.B., J.C.L., The Mass and Holy Communion: Inter-Ritual Law.
236. Linenberger, Rev. Herbert, C.PP.S., J.C.L., The False Denunciation of an Innocent Confessor.
237. Lynch, Rev. George Edward, A.B., S.T.L., J.C.L., Coadjutors and Auxiliaries of Bishops.
238. Lynch, Rev. Timothy, M.S.SS.T., J.C.L., Contracts between Bishops and Religious Congregations.
239. Lowry, Rev. James Martin, A.B., J.C.L., Dispensation from Private Vows.
240. McClunn, Rev. Justin David, A.B., S.T.L., J.C.L., Administrative Recourse.
241. McGarvey, Rev. Thomas Joseph, A.B., S.T.L., J.C.L., Bination.
242. McGrath, Rev. James, A.B., J.C.L., The Privilege of the Canon.

243. MARBACH, REV. JOSEPH FRANCIS, A.B., J.C.L., Marriage Legislation for the Catholics of the Oriental Rites in the United States and Canada.
244. SHIMKUS, REV. BERNARD ALOYSIUS, A.B., J.C.L., The Determination and Transfer of Rite.
245. SMITH, REV. VINCENT MICHAEL, A.B., S.T.L., J.C.L., Ignorance Affecting Matrimonial Consent.
246. WACHTRLE, REV. PAUL ANTHONY, A.B., J.C.L., The Baptism of the Children of Non-Catholics.